"Derek Taylor's *Reading Scripture as the Church* that we have all been waiting for. As well as capturing the rich texture of Bonhoeffer's ecclesiology and scriptural engagement, Taylor brings him into close dialogue with John Webster, Robert Jenson, Stanley Hauerwas, and others. The result is a compelling account of how through Scripture Christ concretely encounters and forms the church for the world. With this book Taylor has made an important contribution to Bonhoeffer studies as well as to theological interpretation of Scripture, missiology, and systematic theology more broadly."

Michael Mawson, senior lecturer in systematic theology and ethics at Charles Sturt University, Australia

"There are few things more basic to the life of the church than reading Scripture, and there are few modern theologians who can teach Christians how to read the Bible more than Dietrich Bonhoeffer. Derek W. Taylor's inspiring and challenging new book sheds light on Bonhoeffer's understanding of how the church is made by God's Word, has engaged in reading it, is gathered around it, and is sent to share it with the world. *Reading Scripture as the Church* is a significant new contribution to Bonhoeffer studies and to a renewal of the church's relationship with the living Word of God."

Stephen Plant, dean and Runcie Fellow at Trinity Hall, University of Cambridge

"In this highly insightful and provocative book, Derek Taylor draws on Dietrich Bonhoeffer, in conversation with Webster, Jenson, and Hauerwas, to argue convincingly for theological interpretation of Scripture as an ecclesial practice of embodied discipleship in the world. We read Scripture not to know Scripture but to know and follow Jesus, present with us as the crucified and risen Lord. Taylor's carefully argued vision challenges theological interpretation to be communal, cruciform, contextually missional, and above all Christocentric."

Michael J. Gorman, Raymond E. Brown Chair in Biblical Studies and Theology at St. Mary's Seminary and University, Baltimore

"In *Reading Scripture as the Church*, Derek Taylor draws deeply and fruitfully on Bonhoeffer's work with a keen eye for discipleship and the church's reading of Scripture. His combination of a missional hermeneutic with a doctrine of the church offers a provocative, constructive vision of how the Bible, church, and practical mission relate. This is a thoughtful and significant book for both scholars and theologically minded pastoral leaders."

J. Todd Billings, Girod Research Professor of Reformed Theology at Western Theological Seminary

"Derek Taylor has written a book on Bonhoeffer that needed to be written. In engaging Bonhoeffer's hermeneutics, an area of Bonhoeffer studies that is underappreciated, Taylor brings fresh insight into what it means for the Bible to be the book of the church. By bringing Bonhoeffer into conversation with significant contributors to theological hermeneutics, Taylor demonstrates the unique contribution Bonhoeffer has to make. This book will appeal both to Bonhoeffer scholars and those interested in how ecclesial commitments and location should shape our approach to hermeneutics."

Joel D. Lawrence, senior pastor of Central Baptist Church, St. Paul, Minnesota, and author of *Bonhoeffer: A Guide for the Perplexed*

"Derek Taylor has discovered a side of Dietrich Bonhoeffer that most people, even scholars, know less well or not at all, which is Bonhoeffer as a guide to how the church should read the Bible. As Taylor explains, Bonhoeffer believed that the Bible is meant to do more than provide religious information. It is inherently a formational book, intended by its very nature to shape a community on mission to live as disciples of Jesus. Taylor knows Bonhoeffer well. He moves comfortably through a wide range of sources. He writes well too. He is clear, winsome, and always insightful. This book stands at the crossroads of Bonhoeffer as theologian, visionary, pastor, and preacher, which is true to who Bonhoeffer was. It provides a new angle of vision on this important and relevant figure of history. I highly recommend it as a book for pastors, not simply scholars."

Gerald L. Sittser, professor of theology at Whitworth University, author of *Resilient Faith: How the Early Christian "Third Way" Changed the World*

"Derek Taylor brings his considerable analytical ability to the important topic of biblical interpretation, offering us a deeply considered proposal building on the work of Bonhoeffer and others, on the sense in which the church is the context for reading the Bible. This book is not to be missed."

Darren Sarisky, senior research fellow in religion and theology at Australian Catholic University

"This book is a great idea; it's high time for a fuller engagement with Bonhoeffer's theological hermeneutics. Even those with a few misgivings will benefit from Derek Taylor's appropriation of the core theme: reading Scripture faithfully involves hearing the voice of the risen Christ and together following him."

Daniel J. Treier, Gunther H. Knoedler Professor of Theology, Wheaton College Graduate School

NEW EXPLORATIONS IN THEOLOGY

READING SCRIPTURE AS THE CHURCH

DIETRICH BONHOEFFER'S HERMENEUTIC OF DISCIPLESHIP

DEREK W. TAYLOR

Academic

An imprint of InterVarsity Press
Downers Grove, Illinois

InterVarsity Press
P.O. Box 1400, Downers Grove, IL 60515-1426
ivpress.com
email@ivpress.com

InterVarsity Press® is the book-publishing division of InterVarsity Christian Fellowship/USA®, a
movement of students and faculty active on campus at hundreds of universities, colleges, and schools
of nursing in the United States of America, and a member movement of the International Fellowship
of Evangelical Students. For information about local and regional activities, visit intervarsity.org.

Cover design: Cindy Kiple
Interior design: Beth McGill

ISBN 978-0-8308-4918-5 (print)
ISBN 978-0-8308-4919-2 (digital)

Printed in the United States of America ∞

InterVarsity Press is committed to ecological stewardship and to the conservation of natural resources
in all our operations. This book was printed using sustainably sourced paper.

Library of Congress Cataloging-in-Publication Data
A catalog record for this book is available from the Library of Congress.

| P | 25 | 24 | 23 | 22 | 21 | 20 | 19 | 18 | 17 | 16 | 15 | 14 | 13 | 12 | 11 | 10 | 9 | 8 | 7 | 6 | 5 | 4 | 3 | 2 | 1 |
| Y | 38 | 37 | 36 | 35 | 34 | 33 | 32 | 31 | 30 | 29 | 28 | 27 | 26 | 25 | 24 | 23 | 22 | 21 | 20 |

To Lauren,

the occasion for my joy,

and to Theo and Micah,

bearers of disruptive grace.

Contents

Preface

I STUMBLED INTO HERMENEUTICAL DEBATES as a college student. The biblicism I inherited from my evangelical upbringing collided with Karl Barth's christocentric actualism. Is Jesus the Word of God, or is Scripture? Is God's Word statically embedded in the text, or does it come alive in the freedom of God's grace? Matters became even more confusing when I happened upon N. T. Wright and his unique version of theological historicism. I remember being drawn to all three. Surely the text itself, precisely in its textuality, holds value. But surely God must be active in our knowledge of God. And history must matter too, right? Which is it? Is the truth of Scripture found in the words themselves? In God's voice? In history? Some combination thereof? This conversation, as I understood it, was never merely theoretical. I felt each alternative pressing me not only toward different sets of interpretive virtues but toward different ways of being Christian. Still a theological neophyte, I remember feeling trapped, pulled three ways at once.

As I struggled to sort through these options, another possibility emerged on my theological radar. It seemed to cut straight through the tension. The memory is still crisp in my mind. I recall exactly where I was sitting in the coffee shop. I remember the drink on the table in front of me. I remember the way the book felt in my hands. The title alone—*The Art of Reading Scripture*[1]—was enough to disrupt my hermeneutical assumptions. I dove

---

[1]Ellen F. Davis and Richard B. Hays, eds., *The Art of Reading Scripture* (Grand Rapids, MI: Eerdmans, 2003).

headlong into contemporary debates about the theological interpretation of Scripture. Without laying aside my earlier conversation partners, I learned to reframe their insights within the horizon of the church. I learned that the community of faith—with its unique language, traditions, and practices—possessed resources that could help guide readers into the text. From this new vantage point, I felt like I was reading Scripture with fresh eyes. The momentum of this breakthrough propelled me to grad school and shaped the early stages of my research.

My youthful enthusiasm began to fade, however, one Saturday afternoon. I had escaped to the library for some last-minute sermon preparation. I remember turning to a particular commentary that claimed to be theological in nature. As far as I recall, the commentary evidenced no glaring shortcomings. But I remember feeling underwhelmed, like the words lacked life. The central point of this particular work of theological interpretation was that the Bible, when read properly, confirms the church's doctrinal tradition. In this instance, a hermeneutical lens shaped by inherited belief produced interpretive outcomes that confirmed the inheritance. This seemed unsurprising, to say the least. I remember feeling that in this instance Scripture was functioning more like an echo chamber than a medium of God's address.

This is, of course, just one experience. I have since read many lively works of theological interpretation. I recognize, too, that the threat of confirmation bias lurks no matter what reading method one employs. Yet I haven't been able to shake the troubling feeling I had that Saturday afternoon. When a hermeneutical system explicitly prioritizes held belief and custom, the danger of interpretive circularity seems especially serious. I had learned to read Scripture in the church, but how then could Scripture critique the church? By what leverage could Scripture stand against the church as a living word of judgment and truth? How could Scripture change me? It felt as if I had purchased a tidy hermeneutical schema at the expense of Christ's surprising livelihood. If I already know where I'll end up, why read at all? I would later learn to label this problem "ecclesiocentrism." The Barthian in me began to squirm.

I didn't know it at the time, but my hermeneutical wrestling had set me up to discover Dietrich Bonhoeffer. In a 1932 address to an ecumenical audience, he laments the church's hermeneutical impotence. We are only able to read *for* ourselves, he claims. We have lost the ability to read *against* ourselves.[2] We have lost the ability to hear Scripture as what it is, as Christ's address to his people. Importantly for my developing imagination, Bonhoeffer raised this hermeneutical challenge without downplaying the significance of the church as an interpretive community. Reading him, I felt like my earlier conversation partners began to synthesize into a coherent position.

This book represents my attempt to sketch this position. As the brief map of my intellectual journey makes clear, this position represents both an *affirmation* of the theological interpretation of Scripture movement and a *critique* of the movement. The various concerns that animate my critique share a common core: I worry about the ecclesiocentric tendencies of theological interpretation. Any attempt to read "in the church" always assumes a particular vision of what the church is and what it means to be in it. The assumptions we make at this seemingly preinterpretive level exert great impact on our reading. The danger is that this impact becomes a hindrance rather than a help. I worry, for instance, that our assumptions about reading "in the church" can limit our ability to hear voices that fall on the margins, beyond the purview of what "counts" as theological interpretation. In a similar manner, I worry that theological interpretation can inculcate a habit of reading "in" the church before the church then (if at all) moves "out" into the world. I worry, in other words, about theological interpretation's tendency to rely on an inflated account of ecclesial boundaries. It comes as no surprise, then, that the practice often comes across as distinctly Western, nonmissional, and nonliberative. I consider this a grave shortcoming. In order to live up to its name, ecclesial hermeneutics needs a richer ecclesiology. While these animating concerns are not always at the forefront of my argument, careful readers will hear them underlying the constructive proposal that unfolds in this work.

---

[2]Bonhoeffer, *Ecumenical, Academic, and Pastoral Work: 1931–1932*, DBWE 11:377-78.

Acknowledgments

If Bonhoeffer has taught me anything, it is that there can be no theology apart from community. I therefore take great delight in thanking the many friends and teachers who made this book possible. Initial encouragement from Ellen Charry and George Hunsinger set me on the path that led to this work. Conversations with Willie Jennings refined my thinking and altered the direction of my research. Stephen Chapman, Edgardo Colón-Emeric, and Kavin Rowe, besides shaping the way I read the Bible, each read an earlier version and offered valuable feedback. Matt Jantzen has been a faithful conversation partner along the way; his way of being Christian has deeply shaped the way I see God and the world. Kristen Johnson, Kurt Heineman, and Colin Yuckman all read portions of this work and offered timely encouragement. Todd Billings was abundantly generous in offering guidance; besides clarifying my own thinking, his wisdom was crucial in helping transition a dissertation into a book. The many members of the Emmaus community—both at Hope College and Whitworth University—have taught me what it looks like when Scripture comes alive. Jerry Sittser and Jim Edwards read the work at its concluding stages and helped me fine-tune the argument. The support of Clifford Green and the German-American Bonhoeffer Research Network were essential in honing my reading of Bonhoeffer's hermeneutic. Dale Soden and the Whitworth University Weyerhaeuser Center for Faith and Learning were gracious in supporting this work in its final stages. Throughout the process, working with David McNutt and the editorial staff at InterVarsity Press has been a great pleasure. Of course, not everyone mentioned will agree with everything I've written; I could have listened more deeply to their wisdom. Yet to them, and many unnamed others, I offer sincere thanks.

A few people deserve special acknowledgement. My parents, Steve and Janet Taylor, first introduced me to the biblical story and instilled within me a desire to follow Jesus. Their love is one of the great gifts of my life, a sign of God's goodness.

Adam Neder drew me into the world of theology and has been a consistent conversation partner throughout this book's process. Both the content of his teaching and also—indeed, more importantly—the posture of his theological life have forever altered the way I think about God.

Greg Jones was the first to suggest that Bonhoeffer might helpfully speak to the questions I was asking. His uncanny ability to the cut to the heart of complicated questions set this project in motion. If there is anything constructive and creative in these pages, I owe it to Greg's guidance.

Patrick Dunn has surely been my most careful and critical reader, which I take to be a sign of true friendship. His capacious theological imagination has left its imprint on all aspects of this book.

In the most literal sense, this book wouldn't exist without the love of my wife, Lauren. Without her I never would've started, and I certainly wouldn't have finished. Lauren is herself a beautiful reader of Scripture; her insightful pastoral eye and deep sense of practical wisdom have shaped everything about me and the way I think. While Lauren did everything she could to ensure this book's completion, Theo and Micah did everything they could to prevent it. For this I am also deeply thankful. The disruptive presence of young children keeps one's feet on the ground, precisely where they ought to be if one is to read Scripture well. To Lauren, Theo, and Micah, I dedicate this book.

Abbreviations

DBWE 1   Bonhoeffer, Dietrich. *Sanctorum Communio: A Theological Study of the Sociology of the Church.* Edited by Clifford J. Green. Translated by Reinhard Krauss and Nancy Lukens. DBWE 1. Minneapolis: Fortress, 1998.

DBWE 2   Bonhoeffer, Dietrich. *Act and Being: Transcendental Philosophy and Ontology in Systematic Theology.* Edited by Hans Richard Reuter and Wayne Whitson Floyd. Translated by Martin H. Rumscheidt. DBWE 2. Minneapolis: Fortress, 1996.

DBWE 3   Bonhoeffer, Dietrich. *Creation and Fall: A Theological Exegesis of Genesis 1–3.* Edited by John W. de Gruchy. Translated by Douglas Stephen Bax. DBWE 3. Minneapolis: Fortress, 1997.

DBWE 4   Bonhoeffer, Dietrich. *Discipleship.* Edited by Geffrey B. Kelly and John D. Godsey. Translated by Barbara Green and Reinhard Krauss. DBWE 4. Minneapolis: Fortress, 2003.

DBWE 5   Bonhoeffer, Dietrich. *Life Together and Prayerbook of the Bible.* Edited by Geffrey B. Kelly. Translated by Daniel W. Bloesch and James H. Burtness. DBWE 5. Minneapolis: Fortress, 1996.

DBWE 6   Bonhoeffer, Dietrich. *Ethics.* Edited by Clifford J. Green. Translated by Reinhard Krauss, Charles C. West, and Douglas W. Stott. DBWE 6. Minneapolis: Fortress, 2009.

DBWE 8   Bonhoeffer, Dietrich. *Letters and Papers from Prison.* Edited by John W. de Gruchy. Translated by Isabel Best et al. DBWE 8. Minneapolis: Fortress, 2009.

DBWE 9   Bonhoeffer, Dietrich. *The Young Bonhoeffer: 1918–1927.* Edited by Paul Duane Matheny, Clifford J. Green, and Marshall D. Johnson. Translated by Mary C. Nebelsick and Douglas W. Stott. DBWE 9. Minneapolis: Fortress, 2003.

DBWE 10   Bonhoeffer, Dietrich. *Barcelona, Berlin, New York: 1928–1931.*
           Edited by Clifford J. Green. Translated by Douglas W. Stott.
           DBWE 10. Minneapolis: Fortress, 2008.

DBWE 11   Bonhoeffer, Dietrich. *Ecumenical, Academic, and Pastoral*
           Work: 1931–1932. Edited by Victoria J. Barnett et al. Translated
           by Douglas W. Stott et al. DBWE 11. Minneapolis: Fortress, 2012.

DBWE 12   Bonhoeffer, Dietrich. *Berlin: 1932–1933.* Edited by Larry L.
           Rasmussen. Translated by Douglas W. Stott, Isabel Best, and
           David Higgins. DBWE 12. Minneapolis: Fortress, 2009.

DBWE 13   Bonhoeffer, Dietrich. *London: 1933–1935.* Edited by Keith W.
           Clements. Translated by Isabel Best. DBWE 13. Minneapolis:
           Fortress, 2007.

DBWE 14   Bonhoeffer, Dietrich. *Theological Education at Finkenwalde:*
           1935–1937. Edited by Mark Brocker and H. Gaylon Barker.
           Translated by Douglas W. Stott. DBWE 14. Minneapolis:
           Fortress, 2013.

DBWE 15   Bonhoeffer, Dietrich. *Theological Education Underground:*
           1937–1940. Edited by Victoria J. Barnett. Translated by Vic-
           toria J. Barnett et al. DBWE 15. Minneapolis: Fortress, 2012.

DBWE 16   Bonhoeffer, Dietrich. *Conspiracy and Imprisonment: 1940–*
           1945. Edited by Mark S. Brocker. Translated by Lisa E. Dahill.
           DBWE 16. Minneapolis: Fortress, 2006.

IJST   *International Journal of Systematic Theology*

JTI   *Journal of Theological Interpretation*

MT   *Modern Theology*

SJT   *Scottish Journal of Theology*

Introduction

HERMENEUTICS AS AN ECCLESIAL PRACTICE

I HAVE WRITTEN THIS BOOK for those who wish to think carefully about Scripture and its interpretation. I have written it under the guiding conviction that the church stands as the locus and agent of faithful reading. Many recent proponents of theological interpretation are guided by similar judgments; indeed, one could argue that this is the unifying center of the movement.[1] Underlying this shared conviction, however, are very

---

[1] When I speak of "theological interpretation," I have in mind the contemporary movement within English-language biblical and theological studies that has emerged over the past few decades and that has focused, broadly speaking, on interpreting the Bible in a distinctly Christian manner. For an introduction to the movement, see J. Todd Billings *The Word of God for the People of God: An Entryway to the Theological Interpretation of Scripture* (Grand Rapids, MI: Eerdmans, 2010); Stephen E. Fowl, *Theological Interpretation of Scripture* (Eugene, OR: Cascade Books, 2009); Daniel J. Treier, *Introducing Theological Interpretation of Scripture: Recovering a Christian Practice* (Grand Rapids, MI: Baker Academic, 2008); Daniel J. Treier and Kevin J. Vanhoozer, *Theology and the Mirror of Scripture: A Mere Evangelical Account* (Downers Grove, IL: InterVarsity Press, 2015); and Kevin Vanhoozer, "Introduction," in *Dictionary for Theological Interpretation of the Bible*, ed. Kevin J. Vanhoozer, Craig G. Bartholomew, Daniel J. Treier, and N. T. Wright (Grand Rapids, MI: Baker Academic, 2005), 19-26. The original theory underlying theological interpretation began to emerge in the 1990s; see Stephen E. Fowl, *Engaging Scripture: A Model for Theological Interpretation* (Malden, MA: Blackwell, 1998); Kevin Vanhoozer, *Is There a Meaning in This Text?: The Bible, the Reader, and the Morality of Literary Knowledge* (Grand Rapids, MI: Zondervan, 1998). Francis Watson, *Text and Truth: Redefining Biblical Theology* (Grand Rapids, MI: Eerdmans, 1997); and idem, *Text, Church, and World: Biblical Interpretation in Theological Perspective* (Grand Rapids, MI: Eerdmans, 1994). The emergence of theological interpretation has inspired a number of efforts to put it into practice (though, as will become clear, this book intends to challenge common assumptions about what it means to "practice" theological interpretation). See, as notable examples, *Belief: A Theological Commentary on the Bible*, ed. Amy Plantinga

different sets of assumptions about how, precisely, the church fulfills its hermeneutical responsibility. By interrogating those assumptions, this book aims to clear the way for a creative and constructive account of theological interpretation, one that penetrates to the very root of what is actually going on when we read the Bible.

I follow Dietrich Bonhoeffer's lead toward this end. At the beginning of *Creation and Fall*, the published version of his lectures on Genesis delivered at Berlin in the winter semester of 1932–1933, the twenty-six-year-old theologian presciently anticipated contemporary trends. "Theological exposition takes the Bible as the book of the church," he boldly claims, "and interprets it as such."[2] For most of church history, Bonhoeffer's claim would have seemed tautological. What other purpose could Scripture have? Who else would read it? And why? But in an academic context where the modern-critical agenda held sway, Bonhoeffer shamelessly prefaced his interpretive work with this traditional claim. Whereas many of his contemporaries focused their interpretive efforts on making Scripture intelligible in its original historical or religious context, Bonhoeffer embarked on a qualitatively different task. He set out to hear Scripture as the word of God. Unsurprisingly, most scholars at the time ignored the work or scorned its seemingly uncritical method.[3] Yet based on the sympathetic response it received from students, Bonhoeffer's newfound interpretive agenda blew like a fresh breeze through the lecture halls of Berlin.[4] The Bible not only spoke back then—it continues to speak today. And hearing this word, he unequivocally proclaimed, is a distinctly ecclesial enterprise, a practice of the church.

Scripture's Migration from the Church

Unpacking precisely how and why this is the case constitutes my fundamental goal in this book. Though Bonhoeffer himself is rarely acknowledged as a forebear of the contemporary turn toward theological interpretation, he

---

Pauw and William C. Placher (Louisville, KY: Westminster John Knox); *The Brazos Theological Commentary on the Bible*, ed. R. R. Reno (Grand Rapids, MI: Brazos Press); and the *Journal of Theological Interpretation*.

[2]Dietrich Bonhoeffer, *Creation and Fall: A Theological Exegesis of Genesis 1–3*, DBWE 3:22.

[3]John W. de Gruchy, "Editor's Introduction to the English Edition," in Bonhoeffer, *Creation and Fall*, DBWE 3:5-6.

[4]De Gruchy, "Editor's Introduction," 1.

should be, for his remarks foreshadow its defining contours. Behind Bonhoeffer's bold hermeneutical claim lies the story of modern historical criticism. The narrative of its emergence has been well rehearsed, and we need not rehash it here.[5] For my larger purposes in this book, the basic point to note can be stated directly: though the emergence of the modern-critical paradigm was explicitly funded by the quest to secure reliable knowledge, ecclesiological assumptions came embedded within it.[6] Spinoza laid the groundwork on which this paradigm would be built when he famously began his *Theologico-Political Treatise* by purifying his interpretive method of ulterior influences: "I deliberately resolved to examine Scripture afresh, conscientiously and freely, and to admit nothing as its teaching which I did not most clearly derive from it."[7] When Kant proposed "no imperative 'Believe!' but only a free *credo*,"[8] the trajectory of modern biblical hermeneutics

---

[5]See especially Hans W. Frei, *The Eclipse of Biblical Narrative: A Study in Eighteenth and Nineteenth Century Hermeneutics* (New Haven, CT: Yale University Press, 1974). Also note Matthew Levering, *Participatory Biblical Exegesis: A Theology of Biblical Interpretation* (Notre Dame, IN: University of Notre Dame Press, 2008), 17-62. Scriptural texts were not literally taken out of the church. Rather, the basic assumption was that in order for one to read Scripture well within the church, one must first read without the church. For a helpful articulation of this mindset, and one that avoids common stereotypes, see John Barton, *The Nature of Biblical Criticism* (Louisville, KY: Westminster John Knox, 2007).

[6]These methodological issues are bound up with more fundamental commitments about the nature of history and historical existence. Whereas in a premodern world one could trust metaphysical paths to lead one to certainty, the fundamentally nonmetaphysical nature of modern epistemology requires another means of ascertaining knowledge. Hence, the importance of method and technique.

[7]Baruch Spinoza, *Theological-Political Treatise*, trans. Samuel Shirley, 2nd ed. (Indianapolis, IN: Hackett, 2001), 5. This is not to suggest that Spinoza himself bears responsibility for the emergence of the critical hermeneutical paradigm but merely that he captures key features of its animating ethos. On Spinoza's hermeneutic, see Levering, *Participatory Biblical Exegesis*, 108-18. It is, of course, impossible to label any one person as the founder of biblical criticism. Regarding various progenitors of the movement, see Barton, *Nature of Biblical Criticism*, 118-30.

[8]Immanuel Kant, "The Conflict of the Faculties," in *Religion and Rational Theology*, ed. and trans. Allen W. Wood and George di Giovanni (Cambridge: Cambridge University Press, 1996), 249. As with most movements, modern hermeneutics emerged in different iterations. Schleiermacher, for example, famously suggested that the goal of hermeneutics is to understand an author better than he understands himself; see F. D. E. Schleiermacher, *Hermeneutics and Criticism: And Other Writings*, ed. and trans. Andrew Bowie (Cambridge: Cambridge University Press, 1998), 33. Even as this highly romantic approach diverges from the rigid objectivism implied in other Enlightenment thinkers, it likewise implies a universal method. Schleiermacher declares: "We must reject the suggestion that in virtue of their divine inspiration the sacred books demand a hermeneutical and critical treatment different from one guided by the rules which obtain elsewhere." F. D. E. Schleiermacher, *The Christian Faith*, ed. H. R. Mackintosh and J. S. Stewart (London: T&T Clark, 1999), 600.

was set. The key presupposition underlying its emergence, as Jon Levenson suggests, is that scholars "eliminate or minimize their communal loyalties, [or] see them as legitimately operative only within associations that are private, nonscholarly, and altogether voluntary."[9]

Of course, this methodological decision does not prohibit Scripture from serving the church's ends. After all, the majority of critical biblical scholars would claim to do their work, in one way or another, for the sake of the church. But it does require that in order for interpretation to reach these ends it must first pass through a general process—Scripture must be read "like any other book."[10] As Gabler paradigmatically depicts the matter in his famous distinction between "biblical" and "dogmatic" theology, a reconstructive and descriptive task—the criteria for which are universal and scientific in nature—must precede the church's particular and normative use.[11] To borrow Ricoeur's terminology, interpretation was thereby "deregionalized"; a general hermeneutic replaced a mode of reading suited to a particular text or domain.[12] Within this hermeneutical paradigm, Scripture may be read *for* the church, but it should not be read *in* and *as* the church. The church may be good for some things—but scriptural hermeneutics is not one of them.

SCRIPTURE'S ECCLESIAL HOMECOMING

If the pursuit of hermeneutical objectivity prompted Scripture's migration from the church to the academy, its homecoming would, perhaps surprisingly,

---

[9]Jon D. Levenson, *The Hebrew Bible, the Old Testament, and Historical Criticism: Jews and Christians in Biblical Studies* (Louisville, KY: Westminster John Knox, 1993), 118. Also see Thomas Howard, *Protestant Theology and the Making of the Modern German University* (Oxford: Oxford University Press, 2006), 201-11.

[10]Benjamin Jowett, "On the Interpretation of Scripture," in *Essays and Reviews: The 1860 Text and Its Reading*, ed. Victor Shea and William Whitla (Charlottesville: University Press of Virginia, 2000), 482.

[11]Johann P. Gabler, "An Oration on the Proper Distinction Between Biblical and Dogmatic Theology and the Specific Objects of Each," in *Old Testament Theology: Flowering and Future*, ed. Ben C. Ollenburger (Winona Lake, IN: Eisenbrauns, 2004), 497-506. Also see William Wrede's work from a century later, "The Task and Methods of 'New Testament Theology,'" in *The Nature of New Testament Theology*, ed. Robert Morgan (London: SCM Press, 1973), 68-116.

[12]Paul Ricoeur, "The Task of Hermeneutics," in *Hermeneutics and the Human Sciences*, ed. and trans. John B. Thompson (Cambridge: Cambridge University Press, 1981), 43. "The real movement of deregionalisation begins with the attempt to extract a general problem from the activity of interpretation which is each time engaged in different texts" (Ricoeur, "Task of Hermeneutics," 45).

follow a similar path. Given the nature of this text, what interpretive posture constitutes true hermeneutical *Sachlichkeit*? What does it mean to be "objective" when reading Scripture? Karl Barth was one of the first to raise this question within the context of modern Protestant theology. Rejecting the epistemological presupposition governing the critical enterprise, he proposed a form of interpretive objectivity controlled not by universal criteria but by the subject matter itself.[13] Barth's claim was simple yet revolutionary: Christian readers must practice a form of interpretive objectivity suitable to the unique object of the reading process, namely, the living and self-revealing God. With this discovery, he found himself in a radically new hermeneutical situation. He, the reader, was the one addressed.[14] Barth was eager to note the irony: in this new situation, he could in fact be more objective than modern hermeneutics would allow, more critical than the critics.[15] To read as one unaddressed, in the mythically neutral domain of historicist study, would be to read something other than the Christian canon and to hear something other than God's living voice.

As a student, Bonhoeffer excitedly embraced Barth's hermeneutical revolution, and it changed the trajectory of his theological career.[16] He learned from Barth that all theological language emerges in response to God's revelatory grace. Bonhoeffer quickly made this insight his own. More readily than Barth, he pressed this logic into the realm of the church. The revelatory word that constitutes the theological enterprise is the very same word that

---

[13]The definitive study of Barth's early hermeneutic is Richard E. Burnett, *Karl Barth's Theological Exegesis: The Hermeneutical Principles of the* Römerbrief *Period* (Grand Rapids, MI: Eerdmans, 2004).

[14]See John Webster, "Barth's Lectures on the Gospel of John," in *Thy Word Is Truth: Barth on Scripture*, ed. George Hunsinger (Grand Rapids, MI: Eerdmans, 2012), 125-50. Some genealogies of the emergence of theological interpretation label Barth a forebear of the movement (e.g., Treier, *Introducing Theological Interpretation of Scripture*). Others grant him little significance (e.g., Fowl, *Theological Interpretation of Scripture*).

[15]Karl Barth, *The Epistle to the Romans*, trans. Edwyn C. Hoskyns (Oxford: Oxford University Press, 1968), 8. As Bonhoeffer would later suggest, echoing Barth's earlier insight, one must interpret the Bible in "orientation to substance [*Sachlichkeit*]" (Bonhoeffer, *Theological Education at Finkenwalde: 1935-1937*, DBWE 14: 417). See Michael Mawson, "Scripture," in *The Oxford Handbook of Dietrich Bonhoeffer*, ed. Michael Mawson and Philip G. Ziegler (Oxford: Oxford University Press, 2019), 130.

[16]The earliest and clearest evidence of Barth's strong influence is Bonhoeffer's 1925 student paper, "On the Historical and Pneumatological Interpretation of Scripture" (in Bonhoeffer, *The Young Bonhoeffer: 1918-1927*, DBWE 9:285-300). The paper's passing grade of "satisfactory" was the lowest Bonhoeffer would receive for his work in systematic theology, evidence that Barth's theology of revelation sat uneasily with Bonhoeffer's Berlin professors.

constitutes the church as the social corollary of God's address. Hearing God's voice and being called into the community of God's people are, theologically speaking, one and the same event. Thus, a simple methodological commitment animates Bonhoeffer's theological imagination: we speak rightly about God when we speak in and as the church. With this, he gave concrete ecclesial dimensions to Barth's theological breakthrough. God's voice, ecclesial existence, and faithful reading are inseparably bound.

While theological resources prompt Bonhoeffer's hermeneutical return to the church, another set of resources emerges from the world of philosophy. In response to what David Tracy calls "the Enlightenment belief in a purely autonomous consciousness,"[17] twentieth-century philosophical hermeneutics has forcefully reasserted the situatedness, historicity, and community-dependent nature of human thought. Here Heidegger and Gadamer lead the way; our mode of being in the world carries interpretive significance, and preunderstanding is not the enemy of hermeneutics but its very possibility. Wittgenstein and others show that the historicity and contingency of language do not constitute a tainted accretion behind which truth lies hidden but the very vehicle of meaning in its truest form. Bourdieu points to modes of understanding embedded within practice, and philosophers like MacIntyre teach that tradition is not only inherent but necessary to rationality. Indeed, all paradigms of thought are historically contingent (Kuhn), and all knowledge has a subjective pole (Polanyi). With regard to texts per se, LaCocque and Ricoeur follow this train of thought when they contend that "the text exists, in the final analysis, thanks to the community, for the use of the community, with a view to giving shape to the community."[18] With regard to the specific act of interpreting texts, many have come to suggest that textually mediated "meaning" is not as stable or accessible as was once thought. Stanley Fish famously suggests, for example, that rather than an objective property carried within the text and unearthed by proper methods, meaning is the product of the reading strategy brought to bear upon it.[19]

---

[17]David Tracy, *Plurality and Ambiguity: Hermeneutics, Religion, Hope* (1987; repr., Chicago: University of Chicago Press, 1994), 16.

[18]André LaCocque and Paul Ricoeur, *Thinking Biblically: Exegetical and Hermeneutical Studies*, trans. David Pellauer (Chicago: University of Chicago Press, 1998), xiii.

[19]Stanley Fish, *Is There a Text in This Class?: The Authority of Interpretive Communities* (Cambridge, MA: Harvard University Press, 1980).

With the help of Hans Frei and George Lindbeck, these insights acquired distinctly theological shape and gained wide influence within Anglophone theology. Frei's *Eclipse of Biblical Narrative* has become a standard genealogy of the demise—and potential rebirth—of a distinctly Christian mode of scriptural interpretation. As he writes elsewhere, "The literal meaning of the text is precisely that meaning which finds the greatest degree of agreement in the use of the text in the religious community. If there is agreement in that use, then take that to be the literal sense."[20] Lindbeck, Frei's Yale colleague, adds ecclesiological depth to this emerging hermeneutical vision. Drawing from a wide of array of philosophical, sociological, and anthropological resources, he argues for a "cultural-linguistic" account of rationality internal to the logic and grammar of a particular community.[21] With insights like these, theologians began to move beyond modern critical assumptions. They were coming to see that the church's particular resources, far from being distortive, are hermeneutically foundational.

In recent decades, Bonhoeffer's trailblazing route back to the church has become a well-worn path. Drawing from these trends, Christian interpreters have felt emboldened not only to tolerate but to prioritize and accentuate the particularity of their ecclesial vantage point and the unique form of thinking constituted by its language, traditions, and practices.[22] Echoing Bonhoeffer's paradigmatic claim, Stephen Fowl captures the heart of the

---

[20]Hans W. Frei, *Types of Christian Theology*, ed. George Hunsinger and William C. Placher (New Haven, CT: Yale University Press, 1992), 15. Also see idem, "The 'Literal Reading' of Biblical Narrative in the Christian Tradition: Does It Stretch or Will It Break?," in *The Bible and the Narrative Tradition*, ed. Frank McConnell (New York: Oxford University Press, 1986), 36-77, in which Frei suggests that the very concept of a *sensus literalis* belongs within the context of a sociolinguistic community that agrees upon the rules for reading its sacred text (Frei, "Literal Reading," 67-68).

[21]George A. Lindbeck, *The Nature of Doctrine: Religion and Theology in a Postliberal Age* (Louisville, KY: Westminster John Knox, 1984). See especially 32-41 and 112-38. For more on the church as a culture, see my discussion in chap. 7 of the present work.

[22]While broader philosophical movements have undoubtedly influenced contemporary theological trends, not all proponents of ecclesial hermeneutics equally appreciate the insights of philosophy. For example, Stephen Fowl no longer thinks that a general theory of textual meaning derived from philosophical hermeneutics is crucial to interpreting Scripture theologically. See Stephen E. Fowl, "Further Thoughts on Theological Interpretation," in *Reading Scripture with the Church: Toward a Hermeneutic for Theological Interpretation*, ed. A. K. M. Adam, Stephen E. Fowl, Kevin J. Vanhoozer, and Francis Watson (Grand Rapids, MI: Baker Academic, 2006), 125-26. This claim slightly modifies his earlier argument in *Engaging Scripture*, which grants more significance to philosophical resources.

movement when he writes, "Reading Scripture theologically is first and foremost a practice of the church. It does not depend on the support of academics for its survival."[23] Elsewhere he claims that the church is the "location where such a reading will be most at home," which is why ecclesiology "provides both the direction for theological interpretation and the standards against which such readings can be judged."[24]

The repercussions of this assertion have been wide ranging. R. R. Reno points to its distinctly doctrinal implications by suggesting that the church's teachings are not distortive but clarifying.[25] For the church to read well, it must read within the framework of the rule of faith.[26] Many have likewise noted that if we return interpretation to the church, liturgical practice gains hermeneutical significance. James Fodor asserts, for instance, that "worship is Scripture's home, its native soil, its most congenial habitat. . . . It is in the liturgy . . . that Christians are schooled and exercised in the scriptural logic of their faith."[27] If this is the case, then the proper reader is not the autonomous academic but the worshiping community.[28] Likewise, distinctly theological virtues and habits formed through ecclesial practices become prerequisites for interpretation,[29] and, as Richard Hays claims, faith—rather than neutrality or objectivity—stands as "the epistemological precondition for reading Scripture well."[30] Hays goes on to suggest that this reading is "a skill

---

[23]Fowl, *Theological Interpretation of Scripture*, 23.

[24]Stephen E. Fowl, "Introduction," in *The Theological Interpretation of Scripture: Classic and Contemporary Readings*, ed. Stephen E. Fowl (Malden, MA: Blackwell, 1997), xix.

[25]R. R. Reno, "Series Preface," in Jaroslav Pelikan, *Acts*, Brazos Theological Commentary on the Bible, ed. R. R. Reno (Grand Rapids, MI: Brazos Press, 2005), 11-16.

[26]For the classic example, see Augustine's *On Christian Doctrine* 3.2, trans. J. F. Shaw, in *Nicene and Post-Nicene Fathers*, 1st series, ed. Philip Schaff (Peabody, MA: Hendrickson, 1999), 2:513-97. For leading recent examples, see Robert W. Jenson, *Canon and Creed* (Louisville, KY: Westminster John Knox, 2010); R. W. L. Moberly, *The Bible, Theology, and Faith: A Study of Abraham and Jesus* (Cambridge: Cambridge University Press, 2000); C. Kavin Rowe, "Biblical Pressure and Trinitarian Hermeneutics," *Pro Ecclesia* 11, no. 3 (2002): 295-312, and David S. Yeago, "The New Testament and Nicene Dogma: A Contribution to the Recovery of Theological Exegesis," in Fowl, *Theological Interpretation of Scripture: Classic and Contemporary Readings*, 87-101.

[27]James Fodor, "Reading the Scriptures: Rehearsing Identity, Practicing Character," in *Blackwell Companion to Christian Ethics*, ed. Stanley Hauerwas and Samuel Wells, 2nd ed. (Malden, MA: Blackwell, 2011), 155.

[28]See Stephen E. Fowl and L. Gregory Jones, *Reading in Communion: Scripture and Ethics in Christian Life* (Grand Rapids, MI: Eerdmans, 1991).

[29]Fowl, *Engaging Scripture*, 62-96.

[30]Richard B. Hays, "Reading the Bible with Eyes of Faith: The Practice of Theological Exegesis," *JTI* 1, no. 1 (2007): 5.

for which we are trained by *the Christian tradition*."[31] While not all would agree with the classical claim, exemplified in Saint Hilary of Poitiers's bold assertion that "those who are situated outside the church are not able to acquire any understanding of the divine discourse,"[32] it is undeniably the case that many scholars today have recovered the Augustinian priority of the church as a hermeneutical presupposition.[33] Scripture, we have learned to claim, has a distinct *Sitz im Leben*, a natural home. Not only can we read Scripture *for* the church's unique ends, we can—and indeed must—read Scripture *in* and *as* the church in order to reach these ends.

This book enters the debate at just this point. Ecclesiology has obviously carried great weight in recent conversations about theological interpretation, but rarely has ecclesiology itself become an object of theological focus within them. When we say that Scripture is the book of the church, what do we mean by *church*? Which church do we have in mind? As much as this question remains unaddressed, ecclesial hermeneutics remains ecclesially ambiguous. In this book, therefore, I ask an ecclesiological question as a means of answering a hermeneutical one. I set out deliberately to consider what it means to read in, as, and for the church. Which aspects of the church are hermeneutically salubrious? What practices come embedded within it? And how does this influence the shape and ends of faithful interpretation?

HERMENEUTICS, ECCLESIOLOGY, AND DISCIPLESHIP

In order to lay the groundwork for the constructive proposal that unfolds in this work, it will be useful here to gesture toward working definitions of three key terms that often lack clear meaning: *hermeneutics*, *ecclesiology*, and *discipleship*.

Hermeneutics. *Hermeneutics* is a notoriously ambiguous word with no unifying definition.[34] As Simone Sinn helpfully notes, we have "no common

---

[31]Hays, "Reading the Bible with Eyes of Faith," 14.

[32]Cited by David S. Yeago, "The Bible," in *Knowing the Triune God: The Work of the Spirit in the Practices of the Church*, ed. James J. Buckley and David S. Yeago (Grand Rapids, MI: Eerdmans, 2001), 49.

[33]"For my part, I should not believe the gospel except as moved by the authority of the Catholic Church." Augustine, *Against the Epistle of Manichaeus Called Fundamental* 5, trans. Richard Stothert, in *Nicene and Post-Nicene Fathers*, 1st series, ed. Philip Schaff (Peabody, MA: Hendrickson, 1999), 4:129-50.

[34]See Stanley E. Porter and Jason C. Robinson, *Hermeneutics: An Introduction to Interpretive Theory* (Grand Rapids, MI: Eerdmans, 2011), 299.

reference point for the many different disciplines that deal with hermeneutical issues," and as a result "the hermeneutical field is very complex and
there is no general theory to hermeneutics as a whole."[35] As a means of un-
tangling the diversity of the subject, Sinn highlights three basic strands:
hermeneutics as (1) the process of interpretation, (2) the phenomenon of
understanding, and (3) the nature of human existence. The first is a methodological question, and it deals with the principles of interpreting texts.
The second is an epistemological question, and it deals with the process of
encountering meaning in a text. The third is an ontological question, and it
deals with the significance of understanding for human nature itself.[36]

In this project, I am ostensibly concerned with the act of reading Christian
Scripture (hermeneutics as an interpretive question). But by moving this act
within the life of the church I am complexifying matters. As Christians, we
seek to interpret a text as a means of knowing the triune God revealed in
Jesus Christ (hermeneutics as an epistemological question), which is bound
up with patterns of life in the world and modes of understanding self and
others vis-à-vis the risen Lord (hermeneutics as an ontological question).
Whereas contemporary discussions about "theological interpretation" tend
to exist within the domain of hermeneutics in the first sense, it will become
clear as this project unfolds that the three cannot be neatly teased apart.
Following Bonhoeffer, I claim that reading Scripture in relationship to the
risen Christ forces us to distinguish between understanding the text's basic
linguistic sense and, as he puts it, "hearing it correctly" as a concrete word
of the present Christ.[37] It is possible, Bonhoeffer implies, to have one without
the other. It is possible to offer good readings (hermeneutics in the first
sense) that nevertheless fail to conform to Christ's ongoing existence and
that are therefore hermeneutically deficient. In such a situation, "The words
are correct, but they have no weight."[38]

This claim is significant, and I explore it in greater detail in chapter two.
For now it is worth noting that by calling to mind this distinction I am not
intending to invoke the traditional contrast between what a text meant back

---

[35]Simone Sinn, "Hermeneutics and Ecclesiology," in *The Routledge Companion to the Christian Church*, ed. Gerard Mannion and Lewis S. Mudge (New York: Routledge, 2008), 583.
[36]Sinn, "Hermeneutics and Ecclesiology," 576.
[37]See Bonhoeffer, *Discipleship*, DBWE 4:181.
[38]Bonhoeffer, *Ethics*, DBWE 6:371.

then and what it means for us today.[39] Nor is this a simple recitation of the argument that texts do not carry meaning apart from the act of interpretation, as true as this claim is. In this book I embark on a more properly theological project of rethinking what it means for a text to "mean" in light of Christ's ongoing work of calling and shaping his community and what implications this has for the process of pursuing this meaning through the act of reading.

Ecclesiology. I pursue the hermeneutical question by means of the ecclesiological because, as I demonstrate in subsequent chapters, what we mean by *church* determines what we mean by hermeneutical faithfulness generally and interpretive faithfulness specifically.

While *church* may seem more straightforward than *hermeneutics*, things are not always so clear. Fowl is one of the few to note that a genuinely ecclesial hermeneutic must navigate the vagueness and imprecision of ecclesiology.[40] Markus Bockmuehl similarly suggests that when conversations about theological interpretation do turn their attention to the church, the term "can remain notably abstract and detached."[41] Particular proposals for an ecclesial hermeneutic frequently fail to proceed "to an account of the church in which this ecclesial hermeneutic actually resides."[42]

Overcoming this lacuna in recent conversations about theological interpretation is no easy task, for ecclesiology is a complex and multifaceted doctrine. To say straightforwardly what the church *is* is notoriously difficult. One reason for this is that the Bible employs a great diversity of images and metaphors to convey the reality of God's people. Paul Minear famously suggests that one can find ninety-six different images for the church in Scripture.[43] A similar complexity emerges from the perspective of systematic

---

[39]On this distinction, see Krister Stendahl, "Biblical Theology, Contemporary," in *The Interpreter's Dictionary of the Bible*, ed. George A. Buttrick et al. (Nashville, TN: Abingdon, 1962), 1:418-32. For convincing arguments against the value and usefulness of this distinction, see Fowl, *Engaging Scripture*, 35-40; and Nicholas Lash, "What Might Martyrdom Mean?" in *Theology on the Way to Emmaus* (Eugene, OR: Wipf & Stock, 1986), 75-92.

[40]See Fowl, *Engaging Scripture*, 2n1.

[41]Markus Bockmuehl, *Seeing the Word: Refocusing New Testament Study* (Grand Rapids, MI: Eerdmans, 2006), 58. Here Bockmuehl engages in specific dialogue with Francis Watson, *Text, Church, and World*. On the idealism of "church" in Watson, also see Christopher Rowland, "An Open Letter to Francis Watson on *Text, Church and World*," *SJT* 48, no. 4 (1995): 507-17.

[42]Bockmuehl, *Seeing the Word*, 58.

[43]Quoted in Avery Dulles, *Models of the Church* (New York: Doubleday, 1978), 23.

theology, for theologians commonly recognize that ecclesiology is a synthetic doctrine, which means that many theological loci are included within or implicated by the doctrine of the church. Moreover, ecclesiology as a specific doctrinal locus is a peculiarly modern phenomenon—perhaps even a twentieth-century phenomenon—emerging as a distinct object of systematic study only as Christendom begins to wane and the church emerges as one among other religious and social options. Because of its relative youth among Christian doctrines, ecclesiology carries less precision than other loci like Christology or the doctrine of the Trinity. On top of all this, of course, loom the theological fractures that mar the post-Reformation landscape.

For these reasons, when theologians use the word *church*, the referent is not always clear. Do they mean by it a community, institution, universal body, invisible entity, or something else entirely? To make matters even more confusing, many theologians maintain that *church* cannot be exhausted by a single image or description. For example, in *Models of the Church*, Avery Cardinal Dulles writes, "In order to do justice to the various aspects of the church, as a complex reality, we must work simultaneously with different models. By a kind of mental juggling act, we have to keep several models in the air at once."[44] Whereas Dulles hesitates to offer a synthetic ecclesiology that incorporates various models and images into one integrative whole, I take a different approach in this project, as will become evident below.

Discipleship. More clearly than the English term *discipleship*, Bonhoeffer's German term *Nachfolge* conveys a sense of "following after" the one who is "walking ahead of me, step by step."[45] While the notion of following after God is attested broadly throughout Scripture, its unique texture emerges in the Gospels.[46] Jesus calls, the disciples relocate their bodies behind him, and their lives come to bear the impression of his ongoing movement as they are drawn along into walking his path. For these first

---

[44]Dulles, *Models of the Church*, 14. Dulles seeks a "balanced ecclesiology" that incorporates major affirmations of each model. In so doing, he explicitly rejects a synthetic move: "The peculiarity of models, as contrasted with aspects, is that we cannot integrate them into a single synthetic vision" (*Models of the Church*, 14).

[45]Bonhoeffer, *Discipleship*, DBWE 4:176.

[46]On the Old Testament theme of "walking in God's ways," see Bonhoeffer, *Theological Education Underground: 1937–1940*, DBWE 15:504.

followers, therefore, discipleship is not one component of their existence alongside others. Rather, it functions as the overarching framework within which their identity and history gain meaning. The notion of discipleship, then, is no mere metaphor or illustration for more basic theological categories. Nor does it deal with only certain elements of Christian life instead of others (say, matters of piety instead of matters of politics). As Bonhoeffer uses the term in his mature work, *discipleship* depicts the essence of Christian existence and thus serves as a structuring theological concept. All dimensions of Christian life and practice fall within its scope. Therefore, the term is fundamental to the very definition of the church.[47] As Bonhoeffer claims, the only explanation for the church's existence is that "Jesus himself calls" and "the disciple walks behind Jesus."[48] All ecclesial activity—indeed, the very being of the *ecclesia* itself—takes shape within this walking.[49]

Bonhoeffer's account of discipleship is thoroughly christological. It relies upon the conviction that Christ has been raised from the dead, that he remains singularly and independently himself, and that through the Spirit he continues to walk with his people. Barth captures Bonhoeffer's insight when he notes that the risen Jesus is not indolently resting in place but "strides through the ages still left to the world."[50] This striding, and the calling that accompanies it, gives the church its nature and shape. Indeed, the very possibility of ecclesial existence is predicated upon the out-aheadness of the risen One. "God does not allow us to walk a path . . . on which he would not precede us," Bonhoeffer claims.[51] As he puts the matter in his prison writings, Christian life consists of being continually propelled into walking Jesus' path.[52] Discipleship is relevant for the questions of this book because the

---

[47]Indeed, it is precisely when the substance of the church is most at risk of being compromised by false allegiance that the concept of discipleship becomes most prominent in his thinking and writing. See Michael J. DeJonge, *Bonhoeffer on Resistance: The Word Against the Wheel* (Oxford: Oxford University Press, 2018), 109-18.

[48]Bonhoeffer, *Discipleship*, DBWE 4:57-58.

[49]On the importance of "the way" as a theologically rich motif in Bonhoeffer's writings, and one that is foundational for understanding his ethical vision, see Brian Brock, "Bonhoeffer and the Bible in Christian Ethics: Psalm 119, the Mandates, and Ethics as a 'Way,'" *Studies in Christian Ethics* 18, no. 3 (2005): 7-29.

[50]Karl Barth, *Church Dogmatics*, vol. IV/3.2, *The Doctrine of Reconciliation*, ed. G. W. Bromiley and T. F. Torrance, trans. G. W. Bromiley (Edinburgh: T&T Clark, 1962), 663.

[51]Bonhoeffer, *Theological Education Underground*, DBWE 15:504.

[52]Bonhoeffer, *Letter and Papers from Prison*, DBWE 8:480.

church reads Scripture precisely within this movement. Indeed, as I will argue in the chapters that follow, the movement of discipleship is the very reason the church approaches Scripture in the first place. Without it, there would be no hermeneutical question.

Rethinking the Church's Hermeneutical Dimensions

The dynamism and relationality inherent to the concept of discipleship suggest a constructive way of reframing the ecclesiological question. Most ecclesiologies are structured according to certain metaphors or models of the church. This approach has the benefit of connecting directly to a particular biblical image. The downside, however, is that synthetic and coherent accounts of the church become uniquely challenging. Whereas models tend to operate according to spatial logic, the notion of discipleship invites us to think of the church in terms of relationships, which in turn allows us to overcome the static and competitive dimensions of metaphorical thinking. While it is difficult to imagine the essence of an object being simultaneously x and y (hence the necessity of Dulles's juggling metaphor and the concomitant challenge of a synthetic ecclesiology), it is far easier to imagine one object simultaneously existing in different identity-defining relationships. Depicting the church in terms of relationships rather than images, metaphors, or models allows us to achieve a level of breadth and coherence that most ecclesiological reflection cannot.

In this work I propose construing the church as the unique entity that exists at the intersection of four identity-defining relationships. The church simultaneously exists (1) in relationship to the risen Christ, (2) in relationship to its historical-institutional past, (3) in relationship to a concrete communal location, and (4) in relationship to the world. Each relationship carries important hermeneutical implications, shaping the nature and practice of scriptural interpretation. In addition, each relational dynamic allows us to incorporate key insights from the array of biblical images for the church without being beholden to the particular logic governing a given image.

Each of this book's four parts focuses on one of these relationships. More than a mere act of four-ball juggling, I hope to show that these relational dimensions cohere to shape the church as one hermeneutical community.

This in itself is noteworthy, for I contend that proponents of theological interpretation frequently highlight one of these relationships (and thus grant it hermeneutical significance) yet fail to adequately account for the others. I hope to demonstrate that a relational approach to ecclesiology does greater justice to the complexity of the church's hermeneutical task.

To be clear, I am not proposing that if we want to read Scripture faithfully, we must adopt one normative ecclesiology in contrast to others on offer. Likewise, I do not mean to suggest that an ecclesiology that foregrounds one particular relational dimension is necessarily deficient. I am suggesting, rather, that these four relationships characterize the true church wherever it is present, regardless of the precise form it may take. These four relationships are true of all true churches, and thus exert force on the church's practice of reading Scripture.

Luke 24 and christological interpretation. The resurrection stories in Luke 24 serve as the imaginative stimulus for this synthetic possibility. Within the three stories that compose this passage—the women at the tomb, the disciples on the road to Emmaus, and Jesus' visitation of the eleven—a cluster of factors concurrently shape the emergence of the first post-resurrection community. These stories are especially pertinent to my interests because they all center on the idea of understanding. For Luke, it seems, the resurrection carries hermeneutical consequence. Moreover, the latter two stories explicitly locate this understanding vis-à-vis the interpretation of Scripture. As Walter Moberly claims of the Emmaus Road story, "It is imaginatively as weighty a story about biblical interpretation and Christ as one could hope to find."[53] Unsurprisingly, Luke's resurrection account is commonly cited as justification for upholding the christological dimension of scriptural hermeneutics (the first of the four relationships I outlined above). Richard Hays notes of the Emmaus Road story, for example, that "the risen Jesus becomes the definitive interpreter" and the one who graciously grants understanding to his followers.[54] Hays points to the disciples' passivity in this text—"their eyes were kept from recognizing him" (Lk 24:16) and then during the meal "were opened" to see him (Lk 24:31). By taking

---

[53]R. W. L. Moberly, *Bible, Theology, and Faith*, 45.
[54]Richard B. Hays, "Reading Scripture in Light of the Resurrection," in *The Art of Reading Scripture*, ed. Ellen F. Davis and Richard B. Hays (Grand Rapids, MI: Eerdmans, 2003), 229.

agency away from the disciples in this way, the text suggests that Christ is the chief hermeneutical agent, the one who alters their faculties of perception and creates genuine understanding.[55]

This challenges what we normally mean when we talk about "understanding Scripture," for the disciples' new understanding is not reducible to the gift of new knowledge about the text.[56] We can presume that after Jesus "interpreted to them the things about himself in all the scriptures" (Lk 24:27), the disciples possessed all the biblical data necessary. Yet still they do not understand.[57] And when Jesus does open their eyes, he does not dispense new information.[58] This compels us to wonder whether our normal categories of understanding can adequately account for the miracle of knowing Jesus in and through Scripture. We are faced with the question: What must happen for accurate knowledge about the Bible to produce a perception of its significance? How does genuine understanding arise?

Rather than producing new data about the text, the uniqueness of Jesus' interpretation lies in the way he frames the telos of the interpretive process: "Beginning with Moses and all the prophets, he interpreted to them the things *about himself* in all the scriptures" (Lk 24:27, emphasis added). Here Jesus paints himself, not the text, as the ultimate goal of the hermeneutical process. As Jesus says in John's Gospel, "You search the scriptures because you think that in them you have eternal life; and it is they that testify on my behalf. Yet you refuse to come to me to have life" (Jn 5:39-40). First John 1 paints a similar picture of the logic of Scripture: we have seen Jesus with our own eyes (1 Jn 1:1), the author writes, and now we declare him to you in writing so that you may know him too (1 Jn 1:3-4). The point is simple, yet

---

[55]Hays, "Reading Scripture in Light of the Resurrection," 231. This becomes even more obvious in the next pericope: "He opened their minds to understand the scriptures" (Lk 24:45).

[56]Of course, neither does it bypass or transcend the text. The interpretation is necessary but not sufficient. Indeed, the active verb depicting the disciples' agency in convincing Jesus to stay with them—"they urged him strongly" (Lk 24:29)—comes sandwiched between the two passives, suggesting that their action in response to hearing the interpretation is somehow related to Jesus' action in delivering understanding.

[57]Similarly, in the next pericope Jesus explicitly reminds the disciples that while he was still with them before the crucifixion, he had already taught them everything written about him in Scripture (Lk 24:44). Like the two disciples on the way to Emmaus, the eleven possessed all the data necessary. Thus this pericope forces the same distinction upon us: prior to encountering the resurrected Christ, the disciples had all the biblical knowledge they needed, yet they failed to understand.

[58]See Hays, "Reading Scripture in Light of the Resurrection," 230.

it provides a fundamental orientation to the interpretive process. We do not read Scripture in order to know Scripture. We read Scripture in order to come to Jesus.

These Johannine texts corroborate the hermeneutical implications of the Luke 24 stories. Ultimately, understanding arises in a moment of grace, in a christological event. It is this grace that grants the disciples a new way of knowing. And while this hermeneutical grace comes through the text, it cannot be reduced to a mere textual encounter. This new mode of knowing Scripture is rightly deemed christological not because knowledge about Christ is subsequently imported to the text as an interpretive key (a common model of "christological exegesis"). Rather than moving from Jesus back to the text, the disciples move from the text to Jesus. The moment of illumination is not about knowing Scripture as much as it is about knowing Christ himself.

Undoubtedly, then, Luke 24 stresses the christological context of interpretation. But this is not the only context. After all, Jesus' presence in the act of interpretation does not, in itself, produce understanding. I mention Luke 24 here in the introduction because as much as it offers hermeneutical insight, it implies that the process of understanding is both christological and multidimensional. In this text, the four above-mentioned relationships—the christological, historical-institutional, communal, and missional—all exert influence, together shaping both the nature of the disciples' newly emerging identity and the nature of the hermeneutical moment.

For the disciples, the christological event of understanding, though radically new, does not emerge out of thin air. Christ's gift of understanding occurs within the context of a historical narrative that gives it shape. Understanding arises in conversation with knowledge, hopes, and traditions inherited from the past. The memory of the women at the tomb is an integral component of their newfound understanding (Lk 24:6, 8). And along with recalling the written traditions, the Emmaus disciples bring a particular historical narrative to the event of understanding—"we had hoped that he was the one to redeem Israel" (Lk 24:21).

At the same time, the event of understanding is communal, emerging from concrete acts of togetherness, friendship, and hospitality. For the Emmaus disciples, understanding arises as Christ's own presence and their inherited hopes coalesce in a concrete act of bodily togetherness.[59] The hermeneutical significance of the first two relational dynamics is actualized in a shared space around a shared meal.

Finally, the event of understanding is missional, for the process of understanding is bound up with movement and proclamation. The women immediately went and "told all this to the eleven and to all the rest" (Lk 24:9), and the Emmaus disciples, upon seeing Christ, immediately "told what had happened on the road" (Lk 24:35). The missional dimensions are most obvious in the final pericope. After opening their minds to understand Scripture (Lk 24:45), Jesus proceeds to lay the groundwork for mission by insisting that his name be proclaimed to all nations (Lk 24:47). In Luke 24, the hermeneutical moment is simultaneously a missional moment.

Surveying the argument. Inspired by the example of Luke 24, I contend that while understanding is fundamentally a gift arising from the community's relationship with the risen One, it simultaneously involves relationships with the institutional past, a local gathering, and the wider world. In each of the book's four parts I explore one of these church-defining relationships. Each part follows a similar pattern. I first engage in a close reading of a leading representative (or representatives) of that particular approach to ecclesial hermeneutics before then inviting Bonhoeffer into the conversation. Each of these conversations achieves a twofold purpose. The first is descriptive and analytical. It allows me to investigate the logic underlying a particular approach to theological interpretation and to show how theological commitments regarding the nature of the church subsequently determine the nature of the hermeneutical enterprise within it. In each section, in other words, I argue from the top down in order to demonstrate that different conceptions of God, Christ, and church fund different conceptions of the hermeneutical task. What is God up to in Jesus (Christology)? Why might Jesus call people to himself (ecclesiology)? And why might this God give this book to these people (scriptural hermeneutics)? Pursuing the descriptive component of my argument in this manner holds value for those interested in navigating the diversity of conversations about theological

---

[59]See Stanley Hauerwas, "The Insufficiency of Scripture: Why Discipleship Is Required," in *Unleashing the Scripture: Freeing the Bible from Captivity to America* (Nashville: Abingdon, 1993), 47-62.

interpretation, for it provides theological rationale for identifying and categorizing the different theologies of interpretation on offer today.

But my main goal is not to categorize. The descriptive task leads me into a corrective and constructive task. It will become evident that while much is to be gleaned from recent contributions, they are not beyond critique. By drawing attention to their underlying theological presuppositions, I hope to interrogate recent proposals. This is where Bonhoeffer proves his worth. His complex theological imagination allows me to diagnose one-sided tendencies prevalent in many discussions about biblical interpretation. I contend that hermeneutical proposals that foreground the church commonly rely upon truncated ecclesiological commitments. This means that only one dimension of the church does the bulk of the hermeneutical heavy lifting. This mistake is theoretically deficient because it fails to account for various relationships that characterize the church. Moreover—and perhaps most importantly—this failure exerts a distorting effect at the practical level by overburdening certain practices while neglecting others. The respective parts of this book provide examples of how this plays out in particular cases.

Beyond merely diagnosing this situation, Bonhoeffer points toward a constructive and integrative alternative, what I call a hermeneutic of discipleship. As I demonstrate in the following chapters, Bonhoeffer contrasts two modes of biblical exposition—the universal and the concrete. The former remains stuck at the level of abstraction and thus cannot become truly theological. The latter, a gift of grace, is what happens when Christ becomes personally present to the church through proclamation and sacrament. Theological interpretation is what happens in this latter situation. Theological interpretation is what happens whenever the words of Scripture become concrete here and now. For Bonhoeffer, therefore, the possibility of theological interpretation is distinctly ecclesial. To read "as the church" is to read attentively to Christ's concrete voice. This means that even biblical claims as seemingly straightforward as "love your neighbor as yourself" (Mt 22:39) and "turn the other cheek" (Mt 5:39) remain lifeless abstractions apart from Christ.[60] Though perhaps possessing spiritual-aesthetic appeal, such claims are, in and of themselves, notably devoid of specific content. The

---

[60]For example, see Bonhoeffer's lecture, "On the Theological Foundation of the World Alliance," in *Ecumenical, Academic, and Pastoral Work: 1931–1932*, DBWE 11:356-74.

abstract becomes particular only when Christ speaks the words, which is just what the church hopes for when it reads the Bible.

I argue that reading as the church, precisely because it is concrete and not universal, cannot be reduced to a method or an interpretive strategy. Theological interpretation is a capacious category, able to accommodate a whole host of reading strategies, styles, methods, and procedures. On one level, this claim intends to forestall any facile attempt to pit theological reading against critical reading. On a deeper level, my argument about reading as the church intends to broaden and complexify the way we imagine the act of faithful reading. I do so not to make the task more complicated but to open our eyes to the possibility that "theological interpretation" happens in innumerable ways, styles, and modes. Our efforts to adjudicate do not lend themselves well to the practice of theological interpretation. In fact, it is precisely as we attempt to adjudicate the practice of faithful reading that we are most tempted to adopt certain distortive assumptions. When we begin reflecting on what counts as good interpretation, we usually operate at the intellectual level, as if hermeneutical faithfulness were enacted entirely within one's brain, guided by a specific set of assumed criteria or norms. Following Bonhoeffer's understanding of the church, I argue for the impossibility of this account of interpretation. To read as the church is not to read in search of (or in light of) any particular set of ideas but to read in search of a person, the risen Christ. To read as the church, therefore, is not to read with any particular method but to read in a particular place (the community concretely gathered around Christ) and in a particular posture (hopefully attentive to Christ's presence through the Spirit). I contend that Bonhoeffer's notion of discipleship conveys this sense of place and posture. And as I argue in the respective sections of this book, his notion of discipleship is a complex reality, encompassing the church in its multiple relationships. Following his lead, therefore, helps us examine the various dimensions and possibilities of hermeneutical faithfulness.

It thus becomes evident that the coherence of my project owes much to Bonhoeffer. His voice serves as the keynote that allows me to draw diverse voices into harmony. In each of the four parts that compose this book I lay out key dimensions of Bonhoeffer's scriptural hermeneutic. What emerges from this is a theologically nuanced picture of Bonhoeffer as a reader of the

Bible. This contribution is noteworthy in its own right. Given the centrality of Scripture in Bonhoeffer's theological imagination, a disproportionately small amount of scholarly attention has been paid to it.[61]

I begin chapter one by listening to John Webster. Webster is particularly relevant for this project, for he masterfully depicts the church in its constitutive relationship to God. In classical terminology, he speaks of the church as the *creatura verbi*, the creature of the word. In chapter two, I invite Bonhoeffer to diagnose a lingering tendency within Webster's work. Bonhoeffer fundamentally agrees with the priority Webster places on divine speech, but he does so while remaining alert to the temptations of hermeneutical immateriality and passivity that often accompany word theologies. Bonhoeffer's concept of discipleship is helpful at precisely this point because it integrates incarnation and resurrection within one Christology. The chapter concludes by laying the groundwork for a Bonhoefferian hermeneutic of discipleship.

The second step toward arguing for a hermeneutic of discipleship is to show that Christ's call creates a community with a social history. Precisely as the *creatura verbi* the church is also an institution stretching through time. I begin by engaging Robert Jenson's ecclesial hermeneutic (chapter three)

---

[61]Most significant is Martin Kuske's work, *Das Alte Testament als Buch von Christus: Dietrich Bonhoeffers Wertung and Auslegung des Alten Testaments* (Göttingen: Vandenhoeck & Ruprecht, 1971), which appeared in English as *The Old Testament as the Book of Christ: An Appraisal of Bonhoeffer's Interpretation*, trans. S. T. Kimbrough Jr. (Philadelphia: Westminster Press, 1976). Other leading secondary works include Brock, "Bonhoeffer and the Bible in Christian Ethics"; Fowl and Jones, *Reading in Communion*, 135-64; Nadine Hamilton, "Dietrich Bonhoeffer and the Necessity of Kenosis for Scriptural Hermeneutics," *SJT* 71, no. 4 (2018): 441-59; Geffrey B. Kelly and F. Burton Nelson, "Dietrich Bonhoeffer's Theological Interpretation of Scripture for the Church," *Ex Auditu* 17 (2001): 1-30; Frits de Lange, *Waiting for the Word: Dietrich Bonhoeffer on Speaking About God*, trans. Martin M. Walton (Grand Rapids, MI: Eerdmans, 1999); Mawson, "Scripture"; Stephen J. Plant, *Taking Stock of Bonhoeffer: Studies in Biblical Interpretation and Ethics* (Burlington, VT: Ashgate, 2014); Brad Pribbenow, *Prayerbook of Christ: Dietrich Bonhoeffer's Christological Interpretation of the Psalms* (Lanham, MD: Lexington Books, 2018); John Webster, "'In the Shadow of Biblical Work': Barth and Bonhoeffer on Reading the Bible," *Toronto Journal of Theology* 17, no. 1 (2001): 75-92; Richard Weikart, "Scripture and Myth in Dietrich Bonhoeffer," *Fides et Historia* 25, no. 1 (1993): 12-25; Sean F. Winter, "Bonhoeffer and Biblical Interpretation: The Early Years," *Bonhoeffer Legacy* 1, no. 1 (2013): 1-15; idem, "'Present-ing' the Word: The Use and Abuse of Bonhoeffer on the Bible," *Bonhoeffer Legacy* 2, no. 2 (2014): 19-35; Ralph K. Wüstenberg and Jens Zimmermann, eds., *God Speaks to Us: Dietrich Bonhoeffer's Biblical Hermeneutics* (Frankfurt am Main: Lang, 2013); and Jens Zimmermann, "Reading the Book of the Church: Bonhoeffer's Christological Hermeneutics," *MT* 28, no. 4 (2012): 763-80.

before turning to Bonhoeffer (chapter four) as a means of forging a constructive synthesis between institutional and christological logics that might otherwise seem incommensurate. Whereas highly institutionalized hermeneutics threaten to conflate Christ into the church, Bonhoeffer suggests that the telos of institutional life is an encounter with Christ himself, the one who is free for the church precisely in being free from it. Given this account of the Christ-church relationship, Bonhoeffer points toward a set of christologically redefined historical-institutional practices.

The third step toward arguing for a hermeneutic of discipleship is to demonstrate the importance of togetherness. Through examining Stanley Hauerwas's ecclesial politic (chapter five) and Bonhoeffer's social Christology (chapter six), I argue that the two lines of thinking I pursued in parts one and two converge in the community, at the nexus of bodies gathered. The church exists simultaneously in relationship to the risen Christ and its historical-institutional past—and precisely in these two relational dynamics it exists concretely as a local gathering. In fact, I argue that the two previous ecclesiological dimensions remain hermeneutically vacuous without concrete practices of togetherness that sustain the process by which the community discerns Christ's voice and enacts its institutional identity.

The fourth and final step toward arguing for a hermeneutic of discipleship is to depict the act of interpretation in relation to the world. What does it mean for theological interpretation that the church is a missional community? In chapter seven I highlight a tension between two different strands of missional ecclesiology, which I call the culturalist and secularist options. I also argue that the practice of theological interpretation today commonly relies upon a strongly normative depiction of the church that cannot adequately account for the diversity of the gospel's crosscultural movement. The basic reason animating this situation is simple: if reading Scripture is something that happens within the culture of the church, then any missionary movement beyond the culture of the church is a movement away from the context of hermeneutical faithfulness. Hermeneutical faithfulness and missional movement remain, at best, sequentially ordered events. In chapter eight I address these shortcomings by reading Dietrich Bonhoeffer as a missional theologian. In his mature theology he gestures toward a church that lives always in and for the world, and does so without compromising its confessional distinctiveness. Building on Bonhoeffer's missional ecclesiology, I propose that missionary movement and intercultural encounter are ingredients within the process of hermeneutical faithfulness, not merely its proper outcome. Mission, at least in part, is how the church learns to see.

While my animating concerns are deeply theological, they are altogether practical. Indeed, theological articulations always touch ground in performative outcomes, in lived expressions that reveal the "functional theology" operative in any community of faith.[62] For this reason, a properly theological account of hermeneutical faithfulness is impossible without attention to the actual activities involved in the reading process. Bonhoeffer understood this well, and he proves himself to be a pastoral theologian by the facility with which he moves back and forth between theoretical and practical registers. Following Bonhoeffer's example, I hope to make a constructive claim not only about the theology of Scripture but also about the practices and habits that sustain faithful reading. As I understand things, the two are inseparable.

At its most basic, then, this is a project about Jesus, his followers, and their use of a book in their ongoing acts of following. Stephen Sykes famously suggests that Christianity is "an essentially contested concept."[63] It follows, moreover, that one's claim about the essence of this concept shapes the way one construes the task of reading Scripture as a Christian practice. As I understand Christianity, its essence lies in Jesus, "the absolutely unique, historic one" raised to new life by the Father through the Spirit.[64] As Bonhoeffer bluntly puts the matter: "Christianity arises out of the encounter with a concrete human being: Jesus."[65] Following Bonhoeffer, I center my vision of faith—and hence of all theological loci, including theological hermeneutics—on the "ongoing presence of the synoptic Jesus."[66] Neither the church nor its reading (nor any other of its practices) makes sense apart from the process of following after its irreducibly singular Lord. The universality and lordship of this particular Nazarene creates the church. The

---

[62]Billings, *Word of God for the People of God*, 15.
[63]Stephen Sykes, *The Identity of Christianity: Theologians and the Essence of Christianity from Schleiermacher to Barth* (Philadelphia: Fortress, 1984), 251.
[64]Bonhoeffer, *Theological Education at Finkenwalde*, DBWE 14:424.
[65]Bonhoeffer, *Letters and Papers from Prison*, DBWE 8:490.
[66]Bonhoeffer, *Discipleship*, DBWE 4:184.

space Jesus creates by calling people to himself is the church's hermeneutical space, the space in and for which his followers faithfully engage their text. Not only does Jesus promise to be always present to his followers (e.g., Mt 28:20), he promises continually to speak to them in the present—"Let anyone who has an ear listen to what the Spirit is saying to the churches" (Rev 2:7). In this project I paint a picture of what this listening entails. What ultimately emerges from this account of Christ and the fourfold account of the church that corresponds to him is a hermeneutic of discipleship, a way of thinking of Scripture that takes place in the wake of Christ's ongoing action and aims at participation in it.

PART ONE

The Church as Creature of the Word: Hermeneutics and the Risen Christ

1

Reading in the Domain of
the Risen Christ

A CONVERSATION WITH JOHN WEBSTER

OUR FIRST STEP toward a holistic account of reading in the church is to listen to John Webster. He offers a theologically rich depiction of the church as it exists in relationship to God's action in the risen Christ. In terms of classical Reformation theology, he points us toward an account of the church as the *creatura verbi*, the creature of the word.[1]

Such a goal will immediately elicit reactions, for it is often feared that "word theologies" erode genuine ecclesiological reflection. Henri de Lubac, for example, notes the risk of spiritualism and the subtle slide toward "ecclesial Monophysitism" that can arise in Protestant accounts of the church.[2] This argument quickly becomes hermeneutical. It is precisely the thinness of Reformation ecclesiologies, so the argument goes, that cedes space for historical-critical practices to flourish.[3] It would seem, then, that

---

[1]On the *creatura verbi*, see Christoph Schwöbel, "The Creature of the Word: Recovering the Ecclesiology of the Reformers," in *On Being the Church: Essays on the Christian Community*, ed. Colin E. Gunton and Daniel W. Hardy (Edinburgh: T&T Clark, 1989), 110-55. According to Schwöbel, this ecclesial dynamic remains a "forgotten heritage" that nevertheless holds great theological potential ("Creature of the Word," 110).

[2]See Henri de Lubac, *Catholicism: Christ and the Common Destiny of Man*, trans. Lancelot C. Sheppard and Sister Elizabeth Englund (San Francisco: Ignatius Press, 1988), 75.

[3]For a recent example of this argument, see Michael C. Legaspi, *The Death of Scripture and the Rise of Biblical Studies* (Oxford: Oxford University Press, 2010). For a recent defense of the Protestant Scripture principle in light of such critiques, see Kevin J. Vanhoozer, *Biblical*

reestablishing a traditionally Catholic ecclesiology would provide the tools necessary to articulate a theologically rigorous account of Christian interpretive practices. Such logic has driven much of the recent effort to recover a distinctly theological interpretation of Scripture.[4]

Given this reasoning, it might seem strange to argue for a theological mode of reading grounded in the church as the *creatura verbi*. Can this fund a distinctly ecclesial form of interpreting Scripture? If church vanishes behind word, as critics worry, then surely little hermeneutical gain is found in this manner of reflection. Ecclesiological spiritualism would leave us hermeneutically empty-handed.

It will become evident in what follows that even as I reference the Catholic criticism of word theologies, I am not necessarily seeking to chart a via media between them. The ecclesial hermeneutic that emerges in this book remains distinctly Protestant. This in itself is a helpful contribution, for much recent discussion about the theological interpretation of Scripture has subtly elided the difference between Protestant and Catholic theologies of church and Scripture. Here in part one I note some common Catholic criticisms because they helpfully highlight real liabilities lurking within Protestant ecclesiology. Granting unique priority to the one who creates the church is not an excuse to neglect the real significance of the church's agency, as some fear. Instead, as I argue here, it gives a distinct shape to our theological depiction of the community's material, social, and historical dimensions.

JOHN WEBSTER AND CHRISTOLOGY AS "NEGATIVE ECCLESIOLOGY"

Toward this end, I turn now to engage Webster, one of contemporary Protestantism's most able theological representatives. His theology of Scripture reads as a sustained hermeneutical manifesto, an attack on what he calls the

---

Authority After Babel: Retrieving the Solas *in the Spirit of Mere Protestant Christianity* (Grand Rapids, MI: Brazos Press, 2016).

[4]The general trend toward *ressourcement* theology has roots in de Lubac's magisterial work, *Medieval Exegesis: The Four Senses of Scripture*, 4 vols. (Grand Rapids, MI: Eerdmans, 1998). This trend's impact on Protestant interpretive thought is readily evident; see, as a prime example, David Steinmetz, "The Superiority of Pre-Critical Exegesis," in *The Theological Interpretation of Scripture: Classic and Contemporary Readings*, ed. Stephen E. Fowl (Malden, MA: Blackwell, 1997), 26-38.

"dogmatic mislocation" of Scripture and interpretation within modern theology.[5] He "resists the quasi-axiomatic status accorded to an anthropology of the interpreting subject" prevalent in modern hermeneutical theory and instead gives "sustained attention to a figure who has virtually disappeared from theological hermeneutics in the modern era, namely Jesus."[6]

In order to make this claim, he takes great care, especially in his later works, to ground God's outward activity in God's wholly realized life in eternity.[7] By stressing divine perfection he attempts to resist trends in twentieth-century theology that reconceptualize the church's traditional ontological language. The problem with these approaches, Webster suggests, is that while rightly accounting for the humanity of Jesus, they risk neglecting the prevenience of divine being and work.

The ramifications of this neglect ripple across the spectrum of theological reflection. They are especially acute in the hermeneutical realm, particularly as they lead to accounts of hermeneutical space divorced from divine action. While a revisionary approach to divine being does not necessarily entail hermeneutical naturalism, Webster alerts us to the coincidence of the two by suggesting that the "naturalization" of the biblical text and the act of reading it are direct corollaries of the naturalization or historicization of the church's talk about God. Indeed, as a discrete discipline, hermeneutics emerged in tandem with the separation of the Bible from theology, which itself mirrored a more fundamental separation between divine action and historical reality. In this sense, modern hermeneutical reflection emerges from historicist soil.[8]

---

[5]John Webster, *Holy Scripture: A Dogmatic Sketch* (Cambridge: Cambridge University Press, 2003), 49. Also see idem, "The Dogmatic Location of the Canon," *Neue Zeitschrift für systematische Theologie und Religionsphilosophie* 43, no. 1 (2001): 17-43.

[6]John Webster, "Hermeneutics in Modern Theology: Some Doctrinal Reflections," *SJT* 51, no. 3 (1998): 308.

[7]John Webster, *The Domain of the Word* (London: T & T Clark, 2012), 7. His reliance on post-Reformation orthodoxy is clearest in idem, "*Omnia . . . Pertractantur in Sacra Doctrina Sub Ratione Dei*: On the Matter of Christian Theology," in *God and the Works of God*, vol. 1 of *God Without Measure: Working Papers in Christian Theology* (London: Bloomsbury T&T Clark, 2016), 3-12.

[8]This is why Hans Frei claims, "Generally . . . hermeneutics and biblical-historical criticism grew up together" (Frei, *The Eclipse of Biblical Narrative: A Study in Eighteenth and Nineteenth Century Hermeneutics* [New Haven, CT: Yale University Press, 1974], 104). He argues that whereas classical interpreters assumed that the literal and historical senses of Scripture were identical, the emergence of a gap between the two senses conditioned the emergence of the hermeneutical

Webster responds by going straight to the root. He contends that "the tide of God's loving acts toward creatures" flows from the "infinite ocean" of God's being.[9] An account of "God's infinitely deep, fully realized life" *in se* serves as the foundation for theological hermeneutics.[10] Care is required here, lest this emphasis on eternity draw focus away from history. While Webster may seem susceptible to this danger, as critics sometimes fear, he consistently insists that attention to God's perfection need not entail the neglect of the economy. Though the economy obviously takes priority in the order of intellect, this "should not be mistaken for the drastically different (and calamitous) dogmatic claim that the only significant distinctions are those enacted in the theater of God's external works."[11] Real distinction exists on both sides of the economic-immanent divide, for the eternal intratrinitarian relation between paternity and filiation is intrinsic to divine perfection.[12] In this sense, Webster is careful to note that "the primacy of theology proper should not be so inordinately emphasized that the glory of God's works of nature and grace is diminished."[13] The eternal processions that constitute God's perfection ground and make possible the economic missions, which is why Webster insists that eternal divine being includes evangelical movement, a secondary though no less real expression of God's love. While God's being does not depend on the missions, they are no mere epiphenomena; God's outer works—within the realm of which falls the church's hermeneutical enterprise—remain aspects of the doctrine of God.

---

task in its modern form. Schleiermacher stands as a prime example. Often called the father of modern hermeneutics, he presupposes that historical distance, hence misunderstanding, is the interpretive norm. The solution to this situation is interpretive activity that bridges the gap between then and now by using interpretive skill to dig through the text to its original underlying experience. Lost within a vision like Schleiermacher's, Webster suggests, is the sense in which God's agency is involved in spanning the perceived hermeneutical gap. On the relation between historicism and historical criticism more generally, see Roy A. Harrisville and Walter Sundberg, *The Bible in Modern Culture: Baruch Spinoza to Brevard Childs* (Grand Rapids, MI: Eerdmans, 2002); and Jonathan Sheehan, *The Enlightenment Bible: Translation, Scholarship, Culture* (Princeton, NJ: Princeton University Press, 2007).

[9]John Webster, "Perfection and Participation," in *The Analogy of Being: Invention of the Antichrist or Wisdom of God?*, ed. Thomas Joseph White (Grand Rapids, MI: Eerdmans, 2011), 381.

[10]Webster, *Domain of the Word*, xi.

[11]Webster, "Perfection and Participation," 383.

[12]Webster, *Domain of the Word*, 33.

[13]Webster, "*Omnia . . . Pertractantur*," 9.

This account of God's being allows Webster to situate historical realities within the scope of divine work. Paradigmatically, this means that Jesus' historicity does not compete with but is enabled by divine activity. Webster thus insists that the church's understanding of Jesus must be "undergirded by an immensely powerful theology of God's perfection."[14] He intends for this claim to counteract a particular christological error. "One illuminating way to write the history of modernity would be to envisage it as the story of the steady eclipse in the belief in Jesus' presence." Once Jesus ceases to be seen as a "presently operative and communicative figure . . . other doctrinal areas expand to fill the gap vacated by his removal."[15]

Prime among them is ecclesiology. Stated simply, Webster fears that talk of church comes to fill in for talk of Christ. Consequently, he understands much of his dogmatic work as what he calls "negative ecclesiology," a prophylactic measure against dogmatic distortion. By means of turning to a classical account of divine being and a corresponding account of Jesus' perfection, he attempts "to win back to Christology" territory that has been annexed by talk of the church.[16]

At this point Webster may seem to confirm critics' worst fears that word theologies carry an antiecclesiological bent. I will address this concern more fully below, for it carries some truth. For now, in fairness to Webster, we should note the specificity of his theological agenda. The negative tone of his ecclesiology is elicited not by the nature of the church per se but by perceived ecclesiological shortcomings in recent theology.

Webster has one particular such shortcoming in mind: the blurring of the distinction between word and church. This danger is evident, for example, within "communion ecclesiologies" that make the church the means of Christ's presence to the world.[17] While these ecclesiologies have the virtue of accounting for the church's visibility, they risk implying what Calvin refers to as the *crassa mixtura* between God and God's people.[18] In being

---

[14]Webster, *Domain of the Word*, 83.

[15]John Webster, *Word and Church: Essays in Christian Dogmatics* (London: T&T Clark, 2002), 2-3.

[16]Webster, *Word and Church*, 3.

[17]See Robert W. Jenson, *The Works of God*, vol. 2 of *Systematic Theology* (Oxford: Oxford University Press, 1999), 213. I offer more on this in chap. 3.

[18]At this point, Webster's Reformed heritage becomes especially pronounced. He believes that contemporary communion ecclesiologies replicate Osiander's error of proffering a "gross

heavily invested in an ontological union between Christ and church, these accounts of the church risk implying a "porous Christology" and thereby eliding the "utter difference" between God and creatures.[19] The hermeneutical danger here can only be stated briefly in anticipation of a fuller treatment in chapters three and four: when the difference between Christ and the church is collapsed and the alterity of the text compromised, readers find themselves within a hermeneutical space that lacks the leverage by means of which Scripture can become God's speech *to* the church. Consequently, a church that should be listening instead finds itself speaking. In this sense, the *crassa mixtura* presses toward a particular instantiation of hermeneutical naturalism.

For now, we should note that Webster's account of the Trinity and Christology produces an ecclesiology not confined to natural or social categories. The *creatura verbi* has its being within the triune economy of grace as the "first fruits of God's utterance."[20] Hence, he confidently proclaims, "'Church' is not a struggle to make something happen, but a lived attempt to make sense of, celebrate and bear witness to what has already been established by God's grace."[21] The church exists because Christ calls people to himself. The *creatura verbi*, therefore, is the collection of people gathered around the risen One, the space that exists because of his grace and in the wake of his call.

In its response to the "already" of God's grace, the church certainly possesses social dimensions. In this, Webster remains alert to the danger of construing the church in a one-sidedly invisible manner. Yet he distinguishes his position by noting that the church is not identical *simpliciter* with its visibility. Its social-material dimensions always take shape in the wake of the risen One.[22] As the *creatura verbi*, its being is a gift, never its own creation, which implies that the church's visible existence is not a social project but remains derivative of its primary task of attending to Christ.

---

mixture of Christ with believers"; see John Calvin, *Institutes of the Christian Religion*, trans. Henry Beveridge (Peabody, MA: Hendrickson, 2008), 481-82 (3.11.10).

[19]John Webster, "The Church and the Perfection of God," in *The Community of the Word: Toward an Evangelical Ecclesiology*, ed. Mark Husbands and Daniel J. Treier (Downers Grove, IL: InterVarsity Press, 2005), 87.

[20]Webster, *Holy Scripture*, 71.

[21]John Webster, "The Church as Witnessing Community," *Scottish Bulletin of Evangelical Theology* 21, no. 1 (2003): 28.

[22]See Webster, "*Omnia . . . Pertractantur*," 178.

FUNDAMENTAL ASYMMETRY AND ECCLESIAL ACTIVITY

This brief tour through the logic of Webster's theology reveals how dogmatic work in the doctrine of God pays off in the doctrine of the church. From a vantage point in his ecclesiology, it becomes clear that prioritizing Christ over the church resources a specific account of ecclesial activity. In all that it does, the church is fundamentally a hearing church, a church that has its being in the act of turning toward Christ's voice.[23] Here we arrive at the heart of Webster's hermeneutical insight. Emphasizing the livelihood and loquaciousness of the risen One places the interpreter in a particular hermeneutical orientation. Because Holy Scripture is an alien reality, an exogenous element of communal life, the church is essentially "a domain of receiving."[24] Hence all ecclesial activity, hermeneutical or otherwise, grows from the same core task—to receive the gospel.[25] Therefore the church must read, Webster claims, from a posture of "self-renunciation before the presence and action of God."[26]

The threat of hermeneutical passivity. A certain danger looms at this point. Webster's emphasis on ecclesial passivity calls to mind the Catholic claim against Protestant ecclesiology. Balthasar's famous appraisal of the early Barth gives voice to this criticism: "Actualism, with its constant, relentless reduction of all activity to God . . . leaves no room for any other center of activity outside of God. In relation to God, there can only be passivity."[27] While Webster's account of ecclesial agency is not identical to that of early Barth, his notion of interpretation as "active passivity or passive activity"[28] nevertheless seems to fall within the range of Balthasar's critique. Moreover, by prioritizing the divine address and the hermeneutical necessity of renunciation in relation to it, it might seem that Webster offers an inherently eventful account of the church that lacks historical stability and concrete creaturely dimensions. All forms of human activity, it would seem, are at best ancillary to the true being of the church.

---

[23]John Webster, "The Visible Attests the Invisible," in Husbands and Treier, *Community of the Word*, 111.

[24]Webster, *Domain of the Word*, 25; and idem, "Visible Attests the Invisible," 110.

[25]Webster, "Church as Witnessing Community," 21.

[26]Webster, *Holy Scripture*, 72.

[27]Hans Urs von Balthasar, *The Theology of Karl Barth*, trans. Edward T. Oakes (San Francisco: Ignatius Press, 1992), 105.

[28]Webster, *Holy Scripture*, 72.

Balthasar's critical insight has reappeared in several iterations. Others have alleged, for example, that a theology of the word presses toward to a "bifurcation" of the true church (an invisible spiritual reality) from the empirical church (a visible historical reality).[29] Word theologies, therefore, threaten to devolve into a form of "ecclesiological Nestorianism" in which the church consists of something like two natures only occasionally united.[30] This "ecclesiological occasionalism" threatens to undermine any sense of continuity in ecclesial existence.[31] Suffering from a christological constriction, Protestant ecclesiology one-sidedly emphasizes God's revelatory action in Christ and thereby leaves no space for ongoing historical and ecclesial activity to participate in God's grace. In short, theologies of the word seem to represent an especially acute instance of what Yves Congar refers to as the "absence in Protestant thought of a genuine ecclesiology."[32] However we parse the issue, the danger is that the church's visible dimensions are reduced to the level of a "mere secular institution."[33] As a supernatural body, the church is but a fleeting moment. In this case, its perduring spatial dimensions remain disconnected from God's activity. The church's concrete activity borders on meaninglessness; as Balthasar memorably puts the matter, "God is in heaven, and man wanders here alone on his poor earth."[34]

This line of critique forces the question upon us: Can hermeneutical practices within the *creatura verbi* achieve anything significant? Balthasar gets to the heart of this problem: "Viewed from above, the Church completely coincides with God's Word; but, viewed from below, all her attempts to give expression to this Word are radically fallible."[35] As a secular space, the church will certainly engage in visible activities, but is this anything more than a mere "wandering alone" that remains "radically fallible"? If not, it would

---

[29]Nicholas M. Healy, "The Logic of Karl Barth's Ecclesiology: Analysis, Assessment and Proposed Modification," *MT* 10, no. 3 (1994): 258-59.

[30]Karl Rahner, "Membership of the Church According to the Teaching of Pius XII's Encyclical *Mystici Corporis Christi*," in *Theological Investigations*, vol. 2, *Man in the Church*, trans. Karl-Heinz Kruger (New York: Crossroad, 1975), 70.

[31]Stanley Hauerwas, *Character and the Christian Life: A Study in Theological Ethics* (San Antonio: Trinity University Press, 1975), 173.

[32]Yves M.-J. Congar, *Tradition and Traditions: An Historical and Theological Essay*, trans. Michael Naseby and Thomas Rainborough (London: Burns & Oates, 1966), 422.

[33]Lubac, *Catholicism*, 75.

[34]Balthasar, *Theology of Karl Barth*, 365.

[35]Balthasar, *Theology of Karl Barth*, 107.

seem that within the *creatura verbi* the church's hermeneutical endeavors amount to nothing more than a chasing after the wind. If this is the case, can the church really function as a hermeneutical space?

Bonhoeffer between Balthasar and Barth: the christological unity of act and being. The charge of "ecclesiological Nestorianism" obviously calls to mind christological debates. Without taking the analogy between incarnation and ecclesiology too seriously, one basic insight emerges from this comparison: as in Christology, the issue here becomes not whether the church is constituted by divine and creaturely dimensions, but how they relate. If the danger is a one-sided eventfulness that severs the two, the solution requires a precise and nuanced account of their relation, one that places priority on divine action yet does not thereby neglect the historicity and creatureliness of the church.

Here Bonhoeffer becomes especially valuable for my argument, for he was one of the first theologians to criticize the actualistic and anti-ecclesiological tendencies in Barth's theology of the Word. Though it is not commonly recognized, Balthasar's famous criticism of Barth's ontology of grace draws from Bonhoeffer's much earlier criticism. As the very title of his book, *Act and Being*, makes clear, Bonhoeffer insists on holding event and ontology together. Balthasar notes that "Bonhoeffer already realized this [i.e., the inseparability of event and ontology] in 1931 in his penetrating study *Akt und Sein*, which tried to unify a theology of actualism with a theology of being-in-Christ, that is, an ontology of the Church."[36] Balthasar's more famous critique echoes Bonhoeffer's original insight: Barth fails to take sufficient account of what God has actually done in Jesus and, consequently, underplays the extent to which the ongoing historicity of the church community is central to revelation. As Balthasar rephrases the matter: "God's revelation can only be an event if something actually takes place."[37] There can be no act without being, no being without act.

According to Bonhoeffer, Barth rightly responded to modern theology's loss of transcendence. Given various trends that objectified, historicized, or humanized revelation, Barth forcefully responded by flipping modernity on its head: God is the subject, not the object, of revelation. God always

---

[36]Balthasar, *Theology of Karl Barth*, 365.
[37]Balthasar, *Theology of Karl Barth*, 364.

remains Lord over the knowledge of God. Bonhoeffer eagerly followed Barth in making this basic methodological move. But working within Barth's reorientation of theology, he sought to offer a corrective voice. He sensed that in one-sidedly emphasizing divine subjectivity, Barth swung the pendulum too far. Barth successfully prevented God's objectification, but did so at the expense of revelation's historicity and continuity. Analogous to Kant's transcendental subject, God becomes for Barth sheer subjectivity, an actor who remains always outside of space and time.[38]

Several implications follow from this. Bonhoeffer believed that Barth's subject-concept of revelation entails a merely formal and negative account of divine freedom, i.e., a freedom *from* creaturely realities.[39] Moreover, he believed that Barth's stress on the eventful and gratuitous nature of divine discourse implies that God's word is always arriving but never actually present.[40] This account of revelation, as Bonhoeffer understands it, consists of a timeless event that enters history but leaves no lasting effect. If this is the case, the church may indeed exist in relationship to God. What is much less certain is the extent to which the church can also exist as a temporal entity in history.

Much could be said about Balthasar's complex criticism of Barth and its likeness to Bonhoeffer's. The relevant issue for my argument at this point is the way Bonhoeffer charts a path beyond Barth. Given the apparent impasse between an act-concept of revelation and a being-concept of revelation, Bonhoeffer proposes a unique third option: revelation takes the form of a *person*.[41]

Bonhoeffer's basic insight is that the concept of person unites both act and being dimensions of revelation. It includes both existential encounter (i.e., act) and historical continuity (i.e., being). Though Bonhoeffer is certainly not beholden to phenomenological descriptions, basic observations about human personhood help elucidate his use of the term *person*. When I encounter another person, I am encountering not a mere object to be

---

[38]Michael P. DeJonge, *Bonhoeffer's Theological Formation: Berlin, Barth, and Protestant Theology* (Oxford: Oxford University Press, 2012), 74-75.

[39]See DeJonge, *Bonhoeffer's Theological Formation*, 8-9.

[40]Dietrich Bonhoeffer, *Act and Being*, DBWE 2:90-91.

[41]See Bonhoeffer, *Act and Being*, DBWE 2:115, 128. The best recent exposition of this theme is found in DeJonge, *Bonhoeffer's Theological Formation*, 56-82. DeJonge refers to Bonhoeffer's unique alternative to act and being as a "person-concept of revelation" (75).

known but another subject who stands over against me. At the same time, this encounter is not a timeless moment but a historical event with past and future dimensions. A person, according to Bonhoeffer, is neither sheer event nor sheer object but a unification of eventfulness and objectivity in the distinct personhood of the other. For this reason, as Michael DeJonge writes, "Person, as a concept of contingent revelation in continuity, is the conceptual foundation for a theology that solves the problem of act and being."[42]

Bonhoeffer is therefore able to claim that revelation is neither an absolute event nor a stagnant ontological given but "the being of the person of Christ in the community of persons of the church."[43] He claims that as person God encounters humanity from the outside and remains permanently distinct from the knowing subject (thereby incorporating the important contribution of act theologies). Yet he simultaneously claims that the person of Christ always exists in and with the community of people that is his body, such that his person is marked by a degree of historical continuity (thereby incorporating the important contribution of being theologies). Christ as person always stands over against the community of human persons and yet precisely in this freedom remains personally present to it.

While Bonhoeffer directs his argument in *Act and Being* toward both act and being concepts of revelation, we are here concerned with the way he moves beyond Barth. Barth's fateful mistake, Bonhoeffer suggests, is that he thinks of God strictly as a subject and thereby fails to understand God as person.[44] Given Barth's one-sidedly dialectical approach to theology, God acts as a divine subject who either remains hidden in eternal nonobjectivity or, if momentarily present in an event of grace, overwhelms creaturely reality. God can act from a divine distance but cannot be genuinely present with humanity in so doing.[45]

But new options emerge when we realize that in Christ "the being of God is God's being person [*das Sein ist sein Personsein*]."[46] For Bonhoeffer, this

---

[42]DeJonge, *Bonhoeffer's Theological Formation*, 77.

[43]Bonhoeffer, *Act and Being*, DBWE 2:125.

[44]Bonhoeffer, *Act and Being*, DBWE 2:125.

[45]To be fair to Barth, he eventually learned to reinscribe this actualism within Christology, thereby maintaining his early emphasis on divine freedom while also accounting for God's presence—indeed, God's very humanity—in Jesus Christ. See Karl Barth, *The Humanity of God*, trans. John Newton Thomas and Thomas Wieser (Louisville, KY: Westminster John Knox, 1960), 37-68.

[46]Bonhoeffer, *Act and Being*, DBWE 2:115.

means that revelation is not an object at our disposal, but neither is it simply a word spoken from an eternal distance. Revelation is a person. By turning to the concept of person as a third way beyond the impasse of act and being, Bonhoeffer adds incarnational thickness to theologies of the Word. The *creatura verbi*, then, is not a mere echo of a distant divine voice but is the community that correlates to and participates in God's very presence in the person of Christ.

It is clear, then, that Bonhoeffer has arrived at his solution to the problem of act and being in a strictly theological manner. Though he shares certain affinities with dialogical philosophy and the philosophy of personalism (both of which were gaining popularity in the 1920s as alternatives to idealism's subject-object paradigm), Bonhoeffer's concept of person is ultimately won not through phenomenological observation but through the experience of encountering Christ in the church. From a purely philosophical perspective, act and being remain perpetually in tension. There is no philosophical solution to the dilemma. But in the miracle of the incarnation, Bonhoeffer claims, God has done the impossible. Jesus Christ enacts divine transcendence squarely within human history. As *transcendent* person, God is with us yet never at our disposal. As transcendent *person*, God is present in a way that does not annihilate our human personhood. Whereas Bonhoeffer believed that Barth's one-sidedly dialectical theology posits a God who is present at humanity's expense, Bonhoeffer here articulates an account of God as person who is essentially *pro nobis*. When we encounter Christ in the church, we see that God does not act in history as a mere revealing subject; rather, God has *entered* history as an incarnate person, and as such God exists always with us and for us. For sure, Christ's freedom cannot be collapsed into his promeity; the miracle of the incarnation is that God has sacrificed none of God's divinity in entering history. Given the reality of Christ's presence in the church, however, Bonhoeffer would have us see that we cannot posit divine reality without simultaneously thinking of this reality's personal presence with us.[47]

Bonhoeffer's person-concept of revelation remains a structuring feature of his theology throughout his career. All of his thinking circles around

---

[47]See Philip Ziegler, "Christ For Us Today—Promeity in the Christologies of Bonhoeffer and Kierkegaard," *IJST* 15, no. 1 (2013): 25-41.

Christus praesens. This is especially true when it comes to ecclesiology. Bonhoeffer's person-concept of revelation allows him to appropriate Barth's account of divine freedom in a way that leaves genuine space for a concrete community. The key here lies in his move from a merely formal to a substantial account of freedom. He succinctly gets to the heart of the matter: "God freely chose to be bound to historical human beings. . . . God is not free *from* human beings but *for* them."[48] The implications for ecclesiology lie close at hand: "God *is* present, that is, not in eternal non-objectivity but . . . 'haveable,' graspable in the Word within the church."[49] Given Christ's free personal presence to his people, the church takes on central significance as the site and bearer of divine revelation. And because the church is constituted not merely by a divine word but by a divine person, it shares in Christ's own continuity. The church exists, for Bonhoeffer, wherever Christ's "living person is at work."[50] As he argued in his earlier work, *Sanctorum Communio*, "There is no relation to Christ in which the relation to the church is not necessarily established as well."[51] Not only does Christ's presence give the church its existence, it also shapes the inner dynamics of communal life. Thus, Bonhoeffer claims that the church is structured as a genuine community that is with-one-another (*miteinander*) and for-each-other (*füreinander*) precisely because Christ exists always with and for others.[52] The structure of the community shares in the structure of Christ's own person. Bonhoeffer ties these threads together in his famous claim that "the church is Christ existing as community [*die Kirche ist Christus als Gemeinde existierend*]."[53]

Ecclesiology and fundamental asymmetry. It is clear, then, that Bonhoeffer articulates an account of the *creatura verbi* that succeeds at upholding the historical dimensions of the church. With this, he avoids the ecclesiological dangers of word theologies. But we should pause to ask: What would Webster say in response? It is worth noting at this point that Webster's

---

[48]Bonhoeffer, *Act and Being*, DBWE 2:90-91, emphasis added.
[49]Bonhoeffer, *Act and Being*, DBWE 2:91.
[50]Bonhoeffer, *Act and Being*, DBWE 2:135.
[51]Bonhoeffer, *Sanctorum Communio: A Theological Study of the Sociology of the Church*, DBWE 1:127.
[52]Bonhoeffer, *Sanctorum Communio*, DBWE 1:178.
[53]Bonhoeffer, *Sanctorum Communio*, DBWE 1:211.

early work on scriptural hermeneutics favorably draws from Bonhoeffer; indeed, Bonhoeffer provides Webster with a concrete example of what it means to "read within the economy of grace."[54] But still we must ask, How would Webster's efforts of "negative ecclesiology" respond to Bonhoeffer's claim that the church is Christ existing as community? Does Bonhoeffer's reasoning subsume Christ into his community? Is this the *crassa mixtura* Webster hopes to avoid?

At this point the distinctly Protestant nature of Bonhoeffer's ecclesiology comes to the fore. As Eberhard Bethge notes, Bonhoeffer never intended his ecclesiological formulation—Christ existing as community—to be true in reverse.[55] The community exists because Christ is present; Christ is never present simply because a community exists. Priority belongs to the Lord. The structure of Bonhoeffer's person-concept of revelation is important at this point. Precisely because Christ is *free*, he can be free *for* his people; his presence is the very enactment of his freedom. In this sense, an important distinction between God and humanity remains intact. Bonhoeffer writes, anticipating Webster's critique, that we must "rule out any idea of a mystical fusion between church-community and Christ."[56] If a stress on distinction presses toward invisibility, and if a stress on unity presses toward the objectification of grace, Bonhoeffer's ability to walk the fine line of unity-in-distinction allows him to emphasize the concrete aspects of ecclesial existence without undermining the sense in which the church must always receive grace anew. Or to put the matter in terms of his person-concept of revelation, Christ is present (thereby securing the unity of God and human in the church), but Christ is present as a divine person (thereby securing the distinction). Bonhoeffer would ultimately respond to the charges leveled

---

[54]For Webster's positive evaluation of Bonhoeffer, see Webster, *Domain of the Word*, 26; idem, *Holy Scripture*, 78-85; and idem, "'In the Shadow of Biblical Work': Barth and Bonhoeffer on Reading the Bible," *Toronto Journal of Theology* 17, no. 1 (2001): 75-92. On the similarities between Bonhoeffer's and Webster's scriptural hermeneutics, see Nadine Hamilton, "Dietrich Bonhoeffer and the Necessity of Kenosis for Scriptural Hermeneutics," *SJT* 71, no. 4 (2018): 441-59. For Webster's positive evaluation of Bonhoeffer's *Ethics*—with some reservations due to Bonhoeffer's Lutheran Christology—see Webster, *Virtue and Intellect*, vol. 2 of *God Without Measure: Working Papers in Christian Theology* (London: Bloomsbury T&T Clark, 2016), 12-17. For analysis of some of the key differences between the two, see chap. 2 of the present book.

[55]Eberhard Bethge, *Dietrich Bonhoeffer: A Biography*, rev. ed., ed. Victoria J. Barnett, trans. Eric Mosbacher et al. (Minneapolis: Fortress, 2000), 84.

[56]Bonhoeffer, *Discipleship*, DBWE 4:220.

against word theologies by claiming that the church indeed remains needy, but it never wanders alone.

In the chapters to come I will unpack the hermeneutical implications of Bonhoeffer's person-concept of revelation and a related account of the church as the communal person of Christ. For now, the relevant point is that Bonhoeffer's person-concept of revelation allows him to distinguish his position from Barth's highly actualistic account of divine presence while nevertheless remaining within the scope of the Barthian turn to revelation. Bonhoeffer helps us see, in other words, how an account of the church as the *creatura verbi* can avoid the common missteps that beset Protestant ecclesiology. The ongoing historicity of the church is indeed central to revelation, but only because Christ is personally present to the community, calling it to himself. Thus, act takes priority, for Christ constitutes the church. But there can be no act without being, for Christ constitutes the church by being personally present to it.

Bonhoeffer's ability simultaneously to distinguish and unify captures the best of the Protestant ecclesiological impulse without lapsing into its common errors. At the heart of a healthy Protestant vision lies what Christoph Schwöbel calls the "fundamental asymmetry" between divine and human agency, the ability to imagine a church that is both united to God's activity and yet asymmetrically ordered in relation to it.[57] This theological sensibility was originally intended to temper inflated accounts of ecclesial practices—most infamously, the practice of selling indulgences. In response to this inflation, Martin Luther prioritized God's gracious initiative in salvation, thereby preventing ecclesial activity from overreaching its capacity.

Given the particular pastoral danger that animates this sensibility, Schwöbel observes that a certain critical tone characterizes Protestant theology: "Against the misguided . . . identification of God's action and a specific form of human action, this distinction had to be stressed as much as possible."[58] The extent to which the Reformers were able to sustain this balance is a point of debate, and it is likely true that Luther's polemical context contributes to his tendency at times to stress distinction at the expense of identity. Yet Schwöbel reminds us, "One can only accuse Luther's

---

[57]Schwöbel, "Creature of the Word," 120.
[58]Schwöbel, "Creature of the Word," 137.

ecclesiology of onesided spiritualism if one interprets the distinction between *opus Dei* and *opus hominum* as a rigid separation and overlooks the
essential relation of divine and human action in the church."[59] Learning
from Luther, Bonhoeffer was keenly attuned to this, as his person-concept
of revelation makes clear. The response to the charge of ecclesiological
Nestorianism is not to abandon the Reformation vision of the *creatura verbi*
but to relearn the importance of the fundamental asymmetry and ordered
unity of divine and human grounded in Christ and his community.

This christologically grounded distinction funds a particular form of
ecclesial activity. Because of the fundamentally asymmetrical nature of the
unity between Christ and the church, *passive* and *active* do not exist on the
same plane; they are not of equal type and consequently do not compete
for space. Bonhoeffer recognizes this when he asserts that faithful activity
assumes a particular anthropology. Within the *creatura verbi,* the very
being of the human has antecedently been determined by Christ's address.
He explains the significance of this by distinguishing *esse* from *habitus.* The
former determines the latter; in relation to God, Christian *esse* is being a
sinner forgiven; Christian *habitus* is the "activity of faith" that follows from
being forgiven.[60] In its passivity, faith is not one act among others in the
Christian life. Rather, faith is the basic orientation of all human activity,
the framework within which all other activity is carried out. As Webster
helpfully puts it, the activity of faith is "human activity bent to the service
of God."[61]

Faith, in this sense, is not fundamentally a matter of content but of existential and spiritual bearing. Faith is our response to God's address, an act
of letting happen, an act of reception. The passivity of faith does not negate
activity but determines its basic shape. For a church created by God's word,
all visible activity arises from this orientation. As Bonhoeffer was keenly
aware, the activity of faith is necessarily visible behavior. Yet as the activity
of faith, it remains alert to its *esse.* The activity of faith recognizes that it will
be the means by which the church participates in Christ's ongoing activity,
even as it never presumes its activity to be identifiable with his. In this,

---

[59]Schwöbel, "Creature of the Word," 130.
[60]Bonhoeffer, *Berlin: 1932–1933*, DBWE 12:231.
[61]Webster, "Visible Attests the Invisible," 107.

Bonhoeffer's account of the "activity of faith" operates according to a similar material logic as does Webster's "passive activity"; yet drawing from his person-concept of revelation, it avoids the potentially distortive implications of passivity.

A Theology of Reading Within the *Creatura Verbi*

Having laid the ecclesiological groundwork, we can now ask the more specific question: What does the activity of faith imply about the nature of reading Scripture? As an activity of faith, the church's practice of reading Scripture remains alert to the fundamental distinction between interpretive productions and divine gift. As Stephen Plant observes of Bonhoeffer, "In the Bible it is God who speaks."[62] This is not to deny the importance of readerly activity in all its dimensions; instead, it places an important caution sign above all of it. As Bonhoeffer argues, "We must read this book with all of our human resources." But this is not an event of making happen. Within christological space, hermeneutical activity is essentially an act of hope that "through the Bible in its fragility God comes to meet us as the Risen One."[63] In this particular sense, reading is a mode of listening, an activity by which the interpreting subject becomes attentive and hopeful. As the creature of the Word, the church is a hermeneutical space of expectation. Having received its very being from the gratuitous presence of the risen One, the church engages in practices that continue to hope for this presence anew.

Webster is particularly helpful at this point because he carefully lays out the hermeneutical implications that follow from prior theological analyses of God and church. A God who exists in divine freedom is not a God human beings can reach by means of unaided creaturely capacities.[64] Knowledge of God is necessarily a gift. Hence, we must situate the creaturely knowledge of God within the realm of God's self-giving desire, God's active willingness to share divine self-knowledge with creatures. God gives this knowledge, of

---

[62]Stephen J. Plant, *Taking Stock of Bonhoeffer: Studies in Biblical Interpretation and Ethics* (Burlington, VT: Ashgate, 2014), 92.

[63]Bonhoeffer, *Berlin: 1932–1933*, DBWE 12:331.

[64]Webster takes this axiom to be dogmatically foundational. See, e.g., John Webster, *God and the Works of God*, 8-9. Here he echoes Kierkegaard's belief in an "infinite qualitative distinction" between time and eternity, a belief that famously shapes Barth's hermeneutical vision in the second edition of his *Der Römerbrief* (1922).

course, by speaking to humanity in and as Jesus Christ. Mediated by the written witness of the prophets and apostles, this speech reverberates through history. By means of the voice of the text we encounter the voice of God in Christ.[65]

Because we are dealing with a living and active God, we cannot limit God's activity with regard to the text to the process of textual production (a process usually depicted in terms of *inspiration*). Webster therefore claims that even during the reading process itself, God remains active.[66] God's revelatory activity initiated the texts, has sustained them through time, and remains operative in our reading today. When reflecting on the hermeneutical enterprise, we are dealing with revelation in the present tense.[67] God has spoken, and, as the risen One, God continues to speak.

Within the domain of the risen Christ, therefore, textual language is more than a means of transferring information; it is—or at least it can become—the means of Christ's address, the means by which Christ's word "strikes home" to the reader.[68] Emphasizing the verbal agency of the resurrected One thereby prevents the church from treating the text as an inert object. Revelation includes textuality but is not limited to textuality. At least one implication follows that contains huge significance for my thesis in this book: within the *creatura verbi* we must differentiate between understanding

---

[65]For a more thorough and nuanced account of this logic, see Barth's notion of the three forms of the one Word of God in Karl Barth, *Church Dogmatics*, vol. I/1, *The Doctrine of the Word of God*, ed. G. W. Bromiley and T. F. Torrance, trans. G. T. Thomson and Harold Knight (Edinburgh: T&T Clark, 1980), 457-537. Webster utilizes a constructive notion of sanctification and inspiration to explain this possibility: "Sanctification is the act of God the Holy Spirit in hallowing creaturely processes, employing them in the service of the taking form of revelation within the history of the creation" (Webster, *Holy Scripture*, 17-18). For an account of double agency discourse, see Nicholas Wolterstorff, *Divine Discourse: Philosophical Reflections on the Claim That God Speaks* (Cambridge: Cambridge University Press, 1995). Also see Scott Swain, *Trinity, Revelation, and Reading: A Theological Introduction to the Bible and Its Interpretation* (London: T&T Clark, 2011), 35.

[66]Webster, *Holy Scripture*, 71.

[67]See Christopher R. J. Holmes, "Revelation in the Present Tense: On Rethinking Theological Interpretation in Light of the Prophetic Office of Jesus Christ," *JTI* 6, no.1 (2012): 23-42.

[68]The notion of Scripture's "becoming" might seem to downplay or even undermine its status as the word of God, but Bruce McCormack argues otherwise in "The Being of Holy Scripture Is in Becoming: Karl Barth in Conversation with American Evangelical Criticism," in *Evangelicals and Scripture: Tradition, Authority, and Hermeneutics*, ed. Vincent Bacote, Laure C. Miguélez, and Dennis L. Okholm (Downers Grove, IL: InterVarsity Press, 2004), 55-75. The notion of "striking home" comes from Ernst Fuchs, *Studies of the Historical Jesus*, trans. Andrew Scobie (Naperville, IL: Allenson, 1964), 196-98, 202.

the text qua text and understanding God's word to the church in and through it.[69] Hearing the text, in other words, is not tantamount to hearing God, even as the latter is inseparably bound to the former. The same directionality that characterizes the God-church relationship also characterizes the God-Scripture relationship. Within the *creatura verbi*, therefore, one must grant "hermeneutical breathing space"[70] to the interpretive process. That is to say, one must respect the critical gap between text and interpretation that leaves room for newness and thereby prevents interpreters from exhausting the text or undialectically equating it with God's voice.

Here I continue to affirm the fundamental asymmetry that is basic to the logic of ecclesiology in the domain of the risen Christ. This distinction applies to bibliology as well. If God remains Lord over knowledge of God, it follows that Scripture has no revelatory authority independent of God's gracious initiative. Accordingly, within a hermeneutical space determined by Christ's address, the interpreter cannot pry revelatory meaning from Scripture as if it were a predicate of the text itself, a quantity to be abstracted through textual practices (whether historical, critical, theological, or any other sort).

While emphasizing God's freedom in revelation should not undermine the commonplace practice of reading the text, it does require us to situate this practice theologically. We again see the value of theological ordering. The conception of divine transcendence operative in Webster's doctrine of God frees him to recognize that human exegetical activity and divine revelatory activity need not stand in a competitive relationship.[71] Since God is wholly other, the two do not exist on the same plane. Thus the human activity of reading can exist within the domain of God's free action. The same Spirit who inspired the biblical authors without setting aside their creatureliness also inspires readers, qua readers, to receive their textual witness.

---

[69]Gerhard Ebeling, *Word and Faith*, trans. James Waterson Leitch (Philadelphia: Fortress, 1963), 318.

[70]Garrett Green, *Theology, Hermeneutics, and Imagination: The Crisis of Interpretation at the End of Modernity* (Cambridge: Cambridge University Press, 2000), 183.

[71]Webster, *Holy Scripture*, 68-73. For a helpful articulation of how a doctrine of God's transcendence can fund a noncompetitive account of agency, see Kathryn Tanner, *Jesus, Humanity, and the Trinity: A Brief Systematic Theology* (Minneapolis: Fortress, 2001), 1-34.

Tying these points together, we now see how Christ's presence through the Spirit constitutes the church's hermeneutical situation. With regard to the resurrected One who constitutes the church, there are no indeterminate readers. "Through baptism the Christian reader *has been* placed in the sphere of church and canon."[72] Webster therefore resists a certain interpretive tendency prevalent in modern hermeneutics: the treatment of Christian reading as an iteration of a general phenomenon of reading. Though analogous to other acts of reading, reading Scripture within the church "is in its deepest reaches *sui generis*."[73] Such reading "is an instance of itself."[74] Establishing the "overlaps between Christian and other reading," while helpful in some regards, "eclipses what in fact is most interesting about what happens when Christians read the Bible: that the Bible as text is the *viva vox Dei* addressing the people of God and generating faith and obedience."[75]

While Webster follows recent trends in theological interpretation by highlighting interpretation's ecclesial home, his emphasis on Christ's priority over the community leads him to nuance his ecclesial hermeneutic in important ways. Because the church is created by an external word, he treads carefully when addressing the ecclesiality of interpretation. "There is a proper externality to Scripture in relation to the church, not because Scripture exists in abstraction from its audience, but because in attending to Scripture the church is not attending to its own voice but to that of the unconfined and self-announcing Risen One from whose mouth Scripture issues."[76] While he insists that those who read Scripture are the redeemed, he is equally clear that, in the most technical sense, Scripture does not *belong* to the church. "Scripture is not the church's book, something internal to the community's discursive practices; what the church hears in Scripture is not its own voice."[77] Rather than belonging to the church, Scripture belongs to the risen Christ.

Here we see the hermeneutical corollary to an ecclesiology that accents Christ's constitutive address: the text belongs *in* the church even as it does

---

[72]Webster, *Domain of the Word*, 73.
[73]Webster, *Holy Scripture*, 72.
[74]Webster, "Hermeneutics in Modern Theology," 317.
[75]Webster, "Hermeneutics in Modern Theology," 317.
[76]Webster, *Domain of the Word*, 44-45.
[77]Webster, "Visible Attests the Invisible," 110.

not belong *to* the church. This further suggests that interpretation is not properly theological simply in virtue of its audience (e.g., church goers rather than academicians); nor is interpretation theological in virtue of tutelage in a particular tradition.[78] Instead, interpretation is theological in virtue of its relationship to the present Christ, who calls the church into being, gifts it with the canon, and continues to address it through the textual medium of revelation.

THE PRACTICE OF READING WITH THE *CREATURA VERBI*

This interplay between Scripture as an entity external to the community and the reading of it as an internal practice gives particular shape to the nature of hermeneutics within the *creatura verbi*. The "how" of God's speech—and thus the proper externality of Scripture to the church—remains a gift of grace beyond analytic control or manipulation. Theological reflection in relation to God's free speech faithfully fulfills its duty not by explaining the logic of this speech but by sketching the theological domain in which the church receives it. Yet here we press further by considering the how of the church's listening. Unlike the how of God's speech, this properly becomes an object of concrete focus.[79] This is not to say that the reception of revelation is a natural event or a capacity inherent to creatures. We continue to affirm that creatures only know God through God's grace. But just as God speaks by means of written human words, the church hears by means of an array of enacted human practices. And just as the written words remain open to critical analysis (even as this analysis does not, in and of itself, lead to God's voice), so too the church's practices of listening remain an object of concrete reflection (even as this reflection will never guarantee that the church hears).

The hermeneutical vision that has emerged to this point possesses a certain theological tidiness. As concepts, the theological building blocks used to depict hermeneutical space within the *creatura verbi* fit together nicely. The danger, however, is that we confuse theological coherence for practical usefulness. The idea of reading as an activity of faith can easily

---

[78]Webster, *Domain of the Word*, 32.

[79]See Rudolf Bultmann, "How Does God Speak to Us Through the Bible?," in *Existence and Faith: Shorter Writings of Rudolf Bultmann*, trans. Schubert M. Ogden (New York: World, 1960), 167.

become mere verbal decoration adorning our preexisting reading practices. Though theologically interesting, it becomes hermeneutically vacuous. Bonhoeffer was sensitive to this threat. The point of a robust doctrine of revelation is not to devalue human action but to give it distinct shape. A doctrine of revelation—because a person is revealed—must fund concrete practices of revelation, which for Bonhoeffer are practices that correspond to Christ's personal presence.

In the following chapters I will elaborate on what this vision entails. For now we can note that Bonhoeffer's commitment to *Christus praesens* shapes his approach to Scripture. When revelation is construed in abstract terms, i.e., without reference to Christ's concrete presence, interpretation quickly devolves into a practice of information gathering. The point of reading, in this case, is to uncover ideas from the text and transplant them to the human mind. In this situation, interpretive method becomes centrally important, for ideas remain susceptible to methodological procedures. A person, however, does not. Thus, Bonhoeffer's person-concept of revelation calls for a qualitatively different sort of interpretive endeavor. This becomes especially clear in two places in Bonhoeffer's writings: first, in a 1932 ecumenical address delivered in Gland, Switzerland, and, second, in a 1936 lecture titled "Contemporizing New Testament Texts."

Ecumenical address in Gland. In June 1931 Bonhoeffer returned from his year studying in New York. Along with his duties as an assistant pastor and lecturer at the University of Berlin, Bonhoeffer became actively involved in the international ecumenical movement. Though growing nationalist sentiments in Germany led many prominent theologians to criticize internationalism, Bonhoeffer eagerly embraced the opportunity. In a gathering of the World Alliance at Gland, Switzerland, in August 1932, just months after the founding of the German Christian movement, Bonhoeffer spoke powerfully into a tense political situation. His reflections on the Bible were particularly pointed. "We prefer our own thoughts to those of the Bible," he suggests. "We no longer read the Bible seriously. We read it no longer *against* ourselves but only *for* ourselves."[80] Those who read for themselves are "the knowledgeable," Bonhoeffer goes on to claim, the ones who know ahead of time

---

[80]Bonhoeffer, *Ecumenical, Academic, and Pastoral Work: 1931–1932*, DBWE 11:377-78, emphasis added.

what the text will bring. But those who hold open the possibility of reading against themselves approach the text as "the starving ones, the waiting ones, as the needy, the hopeful."[81] More than a technical skill, this is an embodied and enacted scriptural sensibility, a matter of "attentiveness and faith."[82]

On one level, Bonhoeffer had no qualms with principles such as peace and love of neighbor, both of which were central to the ecumenical community's reading of Scripture. Indeed, as principles these concepts are beyond critique. But unless they become concrete they remain impotent. At a different ecumenical gathering Bonhoeffer therefore suggests that "the church . . . can proclaim not principles that are always true but rather only commandments that are true today. For that which is 'always' true is precisely not true 'today': God is for us 'always' *God* precisely '*today*.'"[83] This difference between reading abstractly and reading in search of concretion is not a matter of one method versus another. It is a matter of the basic posture that orients the activity of reading. This is why Bonhoeffer suggests to the ecumenical community that a proper hermeneutical posture requires a "change in the church's self-understanding."[84] Pulsing through Bonhoeffer's ecumenical addresses is the underlying conviction that in order for the ecumenical community to hear God's voice in Scripture, it must see itself as a "distinct form of the church itself."[85] In order to read against itself, it must first learn to be the church.

If we lose the ability to read Scripture against ourselves, Bonhoeffer warns, we end up remaking a God in the *imago hominis*. Like Adam and Eve in the garden, the turn toward a voice other than God's and the desire to be like God go hand in hand. Following Luther, Bonhoeffer refers to this as the *cor curvum in se* (the heart turned in on itself).[86] Stuck within itself, the ego remains closed to a word that might approach externally. Reading no longer remains alert to its ongoing need for grace, for the self is the presumed anchor of interpretation. When this happens, interpretive results can be no better than the resources the human reader brings to the act of reading.

---

[81]Bonhoeffer, *Ecumenical, Academic, and Pastoral Work*, DBWE 11:377.

[82]Plant, *Taking Stock of Bonhoeffer*, 44.

[83]Bonhoeffer, *Ecumenical, Academic, and Pastoral Work*, DBWE 11:359-60.

[84]Bonhoeffer, *Ecumenical, Academic, and Pastoral Work*, DBWE 11:356.

[85]Bonhoeffer, *Ecumenical, Academic, and Pastoral Work*, DBWE 11:377.

[86]See Bonhoeffer, *Creation and Fall: A Theological Exegesis of Genesis 1–3*, DBWE 3:103-14.

Contemporizing New Testament texts. In a lecture delivered during his Finkenwalde period, Bonhoeffer expounds on this dilemma. Faced with the weekly task of addressing the congregation, the preacher is inevitably tempted to make Scripture relevant by "contemporizing the text."[87] Two assumptions underlie this temptation: that the text remains inert and useless unless actualized by interpretive agency and that the Archimedean point of interpretation has already been fixed by means of whatever cultural assumptions hold sway. Hidden within such a hermeneutical disposition is the danger that the interpreter becomes the agent of the text's voice. When I seek to justify the text to the present, Bonhoeffer claims, "the *principle of contemporizing resides* within me, in the interpreter . . . I am the subject of contemporizing. . . . In other words, truth is already fixed before I even begin my exegesis of Scripture."[88] When one succumbs to this temptation, one inevitably finds a suitable and usable text, one that has already been tamed by preconceived interpretive interest. Witnessing the Nazification of the church gave Bonhoeffer a unique perspective on this danger. "*This contemporizing* of the Christian message leads directly to paganism," he writes.[89] Hermeneutical practices that aim at contemporizing the text threaten to reduce the God encountered therein to what Bonhoeffer elsewhere calls a divine *Doppelgänger*.[90] Such a God becomes the interpreter's puppet. In one of his most vivid metaphors Bonhoeffer suggests that the one who reads the text from a position of mastery inevitably "trims and prunes [Scripture] until it fits the fixed framework, until the eagle can no longer rise . . . and is instead put on display with clipped wings . . . among other domesticated pets."[91] In contrast, in a letter from that period Bonhoeffer jarringly suggests that within Scripture we ought to find a place utterly repugnant and alien to us, a place that destabilizes our interpretive sensibilities by reorienting our interpretive agenda around the crucified and risen Christ.[92]

Posture versus method. By lifting up the possibility of reading against ourselves and warning of the danger of contemporizing the text, Bonhoeffer

---

[87]Bonhoeffer, *Theological Education at Finkenwalde: 1935–1937*, DBWE 14:413-33.
[88]Bonhoeffer, *Theological Education at Finkenwalde*, DBWE 14:419-20.
[89]Bonhoeffer, *Theological Education at Finkenwalde*, DBWE 14:415.
[90]Bonhoeffer, *Theological Education at Finkenwalde*, DBWE 14:169.
[91]Bonhoeffer, *Theological Education at Finkenwalde*, DBWE 14:414.
[92]Bonhoeffer, *Theological Education at Finkenwalde*, DBWE 14:167-68.

would have us see that revelation, because it is a matter of God's personal presence in Christ, belongs to God. We read in pursuit of knowledge that is never our own. This means, moreover, that no particular interpretive method can guarantee access to this knowledge. It remains always a gift, and as such can never be abstracted from Christ himself. Method, as Bonhoeffer understands it, implies the very opposite. Method emerges from the thinking self and the resources immanent to historical reality. Taken on its own, method becomes a way for the human to manufacture a path into the essence of Scripture.[93] The problem with this, of course, is that it assumes the essence of Scripture to be something other than God's living Word that travels along a path from God to the human. Bonhoeffer states the matter sharply: revelation "excludes every method of reaching it by one's own way."[94]

Instead of method, Bonhoeffer calls the interpretive community to embody a particular form of life. In this work I refer to this form of life as a hermeneutical posture. By *posture* I mean the spiritual energy animating one's reading of Scripture. *Posture* denotes a form of agency that corresponds to Christ's presence. Whereas method grants effectiveness to interpretive practices per se, the notion of posture resituates these practices in relation to Christ and thereby grants their final efficacy to him. For sure, all sorts of textual practices will be helpful and necessary along the way (depending on the context of the interpretive event and the nature of the reading community), but the key issue is not those practices per se but the posture from which they emerge. No particular set of textual practices guarantees such a posture. The danger, as Bonhoeffer realized, was that one could produce technically skilled readings of Scripture that serve merely to echo the interpretive interests brought to the text. As Plant observes, Bonhoeffer believed that even within "the supposed objectivity of scientific biblical criticism he would find an echo of his own opinions rather than the sovereign Word of God."[95] One could deploy the same set of interpretive practices in a posture of receptivity to God's voice or as a mode of propagating a particular interpretive agenda. So while Bonhoeffer in principle had no problem with

---

[93]For a highly qualified—and somewhat tongue in cheek—support of methodology, see Bonhoeffer, *Theological Education at Finkenwalde*, DBWE 14:418.

[94]Bonhoeffer, *Ethics*, DBWE 6:149.

[95]Plant, *Taking Stock of Bonhoeffer*, 45.

historical-critical methods and even advocated for their necessity, he was methodologically much less committed to the practice than were many of his academic peers.

This notion of posture is especially relevant to my central claim in this book. Within a hermeneutic of discipleship we must relocate specifically text-based practices within a more holistic frame of reference determined by the risen One himself. As the Emmaus Road story suggests, the telos of scriptural understanding is not the text but Jesus. In this sense, I am arguing for a set of holistic and embodied hermeneutical practices that, when enacted, sustain the community's ongoing process of becoming attentive to the person of Christ by means of the scriptural text.

Practicing un-mastery. At the heart of a faithful interpretive posture lie practices of un-mastery. Interpretive hubris cannot be tempered by mere good intention, and self-renunciation vis-à-vis the text cannot simply be brought into existence by fiat. Both require intentional activity. Becoming open, expectant, and addressable requires practices of un-mastery that decenter the interpretive subject.[96] When Bonhoeffer suggests that faithful reading of Scripture requires a *sacrificium intellectus*, this is what he has in mind.[97] He is not promoting an anti-intellectualist interpretive agenda or a willful disregard of readerly rigor. He is instead suggesting that if one hopes to hear God's voice in the text, one ought to silence one's own.[98] This requires acknowledging that when one comes to the text, one's intentions are never pure. A reader is always a site of competing interests. One must acknowledge, as much as possible, the presuppositions, agendas, and goals that one imports to the interpretive task. Such self-awareness will by no means guarantee interpretive objectivity, for readers necessarily approach the text with preunderstanding.[99] Yet by intentionally naming and de-centering one's own

---

[96]I borrow this phrase from Sarah Coakley, *God, Sexuality, and the Self: An Essay 'On the Trinity'* (Cambridge: Cambridge University Press, 2013), 43. She modifies John Milbank's notion of "non-mastery" in Milbank, *Theology and Social Theory: Beyond Secular Reason* (Malden, MA: Blackwell, 1990), 6.

[97]Bonhoeffer, *Theological Education at Finkenwalde*, DBWE 14:169.

[98]On this, see Bultmann, "How Does God Speak to Us Through the Bible?," 166-70.

[99]See Bultmann, "Is Exegesis Without Presuppositions Possible?," in *Existence and Faith*, 289-96. He distinguishes between "prejudiced" readings—which we should seek to avoid if we hope to hear from God in the text—and "preunderstanding"—which, as Gadamer and others suggest, is a useful and necessary feature of the hermeneutical process.

agenda, one prevents preunderstanding from devolving into damaging prejudices that determine interpretive outcomes before the actual act of reading.

Practices of un-mastery also require the interpreter to engage in deliberate activities that temper egocentric desires.[100] Bonhoeffer provides several examples that illustrate what such practices entail: remaining "silent in the domain of the church," "letting go of oneself," "bearing the burdens of others," the "practice of service," and even the "practice of asceticism."[101] Such activities constitute the *habitus* that instantiates Christian *esse*. Of course, this list could be extended. For Bonhoeffer, however, two particular forms of un-mastery are fundamentally important to a hermeneutical posture within the *creatura verbi*: confession and prayer.

The former is central to the logic of displacing the ego. "Confession in the presence of another believer is the most profound kind of humiliation. . . . It deals a terrible blow to one's pride."[102] If pride, the desire to be *sicut deus*, is fundamentally an act of turning away from God in order to become the source of one's own knowledge, then a confessional blow to pride paves the

---

[100]Of course, the very otherness of God that calls human action into judgment is also the condition for the unpredictable newness of God's love and grace. As "other," God both judges and saves. Recognizing the different forms of God's salvific presence helps us see that overcoming egocentricity is not the only effect of God's interruptive grace. In recent decades, feminist theology has unmasked the inadequacies of a one-dimensional account of sin as pride that often lurks with much mainline Western theology, as it certainly was within Bonhoeffer's work. See, e.g., Sarah Coakley, "*Kenosis* and Subversion: On the Repression of 'Vulnerability' in Christian Feminist Writing," in *Powers and Submissions: Spirituality, Philosophy and Gender* (Malden, MA: Blackwell, 2002), 3-39; and Judith Plaskow, *Sex, Sin and Grace: Women's Experience and the Theologies of Reinhold Niebuhr and Paul Tillich* (Lanham, MD: University Press of America, 1980). On Bonhoeffer specifically, see Lisa E. Dahill, *Reading from the Underside of Selfhood: Bonhoeffer and Spiritual Formation* (Eugene, OR: Wipf & Stock, 2009). The most relevant point for our particular purposes here is that a complete account of sin's hermeneutical implications requires a more balanced account of sin's social forms. As Rosemary Radford Ruether claims, "Sin has to be seen both in the capacity to set up prideful, antagonistic relations to others and in the passivity of men and women who acquiesce to the group ego" (Ruether, *Sexism and God-Talk: Toward a Feminist Theology* [Boston: Beacon, 1983], 164). This latter point is especially relevant. One of the ways sin thwarts the interpretive process is by buttressing "group ego," thereby generating a hermeneutical echo chamber. Thus the process by which the powerless acquire power is part and parcel with the process by which the community comes to receive a fresh word from God. Said differently, the notions of un-mastery and de-centering for which I have been advocating in this chapter provide space for those who may not otherwise have a voice, thereby allowing the formerly powerless and voiceless to contribute to the hermeneutical process. I consider the communal nature of this process in more depth in chapters five and six.

[101]Bonhoeffer, *Berlin*, DBWE 12:232.

[102]Bonhoeffer, *Life Together and Prayerbook of the Bible*, DBWE 5:111.

way for becoming attentive to the divine voice. The latter, prayer, is the concrete enactment of neediness and the invitation of Christ's presence. "Every attempt at pneumatological interpretation is a prayer; a plea for the Holy Spirit, who alone determines . . . hearing and understanding."[103] By means of confession, prayer, and other practices of un-mastery, the reader tempers interpretive pride and de-centers the interpretive ego, thereby leaving space for the word that only God can bring.

Some may rightly worry that Bonhoeffer's account of practical receptivity looks like mysticism. This is a valid concern because both an inflated ecclesiology (against which Webster reacts) and an inflated account of spiritual experience risk objectifying God's speech. Perhaps this partly explains Webster's reluctance to follow Bonhoeffer's inclinations toward concretion. This danger becomes especially clear when Bonhoeffer's thinking becomes most tangible—during his time at Finkenwalde training and forming students for ministry in the Confessing Church. It is during this stage in his career that outsiders criticized his pastoral vision for becoming overly monastic and hyperspiritualized.

Yet even here Bonhoeffer takes care to distinguish his account of biblical interpretation from spiritual ecstasy or enthusiastic rapture. We indeed wait for God's speech within the congregation, he writes in a letter to a skeptical friend, yet "I enter such a meeting not as one would a Quaker meeting, where I basically would have to await new guidance from the Holy Spirit, but rather as one would enter a battlefield where the word of God is in conflict with all sorts of human opinions."[104] This conflict, he continues, presses the church to Scripture, where God's Spirit fights and where God's word can be concretely located. We need not mystically wait for the coming of God's word, for it is already present when we approach the church's text. The antidote to spiritualism, Bonhoeffer simply suggests, is the act of engaging the text itself and doing so "with an open confession of one's errors."[105] Following Bonhoeffer, we see that a hermeneutical posture predicated on "listening for the word" and enacted via practices of un-mastery such as prayer and confession pressures the interpreter concretely toward the very

---

[103]Bonhoeffer, *The Young Bonhoeffer: 1918–1927*, DBWE 9:298.
[104]Bonhoeffer, *Theological Education at Finkenwalde*, DBWE 14:132.
[105]Bonhoeffer, *Theological Education at Finkenwalde*, DBWE 14:132.

words of Scripture. As he elsewhere claims, the prayer kneeler and the study desk must not be separated.[106]

Attending to the text itself. But what does one actually do at the study desk if one hopes to hear God's voice? How does one embody a posture of faith in the act of reading itself?

Webster helps us see what such a practice entails. Within the *creatura verbi*, "exegetical reasoning is, most simply, reading the Bible, the intelligent (and therefore spiritual) act of following the word of the text" and "and attending to its linguistic detail."[107] As Bonhoeffer suggests, "the exact wording must be taken seriously."[108] This is why Bonhoeffer never abandoned historical-critical tools, even if he challenged how the academy of his day understood the critical enterprise. As he writes in his Christology lectures, "as we live on earth, we must go ahead and use historical criticism, inadequate though it is."[109] Stephen Plant suggests that for Bonhoeffer the choice between critical and theological interpretation was artificial and unhelpful.[110]

---

[106]Bonhoeffer, *Theological Education at Finkenwalde*, DBWE 14:516.

[107]Webster, *Domain of the Word*, 130, 77.

[108]Bonhoeffer, *Theological Education at Finkenwalde*, DBWE 14:541.

[109]Bonhoeffer, *Berlin*, DBWE 12:331. One could argue that the translators have overblown Bonhoeffer's unease with historical-critical practices. The German text—"Sofern wir also auf Erden sind, müssen wir in die Not der historishen Kritik hinen"—less explicitly highlights the *inadequacy* of historical criticism. See Sean F. Winter, "'Present-ing' the Word: The Use and Abuse of Bonhoeffer on the Bible," *Bonhoeffer Legacy* 2, no. 2 (2014): 19-35. The translators of DBWE 12 portray the sense of the German "die Not" with the idea of "inadequacy." Other options are available. For instance, John Bowden's early translation renders this phrase, "we must enter into the *straits* of historical criticism" (Dietrich Bonhoeffer, *Christology*, trans. John Bowden [London: Collins, 1966], 76, emphasis added). Winter suggests: "we must enter into the *necessity/difficulty* of historical criticism" (Winter, "'Present-ing' the Word," 26, emphasis added).

[110]Plant, *Taking Stock of Bonhoeffer*, 45. On Bonhoeffer's training in historical-critical methods at Tübingen and Berlin, see Sean F. Winter, "Bonhoeffer and Biblical Interpretation: The Early Years," *Bonhoeffer Legacy* 1, no. 1 (2013): 1-15. Although Bonhoeffer's encounter with Barth significantly affected his hermeneutical sensibilities by helping him frame interpretive objectivity in light of the living God, Winter observes that Bonhoeffer's introduction to historical-critical methods at Tübingen with Adolf Schlatter actually prepared him for this move. From Schlatter he learned to see the task of critical scholarship oriented toward theological and existential ends (Winter, "Bonhoeffer and Biblical Interpretation," 4). But there is some debate regarding the extent to which Bonhoeffer remained honest to the historical-critical enterprise. See, for instance, the more sober analysis of Helmut Gollwitzer and Gerhard von Rad, both of whom suggest that Bonhoeffer was at times inclined to underplay the historicity of the text and the necessity of historical-critical research (Helmut Gollwitzer, "The Way of Obedience," in *I Knew Dietrich Bonhoeffer*, ed. Ronald Gregor Smith and Wolf-Dieter Zimmermann (London: Fontana Books, 1973), 138-44; and Gerhard von Rad, "Meetings in Early and Later Years," in *I Knew Dietrich Bonhoeffer*, 176-78).

Indeed, historical criticism can play a key role in sustaining a properly theological posture toward the text. "What was distinctive about Bonhoeffer's experience of reading the Bible relative to other texts," Plant writes, "was its *otherness* . . . [and] it is precisely the otherness of the biblical text that historical criticism helps to establish."[111] Whereas the historical-critical enterprise could, as Bonhoeffer vividly puts it, "disintegrate" the canon by distinguishing the sources and "fragmen[ting] . . . textual units into little pieces," thereby leaving "debris and fragments" upon "the field of battle," this is not necessarily the case.[112] Bonhoeffer would suggest that one should dive into the details of the text precisely as a means of reading the text as a whole. Faithful interpretation on this account is a matter of moving ever more deeply into the final form of the text, guided by the simple conviction that this is where God addresses the church.[113] For sure, no method can guarantee that moving into the text will produce such ends. It could end, as it often does, in silence. Such is the nature of reading in relationship to a living God. Moreover, because God speaks freely, we need not theorize in advance how this patient activity of tracing the text will become theologically or spiritually significant. Such significance is always a gift.

Even so, within hermeneutical space constituted by Christ's presence we can confidently expect that exegesis, if it should indeed become the means of this gift, must emerge from a particular spiritual disposition. According to Bonhoeffer, for example, reading Scripture is not a technical skill that can be learned but something that correlates to the reader's spiritual state.[114] Or as Webster puts it, interpretive activity is properly exercised in a "spiritual and ecclesial culture of interpretation by which the regenerate mind is formed, checked and directed."[115] To put the matter differently, the critical

---

[111]Plant, *Taking Stock of Bonhoeffer*, 52.

[112]Bonhoeffer, *Young Bonhoeffer*, DBWE 9:286. Plant notes that the form of biblical criticism prevalent in 1920s Germany was heavily focused on textual and redaction criticism (Plant, *Taking Stock of Bonhoeffer*, 56), hence Bonhoeffer's pejorative comments about fragmenting the canon. As Plant notes, Bonhoeffer's worries about biblical criticism may seem irrelevant to contemporary critical scholars who are less optimistic about digging behind the text and more eager to focus on critically engaging the text in its final form.

[113]On Bonhoeffer's commitment to the final form of the text—rather than a reconstructed "original" or the fragments lying behind the final form—see Nadine Hamilton, "Dietrich Bonhoeffer and the Necessity of Kenosis for Scriptural Hermeneutics."

[114]Bonhoeffer, *Life Together and Prayerbook of the Bible*, DBWE 5:64.

[115]Webster, *Domain of the Word*, 63.

distinction between Christ and his church carries a key performative outcome: it compels the church to acknowledge its exegetical inadequacy. It cannot produce what only God can provide. In this sense, the church's reading practices are built upon the acknowledgment of what it cannot do. This proves profoundly liberating. Because Christ is present, the church need not bear a burden beyond its capacity. The interpreter's primary goal, then, is not to extract meaning from the text or dig behind it in search of its elusive meaning. Such activity, Bonhoeffer suggests, is the hermeneutical corollary of Adam and Eve's sinful activity in the garden.[116] Only God speaks God's word. The exegete is thereby freed to revel in the deep simplicity of the task: to attend expectantly to the words on the page. Faith, not anxiety, drives the exegetical process, and hope, more than cleverness or technique, characterizes readerly activity. In an almost paradoxical way, confessing inadequacy with regard to the exegetical task actually compels the interpreter to become immersed in the text all the more deeply, with a newfound eagerness that emerges only when the interpreter is released of the pressure to produce.

A hermeneutic of "the child." One of the great payoffs of Bonhoeffer's person-concept of revelation and corresponding scriptural hermeneutic is that it reframes human interpretive agency by situating that agency in relation to a person, *Christus praesens*. Though Bonhoeffer never directly connects his person-concept of revelation to a particular form of reading, he seems to intuit the deep freedom that arises in this personal encounter. It is telling, for instance, that he frequently employs personal metaphors when depicting the act of faithful reading. Precisely at the point where we might expect more substantive hermeneutical engagement, Bonhoeffer instead breaks off into a metaphorical analysis of the personal dimensions of reading.

> Just as you grasp the words of someone dear to you not by first analyzing them but merely by accepting them, and just as they may then resonate in your ears for days, simply as the words of this particular person whom we love, and just as in these words the person who spoke them is increasingly disclosed to us the more we "ponder it in our heart" as Mary did, so also should we deal with the word of the Bible.[117]

---

[116]See Bonhoeffer, *Creation and Fall*, DBWE 3:103-14.
[117]Bonhoeffer, *Theological Education at Finkenwalde*, DBWE 14:167.

Elsewhere he suggests, "If we could illustrate [the act of reading] with an example from everyday life, the situation of the one who is reading the Scripture would probably come closest to that in which I read to another person a letter from a friend."[118] Consequently, God's word "is not to be thought to pieces but to be moved by the heart, just as the word of a beloved person dwells in the heart."[119] Bonhoeffer concludes *Act and Being* by suggesting that a person-concept of revelation requires an orientation of pure openness to Christ. This posture, as he suggestively puts it, constitutes "the eschatological possibility of the child."[120] Just as a child unthinkingly attends to a father's words in a seemingly naive act of trust, so too the church looks only to Christ and hopes for the future that only he can provide. This pure orientation toward Christ, Bonhoeffer suggests, is a distinctly personal orientation, as personal as the "prayerful conversation of the child with the father."[121] This personal posture calls forth a particular style of reading Scripture: we must read "word for word like a child," Bonhoeffer claims.[122] As he elsewhere suggests, we must appropriate the text "in a personal way, *word for word*."[123] This word-for-word style of interpretation is not meant as an excuse for anti-intellectual naiveté. To argue as much would be to collapse the fundamental asymmetry that characterizes ecclesiology. It does mean, however, that the style of interpretive activity that corresponds to Christ's personal presence "*must* essentially *be exegesis*," by which Bonhoeffer means "the strict and exclusive reference to the word of Scripture" carried out in childlike hope that through the Bible Christ comes to meet us as the risen One.[124]

---

[118]Bonhoeffer, *Life Together and Prayerbook of the Bible*, DBWE 5:64.

[119]Bonhoeffer, *Theological Education Underground: 1937–1940*, DBWE 15:514. For another example of Bonhoeffer's use of the letter metaphor for reading Scripture, see *Theological Education at Finkenwalde*, DBWE 14:933.

[120]Bonhoeffer, *Act and Being*, DBWE 2:159.

[121]Bonhoeffer, *Act and Being*, DBWE 2:161.

[122]According to the notes of Erich Klapproth, one of Bonhoeffer's students at Berlin, Bonhoeffer began the lecture series with this claim. See de Gruchy, "Editor's Introduction," in *Creation and Fall*, DBWE 3:23n11.

[123]Bonhoeffer, *Theological Education at Finkenwalde*, DBWE 14:494, emphasis added.

[124]Bonhoeffer, *Theological Education at Finkenwalde*, DBWE 14:418, emphasis original. The word *exegesis* is underlined twice in Bonhoeffer's manuscript.

2

Reading in the Wake
of the Incarnate Lord

WEBSTER IS IMPORTANT to the hermeneutic of discipleship I am sketching in this book because he, more rigorously than Bonhoeffer, lays the theological groundwork for a distinctly Protestant account of the church as the creature of the word. He does so, moreover, while managing to uphold a certain account of the church's visibility.[1] The church does not vanish behind the word, as some may fear, but derives real shape from it. Granting this important achievement, this chapter addresses a danger that continues to lurk within his work.

THE THREAT OF AN IMMATERIAL HERMENEUTIC

The problem has to do with the way Webster, in construing the nature of church's hermeneutical activity, emphasizes cognition at the expense of corporeality. This tendency is evident, for example, when revelation becomes fundamentally "the restoration of the creature's knowledge" or when the Spirit's work in interpretation is ordered toward a situation in which "the saints may *know*."[2] Skewed toward matters of knowledge, the telos of revelation

---

[1]See, for example, John Webster, "The Visible Attests the Invisible," in *The Community of the Word: Toward an Evangelical Ecclesiology*, ed. Mark Husbands and Daniel J. Treier (Downers Grove, IL: InterVarsity Press, 2005), 102, where he refers to the church's "spiritual visibility."

[2]John Webster, *The Domain of the Word: Scripture and Theological Reason* (London: T&T Clark, 2012), 22, 53, emphasis original.

becomes "cognitive fellowship," the bestowal of a "new intellectual nature," and a "regenerate intellect."[3]

Though in theory this account of the church's hermeneutical agency is creaturely and visible, it remains an immaterial activity, lacking bodily and spatial dimensions. The mistake, in other words, is that real hermeneutical agency is reduced to mere mental agency. Though visible, the church's hermeneutical activity cannot be seen because it remains hidden in the mind. Put differently, Webster indeed depicts the interpretive enterprise in a way that avoids the charge of passivity and occasionalism, yet he neglects to account for the material processes by which the church seeks understanding through the text. One is led, consequently, to imagine an overly intellectualist account of hermeneutical faithfulness. Though one may claim that reading happens in ecclesial space, the church remains a "space" in only a loosely figurative sense.[4]

Hermeneutical spiritualism. The danger here is not simply that we minimize the humanity of the text itself, a problem sometimes referred to as "docetism of Scripture."[5] This danger is real and must be acknowledged. But I am pressing toward a different problem, something more mundane but nevertheless significant. I suggest we distinguish textual docetism (i.e., a less than fully human text) from what I call hermeneutical spiritualism (i.e., a hermeneutic that underplays the materiality of the process through which one ascertains meaning in and through the text). We have rightly learned to uphold the full humanity of the text. We have even learned to accept historical criticism as an interpretive corollary of textual ontology. We must go one step further. We must uphold the full humanity of the reading process itself. If, as Jens Zimmerman claims, "in entering humanity, God has also entered the ambiguity of language and history . . . [and] the unstable medium of human communication,"[6] then we must acknowledge

---

[3]Webster, *Domain of the Word*, 53, 56.

[4]Darren Sarisky exemplifies this tendency by implying that hermeneutical space is merely a matter of text and reader, not a space in any normal sense of the word (Darren Sarisky, *Scriptural Interpretation: A Theological Exploration* [Malden, MA: Wiley-Blackwell, 2013], 158). He explicitly speaks of this space as a "metaphorical notion" (2). The church becomes more like an ideational field than a matter of spatial extension. The "space" of reading becomes something that fits within the mind.

[5]See, e.g., G. C. Berkouwer, *Holy Scripture* (Grand Rapids, MI: Eerdmans, 1975), 17-18, 92.

[6]Jens Zimmermann, "Reading the Book of the Church: Bonhoeffer's Christological Hermeneutics," *MT* 28, no. 4 (2012): 773.

the instability, ambiguity, and historicity of the process by which we interpret this communication.

An obvious question may emerge at this point: Where would hermeneutics happen if not in the mind? Is not hermeneutics the process of cognitively appropriating the meaning of a text? What else is this agency if not mental? Here Bonhoeffer would have us pause. As I argue below, he challenges basic assumptions about hermeneutics by claiming that more is going on in the process of reading than the mere excavation of meaning. When we read Scripture, our ultimate goal is not to know more but to be different. He thus depicts hermeneutics in more holistic terms, in terms of discipleship.

This is why a denser depiction of reading is necessary. Readers of Scripture do not live in the clouds. The very process of reading is material through and through. A basic phenomenology of reading helps make this case. Our access to the text, our access to literacy, the time we devote to the act of reading, the bodies around which we gather as we read, and the reasons for which we read in the first place are all determined by a complex interplay of social, political, and economic factors. Whenever we read a text, we are doing more than just reading. Accordingly, the posture in which we approach the text is more than just mental. It is always—whether we admit it or not—bound up in a complex nexus of forces and subject to numerous material influences. This does not mean that we must make theological articulation a slave to purely historicist or empiricist articulation. Webster's theological vision remains foundational, and we must continue to be robustly theological in our depiction of the reading subject. But it is necessary to supplement his account of hermeneutical space with a thicker vision that more accurately attends to the multidimensional process by which understanding emerges from a written text that witnesses to a personal God.

God's word and the incarnation of the Word. Toward this end, we should attend to the christological commitments undergirding hermeneutical claims. Christology is rarely neutral, for the way we construe the divine-human relationship in Jesus exposes underlying theological assumptions.[7] I suggest, therefore, that the hermeneutical tendency that is evident in

---

[7]See Leonardo Boff, *Jesus Christ Liberator: A Critical Christology for Our Time*, trans. Patrick Hughes (Maryknoll, NY: Orbis, 1978), 265-66.

Webster has analogies in the cluster of christological mistakes that devalue Christ's body as a site of meaning by elevating the significance of the immaterial aspects of existence. I suggest, in other words, that Webster's inclination toward the disembodied and cognitivist elements of hermeneutical faithfulness correlates with a deeper christological tendency.

This tendency is evident in a number of places in Webster's later work. It becomes especially clear in the following passage as Webster interacts with the Puritan theologian John Owen. After affirming Owen's belief that Christian faith ultimately depends on "invisible things," Webster writes,

> If this is so, then the matter of revelation . . . is not simply identical with the form or medium of revelation. . . . Revelation is not an historical quantity *tout court*, even—especially—in the hypostatic union and the Son's temporal exercise of his offices. There is, of course, historical form which theological reflection may not pass over; but that form has not only an unforgettable density but also a finality, and therefore an instrumental character, such that spiritual intelligence may not terminate there. Revelation beckons theological intelligence to consider the cause of revelation, and to receive it as an embassy of that which cannot be resolved into or exhausted by historical manifestation. Each act and word of the incarnate one has force only because he has come down.[8]

On the one hand, one could claim that his passage simply reproduces the Reformed tendency to maintain the word's freedom in the incarnational union. In itself this is not objectionable; as within ecclesiology, we are dealing with a unity-in-distinction. Yet there is cause for concern. When Jesus' historical form becomes merely instrumental, as Webster suggests, we rightly wonder if balance has been lost. If the historicity of the man from Nazareth is a steppingstone for intellectual ascent, it is easy to see why hermeneutical faithfulness becomes an immaterial affair. Within this vision, the hermeneutical enterprise becomes a matter of transcending the materiality of our existence as we strive for invisible things.

At this point, Rowan Williams's critique of the early Barth continues to hold relevance, for it shines light on the christological assumptions operative in Webster's theology. Williams worries that Barth's theological

---

[8]John Webster, *God and the Works of God*, vol. 1 of *God Without Measure: Working Papers in Christian Theology* (London: Bloomsbury T&T Clark, 2016), 6.

imagination is hamstrung by modernity's preoccupation with knowledge. This plays out christologically in an undue emphasis on the *extra calvinisticum*.[9] The presupposition that conditions this tendency in Barth's early theological work, Williams suggests, is that an "epistemological gulf" separates divine and created being.[10] Animated by this worry, Barth construes the incarnation as an epistemological bridge, a means by which God delivers knowledge from one side of the gulf to the other. When this happens, Jesus' flesh functions as a "concealing exterior vehicle"; it becomes the medium by which the word achieves its revelatory goals without sacrificing its divinity.[11] Elsewhere Williams refers to this epistemologically conditioned account of the incarnation as a "sophisticated technique for ensuring that such non-worldly truth is accurately communicated."[12] When viewed within an epistemic paradigm, the flesh of Jesus, his human history as the man from Nazareth, remains extrinsic to divine revelation. At best, his materiality becomes a matter of ancillary significance, something to be surpassed and set aside on the cognitive quest for the immaterial knowledge hidden within.

It is certainly true that God is a communicative agent and that speech is essential to God's eternal being. And it is true that placing priority on God's agency as the speaker helpfully safeguards God's freedom from historical forces. But, as Bonhoeffer knew well, theological care is necessary at this point. He observes, for instance, that emphasizing God's free speech "runs the risk of neglecting the historicity of Jesus."[13] Bonhoeffer would have us see, in other words, that one particular danger with construing the church as the *creatura verbi* is that we imply a Word without flesh. When this happens, we are subsequently pressured to reduce the activity of faith in relation to verbal reception. When the word that creates the church is reduced to a purely verbal entity lacking historical and fleshly dimensions, the successful hermeneutical endeavor is likewise reduced to an upward climb toward invisible things.

---

[9]Rowan Williams, "Barth and the Trinity," in *Wrestling with Angels: Conversations in Modern Theology*, ed. Mike Higton (Grand Rapids, MI: Eerdmans, 2007), 112.

[10]Rowan Williams, "Barth and the Trinity," 127.

[11]Rowan Williams, "Barth and the Trinity," 127.

[12]Rowan Williams, *On Christian Theology* (Malden, MA: Blackwell, 2000), 132.

[13]Bonhoeffer, *The Young Bonhoeffer: 1918–1927*, DBWE 9:441.

Webster occasionally speaks of nonmental aspects of hermeneutical faithfulness. He speaks, for example, of the importance of Christian fellowship in the reading process. I am suggesting, however, that within his account of Christian practices, Christian bodies remain conspicuously absent, while the Christian mind receives disproportionate attention. *Nous* (mind) rises over *soma* (body). Whether this tendency has direct provenance in christological shortcomings is, of course, difficult to say with certainty. I would venture to suggest, however, that the nature of Webster's christological vision and the absence of bodies in his theological reflection coincide to such a degree that considering the relationship might bear constructive fruit. Regardless of how we diagnose this particular issue in Webster, I suggest that directing attention to the fleshliness of God's *verbum* helps allay the disembodied hermeneutical tendencies especially prevalent within theologies that consider the church to be the *creatura verbi*.[14]

TOWARD A BONHOEFFERIAN HERMENEUTIC OF DISCIPLESHIP

Bonhoeffer helps us at this point in two important ways. First, his christological attack on idea-thinking radically undermines intellectualist accounts of revelation. This becomes especially clear in his Christology lectures and remains an animating feature of his theology throughout his career. Second, by articulating a spatial account of the church that corresponds to Christ's own incarnate materiality, he forestalls the possibility of rendering Christian faithfulness invisible. This becomes especially clear in *Discipleship*.[15]

The Christology lectures. In the previous chapter I began to suggest that for Bonhoeffer the pretensions of the knowing subject stand in an antithetical relationship to the word of God. Whereas the knowing self seeks to pull ideas within the realm of ego, thereby trapping reality within the *cor curvum in se*, the presence of Jesus approaches externally, *extra nos*, thereby exploding the knower's self-constituted echo chamber and creating the possibility of genuine theological knowledge.[16]

---

[14]To raise this charge against Webster is not to say that his theology lacks attention to practice. For sure, his rich reflections on God's glory lead into proclamation. For a beautiful example of Webster's own preaching, see John Webster, *Confronted by Grace: Meditations of a Theologian*, ed. Daniel Bush and Brannon Ellis (Bellingham, WA: Lexham Press, 2014).

[15]Bonhoeffer, *Discipleship*, DBWE 4.

[16]This is why genuine theological knowledge necessarily entails genuine sociality. As much as this is the case, we have good reason to see Bonhoeffer's Finkenwalde experiment as a culmination

Bonhoeffer's clearest and most penetrating attack on theology's intellectualizing ambitions emerges in his Christology lectures, delivered in Berlin during the politically tense summer of 1933. He begins these lectures by noting that human thought inherently attempts to catalog objects. When seeking to understand an object, the human knower asks, "How does this object X fit into the classification that I already have at hand."[17] Here the human mind—what Bonhoeffer calls "the immanent logos of human beings"[18]—exerts power over the object of knowledge precisely by supplying ahead of time the categories of classification. But what happens when the human logos meets a counter Logos (*Gegenlogos*) that doesn't easily fit into preconceived mental compartments? Sensing that "its autonomy is being threatened from outside,"[19] the natural urge of the human logos is to persist in its quest to secure knowledge. It does so by reducing the *Gegenlogos* to an idea that can be manipulated and classified like other objects of thought. The problem, of course, is that for Christian theology the *Gegenlogos* is Jesus Christ himself. Faced with the startling presence of this particular object, humanity's inherent lust for control emerges in the form of *how* questions. Just as in the natural sciences, for instance, where humans ask how objects relate to each other, here the theologian asks how it is possible for Christ to exist, how it is possible that two natures cohere in one person, or how it is possible that this person is present. By asking *how* questions, the human logos attempts to reduce the Word of God to the level of other objects that the human logos can classify and control. Precisely by intellectualizing the *Gegenlogos*, the human knower has evaded the challenge of Christ's presence.

But what happens, Bonhoeffer continues, if

> the counter Logos suddenly presents its demand in a wholly new form, so that it is no longer an idea or a word that is turned against the autonomy of the [human] logos, but rather the counter Logos appears, somewhere and at some

---

of his early theological trajectory. If the Word of God breaks open the *cor curvum in se*, then genuine life together becomes a necessary corollary of God's revelatory presence in Christ. See Derek W. Taylor, "What's This Book Actually About?: *Life Together* and the Possibility of Theological Knowledge," *The Bonhoeffer Legacy* 6, no 1 (2020).

[17]Bonhoeffer, *Berlin: 1932–1933*, DBWE 12:301.

[18]Bonhoeffer, *Berlin*, DBWE 12:302.

[19]Bonhoeffer, *Berlin*, DBWE 12:302

time in history, as a human being, and as a human being sets itself up as judge over the human logos and says, "I am the truth," I am the death of the human logos, I am the life of God's Logos, I am the Alpha and the Omega? Human beings are those who must die and must fall, with their logos, into my hands. Here it is no longer possible to fit the Word made flesh into the logos classification system. Here all that remains is the question: Who are you?[20]

This, Bonhoeffer goes on to claim, is the question of "dethroned human reason." Whereas human reason in its classificatory mode asks *how* questions, human reason dethroned by the person of Christ can only ask the *who* question. Whereas the *how* question emerges from the *cor curvum in se* and the possibilities immanent to the human, the *who* question arises in the wake of the personal presence of the risen Christ. For Bonhoeffer, the *how* question is really an attempt to idealize and thus intellectualize Christ, an attempt to turn Christ into an abstraction.[21] Christ in nonpersonal form (i.e., in the form of an idea, a power, an influence, a morality, even a religious personality) is a Christ that fits within the human classificatory system. Christ in personal form, however, shatters the pretentions of the knowing I. As Stephen Plant aptly summarizes the matter, "it is not the job of the human *logos* to make sense of the *Logos* of God; it is the job of God's *Logos* to make sense of us."[22]

This, of course, is not an excuse to abandon the theological enterprise, as if all intellectual work were necessarily unfaithful. But it does remind us how this enterprise ought to proceed.

> The "who question" can only be asked of Jesus by those who know that it is being asked of them. . . . Strictly speaking, the "who question" can be asked only within the context of faith. . . . As long as the christological question is one asked by our logos, it always remains within the ambiguity of the "how question." But as soon as it stands within the act of faith, *it becomes a form of knowledge*, which has the possibility of posing the "who question."[23]

---

[20]Bonhoeffer, *Berlin*, DBWE 12:302.

[21]On Bonhoeffer's resistance to abstraction, Franklin Littell's early analysis rings true: "From the beginning he was stubbornly opposed to mere abstraction, to Christian principles, ideals, or proclamations separated from a community of witness, divorced from the concrete realities of the historical situation." Franklin H. Littell, "The Question: Who Is Christ for Us Today?, in *The Place of Bonhoeffer: Essays on the Problems and Possibilities in His Thought*, ed. Martin E. Marty, (New York: Association Press, 1962), 28.

[22]Plant, *Taking Stock of Bonhoeffer*, 45.

[23]Bonhoeffer, *Berlin*, DBWE 12:307, emphasis added.

Bonhoeffer here claims that revelation creates its own form of knowledge. In this he continues with the agenda laid out in *Act and Being*. In that earlier work he begins to fundamentally rethink what knowledge means vis-à-vis the living Christ. A bold thesis emerges: "The concept of revelation," he claims, "must . . . yield an epistemology of its own."[24] The way we know other things doesn't work for the way we know Jesus. There is indeed a certain paradox in play here. Faithful theologians pursue knowledge they are unable to possess, knowledge that remains only and always a gift. As soon as we turn Christ into a thought-form, we have abstracted revelation from the living person and relocated it in the human mind. In this case, revelation is rendered an existing object that can be had apart from Christ's personal presence.

In *Act and Being*, Bonhoeffer solves this dilemma by referencing "the paradoxical occurrence of revelation without the reflexive answer of consciousness."[25] His Christology lectures press further into the seemingly paradoxical nature of authentic God-knowledge. "But can *we* then really ask the question, *who?* Can we, when we ask *who*, really mean anything other than *how?* No, we cannot. The mystery of *who* remains hidden from us. The ultimate question for critical thinking is that it *must* ask *who* but it *can* not."[26]

This paradox is not meant to be paralyzing. The concrete payoff of pursuing the paradox of revelation in personal terms lies in the way Bonhoeffer specifies the posture and place of theological activity. The posture and place correspond to Christ's personal presence. "One can legitimately ask *who* only after the self-revelation of the other to whom one puts the question. . . . And this in turn means that the christological question can only be asked . . . within the sphere of the church."[27]

To summarize, here we see that by expounding on his person-concept of revelation and pursuing a christological attack on idea-thinking, Bonhoeffer has established the church as the locus of authentic God-knowledge. Indeed, revelation yields an epistemology of its own, and this is an epistemology that

---

[24]Bonhoeffer, *Act and Being*, DBWE 2:31.
[25]Bonhoeffer, *Act and Being*, DBWE 2:159.
[26]Bonhoeffer, *Berlin*, DBWE 12:303.
[27]Bonhoeffer, *Berlin*, DBWE 12:303.

bears the contours of Christ's concrete presence, a way of knowing that takes place only in his wake. When Bonhoeffer claims that Scripture is the book of the church, this line of reasoning must be kept in mind.

Discipleship *and the church's christological visibility.* To read "within the sphere of the church" is therefore not first and foremost to read in light of certain ideas but to read in a certain place—the place of concrete encounter with Christ—and in a certain posture—hopefully attentive to him. This fact helps us add material dimensions to the hermeneutical enterprise. The church, precisely because it corresponds to a historical person who resists being reduced to an idea, is a space that must be thickly and materially depicted. Said more simply, Bonhoeffer contends that the church takes up space on earth because the incarnation takes up space on earth.[28] This is why "any attack on the assertion 'Christ came in the flesh' . . . abolishes the church."[29] In this sense, the church's visibility is not, most properly, a spiritual visibility but a christological visibility—the earthly-historical form of Christ's ongoing existence.

This is not to say that the church is a continuation or extension of the incarnation; rather, the church is a uniquely visible and historical community called into existence by Jesus' own ongoing historical activity. We are not here resorting to naturalistic conceptions of sociality. The church and its visibility remain dependent upon grace. Webster is right in saying that the church's existence is a spiritual event, as Pentecost makes clear. But it is Christ who sends the Spirit, such that the community formed thereby takes its bearings from him, their head. As the *creatura verbi*, the community shares in Christ's visibility.

One of Bonhoeffer's driving concerns in addressing the nature of the church's visibility is to properly articulate humanity's epistemic relationship to God's activity. He wants to insist on the visibility of grace without thereby giving human knowers uncritical access to it. He recognized that in a

---

[28]Bonhoeffer, *Discipleship*, DBWE 4:225-26. Bonhoeffer calls for a church that claims physical space, not only for its worship but also for the daily life of its members. "That is why we must now speak of the *living space* [Lebensraum] of the visible church-community" (Bonhoeffer, *Discipleship*, DBWE 4:232). As Geffrey B. Kelly and John D. Godsey note, Bonhoeffer's index to the 1937 edition of *Nachfolge* refers to this notion of living space under the subject "Incarnation" (Bonhoeffer, *Discipleship*, DBWE 4:232n36). This testifies to the close link between incarnational and ecclesial space in Bonhoeffer's imagination.

[29]Bonhoeffer, *Theological Education at Finkenwalde*, DBWE 14:461.

specifically theological sense, knowledge is power. The undialectical availability of grace would put creatures in a position to control it rather than receive it, to ask the *how* question rather than the *who* question. Thus, he insists that human knowers can never pin down grace in empirical terms.[30] This important distinction becomes evident when he claims that faithful action is visible, but not empirically available.[31]

At this point, christological reasoning continues to lead the way. Though visibly and materially existing as the Son of God in his continuous human history, Jesus' divinity was not statically available to any general onlooker. His divinity, though inseparable from his human flesh, could not be read directly from his face. This is not to claim that his existence was invisible; rather, it is to say that the perception of Jesus' true identity is always a gift of the Spirit. In this sense, Jesus is indeed "spiritually visible." Yet as such he is always a fully material and fleshly being. The way to maintain the distinction between grace and our epistemic access to it is not to immaterialize Jesus or his body, the church, but to accent his lordship—a lordship he enacts in history. To affirm the spiritual dimension of knowledge is to uphold—not belittle—the material nature of revelation.

When our imaginations are tutored by an incarnational account of Christ's historical existence, we see how ecclesial visibility is both a spiritual and christological reality. It is spiritual because the critical gap between Christ and his community prevents human knowers from undialectically equating their knowledge of the church's material structures with God's free grace. Yet it is christological in the sense that it only and always lives in history as a material reality that takes up space like the incarnate One himself. Even if the visibility of Christ's work in the church remains hidden to onlookers, this work takes shape in history as a materially visible community. As I argue more fully below, this carries implications for our conception of the church as a hermeneutical community. Within the community constituted by Christ's address, the activity of faith has spatial and material dimensions, a matter of the body as well as the mind.

---

[30]On this, see Karl Barth, *Church Dogmatics*, vol. IV/3.2, *The Doctrine of Reconciliation*, ed. G. W. Bromiley and T. F. Torrance, trans. G. W. Bromiley (Edinburgh: T&T Clark, 1962), 726.

[31]Bonhoeffer, *Ethics*, DBWE 6:63.

One of the reasons Bonhoeffer is helpful at this point is because of the seriousness with which he takes the Synoptic Gospels as depictions of God's revelation in Jesus Christ. The word that God speaks, and hence the word that creates the church, is the man the Gospels depict. While this claim may sound so simple as to warrant little consideration, it is telling that Webster's work abounds with Pauline theology and the occasional reference to John, but leaves Matthew, Mark, and Luke conspicuously underrepresented. When the Synoptic Jesus does show up, emphasis falls on his "communicative initiative" as the risen One.[32] Webster helpfully draws from Paul as a means of accenting Jesus' resurrected agency. But disconnected from Jesus' historical life, this remains a thin depiction of his agency.

For Webster, when God calls people to himself through Scripture, the accent falls on the arousal and reconstitution of human intelligence and on the generation of knowledge.[33] For Bonhoeffer, in contrast, the accent falls on embodiment: "The aim and objective is not to renew human thoughts about God so that they are correct . . . but that we, with our whole existence and as living creatures, are the image of God."[34] Christ's speech in and through the text shapes not only knowledge but also being, how we think and also how we are. As he writes elsewhere, when Christ speaks he "is always aiming at one thing, *namely, to bind human beings to himself*."[35] Christ calls creatures into a way of life together with him. And while knowledge will surely accrue along the way, the outcome of his call is not merely (or even primarily) cognitive. It results in thick knowledge predicated upon concrete patterns of lived existence.[36] Within the wake of Jesus' call, a way of knowing and a way of being are inextricably connected.

---

[32]See, e.g., Webster, *Domain of the Word*, 35.

[33]Webster, *Domain of the Word*, ix, 19, 61.

[34]Bonhoeffer, *Discipleship*, DBWE 4:282-83.

[35]Bonhoeffer, *Theological Education at Finkenwalde*, DBWE 14:424, emphasis original.

[36]The notion of "thick knowledge" parallels the notion of "thick description" found in Clifford Geertz and others. Drawing from Geertz, Lindbeck suggests that when attempting to describe a particular aspect of religious language or practice, one cannot isolate the particular from the larger cultural and semiotic framework in which it is embedded. The particular must be understood "thickly," that is, within the context of the whole culture of which it is a part; see George A. Lindbeck, *The Nature of Doctrine: Religion and Theology in a Postliberal Age* (Louisville, KY: Westminster John Knox, 1984), 115. On analogy to the notion of thick description, I use the phrase "thick knowledge" to denote the sense in which one's understanding of God cannot be abstracted from the larger framework that makes this knowledge possible, i.e., the life of discipleship itself and all that this life entails. Unlike Lindbeck, I am not primarily concerned

Bonhoeffer's discipleship motif allows him to relate incarnation and resurrection within one christological vision. In fact, this is one of his main theological goals in *Discipleship*, which he achieves by unifying the Synoptic Jesus (incarnation) with the Pauline Christ (resurrection). Many English translations obscure this point. Whereas the original German edition divides the book into two parts—one that engages the Synoptic Jesus and the other the Pauline Christ—English translations often divide part one into three chapters and reduce part two to the fourth and final chapter, thereby rendering the resurrection a mere addendum to what would appear to be the more primary task of analyzing the Synoptic Jesus.[37] When we recognize the original structure, however, we see that Bonhoeffer is making a powerful point: the earthly Jesus' call to discipleship reverberates through the church, confronting us today as it confronted the first disciples back then.[38]

In other words, Bonhoeffer aims in *Discipleship* to hold incarnation and resurrection together, thereby offering an account of "following after" that carries contemporary relevance for the church. Of course, the discipleship motif is most obviously on display in the Gospels. As Bonhoeffer writes, in these texts "the concept of discipleship can express almost the full breadth and content of relations between the disciple and Jesus Christ."[39] And he admits, "In the Pauline texts . . . this concept recedes almost completely into the background. Paul's primary concern is not to proclaim the story of the Lord's earthly life to us, but rather his presence as the risen and glorified Lord."[40]

---

with the process of understanding theological language or practice as a second-order discipline. Rather, I am making an epistemological suggestion, a claim about the very nature of the disciple's own knowledge of the Lord. The disciple's way of knowing indeed has relevance for the task of describing and disseminating this knowledge, but my main point here is that the knowledge itself is bound up in practice and embodiment, in a way of life. As Kavin Rowe suggests, thick knowledge is "a lived way of knowing . . . indissolubly tied to a set of practices" that constitute a concrete pattern of communal life that publicly instantiates the good news of Christ (Kavin C. Rowe, *World Upside Down: Reading Acts in the Graeco-Roman Age* [Oxford: Oxford University Press, 2010], 6).

[37]See, e.g., the highly popular paperback, Dietrich Bonhoeffer, *The Cost of Discipleship*, trans. R. H. Fuller (New York: Touchstone, 1995). The new critical edition of the English translation (DBWE 4) follows Bonhoeffer's original structure and thereby avoids this error.

[38]See Geffrey B. Kelly and John D. Godsey, "Editor's Introduction to the English Edition," in Bonhoeffer, *Discipleship*, DBWE 4:31.

[39]Bonhoeffer, *Discipleship*, DBWE 4:205.

[40]Bonhoeffer, *Discipleship*, DBWE 4:205.

It would seem, then, that attention to the resurrection would diminish the significance of Jesus' call to discipleship. Bonhoeffer recognizes that many readers will reason in this way: "To his first disciples Jesus was bodily present, speaking his word directly to them. But this Jesus died and is risen. . . . Jesus no longer walks past me in bodily form and calls, 'Follow me,' as he did to Levi."[41] Bonhoeffer responds by noting that this line of reasoning must be rejected, for it bifurcates the unity of Jesus and thereby places the church outside of Christ's living presence. "All of these questions refuse to take seriously that Jesus Christ is not dead but alive. . . . He is present with us today, in bodily form and with his word."[42] Consequently, one of Bonhoeffer's fundamental goals in *Discipleship* is to incorporate Paul's new and unique insights into an overarching account of Christ's relationship to his followers. "Paul, albeit with a new terminology, adopts and further develops the concept of discipleship."[43]

Though in *Discipleship* Bonhoeffer rarely engages in explicit discussion with dialogue partners, certain individuals stand in the background. Bultmann is perhaps the most prominent. While Bultmann (as Bonhoeffer reads him) separates the earthly Jesus from the resurrected Christ, referring to the former as the "prehistory" for the church's kerygma, Bonhoeffer allows for no mode of Christ's risen existence to differ from that of the Synoptic Jesus.[44] Bultmann's move, Bonhoeffer believes, not only destroys the unity of Scripture, it turns Jesus into a theological principle, such that he is no longer the singular and embodied Lord. Though Webster and Bultmann obviously differ in many respects, the theology of the word present in both thinkers tends toward the same christological outcome: an

---

[41]Bonhoeffer, *Discipleship*, DBWE 4:201.

[42]Bonhoeffer, *Discipleship*, DBWE 4:201-2.

[43]Bonhoeffer, *Discipleship*, DBWE 4:207. Elsewhere Bonhoeffer writes, "A Pauline doctrinal text is not essentially a dogmatic statement—though it is that as well—but a unique witness to the unique Christ. Although one may say that in the Gospels the miracle of Christ's incarnation and human existence is more perceivable, and in the Epistles the miracle of the cross and resurrection more perceivable, it is never such that in the Gospels, too, the entire crucified and resurrected Christ, and in the Epistles, the entire incarnate human being Christ, is not also attested in all its uniqueness" (Bonhoeffer, *Theological Education at Finkenwalde*, DBWE 14:424-25).

[44]Bonhoeffer, *Discipleship*, DBWE 4:206n10. See Martin Kuske and Ilse Tödt, "Editors' Afterword to the German Edition," in Bonhoeffer, *Discipleship*, DBWE 4:301. For Bultmann, see Rudolf Bultmann, *Jesus and the Word*, trans. Louise Pettibone Smith and Erminie Huntress Lantero (New York: Scriber, 1958), 3-26.

emphasis on the resurrected Pauline Christ and a concomitant devaluation of the incarnation.

In response to this tendency Bonhoeffer boldly proclaims—and this gets to the very heart of his constructive vision in *Discipleship*—that the whole of Scripture "testifies to the ongoing presence of the synoptic Jesus Christ."[45] "The life of Jesus Christ here on earth has not yet concluded,"[46] he continues, which is why "as the Crucified and Risen One, Jesus is at the same time the Christ who is present now."[47]

Christus praesens. The ongoing nature of Jesus' historical existence is one of the most distinctive features of Bonhoeffer's Christology. Those concerned with Christology as a theological locus normally begin their exploration by looking to the incarnation, to that miraculous event in the past in which the two natures were united in one person. Traditional Christology therefore tends to speak of Jesus' history as those years between his birth in Bethlehem and death outside Jerusalem. These years, as the reasoning goes, display the meaning and effects of the incarnational union. On these accounts, the ascended Christ indeed continues to live freely, but his ascended actions are often limited to the epistemological realm—he *makes known* what happened in those thirty years that constitute his history as the incarnate One.[48] It is commonly assumed, in other words, that one must distinguish Christ's historical existence from his ascended existence. One determines his identity; the other proclaims it.

Bonhoeffer, however, begins christological reflection in a very different place—by looking to *Christus praesens*. It is the one we encounter concretely today and not the historical Jesus, the Christ of church doctrine, or even the Christ embodied socially that stands as the proper object of theological reflection. "Christology asks not about what Christ *has done* but rather who Christ *is*."[49] Even though the earthly body of Jesus of Nazareth has ascended into heaven, he remains the incarnate Lord; sitting at the Father's right hand

---

[45]Bonhoeffer, *Discipleship*, DBWE 4:206.

[46]Bonhoeffer, *Discipleship*, DBWE 4:286.

[47]Bonhoeffer, *Berlin*, DBWE 12:310.

[48]On this, see J. Patrick Dunn, "The Presence of the Ascended: History and Incarnation in Barth and Bonhoeffer" (paper presented at the XII International Bonhoeffer Congress, Basel, Switzerland, July 2016).

[49]Bonhoeffer, *Berlin*, DBWE 12:310, emphasis added. He continues, "As the Crucified and Risen One, Jesus is at the same time the Christ who is present now."

does not entail a reversal of the statement in John 1:14 that "Word became flesh." Nor does it entail the end of Jesus' historicity. To be sure, Bonhoeffer would agree with Webster that through the Spirit the risen Christ is free from temporal and spatial circumscription and able to present himself to all times and places.[50] Yet even so, Jesus never ceases to be singularly particular, to be *this* man and no other. He remains the "absolutely unique, historic one."[51] It thus becomes evident that a specific Christology underlies the discipleship motif. It remains Chalcedonian, though it offers a particular rendition of the tradition. It affirms the full humanity and divinity of Jesus but insists that these are not static essences that somehow cohere within the person. The two are united not spatially but historically, in a life. Because Jesus' humanity and divinity are not static entities but dynamic qualities that cohere in a person, he exists as the God-man precisely as he continues to live a personal history that unites these two natures. In this sense, we see how the person-concept of revelation that emerged earlier in Bonhoeffer's career remains operative in *Discipleship*. Indeed, we could even argue that his early idea comes to fulfillment in this later work. If God is known as a person and not as an idea or as an abstract subject, then following is an ingredient in knowing. In *Discipleship*, Bonhoeffer gives a new texture to the epistemology of revelation he began pursuing in *Act and Being*. We know ideas through mental acquisition, we know persons through historical encounter, and we know *this* person by responding to his call and following after him.

This carries important ecclesiological implications. Just as Jesus' humanity and divinity are active, the church's participation in him must be active as well. In this way, the ongoing life of the man from Nazareth creates the possibility of the church. Christians live "in Christ" (e.g., Rom. 8:1; 1 Cor. 1:30) not in that they somehow participate in the divine substance he assumed but to the extent that their histories take shape within the arena of his ongoing life. To be "in Christ," in other words, is the Pauline equivalent of what the Gospels refer to as discipleship. To be in Christ is to participate in his movement in history, to walk his path.[52]

---

[50]Webster, *Domain of the Word*, 42.

[51]Bonhoeffer, *Theological Education at Finkenwalde*, DBWE 14:424.

[52]Bonhoeffer, *Theological Education Underground: 1937–1940*, DBWE 15:505. See Keith L. Johnson, *Theology as Discipleship* (Downers Grove, IL: InterVarsity Press, 2015), 61.

Of course, much more could be said about the Christology that underlies Bonhoeffer's discipleship motif. A full treatment exceeds the limits of this project. Here in part one I gesture toward some of its defining features because it resources the hermeneutical task that I articulate in this book. The main point to note for now is that by unifying Paul with the Synoptics, Bonhoeffer succeeds at construing Jesus' ongoing resurrected existence in spatial terms. Because Jesus is not just an immaterial word or idea, we must think in a concrete and material manner about the modes of his presence. Jesus' ongoing existence calls forth a social space and an array of practices that become the means by which his followers participate in him. Christopher Rowland points toward the hermeneutical ramifications of this christological vision when he reminds us, echoing Bonhoeffer's central insight: "The fundamental learning experience in the Gospels is not the teaching Jesus gave his disciples but their activity in walking with Jesus on the way to Jerusalem."[53] To learn from the risen Lord within the process of discipleship is to learn in a holistic and complex manner, to learn as one who travels with Jesus along the way.

God's word and the crucifixion of the word. This way leads through the cross. "Where you see the Resurrected, you should also see the Crucified."[54] With this, Bonhoeffer upholds Luther's hermeneutical axiom—*crux probat omnia*. The cross is "the center and the paradoxical emblem of the Christian message,"[55] he writes, which is why one's reading of Scripture "should drive him to the cross of Christ."[56] For Bonhoeffer, the turn to Scripture "corresponds exactly to the turn . . . to the cross of Christ."[57]

This requires us to think critically about traditional accounts of the *creatura verbi*. Here we can again consider Webster. While I agree that the risen One speaks to his community with eloquence and radiance, as Webster

[53]Christopher Rowland, "Liberation Theology," in *Oxford Handbook of Systematic Theology*, ed. John B. Webster, Kathryn Tanner, and Iain R. Torrance (Oxford: Oxford University Press, 2007), 643. Here Bonhoeffer would be in full agreement.

[54]Bonhoeffer, *Theological Education at Finkenwalde*, DBWE 14:638.

[55]Bonhoeffer, *Barcelona, Berlin, New York: 1928–1931*, DBWE 10:357. On Bonhoeffer's use of Luther's *theologia crucis*, see H. Gaylon Barker, *The Cross of Reality: Luther's Theologia Crucis and Bonhoeffer's Christology* (Minneapolis: Fortress, 2015).

[56]Bonhoeffer, *Theological Education at Finkenwalde*, DBWE 14:519.

[57]Bonhoeffer, *Theological Education at Finkenwalde*, DBWE 14:419.

forcefully claims,[58] I wonder if this accent threatens to miss something of the cross. Precisely as we emphasize Christ's verbal activity we must also affirm that the one who speaks carries the marks of Golgotha. Christ's is a *cruciform eloquence.*[59] Barth says it well: "Raised from the dead by the power of God, He encounters him in the *despicable and forbidding form* of the Slain and Crucified of Golgotha."[60] Webster deals extensively with Barth's mature theology as it emerges in *Church Dogmatics* IV/3. His account of the risen Christ's verbal activity owes much to Barth's creative exploration of Christ's prophetic office. Yet Webster's reluctance to attend to the cruciform dimensions of Barth's vision reveals a lacuna in his own, and it thereby alerts us to another distortive possibility lurking within ecclesiologies that prioritize the word. So we ask: What does it imply about the church as a hermeneutical community that the word that creates it is despicable and forbidding, a word with holes in his hands and a scar in his sides?

Most obviously, this account of the *verbum* prevents the triumphalism that can result from a strong emphasis on the resurrection. Such triumphalism often enters into hermeneutical debates in the form of a strong account of Scripture's *claritas*. Webster has consistently made the doctrine of clarity a point of emphasis in his hermeneutical theology.[61] As a theological concept, it functions to prioritize God's activity in and through the text. The text is perspicuous not because of some static quality it possesses in and of itself but because God's word is eloquent, radiating out of the text by virtue of its own "inherent potency."[62]

This account of scriptural clarity certainly holds value. By placing priority on God the revealer, it helps uphold the hermeneutical implications of the critical distinction that exists between Christ and his people, thereby serving to chasten interpretive hubris and press toward hermeneutical practices of un-mastery. The danger, however, is that an imbalanced conception of

---

[58]Here Webster himself follows Barth. See John Webster, "'Eloquent and Radiant': The Prophetic Office of Christ," in *Barth's Moral Theology: Human Action in Barth's Thought* (Grand Rapids, MI: Eerdmans, 1998), 125-50.

[59]See Derek W. Taylor, "*Crux Probat Omnia*: Rowan Williams' Scriptural Hermeneutic," *SJT* 69, no. 2 (2016): 140-56.

[60]Barth, *Church Dogmatics*, vol. IV/3.1, *Doctrine of Reconciliation*, 377, emphasis added.

[61]See especially John Webster, "On the Clarity of Holy Scripture," in *Confessing God: Essays in Christian Dogmatics II* (London: T&T Clark, 2005), 33-68.

[62]Webster, "On the Clarity of Holy Scripture," 40.

scriptural clarity that foregrounds Christ's eloquence undermines the practical significance of the asymmetry between Christ and his church. Whereas the asymmetrical nature of the relationship Christ shares with his people should function hermeneutically to press the reading community toward constant repentance, prayer, and other practices of un-mastery, accounts of clarity that remain unchastened by the cross can exaggerate interpretive certainty, thereby vacating this relationship of performative potential. When this happens, the interpretive community situated in relation to the eloquent Christ can employ a conception of clarity to underwrite the God-ordained nature of its knowledge. Having established a critical distinction with one hand, we nevertheless employ a conception of clarity to overcome it with the other. The logic of clarity becomes the logic of control.

But what happens when the doctrine of clarity takes account of the word's cruciformity? What might it mean for the hermeneutical enterprise that the word of Christ that comes to the church through the textual auxiliary is not only "eloquent and radiant" but also "despicable and forbidding"?

Bonhoeffer points toward an answer when he speaks of a light "that looks like the deepest night."[63] As he realized, a cruciform theology of the word not only illumines but also disrupts, not only reveals truth but also places the church itself in question. The cross shatters false religious pretensions, revealing humanity's desire for God's presence to be a mere façade. Although humanity may claim to want God, they cannot bear God's presence, so they kill God. As Bonhoeffer starkly puts it, "The Word become human must be hung on the cross by the human logos."[64] At the cross the disciples' vision of God and God's future is shattered, and thus they flee. For them, the cross is disorienting and darkening, a termination.

This is not, of course, the end of the story. The crucified word raised from the dead confronts the very ones who fled. He whom his followers abandoned issues again the call, "follow me" (Jn 21:19). This is simultaneously a moment of judgment and grace. The Christ who passes through the cross and reconvenes his scattered followers is the one whose very presence compels them to acknowledge their failure, even as that same presence assures them of their forgiveness. Gathering around *this* Jesus entails a process

---

[63]Bonhoeffer, *Theological Education at Finkenwalde*, DBWE 14:598.
[64]Bonhoeffer, *Berlin*, DBWE 12:305.

of confession and reorientation. To encounter the word of the crucified and risen One is to encounter a moment of grace that is simultaneously an invitation to embark upon the ongoing process of unlearning the sinful patterns and habits of human existence. While the word of the resurrected Christ obviously addresses humanity's epistemological problem, the word of the crucified Christ addresses a deeper issue—the very sinfulness and brokenness of human existence. The solution to this problem is not a mere address, though it certainly includes that. The solution is to be called into a new way of life following after the Lord—and to be continually given grace anew to walk the path.

A healthy dose of cruciformity thus challenges any lingering presumptions about the immediacy of the revelatory moment. For Bonhoeffer, revelation entails both the moment of grace that puts one on the road with Jesus and the continual return of grace as the disciple is called step by step.[65] In this sense, revelation is not "all at once" but an ongoing fellowship; being a Christian "is not a matter of a moment but takes time."[66] Indeed, Bonhoeffer suggests that when we embark on the journey of discipleship "a cold fog [rolls] in, which envelopes us completely, so that we no longer see one step ahead of us."[67] To be called by *this* Christ is to abandon the security that comes with ideas and principles and instead to embrace the knowledge that only arises one step at a time.

The *theologia crucis* animates Bonhoeffer's hermeneutical sensibilities. "We seek the will of God, who is utterly alien and repugnant to us," he writes, "whose ways are *not* our ways, and whose thoughts are *not* our thoughts, the God concealed beneath the sign of the cross, where all our ways and thoughts come to an end."[68] This account of God reminds us that the hermeneutical lust for immediacy and certainty must confront the reality of Jesus' crucified body. Precisely because Jesus is present as a crucified agent, the hermeneutical process is marked by elements of silence, watchfulness, and the expectation of judgment.[69] Scriptural clarity, situated in the shadow of the cross, would have more in common with a process of repentance than with a

---

[65]See Bonhoeffer, *Theological Education Underground*, DBWE 15:511.

[66]Bonhoeffer, *Theological Education Underground*, DBWE 15:517.

[67]Bonhoeffer, *Ecumenical, Academic, and Pastoral Work*, DBWE 11:437.

[68]Bonhoeffer, *Theological Education at Finkenwalde*, DBWE 14:168.

[69]See Rowan Williams, *On Christian Theology*, 29-43.

moment of cognition. Unlike readings that seek a revelatory moment of lucidity, the church called into being by the crucified Lord also reads in search of the revelatory moment of crisis, the moment that disrupts one's normal way of being human by placing one next to the crucified Lord. "We ourselves are now the ones who stand convicted."[70] Precisely in this strange form of material visibility, God's grace unsettles the human knower and judges all attempts at mastery. Precisely because Jesus is the slain One, the encounter with his gracious voice is a challenging event. And precisely because he was slain and raised in the *flesh*, the encounter with his gracious voice cannot bypass material processes.

Here it becomes clear that the hermeneutic of "againstness" for which Bonhoeffer advocates is a function of the incarnation, the resurrection, and the cross. If a resurrection hermeneutic emphasizes Christ's living speech and the necessity of a posture of receptivity toward his vocal activity—as Webster reminds us so well—and if an incarnational hermeneutic emphasizes the importance of concretely visible forms of life that follow Jesus on his way, then a cruciform hermeneutic emphasizes the importance of repentance and the correlating ecclesial practices predicated upon the conviction that Christ's call challenges the human community to new forms of thinking and being. Within the community constituted by the word, the hermeneutical process is simultaneously marked by the spatiality of the incarnation, the potent eloquence of the resurrection, and the chastening silence of the cross.

RECONFIGURING THE HERMENEUTICAL SITUATION

My argument in this chapter presses toward a reconfiguration of the church's hermeneutical situation. Within the discipleship motif, Christ is more than a speaker or teacher; he is the One who goes ahead of his followers and leads them into new patterns of existence. Put differently, the word of God does not *mean* something, it *is* something. Therefore, we should not reduce the hermeneutical situation to an encounter between a speaking Christ and a listener. Without abandoning the obviously verbal elements of word theologies, Bonhoeffer presses toward a more complex and holistic vision of

---

[70]Bonhoeffer, *Berlin*, DBWE 12:305.

Christ's action in relation to his people. When Christ speaks, it certainly creates what Webster refers to as "cognitive fellowship." But it is not limited to that. To "hear" Christ's address is not simply to be gifted with new intellectual quantities. Within the framework of discipleship, the hermeneutical goal is more holistic; we read the text as a means of faithfully walking behind our Lord.

Bonhoeffer further suggests that not only the goal but the very process of interpretation must be thickly depicted. Within the church, precisely because it is constituted by Christ's call, we encounter a unique form of knowing, a mode of apprehension distinctive to revelation. "Do not interpret or apply, but do it and obey," Bonhoeffer suggests, for "that is the only way Jesus' word is really heard."[71] As I began to argue in the previous chapter, revelation requires an epistemology unique to itself. In *Discipleship*, Bonhoeffer adds substance to this mode of knowing by insisting that understanding is predicated upon the ongoing process of discipleship. The activity of faith situated receptively vis-à-vis the risen Christ takes concrete shape as a mode of existence caught up in the activity of following. Discipleship, therefore, is not merely the outcome of hermeneutical faithfulness but its very shape and context, the fundamental presupposition of knowing Christ.

Bonhoeffer's person-concept of revelation and related account of discipleship as the appropriate response to the person need not be read as an outright dismissal of the classical subject-object construal of epistemology. It does, however, remind us that the *type* of subject we are matters in our apprehension of this particular object. The danger is we assume that a generic subjectivity is fit to handle this object, an object that is itself a living subject. Bonhoeffer reminds us that true knowledge requires self-involvement: "In order even to see something we need to love it. If we are indifferent toward a person or a thing, *we will never understand it*."[72] This love, of course, cannot overcome generic modes of knowing if it is itself generic. Love, more than a mere idea, is a matter of commitment, a matter of following.

With these insights, Bonhoeffer presages later developments in philosophical hermeneutics that note the interrelatedness of epistemology and

---

[71]Bonhoeffer, *Discipleship*, DBWE 4:181.
[72]Bonhoeffer, *London: 1933–1935*, DBWE 13:389.

practice.[73] To borrow from Bourdieu, the notion of discipleship functions for Bonhoeffer as a christologically defined *habitus*, a form of knowing inscribed in the body by experience.[74] Bonhoeffer's account, of course, remains distinctly theological. According to him, the pursuit of textual knowledge requires interpretation, while the pursuit of Jesus requires obedient action. For this reason, he contrasts the pharisaical pursuit of knowledge with the Christian pursuit of Christ.[75] In terms of the discipleship paradigm, Scripture functions as one of the primary means by which Christ addresses the community, becomes present to it, and draws it along into active fellowship with him.

When situated within the church as the *creatura verbi*, hermeneutical inquiry terminates with Christ himself. We read so as to have communion with him, and though communication is central to this communion, the two are not identical.[76] The question driving the hermeneutical enterprise is always both "What is going on in this text?" (the penultimate hermeneutical question) and Bonhoeffer's famous "Who is Christ actually for us today?" (the ultimate hermeneutical question).[77] We ask the first question only because we have already asked the second.

In other words, we read the text within the activity of discipleship. When we ignore this—when we ignore the material dimensions of the word himself and the embodied nature of following after him—reading threatens to remain stuck in the ideational realm. We end up imagining that the poles of

---

[73]For example, Pierre Bourdieu, "Bodily Knowledge," in *Pascalian Meditations*, trans. Richard Nice (Stanford, CA: Stanford University Press, 2000), 128-63. Also see Maurice Merleau-Ponty, *Phenomenology of Perception*, trans. Donald A. Landes (New York: Routledge, 2014). For an argument for the bodiliness of reason from the perspective of cognitive science, see George Lakoff and Mark Johnson, *Philosophy in the Flesh: The Embodied Mind and Its Challenge to Western Thought* (New York: Basic Books, 1999); and George Lakoff and Rafael E. Núñez, *Where Mathematics Comes From: How the Embodied Mind Brings Mathematics into Being* (New York: Basic Books, 2000). These trends have taken particular theological shape in the praxis-based epistemology of liberation theology. Christopher Rowland directly connects this to the interpretation of Scripture: "The understanding of the Christian scriptures in particular is an activity and a discipline inseparable from the action which is epistemologically fundamental" (Rowland, "Liberation Theology," 643).

[74]See Bourdieu, "Bodily Knowledge," 138.

[75]Bonhoeffer, *Ethics*, DBWE 6:325.

[76]For a recent example that risks conflating communication and communion, see Scott Swain's *Trinity, Revelation, and Reading: A Theological Introduction to the Bible and Its Interpretation* (London: T&T Clark, 2011).

[77]Bonhoeffer, *Letters and Papers from Prison*, DBWE 8:362.

interpretation are the written texts.[78] On this misguided assumption, the skilled interpreter is the one who takes one text (made difficult by cultural and linguistic distance) and turns it into a different text (made accessible by means of interpretive activity). Interpretation becomes a matter of navigating the gap between the then and now so as to present the text in contemporary idiom. Interpretation is reduced to translation, and the task of the interpreter is reduced to something like decoding, giving new arrangement and expression to old words so as to render them accessible.[79] The hermeneutical goal becomes (perhaps implicitly) what Raymond Williams refers to as consumption; interpretation becomes "concerned with understanding an object in such a way that it can be profitably or correctly consumed."[80] Stated more straightforwardly, the danger lies in scriptural interpretation becoming a complex game of information gathering.[81] This danger lurks in all modes of reading. R. R. Reno argues that even much of what passes as "theological exegesis" is essentially abstractive in nature in that it seeks to draw out something theological from the text (e.g., a doctrine or concept).[82]

Within a hermeneutic of discipleship, conversely, the text seeks to draw us along into the path Jesus walks. When we think of the revelatory process in and through the text within the framework of following after Jesus in terms of both patterns of life and patterns of knowing, the hermeneutical task takes on new layers. Contrary to the standard practice, Nicholas Lash suggests that the poles of the interpretive process are not "expressions of 'meaning'" but "patterns of human action." He contends that a faithful interpretation of a biblical text might look like a life of witness.[83] He presses further: "I would wish to argue that the fundamental form of the Christian

---

[78]Nicholas Lash, "Performing the Scriptures," in *Theology on the Way to Emmaus* (Eugene, OR: Wipf & Stock, 1986), 37-46.

[79]See A. K. M. Adam, "Poaching on Zion: Biblical Theology as Signifying Practice," in A. K. M. Adam, Stephen E. Fowl, Kevin J. Vanhoozer, and Francis Watson, *Reading Scripture with the Church: Toward a Hermeneutic for Theological Interpretation* (Grand Rapids, MI: Baker Academic, 2006), 17-34.

[80]Quoted in Lash, *Theology on the Way to Emmaus*, 84.

[81]See Stephen B. Chapman, "Studying the Word of God," in *Scripture*, Christian Reflection: A Series in Faith and Ethics (Waco, TX: Baylor University Institute for Faith and Learning, 2014), 29-36.

[82]R. R. Reno, "Biblical Theology and Theological Exegesis," in *Out of Egypt: Biblical Theology and Biblical Interpretation*, ed. Craig G. Bartholomew et al. (Grand Rapids, MI: Zondervan, 2004), 385-408.

[83]He offers Maximilian Kolbe's life as an example (Lash, *Theology on the Way to Emmaus*, 89-90).

interpretation of scripture is, in the concrete, the life, activity and organization of the Christian community, and that the Christian practice consists . . . in the performance or enactment of the biblical text."[84]

Incarnation and inspiration. Richard Kearney gets at something similar, though from a distinctly philosophical perspective. He suggests that in much hermeneutical discussion "the journey from flesh to text often lacked a return ticket."[85] With the so-called linguistic turn in philosophy (he has in mind the work of Gadamer and Ricoeur in the 1960s) Kearney contends that "we witness an embrace of language at the expense of body." This is not to deny that important insights arose from this movement; it is to say, however, that preoccupation with textual and linguistic representation risks missing something more fundamental to the process of human knowing. According to Kearney, "we find the 'linguistic turn' of hermeneutics tending to veer away from the carnal as a site of meaning, replacing body with book, feeling with reading, sensing with writing."[86] Kearney is making a significant argument about the trajectory of continental philosophy since Heidegger, arguing in a fresh way for the reappropriation of Husserl's emphasis on the primacy of *Leib* (body) as that which constitutes psychic reality.[87] The task of understanding, he suggests, must break free from old dualisms between *nous* and *soma* (mind and body). The danger of the "hermeneutical turn," he contends, is that we lose this unity and consequently trade embodiment for textuality. To put this insight in specifically theological terms, we lose the incarnation of the word behind its textual inspiration.

Kearney and others are attempting to argue philosophically for something that incarnational theology should presuppose: embodiment is integral to knowing. God's speech is "verbal" in a very particular sense. Taking the incarnation seriously, we see that God speaks a life: "In these last days he has spoken to us by a Son" (Heb 1:2). This Son is not a glorified angel, God's most trusted courier—the Son *is* God's speech. The medium is the message. *Verbum* and *carnem* belong together. If we sever this relationship by making the latter a "concealing exterior vehicle," we reductively distort

---

[84]Lash, *Theology on the Way to Emmaus*, 90.

[85]Richard Kearney, "What Is Carnal Hermeneutics?," *New Literary History* 46, no. 1 (2015): 100.

[86]Kearney, "What Is Carnal Hermeneutics?," 100.

[87]See the recent volume, *Carnal Hermeneutics*, ed. Richard Kearney and Brian Treanor (New York: Fordham University Press, 2015).

our doctrine of God. The revealing God becomes essentially a speaker, a vocal being.[88] But if the God of the Bible is the one we seek to understand, we must admit that understanding comes through Christ's flesh, and, if we take Bonhoeffer seriously, it is mediated through our bodies as he calls us to follow him. Christ asks the disciples to put down their nets (Mk 1:17-18) before he asks, "Who do you say that I am?" (Mk 8:29). The following is the condition of the knowing. For sure, Webster's emphasis on cognition carries important insights, for the Spirit gifts human beings with a certain form of knowledge as they undergo the renewal of the mind (Rom 12:2). Yet this mental transformation is also a physical, material occurrence—a matter of laying one's body on the altar (Rom 12:1). To lose sight of the body in our preoccupation with knowledge is to offer an attenuated account of God's revelatory activity.

Kearney's insight is relevant for our discussion, for much of what passes today as theological interpretation is in some sense predicated (if not dependent) upon the linguistic turn in philosophy. We have come to see that language—and hence tradition and narrative—is hermeneutically fundamental. Taken seriously, this claim paves the way for a return to the church as a hermeneutical community. These hermeneutical trends have done much for theological interpretation, not least by showing how "being the church" is a prerequisite for reading faithfully.

In this chapter I have been complexifying this common claim by suggesting that we take discipleship seriously as a hermeneutical category. Reading within the church involves reading in light of language, tradition, and narrative—but it also involves reading in the space created by Christ's incarnation, crucifixion, and resurrection. Webster notes that the so-called linguistic turn in theological hermeneutics often lacks specifically theological dimensions, that talk of text and reader can fill in for talk of God. Here he is surely right, though in making this important assertion against

---

[88]Certainly, a more nuanced account of God's speech-acts would helpfully alleviate some of this one-sidedness. See, e.g., Richard S. Briggs, *Words in Action: Speech Act Theory and Biblical Interpretation* (Edinburgh: T&T Clark, 2001); and Kevin J. Vanhoozer, *The Drama of Doctrine: A Canonical-Linguistic Approach to Christian Theology* (Louisville, KY: Westminster John Knox, 2005), 63-68. However, even within the framework of a theologically serious account of speech-act theory, we must confront the tendency to construe God's "acts" as primarily mental or linguistic in nature.

the standard theological appropriation of hermeneutical philosophy we nevertheless risk replicating its linguistic preoccupation. The danger is not simply that the hermeneutical process underplays divine language but also that it loses touch with the materiality and cruciformity that is basic to Christian faith.

Webster's response: aseity and promeity. At this point, Webster might push back:

> The person and work of the Son can be so identified with his incarnate presence that his eternal pre-existent deity recedes from view; or the post-existence of the Son in his state of exaltation can come to be retracted. In both, Christology is constricted, as the temporal career of the Son is allowed to expand to fill the whole. . . . As a result, ecclesiology tends to be preoccupied with the question: What kind of continuity is there between the incarnate and the ecclesial body?[89]

Webster worries that this tendency is especially evident in certain strands of Bonhoeffer scholarship.[90] The principal danger, he suggests, is that an undue emphasis on God's presence risks collapsing divine freedom into worldly processes, thereby calling God's aseity into question. This tendency, he concludes, "surely needs correction by a robust account of the lordly activity of God in Christ."[91]

Though Webster's early writings deal favorably with Bonhoeffer, as Webster's theology develops and moves in a more classical direction, certain criticisms become more pronounced. Therefore, we must note the important difference of emphasis that separates Bonhoeffer and Webster. This difference becomes especially evident when we recall the importance of promeity in Bonhoeffer's theological imagination: "I can never think of Jesus Christ in his being-in-himself, but only in his relatedness to me."[92] Given this clear theme in his writing, it is worth distinguishing Bonhoeffer himself from certain interpretive trends in Bonhoeffer scholarship. Beginning with John Robinson's *Honest to God*, English language scholarship has been

---

[89]Webster, *God and the Works of God*, 184.
[90]Webster, *Domain of the Word*, 128. In particular, Webster notes Paul D. Janz, *God, the Mind's Desire: Reference, Reason and Christian Thinking* (Cambridge: Cambridge University Press, 2004), 213-20.
[91]Webster, *Domain of the Word*, 128.
[92]Bonhoeffer, *Berlin*, DBWE 12:314.

tempted toward superficial readings of Bonhoeffer as a post-Christian or secular theologian who abandons all recourse to God's objectivity.[93] Webster is right to react critically to these trends.

Bonhoeffer's discipleship motif has great utility at just this point of tension, for it frees him from the constraints of a purely vertical conception of God's presence to creation and thereby allows him to articulate God's sovereignty in a historical register. The ongoing historical presence of the God-man allows Bonhoeffer to overcome the limits of classical metaphysical geometry and thereby uphold God's divine freedom without sacrificing Christ's promeity. God has fully entered history in Jesus, but God has done so freely, as an act of pure grace. More particularly—and this is where the theme of discipleship is so helpful—God realizes this freedom historically. Christ is "above" his people in divine freedom precisely by living "out-ahead" of them as their living Lord.[94] In the journey of discipleship, Jesus retains priority. The path belongs to him. Even being present, the incarnate Christ lives in utter mobility, exercising his sovereign otherness by means of his utter out-aheadness. Therefore, to say that Christ is with us is not to say that we have him under control. Precisely the opposite is the case. Within the discipleship motif, Christ is truly at hand but never in hand.[95] In this sense, Bonhoeffer, with Webster, appreciates the disruptive potential of God's otherness. Yet, he does so in a way that refuses to downplay the concrete nature of life with Christ. Christ's presence is certainly interruptive, yet the goal of this interruption is historical fellowship between the Lord who walks his path and the people who follow along behind.

Another potential danger with this strong accent on promeity is that it lapses from Christocentrism to Christomonism. The Holy Spirit becomes particularly important at just this point. I have followed Bonhoeffer by foregrounding Christ as an irreducibly particular and personal figure, but what about the Spirit? Though the Holy Spirit does not often become a direct object of focus in his work, I contend, in his defense, that the notion

---

[93]John A. T. Robinson, *Honest to God* (Philadelphia: Westminster, 1963). Almost unanimously, recent Bonhoeffer scholarship has deemed this a tendentious misreading.

[94]See André Dumas, *Dietrich Bonhoeffer: Theologian of Reality*, trans. R. M. Brown (London: SCM Press, 1971), 168.

[95]On the idea that God is at hand but not in hand, see Christopher Morse, *The Difference Heaven Makes: Rehearsing the Gospel as News* (London: T&T Clark, 2010), 6.

of discipleship disintegrates without it. There can be no "following after" apart from the mediating activity of a personal Spirit.[96] One of the most common signs that we have slipped into Christomonism is that we reduce the Spirit to a mere manifestation of a certain dimension of Jesus' own identity—perhaps a mode, power, or emanation of Christ himself. Such a move must be resisted, for it would call into question the presence-otherness tension characteristic of Bonhoeffer's discipleship Christology.[97] A personal account of the Spirit as the one Jesus sends allows the church simultaneously to uphold, on the one hand, Christ's irreducible singularity and utter out-aheadness and, on the other, his gracious presence and promeity.[98] Christ strides through history leading the church into the Father's kingdom, and the Spirit spans the gap between Christ and his people, leading them into all truth, conforming them to him, and thereby drawing them along into his ongoing activity.

As with the christological question, this pneumatology deserves fuller treatment than I can give it here. By gesturing toward the Spirit's important

---

[96] As Colin Gunton notes, "the presence of Christ is not *as* but *through* the Spirit, who is the mediator both of Christ's presence and his . . . otherness" (Gunton, "'Until He Comes': Towards an Eschatology of Church Membership," *IJST* 3, no. 2 [2001]: 197, emphasis original). Bonhoeffer similarly claims that the Spirit is independent and personal, not a "neutral power," a "collective spirit," or a general gift that proceeds from Christ's overall activity (Bonhoeffer, *Theological Education at Finkenwalde*, DBWE 14:482).

[97] A similar line of thinking emerges in Jenson's critique of Barth: Robert W. Jenson, "You Wonder Where the Spirit Went," *Pro Ecclesia* 2, no. 3 (1993): 296-304. Jenson suggests that Barth lapses into functional binitarianism by reducing the Spirit to a power of Christ or to Christ's own work of coordination with his congregation. In this sense, the Spirit becomes a mode of Christ and not a distinct person. Jenson suggests that Barth's Spirit-avoidance is closely linked to his avoidance of the church. In this project, I echo Barth's christocentricity, but I attempt to do so without avoiding the church, which is why the Spirit remains important as a singular person of the Trinity.

[98] Unsurprisingly, Bonhoeffer adamantly affirms the *Filioque*. In his estimation, the struggle against the German Christians rendered the doctrine vital to Christian witness, for its absence would open the door to an account of the Spirit not bound to the Jewish flesh of Jesus— e.g., a uniquely *völkisch Geist*. He strongly criticizes the view that "the Spirit also comes through nature and the creation," which would amount to a perverse "deification of the natural" (Bonhoeffer, *Theological Education at Finkenwalde*, DBWE 14:482). He believed that binding the Spirit to Christ undermines the possibility of natural theology and its destructive racial effects. More particularly, he insists that the Spirit comes only through the cross of Christ, thereby suggesting that God's presence in the world today remains always a cruciform presence (see Bonhoeffer, *Theological Education at Finkenwalde*, DBWE 14:481). For Bonhoeffer, in short, the Spirit is always bound to Jesus: "The condition for the coming of the Spirit is the departure of Jesus," and thus the "Spirit comes only from Jesus Christ" (Bonhoeffer, *Theological Education at Finkenwalde*, DBWE 14:481-82).

role, we can at least see that a doctrine of the Trinity is operative within the discipleship motif, even if it is more often implied than expressly stated. Certainly, the Trinity does not exert a structuring role for Bonhoeffer the way it does for many classical theologians, nor does he often speculate about God's being in itself. In both these ways Webster offer resources not present in Bonhoeffer. Even so, we find no evidence that Bonhoeffer questioned the notion of God's triune aseity.[99] As Clifford Green persuasively argues, "the doctrine of the Trinity is an unquestioned presupposition of Bonhoeffer's theology."[100] For Bonhoeffer, promeity assumes aseity. This is why he claims that the doctrine of the Trinity functions to preserve God's wonder and mystery even as God is with us and for us in Jesus.[101]

Webster might raise a final criticism. When writing about the nature of the church's invisibility, he contrasts his position with one that he explicitly locates in Bonhoeffer's *Discipleship*. In particular, he worries about the resonances between Bonhoeffer's ecclesiology and an inflated account of "the concept of 'practice' as it has been developed in social and cultural

---

[99]Even in Bonhoeffer's "nonreligious" writings from prison, it seems unlikely that he had any intention of abandoning inherited orthodoxy. This is evident, for example, in his repeated insistence that he desires to be "theological" and not "liberal" and in his use of the arcane discipline to guard the secrets of Christianity in the midst of the church's worldly life. It is telling that Webster is not fond of Bonhoeffer's most mature work: "The prison texts do not contain the most important or interesting things which Bonhoeffer had to say: there is much more theological good sense on questions of the presentation of the gospel to be found in the Finkenwalde homiletics lectures." John Webster, "'In the Shadow of Biblical Work': Barth and Bonhoeffer on Reading the Bible," *Toronto Journal of Theology* 17, no. 1 (2001): 75.

[100]Clifford J. Green, "Trinity and Christology in Bonhoeffer and Barth," *Union Seminary Quarterly Review* 60, nos. 1-2 (2006), 2. Green agrees with Charles Marsh, who distinguishes between God's "primary objectivity" (which includes notions of aseity and Trinity) and God's "secondary objectivity" (which includes notions of promeity and Christology). Marsh claims that while Bonhoeffer's focus tends to fall on the latter (in contrast to Barth), his emphasis on promeity always presupposes aseity; the latter is never meant to denigrate the former. See Charles Marsh, *Reclaiming Dietrich Bonhoeffer: The Promise of His Theology* (Oxford: Oxford University Press, 1994), 3-31. For a contrary reading of Bonhoeffer and the Trinity, see George Hunsinger's review of *Reclaiming Dietrich Bonhoeffer*, where he claims, "Precisely because of his Ritschlian heritage . . . Bonhoeffer always accepted the axiom that it is impossible to speak of God's being as it is in itself." Hunsinger, review of *Reclaiming Bonhoeffer*, by Charles Marsh, *MT* 12, no. 1 (1996): 122.

[101]See Bonhoeffer, *Barcelona, Berlin, New York*, DBWE 10:461. Regarding the importance of a conception of eternity undergirding Bonhoeffer's thinking, see *Barcelona, Berlin, New York*, DBWE 10:538. On the vital relationship between Trinity and Christology, see Bonhoeffer, *Berlin*, DBWE 12:355: "God who became human is the God of glory; God glorifies himself in the human. This is the ultimate mystery of the Trinity. From 'now unto eternity,' God regards himself as the God who became human."

theory."[102] He suggests that by prioritizing visibility and sociality through emphasizing the theme of practice, contemporary ecclesiologies risk losing sight of God and thereby risk sliding into a form of ecclesiological monophysitism that reduces the church to a purely human reality.[103] These are valid fears, and we would do well to remain alert to them.

In fairness to Bonhoeffer, however, the resonances are less pronounced than Webster suggests. While Bonhoeffer's ecclesiology shares points of overlap with contemporary communion ecclesiologies and the notion of practice that emerges in strands of social theory, his entire theological career is marked both by conversing with social theory and by distinguishing genuine theology from it. Indeed, it is common for Bonhoeffer to delve deeply into philosophical issues only to emerge on the other side having concluded that the philosophical concepts in and of themselves are inadequate for the theological task at hand.[104] Rather than parroting intellectual trends, he frames his ecclesiology within the logic of the gospel. Webster worries about overemphasizing the historicity of the church, its being as an endurable reality, and its social-historical visibility. Bonhoeffer would agree that ecclesiological naturalism looms within such inclinations. He suggests, for example, that certain dangers lurk within a theology that is too strongly focused on the congregation and "too strongly oriented to praxis."[105] He even suggests that an overemphasis on practices risks displacing the importance of the Trinity and Christology, for both "ministry and church spring from the triune God."[106]

Though Webster's worries are valid, he is wrong to criticize Bonhoeffer for his concrete emphasis on ecclesial life. To equate Bonhoeffer's vision with contemporary trends is to miss the unique possibilities his thought presents. This is especially true when thinking about the church as a hermeneutical community. Rather than being the anthropological corollary of a version of social immanentism, thereby funding a form of hermeneutical Pelagianism

---

[102]Webster, "Visible Attests the Invisible," 98.

[103]Webster, "Visible Attests the Invisible," 99.

[104]For a clear example of this tendency, see Bonhoeffer's "Inaugural Lecture: The Anthropological Question in Contemporary Philosophy and Theology," *Barcelona, Berlin, New York*, DBWE 10:389-408.

[105]Bonhoeffer, *Conspiracy and Imprisonment: 1940–1945*, DBWE 16:495.

[106]Bonhoeffer, *Discipleship*, DBWE 4:230. See Clifford Green, "Trinity and Christology in Bonhoeffer and Barth," 12.

that seeks to produce meaning, the notion of practice that emerges within Bonhoeffer's discipleship motif remains thoroughly concrete and yet essentially receptive, predicated upon the gracious otherness and livelihood of the risen Christ.

CONCLUSION: WEBSTER, BONHOEFFER, AND THE CHURCH AS A CHRISTOLOGICAL SPACE

In part one I have suggested that the church's relationship to Christ constitutes the ultimate context of hermeneutical activity. In subsequent chapters I will add depth to this account by considering the various proximate contexts of the hermeneutical enterprise.[107]

The basic hermeneutical liability lurking within the *creatura verbi* is that the word that constitutes the church remains abstract and disembodied. For this reason, I have taken the incarnate and cruciform nature of God's *verbum* with utmost seriousness. It is precisely the lordship of this particular Nazarene that creates the church and gives it shape across time. I have suggested that the space this man creates by calling people to himself is the church's hermeneutical space, the space in and for which Jesus' followers faithfully engage their text. Within this space, engaging Scripture is a material, historical, and spatial event. Meaning—when we are talking about this text and this Lord—is a way of life, an embodiment, a performance. Intellectual understanding and concrete ways of living cannot be segregated. This makes the hermeneutical task at once more complex (for it opens the door to a wide range of potential hermeneutical

---

[107]In speaking of the "ultimate" and "proximate" contexts of interpretation I am riffing on David H. Kelsey. He uses these terms in *Eccentric Existence: A Theological Anthropology* (Louisville, KY: Westminster John Knox, 2009) as a means of framing the contours of a theological anthropology. "Theologically speaking, human beings are God's creatures. The ultimate context into which they are born is God's relating to them as their creator. Human persons are born into complex networks of other beings that interact with one another and with specifically human beings in dynamic systems of energy and energy exchange that constitute their proximate contexts" (Kelsey, *Eccentric Existence*, 160). Stated more simply, the ultimate context of human life is God and God's ways of relating to us; the proximate context is the quotidian, the everyday finite realities that constitute the human person's concrete location in the world (Kelsey, *Eccentric Existence*, 190). While the ultimate cannot be reduced to the proximate, neither can they be severed. To refract Kelsey's anthropological insights into the ecclesiological realm, a properly theological analysis of the church requires that we talk about both God's action in constituting a people (the ultimate context) and also the material and quotidian dimensions that constitute the community as a social reality (the proximate context).

practices) and less sophisticated (for we are no longer beholden to any particular methodological procedure).

The claim that reading occurs within the space of discipleship may leave us asking: But what does this actually mean for how we read the Bible? I began answering this question in chapter one by drawing attention to a hermeneutical posture sustained by practices of un-mastery. As I move on to consider the church's other constitutive dynamics, I will add flesh and bone to this account by noting the importance of concrete acts of togetherness (part three) and missionary encounters with the world (part four). Now, however, I turn to consider the church in relation to its historical-institutional past. Christ's call creates a community that stretches across space and time, which is why the church as a hermeneutical community is marked by a shared institutional history.

PART TWO

The Church as Institution: Hermeneutics and the Ecclesial Past

3

Reading in Light of the Past

A Conversation with Robert Jenson

When Christ calls disciples, he creates the ultimate context in which they faithfully engage their text. As Bonhoeffer demonstrates, this call constitutes the church as a unique structural entity that is grounded in God's grace, resists empirical explanation, and yet remains a visible social reality that corresponds to Christ's ongoing movement as the risen Lord. Yet, other proximate dimensions of existence are implicated in it. For the first disciples, the process of understanding arose as the past—i.e., tradition, narrative, and inherited hopes—came into conversation with the risen Lord. For them, past and future collided in the christological present. Jesus did not bypass the disciples' inherited past but brought it to life by shining his resurrection light upon it. In having their eyes opened, the disciples were not subsequently abstracted from the continuities of their history. Instead, this radically new event required them to learn to see this continuity in new ways. The resurrection forced the disciples to imagine new forms of faithfulness that were at once continuous with their inherited past and yet inflected through the presence of Christ. The New Testament itself is a product of this creative tension. Those who received new sight from the risen Lord did not abandon their old texts and traditions but read them in new ways.[1]

---

[1]See Richard B. Hays, "Reading Scripture in Light of the Resurrection," in *The Art of Reading Scripture*, ed. Ellen F. Davis and Richard B. Hays (Grand Rapids, MI: Eerdmans, 2003), 216-38.

Even in the space of the risen Christ, the institutional past remains hermeneutically consequential.

Or as Bonhoeffer puts it, "Between us and the Bible there stands a *church that has a history*."[2] One cannot understand the Bible, he goes on to suggest, without an awareness of the church's historical dimensions. As he states elsewhere, Scripture "is a book from which the church has for two thousand years already drawn knowledge of the truth; it has not been left to us to discover truth for the first time, God has been revealing it to the church community from that source for centuries."[3] In Bonhoeffer's imagination, hermeneutical space is constituted both by the community's relationship to the risen Christ and by its relationship to its own historical past. Christ's call creates a community with a social history. Precisely as the *creatura verbi* the church is also a historical-institutional body.

Acknowledging the hermeneutical significance of church history calls to mind the common affirmation that Scripture does not stand alone but becomes intelligible in light of tradition. The relationship between Scripture and tradition is, of course, one of the most vexing debates in post-Reformation theology. Taking it up places us squarely within the classical tension between Catholic and Protestant hermeneutics. Before becoming Pope Benedict XVI, Joseph Ratzinger summarizes the situation well when he claims that for Protestantism the word guarantees the ministry of the church, but for Catholicism the ministry of the church guarantees the word. "Perhaps in this reversal of relations between word and ministry lies the real opposition between the views of the church held by Catholics and Reformers."[4]

By prioritizing the church's constitutive relationship to the risen word I am in this project offering a distinctly Protestant account of hermeneutical space. Yet, as I demonstrated in the previous chapter, the Catholic voice deserves attention precisely for its ability to shine light upon potential blind spots in Protestant thought. The various authorities involved in the hermeneutical process must be differentiated and ordered, not placed in

---

[2]Bonhoeffer, *Conspiracy and Imprisonment: 1940–1945*, DBWE 16:495.
[3]Bonhoeffer, *Theological Education at Finkenwalde: 1935–1937*, DBWE 14:517.
[4]Karl Rahner and Joseph Ratzinger, *Revelation and Tradition*, trans. W. J. O'Hara (Freiburg: Herder, 1966), 29. For a recent take on this from a distinctly Catholic perspective, see Joshua R. Brotherton, "Revisiting the *Sola Scriptura* Debate: Yves Congar and Joseph Ratzinger on Tradition," *Pro Ecclesia* 24, no. 1 (2015): 85-114.

competition. Carl Braaten expresses this point well: "The church is the creature of the Word; the Word is prior. But in the order of human experience the church comes before the gospel. We might put it this way: in the order of being (*ordo essendi*) the gospel comes before the church, but in the order of knowledge (*ordo cognoscendi*) the church comes before the gospel."[5] One can ontologically prioritize the ongoing activity of the risen One while insisting that the church provides access to this activity. Christ and tradition, event and institution, revelation and history—together these shape one and the same hermeneutical space.

My goal in part two is neither to untangle all the threads of Scripture-tradition debates nor to highlight all their historical dimensions. Instead, I hope to show how attending to the risen Christ allows us to articulate a coherent vision of the hermeneutical task that accounts for the church's christological and historical-institutional dimensions.

By *institution* I simply mean a historical society with consistent visible structures, a social entity that exists beyond the lifetime of its members. The church is an institution in that its oneness takes form concretely in history.[6] Of course, there are different ways of accenting the institutional dimension of the church. Avery Cardinal Dulles suggests that a sound ecclesiology will uphold the institutional elements of the church without devolving into distortive one-sidedness in which the visible structures become the defining feature of the church's existence, what he calls rigid institutionalism.[7] He notes that hermeneutical implications lie close at hand; an institution can function as a "zone of stability" that allows the community to navigate into an "uncertain present" on the basis of "an esteemed religious

---

[5]Carl E. Braaten, "The Problem of Authority in the Church," in *The Catholicity of the Reformation*, eds. Carl E. Braaten and Robert W. Jenson (Grand Rapids, MI: Eerdmans, 1996), 55.

[6]See Avery Dulles, *Models of the Church* (New York: Doubleday, 1978), 39.

[7]Dulles, *Models of the Church*, 41. Institutionalism entails what Dulles calls a deformed view of the true nature of the church in which the institution becomes the hierarchical machinery of the mediation of grace. According to Dulles, the tendency is not inherent to Catholicism but began to develop in the late Middle Ages and Reformation period as Catholic theologians responded to the Protestant Reformers (Dulles, *Models of the Church*, 41). In the worst cases, this Counter-Reformation impulse resulted in a view of the church as a totalizing institution that exists for the sake of itself, similar to the way a nation-state exists for the good of its citizens. Also see Yves M.-J. Congar, *Lay People in the Church: A Study for a Theology of Laity*, trans. Donald Attwater (Westminster, MD: Newman Press, 1962), 44-45, where he similarly warns against turning ecclesiology into "hierarchology."

past."[8] Examining how the institution performs this hermeneutical function is one of my tasks in chapter three.

ROBERT JENSON'S REVISIONARY METAPHYSIC

My initial guide is Robert Jenson, whose work has been consistently on the cutting edge of ecclesial trends in scriptural hermeneutics.[9] Jenson is a fascinating object of study in his own right, yet I engage him here for a specific purpose. He serves my larger constructive project in two particular ways. On the one hand, he lucidly illustrates the logic of the church's historical and institutional existence and highlights the constructive hermeneutical value of locating Scripture within that history. On the other hand, certain weaknesses in his thinking signal the dangers that might emerge when the hermeneutical dimensions of the church's institutional past become inflated beyond their capacity. In this sense, Jenson's function in part two formally resembles Webster's in part one, though in a materially opposite way. When read together, Webster's revelational hermeneutic and Jenson's institutional hermeneutic seem to stand at odds with each other. For this reason, I return to Bonhoeffer in chapter four as a means of forging a constructive synthesis between christological and institutional logics that might otherwise seem incommensurate. Following Bonhoeffer's lead, I attempt to reinscribe the historical-institutional dimensions of hermeneutical faithfulness within a christological account of ecclesial space.

In order to explore the hermeneutical dimensions of Jenson's theology it will be helpful to highlight their theological underpinnings. These take shape as Jenson provides a unique answer to an old problem. In its appropriation of the theology that preceded Jesus, the church inherited a particularly perplexing task: how to resolve "the old dissonance between the metaphysical principles of the Greeks and the storytelling of the gospel."[10] Jenson worries that by uncritically allowing pagan philosophy to determine its thinking, the church in the West drifted from narrative particularity to metaphysical abstraction, unwittingly pitting the God of its Scriptures

---

[8]Dulles, *Models of the Church*, 47.

[9]See Robert Jenson, *The Triune God: Collected Essays on Scripture*, ed. Brad East (New York: Oxford University Press, 2019).

[10]Robert W. Jenson, *The Triune God*, vol. 1 of *Systematic Theology* (Oxford: Oxford University Press, 1997), 112.

against the God of its theology. At the heart of his project, therefore, is the desire to free the church to read Scripture faithfully.

Perhaps the most telling sign of this theological dilemma is the loss of trinitarian language in much contemporary church life. The way forward, Jenson argues, requires theological reconstruction, which is why he summarizes his project as "an effort of revisionary metaphysics, aimed at allowing one to say things about God that scripture seems to require but that inherited metaphysics inhibits."[11] Axiomatic to his revisionary system is the belief that God is identified with and not merely by the economy of salvation.[12] Whereas much Western theology has insisted upon inserting an analogical interval between God's immanent and economic existence, Jenson maintains that the plot of the life of God and his people is the whole reality of God; "history occurs not only in him but as his being."[13]

Jenson's attempt to blaze a revisionary trail has much to commend it, not least in that it forces the church to attend to the logic of its text with fresh eyes. A full analysis of Jenson's theological vision exceeds the limits of this project, yet in order to set the stage for our analysis of the church, two points are worth highlighting. First, Jenson refuses to import an unbaptized notion of eternity into the theological task. Running against the grain of much of the tradition, he contends that eternity and time are in fact positively, not negatively, related. Like creatures, God has time, but unlike them, God is in no way bound in having it. God does not transcend the contingencies, movements, and passions of history; what God transcends is having any personal limitation thereby.[14]

A close reading reveals that Jenson's unique construal of time and eternity is foundational to his entire theological project. It allows him to reimagine inherited metaphysical beliefs without abandoning the church's traditional language about God. It is at just this point that the revisionary—and to some readers, counterintuitive—nature of his thought becomes most apparent.[15]

---

[11]Robert W. Jenson, "Response to Watson and Hunsinger," *SJT* 55, no. 2 (2002): 230.

[12]Jenson, *Triune God*, 59.

[13]Jenson, *Triune God*, 221.

[14]Jenson, *Triune God*, 66, 138-45.

[15]See, e.g., Simon Gathercole, "Pre-Existence, and the Freedom of the Son in Creation and Redemption: An Exposition in Dialogue with Robert Jenson," *IJST* 7, no. 1 (2005): 38-51; and Oliver Crisp, "Robert Jenson on the Pre-Existence of Christ," *MT* 23, no. 1 (2007): 27-45. Crisp contends that Jenson becomes incoherent in his talk about time:

He contends that the problem that perplexes critics has more to do with their assumptions than with his theology. Some find his account of time unsatisfactory, he claims, "only because we unthinkingly make an (in itself rather naïve) assumption about time: that it glumly marches on. . . . But time, in any construal adequate to the gospel, does not in fact march in this wooden fashion. Time . . . is neither linear nor cyclical but perhaps more like a helix, and what it spirals around is the risen Christ."[16] Here Jenson's driving concern is fairly straightforward: one should construct a theology of time and eternity in light of the New Testament rather than importing a preconceived notion into it.

His christological account of eternity opens space for a radical reimagining of the relationship between Jesus' divine and human natures. This is the second important point to note, for it fundamentally shapes his ecclesiology. By eliminating the gap between God's immanent and economic reality, Jenson suggests that the second person of the Trinity is none other than Jesus, the man from Nazareth. With no ontological shield protecting heaven from earth, the way is opened for a radically Cyrillian account of the communion of attributes.[17] In revising the traditional metaphysical claims that have undergirded much Western theology, Jenson even goes so far as to reject the very existence of the entity normally known as the *logos asarkos* (the unfleshed word, i.e., the eternal logos "before" the incarnation), the invention of which was a "historic mistake."[18] It is the "aggressively incarnate protagonist" of the Gospel narrative who claims, "Before Abraham was, I am" (Jn 8:58), thereby putting his antecedence to Abraham in the present

---

God is temporally infinite. This sounds like the view that God endures through time . . . in which case, like all other things in time, it would seem that God has a past, a present and a future. . . . But Jenson denies this "Aristotelian" picture of divine temporality. What does he replace it with? A notion that God is temporally infinite, but has no past or future and is past and present to himself because he is somehow future to himself. It is rather as if God exists through time by projecting himself backwards in time from his future to his past and present. But what could that possibly mean? (Crisp, "Robert Jenson," 35)

[16]Robert W. Jenson, "Scripture's Authority in the Church," in Davis and Hays, eds., *Art of Reading Scripture*, 35.

[17]As we will see more fully below, Cyril of Alexandria's logic funds Jenson's uniquely narrative account of Scripture. By refusing to divide the protagonist of the Gospels into two subjects, one human and one divine, Cyril provides "theological warrant to read the Gospels whole as God's own story" (Jenson, *Triune God*, 128-29).

[18]Robert Jenson, "Once More the *Logos asarkos*," *IJST* 13, no. 2 (2011): 130.

tense.[19] With this, Jenson's historicist logic stretches as far as it can go. The second person of the Trinity is not an "extra metaphysical entity. . . . He is Mary's child, the hanged man of Golgotha."[20]

These two points are significant for this chapter's argument because they dovetail into a particular conception of ecclesial space. If "Jesus' human action and presence is without mitigation God's action and presence,"[21] and if no heavenly *logos* hides behind the back of the man from Nazareth, an important question arises: Where do we presently locate the risen One? If the second person of the Trinity is inseparable from a historical and material body, where now is that body?[22]

Jenson's answer is unequivocal: *the church*. A body is someone's objective availability to others, he suggests, and the risen One possesses such availability as the community of his people, the body of Christ.[23] More than a mere metaphor, this piece of Pauline theology is an "ontic identification."[24] "The object—the body—that the risen Christ is . . . is the church around her sacraments. He needs no other body to be a risen man, body and soul. . . . Heaven is where God takes space in his creation to be present to the whole of it; he does that in the church."[25] With this, the effects of Jenson's revisionary metaphysic have rippled into ecclesiology. In rethinking the nature

---

[19]Jenson, *Triune God*, 139.

[20]Jenson, *Triune God*, 145.

[21]Jenson, *Triune God*, 144.

[22]Jenson notes that this question carries particular challenges in the modern era. In a Ptolemaic universe, one could physically locate Jesus' literal ascended body above the heavens. But the Copernican revolution rendered this answer implausible. There is no "place" for a heavenly body in modern cosmology. Jenson suggests that this leads to a rise in disembodied pneumatology in modern theology. See Jenson, *Triune God*, 201-6; and idem, "You Wonder Where the Body Went," in *Essays in Theology of Culture* (Grand Rapids, MI: Eerdmans, 1995), 216-24. Interestingly, Colin Gunton suggests that Jenson is overreliant on natural theology at just this point. See Colin E. Gunton, "'Until He Comes': Towards an Eschatology of Church Membership," *IJST* 3, no. 2 [2001]: 198.

[23]Jenson, *Triune God*, 205; idem, *The Works of God*, vol. 2 of *Systematic Theology* (Oxford: Oxford University Press, 1999), 213.

[24]Jenson, *Triune God*, 204. Regarding the nonmetaphorical nature of Paul's "body of Christ" imagery, see Jenson, *Works of God*, 190. Also see Judith Brown, "The Pattern of Theological Truth: An Interview with Robert Jenson," *Stimulus: The New Zealand Journal of Christian Thought and Practice* 22, no. 1 (2015): 32, in which Jenson claims that in its fundamental usage, body-of-Christ language in Paul is not a metaphor; Paul is speaking propositionally. The church is quite literally the place in the world where you look if you want to see Christ. Jenson admits, of course, that after asserting this proposition, Paul proceeds to exploit it metaphorically, e.g., in talking about the head and the feet.

[25]Jenson, *Triune God*, 206.

of God's time and Jesus of Nazareth's role in the triune life, Jenson has suggested a very particular account of ecclesial space—this space is the body of Christ.

INSTITUTIONALIZED HERMENEUTICS

Jenson presses his Cyrillian logic into the being of the church. Just as one cannot imagine a *logos asarkos* in distinction from the man from Nazareth, neither can one imagine an invisible ecclesial entity hiding behind the visible and temporal institution. The church in history is the present tense of Jesus, his availability for the world.[26] Because of this, its visible continuity takes on utmost importance. A church that lacks adequate visibility would be as senseless as a person who lacks a body. For this reason, Jenson stands as an exemplar of my second ecclesiological dimension. Rather than following "the Reformation emphasis that the church is in a special sense 'the creature of the gospel,'" he foregrounds the "traditional question about the founding of the church. . . . That is, [ecclesiology] presumes the actual historical existence of the church and inquires into its origin and nature."[27]

As it does in his doctrine of God, the notion of time takes on great importance in Jenson's ecclesiology. Whereas Protestantism's account of the church, as Jenson understands it, is determined by revelation, his account is governed by a depiction of the church's unique temporal location. "God institutes the church by *not* letting Jesus' Resurrection be itself the End," Jenson writes.[28] At Pentecost, the Spirit frees a human community to be Christ's body during this unique eschatological detour. The church's existence, in other words, is contingent upon the space that has been opened between the resurrection and the second coming.

Within this unique stretch of time, the church has a particular mission: "The purpose that constitutes and distinguishes the church . . . is maintenance of a particular message, called 'the gospel.'"[29] Elsewhere he writes, "Any community that intends to live for more than a moment,

---

[26]Jenson, *Triune God*, 201.
[27]Jenson, *Works of God*, 168.
[28]Jenson, *Works of God*, 170.
[29]Jenson, *Triune God*, 4.

that hopes to remain itself through some term of yesterday-today-and-tomorrow, will have to deal with the fragility of an identity thus stretched across time."[30] Perhaps due to his futurist ontology, Jenson eschews an account of divine sovereignty that would protect the fragile institution as it traverses through time. He instead declares that the "the church's diachronic identity is *as threatened* by the passage of time as is that of any other community."[31]

This claim is significant, and we shall return to it shortly. Here we pause to note, in anticipation of what is to come, that although Bonhoeffer similarly locates Christ's personal presence in the church, he offers a different account of the nature of Christ's relationship to the institution, and thus a different account of the church's survival. Teasing apart this difference will be key to articulating the institutional dimensions of a hermeneutic of discipleship.

Touchstones of continuity: canon and creed. If, as Jenson suggests, the church is a fragile institution threatened by the passage of time, how shall it survive? Jenson's hermeneutical vision begins to emerge as he answers this question. The way to deal with ecclesial fragility, he contends, is through "structures of historical continuity" established by means of "deliberate *institutions* that would be constitutive of [the church's] life."[32]

> Institutions constitute a community's diachronic identity and simply in their own power as institutions establish a purely inner-historical continuity through times. The historical ground of the church's institutions is the events told in the Gospels. And however peculiar a historical event one of these events, the Resurrection, was, the relation of the community thus founded to its historical ground obeys the usual regularities: when one knows the circumstances of the church's historical origin one can predict what general sort of institutions the church must have.[33]

For Jenson, in other words, the church is a historical community that functions as such, which means that particular structures of continuity are necessary to ensure the perpetuation of its identity.

---

[30] Robert W. Jenson, *Canon and Creed* (Louisville, KY: Westminster John Knox, 2010), 3.
[31] Jenson, *Canon and Creed*, 3, emphasis added.
[32] Jenson, *Triune God*, 24-25, emphasis original.
[33] Jenson, *Works of God*, 180.

These structures of continuity also constitute the hermeneutical space within which the church reads Scripture faithfully. They do so, most fundamentally, by bridging the so-called hermeneutical gap. Whereas hermeneutical theory is traditionally predicated upon the distance between the initial recipients of a text and those who attempt to read it in the present, Jenson's account of the church as the institutionally maintained presence of Christ's body undercuts this logic. At just this point Jenson would have us see that modern criticism errs by methodologically presupposing the nonexistence of "one diachronically identical universal church."[34] Guided by this errant commitment, critical historians employ hermeneutical tools and methods to surmount the distance separating them from the text. For Jenson, this is nothing short of a secular enterprise, for it necessarily posits a reading community other than the church and is, by definition, a non-Christian enterprise (even if undertaken by people of faith).[35] In contrast, Jenson avers that "there is *no* historical distance between the community in which the Bible appeared and the church that now seeks to understand the Bible, because these are the same community."[36] Because of this, "past and present do not need to be bridged before understanding can begin, since they are always already mediated by the continuity of the community's language and discourse."[37] At this point, the logic of Jenson's account of hermeneutical space becomes especially clear. To read within the church is to read under the guidance of this mediated continuity.

Had Jesus returned immediately, as some early Christians expected, institutions of diachronic continuity would have been superfluous. The firsthand living memory of the apostles and their disciples would have sufficed to establish communal identity. But Jesus did not soon return, and thus "the telephone-game problem became apparent."[38] When living memory began to fade, it had to be institutionalized. According to Jenson, the Spirit gifted the church with the means of this institutional continuity at precisely this precarious point in its historical life. In particular, the Spirit

---

[34]Jenson, *Works of God*, 280.
[35]Jenson, *Works of God*, 280.
[36]Jenson, *Works of God*, 279.
[37]Jenson, *Works of God*, 280.
[38]Jenson, *Canon and Creed*, 4.

gave the church the canon and the creed, concrete touchstones that forged communal continuity between past and present.[39] Regarding the canon, Jenson writes,

> What Christians call the Bible . . . exists as a single entity because—and only because—the church gathered these documents for her specific purpose: to aid in preserving her peculiar message, to aid in maintaining across time, from the apostles to the End, the self-identity of her message that the God of Israel has raised his servant Jesus from the dead. Outside the community with this purpose, binding these particular documents into one volume would be pointless.[40]

Therefore, in contrast to the "currently fashionable doctrine of literary scholars . . . [which claims] that there is no text other than the logical product of interpretations," Jenson claims that the living community, held intact by institutional structures, anchors the text's stability.[41] One distinct text exists precisely to the extent that one distinct community exists. Because those who read Scripture are members of the same community that canonized it, to read these texts as anything other than Scripture is in fact a form of eisegesis.

Important interpretive implications follow. Given the church's act of canonization, the various texts that compose it are no longer confined to the space of their historical origin. Any particular meanings that may have been necessary to their original composition become secondary to Scripture's meaning as a canonical whole. Consequently, the church must direct its hermeneutical efforts toward just this text and no other.[42] While this assertion seems simple, it actually flies in the face of much modern interpretive practice. Echoing key aspects of Frei's notion of

---

[39]Jenson, *Canon and Creed*, 1-7.

[40]Jenson, "Scripture's Authority in the Church," 27-28. Also see Robert W. Jenson, "On the Authorities of Scripture," in *Engaging Biblical Authority: Perspectives on the Bible as Scripture*, ed. William P. Brown (Louisville, KY: Westminster John Knox, 2007), 53-61.

[41]Jenson, *Triune God*, 40n45.

[42]This is evident in Jenson's own works of scriptural commentary. See Robert W. Jenson, *Song of Songs*, Interpretation: A Bible Commentary for Teaching and Preaching (Louisville, KY: Westminster John Knox, 2005); and idem, *Ezekiel*, Brazos Theological Commentary on the Bible (Grand Rapids, MI: Brazos Press, 2009). This is not to say that he avoids engaging the history behind the text or the text's redactional layers—he indeed engages them in an ad hoc manner. But when he does, his final object of concern remains the text in its received form.

intratextuality, Jenson argues that the authority of the canon cannot be defined in reference to something outside of the story—e.g., historical events, religious experiences, or doctrinal truths. The text is not ultimately about something other than itself, not merely an instrument of reportage. By defining Scripture in terms of its institutional location and canonical form, Jenson loosens the text from its original *Sitz im Leben*. The interpretive enterprise does not terminate after the exegete has extracted linguistic details, reconstructed historical events, or separated the text into its constitutive redactional layers—even as such tasks may at times contribute to the larger interpretive process. For Jenson, this is a liberating realization. With no hermeneutical gap to span, readers of Scripture are free to use various tools of interpretation in an ad hoc manner as means of attending to the literary topography of the text as it comes to the church in canonical form.[43]

This logic coincides with a particular narrative sensibility: "Since we are *in* the story, all procedures that read Scripture for information about some third entity are wrong."[44] In Lindbeck's terminology, which maps nicely onto Jenson's scriptural hermeneutic, the text functions as a narrationally structured symbolic world that the church seeks to indwell.[45] Within historical-institutional space, the various tools used to engage Scripture ultimately serve to move the community within the text. As one of the chief pioneers of this sensibility suggests, "We are to fit our own life into its world, feel ourselves to be elements in its structure of universal history."[46]

---

[43]Jenson, *Works of God*, 274. Among other things, this implies that "even biblical Greek and Hebrew must be familiar somewhere in the life of the church" (Jenson, *Works of God*, 275). Likewise, Jenson strongly warns against the temptation of ever new and more relevant translations (Jenson, *Works of God*, 275n19).

[44]Jenson, "Scripture's Authority in the Church," 31.

[45]George A. Lindbeck, "Postcritical Canonical Interpretation: Three Modes of Retrieval," in *Theological Exegesis: Essays in Honor of Brevard S. Childs*, ed. Christopher Seitz and Kathryn Greene-McKnight (Grand Rapids, MI: Eerdmans, 1990), 26-51.

[46]Erich Auerbach, *Mimesis: The Representation of Reality in Western Literature*, trans. Willard R. Trask (Princeton, NJ: Princeton University Press, 2003), 15. Hans Frei has something similar in mind in his effort to retrieve the precritical notion of Scripture as a realistic narrative: "Biblical interpretation became an imperative need, but its direction was that of incorporating extra-biblical thought, experience, and reality into the one real world detailed and made accessible by the biblical story." Hans W. Frei, *The Eclipse of Biblical Narrative: A Study in Eighteenth and Nineteenth Century Hermeneutics* (New Haven, CT: Yale University Press, 1974), 3.

In this way, Jenson's historical-institutional hermeneutic resonates with larger trends that emphasize narrative as an interpretive category.[47] Yet for Jenson, this is no literary fad. His historical-institutional ecclesiology provides the theological rationale for the intratextual turn.[48] If, as he claims, the canon was shaped "to the general plot and understanding of the church's story as she had been telling it all along,"[49] then it functions precisely to maintain the continuity of the narrative. The church must indwell its story— its "history book," as he calls it—precisely as a means of extending the story through history. The point of reading this text within this community is to become part of its narrative movement. Scripture exerts its authority precisely as it maintains the community's identity in the midst of this movement. Scripture's authority functions, in other words, the way a novel constrains its characters, and this before the novel is finished.[50]

Besides providing the canon and placing readers in an intratextual posture toward it, the church functions as a hermeneutical space in another important sense: it provides a hermeneutical optic. This optic, Jenson suggests, is the Apostles' Creed, which functions as the second important touchstone of continuity. In particular, he suggests that the creed is the church's "critical theory" for Scripture, i.e., the lens that allows the community to see what is really going on in the text. "The community positioned to perceive what a scriptural text is truly up to is the church," he claims, "and the creed is the set of instructions for discerning this agenda." He goes on to assert that "the needed suspicious eye is the eye trained in the church."[51] One must read Scripture in the church, Jenson suggests, because the church provides unique access to its content and the rules for reading it properly. Criticism becomes truly critical, on this reading, not when it dispenses with presuppositions but when it embraces the right ones.

---

[47]In a sense, Jenson's strongly narrativized doctrine of God stands as the doctrinal telos of this hermeneutical trend. His principled resistance to metaphysics prevents him from moving beyond or above the text to a purer realm of theological meaning. God lives God's own life in history, such that no suprahistorical exegetical move is necessary.

[48]Such grounding is often lacking in other proponents of this move, some of whom turn to narrative as a means of valuing Scripture without recourse to God. But, for Jenson, a distinctly Cyrillian logic remains at play. His valuation of narrative and his account of divine being go hand in hand.

[49]Jenson, *Works of God*, 274.

[50]Jenson, "Scripture's Authority in the Church," 32.

[51]Jenson, *Canon and Creed*, 81.

Christ, culture, and catechesis. Together, the touchstones of continuity
help to shape a distinct culture.[52] Jenson declares that the church, under the
aid of the touchstones, "is responsible to cultivate her culture, and can lose
her identity if she does not."[53] By claiming that the church in its diachronic
continuity is Christ's earthly presence, Jenson attempts to cut through the
Gordian knot of Christ-culture debates. Rather than theorizing how these
two entities might relate to each other, Jenson avers, quite simply, that Christ
is a culture. Whereas H. R. Niebuhr's famous typology suggests that Christ
is one thing and culture another, Jenson's account of Christ's resurrected
presence requires him to dispense with this faulty assumption.[54] Christ has
a body that is itself a community of bodies, and together these compose one
identifiable culture.[55]

This line of reasoning safeguards ecclesial stability. Whereas positing an
invisible metaphysical entity lying behind the visible community would
loose the empirical church from any specific form and thereby allow the
community a degree of flexibility in adapting its cultural life, Jenson's claim
that Christ is a culture anchors the empirical form of the community
through time. Christ and his communal body, Jenson implies, are the same
yesterday, today, and forever. This does not, of course, disallow certain
culturally contingent elements from participating in ecclesial life, but it does
suggest the undergirding presence of a normative cultural pattern. The
church's task with regard to competing cultures is not to adapt or modify its
own (perhaps as a means of becoming culturally relevant, a desideratum
Jenson would like to eradicate from the church's imagination) but to remain
consistently itself, to be the culture that Christ is.

Whereas much debate on the relationship between ecclesial and non-
ecclesial cultures theorizes the possibility of an overlap or merging of the
two,[56] Jenson adamantly insists on their difference. "By his resurrection and
ascension, Christ is a political fact among and in competition with the

---

[52]On the church as a culture, see chap. 7 in this book.

[53]Robert W. Jenson, "Christ as Culture 1: Christ as Polity," *IJST* 5, no. 3 (2003): 324.

[54]See H. Richard Niebuhr, *Christ and Culture* (New York: Harper & Row, 1951).

[55]For a critical take on Jenson's view of the church as culture, see Peter Kline, "Participation in
God and the Nature of Christian Community: Robert Jenson and Eberhard Jüngel," *IJST* 13,
no. 1 (2011): 38-61.

[56]For example, Niebuhr's "transforming culture" type in his *Christ and Culture*, 190-229.

polities of this world."[57] He goes so far as to speak of this as a relationship of conflict: "We must expect other polities to make war against us."[58]

Jenson suggests that the church engages in this conflict and thereby maintains its cultural difference through rigorous observance of "discipline at its border."[59] The basic form of this discipline is catechesis, which Jenson calls a "long immersion in the church's dogmatic, liturgical, and moral tradition."[60] Rather than a useful practice that helps to make the church more faithful than it otherwise might be, Jenson considers catechesis a matter of ecclesial survival.[61] In less bellicose imagery, he likens the process of catechesis to the process of learning a language. The church is the community that speaks "Christianese," he writes, and to enter its culture is to enter the logic of its grammar.[62] The threat, then, is that the church might cease to be what she is by abandoning her distinct identity. The catechetical process exists because there must be a way of passage from non-Christian to Christian (however Christianized the former may claim to be) that protects the cultural purity of the latter.[63]

Practical hermeneutical implications lie close at hand. Within historical-institutional space, pedagogy becomes a primary hermeneutical tool. Faithful reading is catechized and disciplined reading, reading that accords with the church's unique culture. For much of Christian history, this

---

[57]Jenson, "Christ as Culture 1," 328. This calls to mind Bellarmine's infamous parallel between the church and nation-states. Jenson suggests that the papacy's occasional behavior as a literal government, complete with ministers of state and even a military, was a perversion—"But it was a perversion of something true" (Jenson, "Christ as Culture 1," 329).

[58]Jenson, "Christ as Culture 1," 329. Though Jenson rejects Niebuhr's typology, some critics suggest that he nevertheless articulates an account of Christ *against* culture; or, more accurately: the culture that Christ is stands against the other cultures and polities of the world. Schwöbel claims, for example, that in Jenson the Christ-culture debate morphs into a church-culture debate; see Christoph Schwöbel, "Once Again, Christ and Culture: Remarks on the Christological Bases of a Theology of Culture," in *Trinity, Time, and Church: A Response to the Theology of Robert W. Jenson*, ed. Colin E. Gunton (Grand Rapids, MI: Eerdmans, 2000), 103-25. While a certain "againstness" characterizes the relationship between church and culture, Jenson unabashedly claims that all cultures have an ecclesial telos, for the church will eventually absorb all cultures. If Niebuhr's view is dualistic, Jenson's view becomes strongly monistic in that it absolutizes the church (see Schwöbel, "Once Again, Christ and Culture," 123).

[59]Jenson, *Works of God*, 205.

[60]Robert W. Jenson, "A Lesson to Us All," *Pro Ecclesia*, 3 no. 2 (1994): 135.

[61]Jenson, "Christ as Culture 1," 324.

[62]Jenson, *Triune God*, 18.

[63]Robert W. Jenson, "Catechesis for Our Time," in *Marks of the Body of Christ*, ed. Carl E. Braaten and Robert W. Jenson (Grand Rapids, MI: Eerdmans, 1999), 141.

hermeneutical vision was assumed and did not need forthright argument. Yet in a post-Christendom context Jenson believes that ecclesial faithfulness requires a new level of intentionality. "The church in the West can no longer suppose that the regular schools or the organs of public opinion . . . will instruct people in a way that is harmonious with the church's instruction. Indeed, we must assume the contrary: that they will inculcate ideological naturalism, moral relativism, and the superiority of all other religions to Christianity."[64] The way forward requires drastic measures: "We may find ourselves willy-nilly emulating the roles of Celtic Christianity or of the Benedictines during the 'dark ages.' If the Church survives in the West as a tiny and despised community, let her attend to the authenticity of her own life . . . with the world viewing this strange body."[65]

Jenson, MacIntyre, and "traditioned rationality." Jenson's allusion to Benedictine communities calls to mind Alasdair MacIntyre's enigmatic suggestion in the closing pages of *After Virtue*. After likening the cultural moment to the emergence of the dark ages in Europe, MacIntyre suggests that "what matters at this stage is the construction of local forms of community in which [traditional forms of life] can be sustained through the new dark ages which are already upon us. . . . We are waiting . . . for another—doubtless very different—St. Benedict."[66] MacIntyre responds to modernity's moral fragmentation, in other words, by insisting on the formation of distinct traditions and the communities necessary to sustain them. In particular, he suggests returning to Aristotelian notions of personhood and virtue in which the excellencies of human action are determined not by universal standards but by their coherence with a communal narrative and hence by the telos toward which communal life is patterned. He builds on these ideas by suggesting that all rational inquiry is tradition specific.[67] "We need to recover . . . a conception of rational enquiry embodied in a tradition," he writes, "a conception according to which the

---

[64]Jenson, "Catechesis for Our Time," 142.

[65]Robert W. Jenson, "It's the Culture," *First Things*, May 2014, 36.

[66]Alasdair MacIntyre, *After Virtue: A Study in Moral Theology*, 2nd ed. (Notre Dame, IN: University of Notre Dame Press, 1984), 263.

[67]Regarding the tradition-specific nature of rationality, see MacIntyre, *After Virtue*, 204-25. Echoing MacIntyre, Jenson speaks of this history as an ongoing communal argument through time; cf. Alasdair MacIntyre, *Whose Justice? Which Rationality?* (Notre Dame, IN: University of Notre Dame Press, 1988), 12, 222.

standards of justification themselves emerge from and are part of a history."[68] If modernity can be defined as an effort to flee the authority mediated by the traditions and institutions of the past,[69] MacIntyre counters by challenging modernity's claim to universal rationality, suggesting instead that rationality is necessarily tradition specific. To flee the past is to flee the very possibility of rational inquiry.

MacIntyre illumines Jenson's guiding logic. Though Jenson's animating concerns differ from MacIntyre's in certain respects—e.g., he is motivated by the particular task of maintaining ecclesial faithfulness rather than broader issues pertaining to the rationality and coherence of moral discourse—he too offers a particular and inherently teleological view of human being. True humanity, Jenson suggests, is found in the church, and humanity's true telos is participation in the triune life.

Setting these two thinkers next to each other is particularly relevant given the goal of this chapter, for it helps make sense of Jenson's underlying hermeneutical logic. The church reads faithfully—it develops a mature hermeneutical rationality, he might say—when it indwells and embodies its specific tradition, when it becomes immersed in the particularity of its story. For Jenson, as we have seen, the structures of diachronic identity constitute this tradition as an inhabitable space, and catechetical and intratextual practices provide the main avenues by which one inhabits it. Jenson's key hermeneutical practices, in other words, function precisely by placing the reader in a traditioned posture. By being absorbed into the culture and shaped to the contours of the story, one is equipped to read in a manner that is faithful to the text's historical-institutional location.

INSTITUTIONALISM AND THE PRESENCE OF CHRIST

At first glance, Bonhoeffer's emphasis on un-mastery and Jenson's emphasis on tradition-based rationality may seem discordant. Whereas Bonhoeffer's suggested hermeneutical orientation directs the reading community toward an extrinsic reality, Jenson seems to imply an insular process. The key to faithful reading, for Jenson, is to move ever more deeply within the church.

---

[68]MacIntyre, *Whose Justice?*, 7.
[69]As Jeffrey Stout has influentially claimed; see Stout, *The Flight from Authority: Religion, Morality, and the Quest for Autonomy* (Notre Dame, IN: University of Notre Dame Press, 1981).

Interpretive faithfulness, it would seem, is internal to the reading culture, such that the church, in and of itself, becomes hermeneutically sufficient.

Jenson's trust in ecclesial culture is notably evident in his account of the resources required to read Scripture faithfully. "The Bible is the Spirit's book, who may do with it what he will," he writes, "and the church as his prophet knows what that is."[70] We should pause to register the boldness of this claim. Jenson is suggesting that the church knows what the Spirit will say. At this point one might raise a concern. Closely linking the Spirit's voice to ecclesial knowledge certainly has the benefit of buttressing the significance of the institution, but does it not also threaten to constrain the Spirit's freedom? Asked more pointedly, if we so closely link the Holy Spirit to an immanent cultural reality, does the Spirit actually need to do anything? If the church already knows what the Spirit will say, why must the Spirit say it? This hermeneutical posture risks reducing the Spirit's work to redundancy. Jenson's institutional hermeneutic would work, it would therefore seem, even if God did not exist. I suggested earlier that language of divine revelatory action ought to exert force on the ground by shaping corresponding practices. Is this the case with Jenson? I worry that for him the language of "Holy Spirit" tends to function as doctrinal decoration masking more basic realities like "institutional memory" or "communal consciousness."[71] A theoretical account of the Spirit's activity in the reading process has become theological adornment without concrete effect. The church has its inherited culture—and for such a hermeneutic, this seems to suffice.

To state the hermeneutical matter a bit differently, Jenson accents the text's regulative mode at the expense of its sacramental mode.[72] Scripture functions for the church analogously to the way foundational cultural artifacts function within other communities. Indeed, as a "documentary relic," Scripture behaves as an essentially secular entity.[73] It operates as a regulative tool at the church's disposal more than as a means of divine address.

---

[70]Jenson, *Works of God*, 276. Also see Robert W. Jenson, "The Religious Power of Scripture," *SJT* 52, no. 1 (1999): 94.

[71]See Jenson, *Canon and Creed*, 15-16.

[72]For the regulative-sacramental distinction, see Michael Horton, *The Christian Faith: A Systematic Theology for Pilgrims on the Way* (Grand Rapids, MI: Zondervan, 2011), 154.

[73]Jenson, *Triune God*, 27. Speaking of Scripture as a secular entity, Katherine Sonderegger writes, "Now, such a book belongs to the world of other books, though it is the best among them. . . . [Its] aim is perfectly general. Against all other books of instruction, all other manuals of culture

Of course, Jenson wants to affirm that Scripture is in some sense an agent that acts in distinction from the community. He maintains, for example, that even as Scripture is a collection of writings put together by the church, it is also the word of God that creates the church.[74] In this sense, it would seem that Scripture functions in both regulative and sacramental modes, as both norm and address. But what precisely does Scripture do? When Scripture does act in a seemingly sacramental way, it acts "to guard the integrity of a message" across time and thereby to preserve the church's cultural authenticity.[75] What Scripture does, in other words, is norm identity. Scripture's sacramental capacity is thereby collapsed into its regulative capacity. Whatever unique voice the text has is made derivative of its more basic culture-forming capacity.

This plays out in practice. Whereas Bonhoeffer's account of Christ correlates with a willed vulnerability vis-à-vis the revealing God and practices that sustain such vulnerability, Jenson's account threatens to reinforce prior commitments. It is perhaps unsurprising that practices such as confession of sin, repentance, and prayer—so vital to Bonhoeffer's hermeneutic—sparsely appear in Jenson's. Absent a serious account of Scripture's sacramentality, the church is tempted toward a hermeneutic characterized by "radical horizontality" in which "interpretation very quickly turns into an advancement of ideologies."[76] Without the necessary critical leverage between Christ's word and the church's reading, the ecclesial optic operative in Jenson and others can serve merely to fund "cultural circularity."[77]

It becomes clear, then, that Jenson's historical-institutional hermeneutic indeed stands in some tension with the christological hermeneutic that emerged in part one. I suggest, however, that this tension is not an impasse. So how shall we move forward? The question for us becomes: Can we

---

or doctrine or piety, against all other histories and law codes, the Bible stands out as the highest." Katherine Sonderegger, *The Doctrine of God*, vol. 1 of *Systematic Theology* (Minneapolis: Fortress, 2015), 520-21; for her critique of Jenson see Sonderegger, *Doctrine of God*, 526.

[74]Jenson, *Works of God*, 276.

[75]Jenson, *Canon and Creed*, 86-87; idem, "On the Authorities of Scripture," 59-60.

[76]Christopher R. J. Holmes, "Revelation in the Present Tense: On Rethinking Theological Interpretation in Light of the Prophetic Office of Jesus Christ," *JTI* 6, no. 1 (2012): 37. The notion of "radical horizontality" comes from Charles Taylor, *A Secular Age* (Cambridge, MA: Harvard University Press, 2007), 209.

[77]On this, see Willie James Jennings, *Christian Imagination: Theology and Origins of Race* (New Haven, CT: Yale University Press, 2010), 209.

appropriate Jenson's insights without sliding into one-sided institutionalism, a task I take up in chapter four. Key to this possibility is reframing the relationship between Christ and the institution.

Underlying ecclesiological distortions. The first step toward this reframing requires that we examine the theological commitments underlying Jenson's ecclesiological one-sidedness. The problem becomes especially evident when we consider the way he relates the agency of Christ to the agency of the community. "Whether the head speaks or the members," he claims, "it is the one Christ who speaks."[78] But this raises an important question. If Christ does not speak "except by his body," as Jenson maintains, who speaks *to* the body? In what sense is Christ external to his people? In what sense can Christ confront, challenge, or reform the community?

Jenson proffers a subtle nuance meant to uphold some semblance of difference between Christ and his people. He writes, for instance, that God's word "always . . . contrives *somehow* to be an 'external' word, a word that cannot be absorbed into the hearer's subjectivity."[79] This claim indeed establishes a degree of freedom for the word, but does it work? Does Jenson's puzzling use of the word *somehow* provide adequate theological anchorage for Christ's otherness? A similar ambiguity emerges in Jenson's articulation of the Eucharist. "The church *is* the body of Christ for the world and for her members in that she is constituted a community by the verbal and 'visible' presence *to* her of that same body of Christ."[80] In other words, the church is the body of Christ because the body of Christ is present to the church. In this sense, the church encounters a divine presence within the community that is (somehow) not identical to it. Jenson expands on how this is possible: "The body of Christ is at once his sacramental presence within the church's assembly . . . and is the church-community herself to the world and her members."[81] The objectivity of Christ, on this account, is found in the bread and cup. The elements are Christ's availability to the community, even as the community is itself Christ's availability to the world.[82] Thus, Christians span the gap between them and their Lord precisely by moving toward the table.

---

[78]Jenson, *Works of God*, 271.
[79]Jenson, *Works of God*, 275, emphasis added.
[80]Jenson, *Works of God*, 168.
[81]Jenson, *Works of God*, 168.
[82]See Jenson, *Triune God*, 204-5.

Does this notion of eucharistic objectivity uphold the freedom and personhood of the risen Christ? Does it account for Jesus' singularity? As some critics have noted, Jenson offers here at best a strained account of Christ's otherness.[83] While he attempts to distinguish Christ's presence to the church from Christ's presence to the world as the church, he frequently resorts to language that stresses identity, thereby blurring whatever subtle distinction he had achieved. This is evident, for example, when he equates God's Spirit with the church's spirit: "A community's spirit is the liveliness that blows through it, the freedom in which it is more than the sum of its parts. . . . It is the church's founding miracle that her communal spirit is identically the Spirit that the personal God is and has."[84] Jenson attempts to uphold the otherness of Christ to the community by means of the objectivity of the eucharistic elements while also stressing the identical nature of communal spirit and Holy Spirit. This is ambiguous at best.

The ecclesiological problem, therefore, is that Jenson provides no convincing theological basis for upholding Christ's externality to the community, no means by which to establish critical leverage between the Lord and his people. By making Christ historically available in the structures, practices, and language of the church, his theology makes it virtually impossible to distinguish the risen One himself from the institution that bears his presence. Christ's singular identity recedes from view.

To sum up the argument to this point, Jenson's revisionary metaphysic leads him to locate Christ's body in and as the church. No invisible entity lies behind the visible. To be in the church is to be in Christ in the fullest sense. Salvation is tantamount to church membership. The process by which one enters the church is itself God's election.[85] Jenson therefore requires institutional structures to bear a great burden. He tasks them with preserving the church's identity—hence the very presence of Christ—as it traverses the strange eschatological detour between ascension and parousia. As I have shown, this radically historicist orientation dovetails into a hermeneutical posture oriented toward communal resources. Reading Scripture

---

[83]As John Webster rightly notes, this account of Christ's otherness reads as an "emergency measure" that does not adequately account for the singularity of the risen One. John Webster, *God and the Works of God*, 186.

[84]Jenson, *Works of God*, 181.

[85]See Jenson, *Works of God*, 178.

well, on this account, requires one to focus inwardly on the community and to trust its inherited cultural artifacts. This means that the structures of diachronic continuity bear a heavy load. They must ward off the identity-compromising dangers the church encounters as it navigates time.

I suggest that this overburdens the institutions. Jenson asks them to do things they were never meant to do, things only the risen One can accomplish. Here we recall that for Jenson the church's identity during its eschatological detour is as threatened as any other community's.[86] This is a startling claim. One might expect him to suggest that Christ guides the community as it journeys toward the eschaton. One might expect Jenson to suggest that the church's relationship to the risen One is such that it is *not* just like any other community. But in his concern to safeguard ecclesial culture, Jenson instead reduces the church to a species of a more basic genus. The church becomes generic.

I deal with the issue of culture and hermeneutics more fully in chapter seven. For now, I want to consider whether we can construe the church's historical-institutional dimensions in a way that treats institutional resources not as a replacement for Christ but as an aspect of the church's attention to him. Toward this end, I claim that Jenson's underlying mistake lies in his tendency to conflate two modes of thinking—the institutional and the christological. In other words, his ecclesiological error derives not simply from his attention to the institution but from his tendency to collapse Christ into it. This holds open the possibility, as I explore more fully in chapter four, of upholding the institutional dimensions of scriptural hermeneutics without necessarily adopting Jenson's entire vision. In a similar manner, the weakness of his scriptural hermeneutic is not a matter of his revisionary metaphysic per se. Rather than being the source of the problem, his revisionary metaphysic poses a particular question—Where now is Christ's body?—which he answers by conflating Christ with his community. It is not the metaphysic itself that leads him to exaggerate the church's institutional dimensions, but his response to its question. This, too, opens space for reimagining the hermeneutical import of the church's historical-institutional identity. To begin moving in this direction, we turn now to begin considering how Bonhoeffer

---

[86]Jenson, *Canon and Creed*, 3.

deals with the institution's survival. How does the church preserve its identity in the midst of chaotic times?

The Church Struggle and the preservation of the church. Jenson's tendency to conflate Christ and the institution obviously differs from the Bonhoefferian vision of discipleship that began to emerge in chapter two. Indeed, Bonhoeffer's discipleship motif stands in explicit tension to ecclesiologies that one-sidedly stress the nearness of Christ to his community. For Bonhoeffer, this was no mere theoretical quibble. A concrete form of this threat became relevant for Bonhoeffer when he participated in the Church Struggle. As his critique of "religion" in his prison writings reveals, he perceived grave christological dangers lurking within the Confessing Church's otherwise noble attempt to resist the tumultuous social and political conditions it faced in Nazi Germany. Bonhoeffer came to the perhaps counterintuitive belief that an overdone concern to preserve the church's identity and guard its inherited structures actually compromised its witness. I suggest that listening to Bonhoeffer in this regard can shed light on Jenson's account of hermeneutical space and point the way toward integrating the church's institutional and christological dimensions.

Several features characterize Bonhoeffer's critique of religion. Here I will only focus on two, for these most helpfully expose the dangers of one-sidedly institutional logic. Bonhoeffer claims that the "religious" posture (1) prioritizes ecclesial preservation as the ultimate good and (2) reduces ecclesial faithfulness to doctrinal purity. In Bonhoeffer's judgment, both tendencies prevent the church from discerning and participating in Christ's work in the world. The religious posture can inquire into the identity of the church, but it struggles to ask Bonhoeffer's famous question: "Who is Jesus Christ for us today?"

From prison, Bonhoeffer was particularly attuned to the reality of a world "come of age." This obviously posed acute questions for Christian life and identity. Similar to the way Jenson responds to the seemingly anti-Christian dimensions of culture today and MacIntyre laments the onset of the new dark ages, Bonhoeffer and many of his contemporaries within the Confessing Church recognized that the formation of faithful Christian identity required deliberate institutional efforts. Years earlier at Finkenwalde, Bonhoeffer began experimenting with what these efforts might entail. Yet as much as he recognized the importance of this task, he also perceived the risks present within it.

The Confessing Church was a broad and multifaceted movement.[87] By the time Bonhoeffer wrote his theological letters from prison in 1944, the movement had effectively been overwhelmed by Nazism. As he reflects back over the movement, he observes its key weaknesses. Even the 1934 Barmen Declaration, a significant theological achievement in its own right, had become an ingredient of the church's unfaithfulness. Facing the threat of doctrinal compromise, some were tempted to double down on Barmen's verbal formula. Bonhoeffer saw that this posture, though seemingly bold, could actually become self-serving; a supposedly brave set of christological conceptualities could correspond to a timid way of life. Fearful of doctrinal contamination, the church was tempted, Bonhoeffer claims, to entrench itself within ecclesial walls, to retreat into an isolated form of Christian existence in which there is no "no risk taking for others."[88] One might think that the grave threat of Nazi ideology would license, at least for a time, a form of sectarianism aimed at "conservative restoration."[89] As I will show below when I examine Bonhoeffer's account of the "arcane discipline," there is some truth in this. Yet Bonhoeffer consistently refuses to slide into one-sided modes of thinking. The allure of restoration led many Christians astray, producing a *cor curvum in se* writ large across the church itself. "Our church, which has been fighting in these years for its self-preservation, as though that were an end in itself, is incapable of taking the word of reconciliation and redemption to . . . the world," Bonhoeffer writes.[90] In prioritizing its own survival, the church had forgotten about its more fundamental call to remain faithful to Jesus and follow after him.

Bonhoeffer thus raises his most stinging critique: from a posture predicated on ecclesial survival, "Jesus disappears from view."[91] With eyes on itself the church became unable to inquire into the whereabouts of Christ. The church became a fearful space, one that operated from a posture of

---

[87]For more on the nature of the Confessing Church, see Victoria J. Barnett's excellent study, *For the Soul of the People: Protestant Protest Against Hitler* (Oxford: Oxford University Press, 1992).

[88]Bonhoeffer, *Letters and Papers from Prison*, DBWE 8:500, 502.

[89]Bonhoeffer, *Letters and Papers from Prison*, DBWE 8:429.

[90]Bonhoeffer, *Letters and Papers from Prison*, DBWE 8:389.

[91]Bonhoeffer, *Letters and Papers from Prison*, DBWE 8:500, emphasis added.

preservation rather than a posture of faith. In such a situation, the task of ecclesial maintenance works at cross-purposes with the logic of discipleship. There is, of course, partial truth in this posture; the church must attend to the authenticity of its identity as it seeks to follow Christ. But contrary to those he criticized, Bonhoeffer inverts these priorities. He recognizes that the church receives its identity not through practices of preservation but when it seeks to stand with Christ—"The church is only the church when it is there for others."[92] Instead of being reduced to an ecclesial cause, faithfulness requires the church to pursue Jesus and thereby stand with him "in the center of the village."[93]

This brings us back to Jenson. Bonhoeffer would have us believe that the process of reading Scripture becomes hermeneutically significant not merely because we read with the proper critical theory (i.e., the creed, as Jenson claims), not merely because readers have been adequately catechized, and not merely because we read with a tradition-based rationality. The process of reading becomes significant because Christ is communicatively gracious, calling the church to follow after him.

To be sure, the church has good reason to read Scripture in light of inherited knowledge. Yet even as we rightly acknowledge doctrine's hermeneutical significance, we recognize, as Barth pithily reminds us, that Christology has "neither words nor a voice."[94] By blurring the distinction between Christ and community, ecclesial readers are tempted to confuse Christ—a living person—with Christology—the church's teaching about that person. To borrow Kathryn Tanner's language, we risk putting "human ideas about God in the place that only God should fill in the Christian life."[95] When we devocalize Christ by reducing his agency to ongoing institutional structures, we are tempted to fill the silence. God's own talk recedes as the church's talk about God grows loud.

I certainly do not mean to equate Jenson's overall theological vision with the conservative factions within the Confessing Church. In many ways, he

---

[92]Bonhoeffer, *Letters and Papers from Prison*, DBWE 8:503.

[93]Bonhoeffer, *Letters and Papers from Prison*, DBWE 8:480, 367.

[94]Karl Barth, *Church Dogmatics*, vol. IV/2, *The Doctrine of Reconciliation*, ed. G. W. Bromiley and T. F. Torrance, trans. G. W. Bromiley (Edinburgh: T&T Clark, 1958), 536.

[95]Kathryn Tanner, *Theories of Culture: A New Agenda for Theology* (Minneapolis: Fortress, 1997), 126.

resonates with Bonhoeffer's criticism of religion.[96] I am claiming, however, that his hermeneutical posture mirrors theirs in key ways, particularly as an overblown anxiety about ecclesial preservation forestalls the ability to attend to the singular identity and action of Jesus. This posture has the benefit of buttressing the church's institutional identity. But it comes at a price. The stability of a diachronically continuous culture is purchased at the expense of the destabilizing presence of the risen One. If the error that lurks within theologies of the word is that the church vanishes behind the word, the danger here is precisely the opposite. In both cases—Christ without a church or a church without Christ—we lose the fundamental logic of the discipleship motif.

The way forward requires that we continue to affirm the asymmetrical unity between Christ and his people. We need an agile ecclesiological imagination that at once upholds both the essential unity between the two as well as Christ's utter out-aheadness. As we have seen, each side of this tension suggests a particular posture and a particular account of hermeneutical practices. The task of imaginative joining requires that we maintain both sides of the tension without falling into one-sided patterns that distort the hermeneutical process.

Conclusion

For both Webster and Jenson, hermeneutical practices derive from underlying theological commitments. Therefore, a neat synthesis between the two is obviously impossible. Yet I hope to show that some form of mediation is both desirable and feasible. In part one, Bonhoeffer's account of God's promeity in Christ tempers otherworldly accounts of divine being. I suggest that Bonhoeffer can function similarly in part two, but to the opposite effect. Though his vision of God's historical presence resonates with Jenson's revisionary metaphysic in key ways, he remains utterly committed to God's concrete otherness, which is actualized in the out-aheadness of the risen One. Jesus is both with and ahead of his community. The danger of a classical vision is that it underplays the former; the danger of a revisionist account is that it underplays the latter.

---

[96]For example, Jenson, like Bonhoeffer, would readily challenge the necessity of metaphysics as a presupposition for religion and the notion that religion is primarily individualistic and inward. See Bonhoeffer, *Letters and Papers from Prison*, DBWE 8:362-63.

Hence, it is important to note that even as Bonhoeffer has helped reveal the weaknesses in Jenson, I do not intend to place the latter's institutional hermeneutic at odds with the former's christological hermeneutic. The goal instead is an account of the institutional and christological elements of the church that coexist in ordered unity. Given a christological depiction of the ultimate context of interpretation, how can the institutional dimensions of the church contribute constructively to the hermeneutical enterprise? Can we uphold the hermeneutical significance of the structures of continuity without requiring them to maintain the church's identity? By distinguishing Jenson's institutional logic from his conflationary tendencies and by noting the difference between his revisionary metaphysic and his use of the "body of Christ" metaphor, I have implied that we can. To this end, I seek in chapter four to emphasize both the church's continuous identity in history and the irreducible particularity of the risen One.

4

Reading in Light of
Christ's Ongoing Reign

As a young doctoral student Bonhoeffer theorized the relationship between the church's empirical and essential forms. Almost two decades later he witnessed a world "come of age." His early theory was thereby put to the test. What precisely did the church inherit from its past? What was necessary? What was contingent? From prison he came to see that the empirical forms that had characterized the church in Germany for generations would no longer suffice for Christian faithfulness. He thus embarked on a creative, even if short-lived process of ecclesiological reflection. Like Jenson, he affirms the institutional nature of the church and institutional practices that sustain ecclesial culture and situate traditioned knowers within it. Yet the world's coming of age forces him to see that the church's institutional inheritance could no longer carry value in itself. He therefore frames institutional practices differently and directs them toward different ends. Rather than ensuring faithfulness or guaranteeing ecclesial preservation, the inheritance orients the community toward Christ, the ground of its identity.

SANCTORUM COMMUNIO

Bonhoeffer's account of the relationship between the church's institutional and christological dimensions first emerges in *Sanctorum Communio*.[1] Here

---

[1]For the most helpful analysis of this work, see Michael Mawson, *Christ Existing as Community: Bonhoeffer's Ecclesiology* (Oxford: Oxford University Press, 2018). Regarding the fundamental

in his first dissertation the young Bonhoeffer aims to think of the church as simultaneously a theological and a sociological entity; the same object is open to two modes of analysis. He analyzes the visible, empirical church (*Kirche*) as a historical institution while he considers the essential, theological community as the creature of Christ (*Gemeinde*).[2] The theological and the sociological come together in his famous phrase, *die Kirche ist Christus als Gemeinde existierend*—the church is Christ existing as community. The essential church that "exists through Christ's action"[3] is always also a "religious community" with all the concomitant social and empirical markers.[4]

The ground of this two-sidedness is Jesus Christ himself. "The word constitutes the unity between essential and empirical church," Bonhoeffer claims.[5] This is the case because Christ relates to the community in both a historical and a theological manner, both horizontally and vertically. Bonhoeffer suggests, in other words, that the relationship between Christ and the church is ambidextrous; Christ is both "the foundation, the cornerstone" of the community and also a "real presence" to it.[6] The empirical church is the "historical result of the work of Jesus Christ" in founding the institution.[7]

---

consistency of Bonhoeffer's thinking throughout his career, see Clifford J. Green, "Editor's Introduction to the English Edition," in Bonhoeffer, *Sanctorum Communio: A Theological Study of the Sociology of the Church*, DBWE 1. Green notes that the notion of "community" that first comes to expression in *Sanctorum Communio* remains foundational to Bonhoeffer's understanding of Christian community as it emerges during his Finkenwalde period. Green even suggests that Bonhoeffer's conception of Jesus from prison as the "man for others" has material ties to this early work. "In light of the foundational role of *Sanctorum Communio* . . . one has to be very careful not to interpret some of Bonhoeffer's later rejections as rejections of his early theological work." Green, "Editor's Introduction," in Bonhoeffer, *Sanctorum Communio*, DBWE 1:7.

[2]Clifford Green notes that *Gemeinde* carries a range of meanings and usages in Bonhoeffer's writing and "therefore presents the most complex translation problem" (Green, "Editor's Introduction," in Bonhoeffer, *Sanctorum Communio*, DBWE 1:14). "In Bonhoeffer's most distinctive and fundamental usage in this book, *Gemeinde* means Christ present as *sanctorum communio*" (Green, "Editor's Introduction," in Bonhoeffer, *Sanctorum Communio*, DBWE 1:14). *Gemeinde* functions for Bonhoeffer not generically as *community* but as a theological specification, which is why it would be misleading to translate it with a purely sociological term. Yet *Gemeinde* must also be distinguished from *Kirche*, which for Bonhoeffer tends to refer to the empirical church and not necessarily the *sanctorum communio*. For this reason, Green tends to translate *Gemeinde* as "church-community." For Green's full articulation of *Gemeinde* in Bonhoeffer, see Clifford J. Green, *Bonhoeffer: A Theology of Sociality*, rev. ed. (Grand Rapids, MI: Eerdmans, 1999).

[3]Bonhoeffer, *Sanctorum Communio*, DBWE 1:137.

[4]E.g., Bonhoeffer, *Sanctorum Communio*, DBWE 1:216.

[5]Bonhoeffer, *Sanctorum Communio*, DBWE 1:226.

[6]Bonhoeffer, *Sanctorum Communio*, DBWE 1:139.

[7]Bonhoeffer, *Sanctorum Communio*, DBWE 1:209.

Given the horizontal dimension of Christ's presence to the community, Bonhoeffer even suggests that the institution itself stands in as Christ's ongoing visible presence in history. Here his ecclesiology parallels Jenson's. Yet, Christ is also significant for the church in his otherness from it and in his gracious presence to it, as the one who actualizes the church in the present through the Spirit.

Given the historical mode of Christ's relationship to the community, the church remains open to sociological analysis. "Where wills unite," Bonhoeffer writes, "a 'structure' is created—that is, a third entity, previously unknown, independent of being willed or not willed by the persons who are uniting."[8] Drawing from Hegel's "The Philosophy of Spirit," he refers to this as the community's "objective spirit."[9] Because of it, those entering a community experience it as "something real outside themselves" and as something irreducible to the sheer conglomeration of members.[10] The objective spirit spans the spatial and temporal dimensions of the community, forges historical continuity, and thereby allows the community to persist as one entity through time. Institutional structures and offices play a key role in this process, for they manifest a community's spirit in history. The similarities with Jenson's structures of diachronic identity are obvious.[11]

But the difference between the two becomes readily apparent. Whereas Jenson implies, in Hegelian fashion, that the community's consciousness *is* God's Spirit, Bonhoeffer refuses to equate the two. "A complete identification between Christ and the church-community cannot be made, since Christ has ascended into heaven."[12] In biblical idiom, Bonhoeffer recognizes that the Spirit blows where it will (Jn. 3:8).[13] Distinguishing Christ from the institution grants the church an eschatological horizon. Bonhoeffer therefore realizes that on this side of the eschaton the *sanctorum communio* and the

---

[8]Bonhoeffer, *Sanctorum Communio*, DBWE 1:98.

[9]Bonhoeffer, *Sanctorum Communio*, DBWE 1:98; for Hegel, see G. F. W. Hegel, "The Philosophy of the Spirit," in *Encyclopedia of Philosophical Sciences in Outline, and Other Critical Writings*, ed. Ernst Behler, trans. Steven A. Taubeneck (New York: Continuum, 1991). On Bonhoeffer's use of Hegel, see David S. Robinson, *Christ and Revelatory Community in Bonhoeffer's Reception of Hegel* (Tübingen: Mohr Siebeck, 2018).

[10]Bonhoeffer, *Sanctorum Communio*, DBWE 1:98-99.

[11]See Michael Mawson, "The Spirit and the Community: Pneumatology and Ecclesiology in Jenson, Hütter and Bonhoeffer," *IJST* 15, no. 4 (2013): 453-68.

[12]Bonhoeffer, *Sanctorum Communio*, DBWE 1:140.

[13]Bonhoeffer, *Sanctorum Communio*, DBWE 1:203, 214.

peccatorum communio always coexist.[14] In history there is no pure church. The church's present form is not its final form; it remains a community on the way.

Yet this fundamental difference between Christ and his people does not negate the theological importance of the empirical community. Rather than being a mere secular veneer covering a properly theological reality, the church's objective spirit plays a significant material role in Bonhoeffer's ecclesiology. "The Holy Spirit uses the objective spirit as a vehicle for its gathering and sustaining social activity." He continues, "Here it becomes clear that in order to build the empirical church both Christ and the Holy Spirit make use of the forms of the life of the objective spirit as they exist historically."[15] The objective spirit not only serves to maintain the church's diachronic identity (a profane task, as Bonhoeffer calls is); it also becomes the means of a divine event.

According to Bonhoeffer, the Holy Spirit uses the objective spirit to actualize the community of Christ in the present. This implies that the relationship between the two is not fixed. The "church can in its essence be understood only as a divine act," Bonhoeffer contends.[16] Even as the community necessarily possesses visible features in history, the gratuity of this event precludes the Holy Spirit from being objectified as an empirical feature of communal life.[17] To echo an important point Bonhoeffer makes elsewhere,

---

[14]Bonhoeffer, *Sanctorum Communio*, DBWE 1:213.

[15]Bonhoeffer, *Sanctorum Communio*, DBWE 1:215.

[16]Bonhoeffer, *Sanctorum Communio*, DBWE 1:277. In *Act and Being*, DBWE 2, Bonhoeffer employs a similar line of thinking when dealing with the relationship between theology and preaching. "Theology is the memory of the church," he claims. It is the "word of the person of Christ, which is preserved as something that exists in the historical church. . . . It stands between past and future preaching." He admits that the notion of theology as institutional memory seems "indistinguishable from profane thinking" (Bonhoeffer, *Act and Being*, DBWE 2:130). In and of itself, institutional memory remains lifeless. It is of value "only where the living person of Christ is itself present and can destroy this existing thing or acknowledge it. . . . The community of faith knows that making general pronouncements makes sense only where Christ confirms it in each instance." Only when "Christ himself speaks these words [of dogma] *hic et nunc* are they really about God" (Bonhoeffer, *Act and Being*, DBWE 2:131).

[17]Bonhoeffer worries that various forms of Christianity—e.g., Anabaptism, Pietism, Kant's secularized concept of the kingdom of God, the religious-socialist Youth Movement—risk undialectically equating the Holy Spirit with the objective spirit of the community, thereby claiming "to have the Realm of God finally present not only by faith but by sight, no longer veiled within the strange forms of a Christian church, but clearly manifested in the morality and holiness of human beings" (Bonhoeffer, *Sanctorum Communio*, DBWE 1:222).

the true church of Christ is visible but not empirically available. The objective spirit becomes the means by which Christ, in the freedom of his life as the risen Lord, exists as church-community.

This is the case in spite of the sinfulness, imperfection, and—on occasion—downright unattractiveness of the church's empirical features. While Bonhoeffer sarcastically acknowledges the "deadly boredom of a publicly visible assembly in which one risks sitting in front of a narrow-minded preacher and next to lifeless faces," he nevertheless claims that "the assembly of believers remains our mother."[18] Gathering together as an assembly, like other ecclesial practices, "is not simply an entrenched traditional habit."[19] As an empirical activity it carries a divine commission: "It is in fact this empirical church in whose womb grows God's sacred treasure, God's own church-community."[20]

In particular, Bonhoeffer believes that the concrete function of the empirical church lies in its ability to sustain preaching and the sacraments.[21] He is clear that, as practices, preaching and the sacraments do not hold value in and of themselves. Rather, their value lies in their ability to direct the community toward Christ and thereby facilitate a gracious encounter. The horizontal serves the vertical. Individuals commit themselves to the historical-institutional community "because they accept that God wills to speak in the empirical church" and because they trust that God has given the church the means and offices by which this speaking can occur.[22] "The objective spirit, fraught with so much contingency, imperfection, and sin, nevertheless has the promise that it can preach the word of God; it becomes the *bearer of the social activity of the Holy Spirit.*"[23] Precisely as the *creatura verbi*, the church exists as an institution in history, which means that institutional practices like preaching and the sacraments direct the church toward a presence not reducible to or derivable from its social features. In this way, Bonhoeffer upholds an asymmetrical unity, valuing the institution without sliding into institutionalism.

---

[18]Bonhoeffer, *Sanctorum Communio*, DBWE 1:228.
[19]Bonhoeffer, *Sanctorum Communio*, DBWE 1:227.
[20]Bonhoeffer, *Sanctorum Communio*, DBWE 1:222.
[21]Bonhoeffer, *Sanctorum Communio*, DBWE 1:226.
[22]Bonhoeffer, *Sanctorum Communio*, DBWE 1:230.
[23]Bonhoeffer, *Sanctorum Communio*, DBWE 1:233, emphasis original.

As I explore more fully below, this carries implications for scriptural hermeneutics. Just as Christ relates to the church in a dual manner, so too Scripture functions in two ways, in both an empirical and a theological sense. Given the unity of objective spirit and Holy Spirit, the text carries a regulative capacity and an ability to serve the community's diachronic identity. In line with Bonhoeffer's sociological mode of analysis, the Bible exists as a historical text within the empirical institution. Just as all communities have a charter, so too the church has its canon. At the same time, because of the distinction between the objective spirit and the Holy Spirit, because the two can never be fixed undialectically, the text also functions in a sacramental capacity as the means by which the Holy Spirit addresses the community and draws it into Christ's ongoing activity.

LETTERS AND PAPERS FROM PRISON

Taken at face value, Bonhoeffer's famous claim that the church is Christ existing as community might seem to imply that institutional structures suffice for producing Christian faithfulness. As we have just seen, however, *Sanctorum Communio* puts forth a nuanced yet important distinction that prevents this reading. This distinction remains an important feature of Bonhoeffer's ecclesiology, even as his theology develops over time. In particular, the onset of the Church Struggle compels him to further grapple with the distinction between the institutional and christological dimensions of the church. As the acute faithlessness of the church in Germany became glaringly apparent, ecclesiological asymmetry took on increased importance. Without severing the connection between the church's empirical life and its conformity to Christ, he became freshly attuned to the importance of the gap between the two.

This gap provides space for the concrete and particularist Christology of *Discipleship* to emerge. In this sense, the discipleship motif represents the maturation of his earlier insights. In *Sanctorum Communio* he argues that Christians commit themselves to the empirical form of the church "not merely out of gratitude for the gift they have already received" but because they "are driven by a desire to receive it ever anew, to be born anew again and again."[24] In terms of discipleship, the institutional structures become

---

[24]Bonhoeffer, *Sanctorum Communio*, DBWE 1:228.

a means by which Jesus' followers encounter their Lord and are daily called to continue following after him.

This sensibility becomes even more apparent in his prison writings. From his cell, Bonhoeffer reflects on society's maturation, its coming of age (*die Mündigkeit*). For generations, the church's institutional structures had been woven into the fabric of European culture, but in this new age it was unclear what their future entailed. This dilemma compelled him toward fresh ecclesiological exploration. In many ways, what emerges in prison is radical for its time—the church should sell its property, find new methods for training ministers, pay pastors congregationally, and distance itself from governmental authorities.[25] At the same time, however, certain components of the church must remain consistent. Bonhoeffer's constructive vision emerges within the context of this tension.

Two options must be rejected: the task of the church in the world is not, as some of his contemporaries were advocating, to retreat into a ghetto and inculcate doctrinal and confessional purity.[26] Nor was the task of the church to fight to expand its relevance through methods of apologetic manipulation and religious propaganda.[27] Both tendencies fall prey to the allure of empirically verifiable faithfulness. Both tendencies are mistaken, in other words, in thinking that in the midst of a changing cultural situation the church must fight to uphold its inherited institutional and empirical forms of life.

In contrast to these options, Bonhoeffer came to believe that in a world come of age, the church must rethink the nature of its public presence and witness—speaking "Christianese" is no longer tantamount to speaking truthfully (contra Jenson), and performing inherited rituals may in fact be an act of faithlessness. To attempt to do by human force and cleverness what only God can do is to turn revelation into a religious object.[28] Even so, the church obviously cannot abandon its structures and

---

[25]Bonhoeffer, *Letters and Papers from Prison*, DBWE 8:503.

[26]Bonhoeffer, *Letters and Papers from Prison*, DBWE 8:428-29.

[27]See Bonhoeffer, *Letters and Papers from Prison*, DBWE 8:363, where Bonhoeffer forcefully refers to such tactics as "religious rape."

[28]Bonhoeffer refers to this as "positivism of revelation." See, e.g., Bonhoeffer, *Letters and Papers from Prison*, DBWE 8:429. For more on this, see Eberhard Bethge, *Dietrich Bonhoeffer: A Biography*, ed. Victoria J. Barnett, trans. Eric Mosbacher et al., rev. ed. (Minneapolis: Fortress, 2000), 882-83.

practices. The question becomes: How can the church's empirical form serve its essential identity?

The notion of the *disciplina arcani*—the "arcane discipline"—is central to his answer.[29] This discipline first emerged in the early church as a means of distinguishing between the sermon, which was often open to the public, and a set of practices carried out in private (e.g., reciting the creed, confessing sin, saying the Lord's Prayer, and participating in the Eucharist). By distinguishing the church's public and private activities, the arcane discipline provided the time and space necessary for the formation of a distinctly Christian pattern of life in the midst of a largely non-Christian context.[30] By reappropriating the discipline, Bonhoeffer implies that even a "nonreligious" posture toward the world is not an excuse to discard the tradition. In this sense, the arcane discipline functions as the counterpoint to the nonreligious Christianity Bonhoeffer espouses from prison. As Eberhard Bethge suggests, "While Bonhoeffer developed his ideas on the nonreligious interpretation of Christianity in a world come of age, he never considered abandoning his connection with the traditional words and customs of the church."[31] He recognizes, in other words, that even as certain traditional

---

[29]The meaning of this phrase in Bonhoeffer's thinking is disputed. Two strands of interpretation are available: the traditional and the revisionary. The traditional is evident, e.g., in Bethge, *Dietrich Bonhoeffer*, 880-83; and John D. Godsey, *The Theology of Dietrich Bonhoeffer* (Eugene, OR: Wipf & Stock, 2015), 254. The revisionary is found in John D. Matthews, "Responsible Sharing of the Mystery," in *Reflections on Bonhoeffer: Essays in Honor of F. Burton Nelson*, ed. Geffrey B. Kelly and C. John Weborg (Chicago: Covenant, 1999), 114-26. Traditionally, the arcane discipline refers to the practice of preserving or guarding the secrets of the faith from public profanation, e.g., by reserving the Eucharist or the creed for the select faithful. Matthews suggests, however, that Bonhoeffer meant to substantiate the word *arcani*. On this reading, Bonhoeffer meant something like, "The discipline or practice of sharing the mystery faithfully," i.e., of translating it into a culturally acceptable idiom. Here I follow the traditional interpretation, which is generally better attested and which, in my estimate, makes more sense of Bonhoeffer's driving concerns in *Letters and Papers from Prison*. Importantly for the traditional reading, the arcane discipline was an important feature of Bonhoeffer's thinking earlier in his career and not merely a product of his prison imagination; see, e.g., Bonhoeffer, *Ecumenical, Academic, and Pastoral Work: 1931–1932*, DBWE 11:313-15; idem, *Berlin: 1932–1933*, DBWE 12:213; and idem, *Theological Education at Finkenwalde*, DBWE 14:551-58. At Finkenwalde Bonhoeffer notes the importance of preserving the mysteries entrusted to the church. He notes that in the Protestant church the only thing resembling the arcane discipline is admission to the Lord's Supper, which, he claims, "represents a final, weak remnant of the arcane discipline" (Bonhoeffer, *Theological Education at Finkenwalde*, DBWE 14:556).

[30]See Stephen E. Fowl and L. Gregory Jones, *Reading in Communion: Scripture and Ethics in Christian Life* (Grand Rapids, MI: Eerdmans, 1991), 33.

[31]Bethge, *Dietrich Bonhoeffer*, 881.

practices lose their social credibility in a new cultural situation, some must be retained and sheltered against profanation.[32]

In this particular sense, Bonhoeffer places special importance upon the church as a historical-institutional entity. But a key question remains— Why? Why is it important to preserve the church in this way? Why not abandon the tradition and rebuild Christianity from the ground up? Here his thinking remains consistent with what emerged in *Sanctorum Communio*. Beyond simply maintaining the identity of the institution, the arcane discipline functions in a profoundly christological manner.

Bethge summarizes it well: "In the *arcanum* Christ takes everyone who really encounters him by the shoulder, turning them around to face their fellow human beings and the world."[33] It functions, in short, as the institutionally mediated means of placing the community in position to encounter Christ and be called into his ongoing work. The discipline provides space to nurture a way of thinking and seeing appropriate to the resurrection, a *modus vivendi* particular to the community of the risen One. Ecclesial faithfulness, therefore, is something that continually happens as the church opens itself to the presence of Christ, and a traditioned faith tutored by the arcane discipline situates the church for this event. To borrow Bonhoeffer's language from another writing, it becomes the means by which the community daily orients itself to the crucified One and allows itself to be called into conversion by him.[34]

For this reason, the arcane discipline is not a withdrawal from the world, and its solution to the struggles of the day is not the mere formation of a counterculture, as tempting as this option must have seemed in the midst of cultural decay. For sure, the task of sustaining the church's historical-institutional dimensions requires the church to attend to its unique culture, and certain practices constitute the church as a distinctive polity. But this culture and this distinctiveness are not themselves the answer. Rather, they situate the church in relation to the One who is. Christian identity, on this account, is always a gift, never an achievement. The value of the church's historical-institutional dimensions lies not in itself but in Christ's

---

[32]Bonhoeffer, *Letters and Papers from Prison*, DBWE 8:373.
[33]Bethge, *Dietrich Bonhoeffer*, 883.
[34]Bonhoeffer, *Conspiracy and Imprisonment: 1940–1945*, DBWE 16:41.

faithfulness to his people. What for Jenson are structures of diachronic identity function for Bonhoeffer as structures of reception, the means by which the community situates itself to receive its identity from the risen One ever anew.

Bonhoeffer recognizes, in other words, that in order to live faithfully the church at all times must ask, "Who is Jesus Christ for us today?" In a turbulent cultural moment, this question carries particular challenges. It may seem more pressing to divert energy elsewhere, perhaps toward the task of preservation or apologetics, two options Bonhoeffer rejects. At precisely this point the arcane discipline proves its usefulness. For Bonhoeffer, the task of developing tradition-based rationality aims at fostering a particular lived orientation. The telos of formation is christological. The church's process of forming traditioned knowers remains fundamentally secular only if it asks about the community's relationship to its past, in which case its purpose would lie within itself. The genuinely theological character of this community arises when it asks about its living Lord: Who is he for us today? Thus, as I explore more fully below, the well-formed community can sustain a posture of openness and orientation toward Christ and thereby exercise modes of knowing that are particular to the ongoing journey of discipleship.

A CHRISTOLOGICAL ACCOUNT OF HISTORICAL-INSTITUTIONAL PRACTICES

Jenson's problem, as we saw in chapter three, is that his revisionary metaphysic poses a question—where now is Christ's body?—that he answers by hypervaluing the institution. This problem takes shape hermeneutically as a tendency to overburden the practices that form traditioned rationality. But, as I argued, these dangers are not inherent to an institutional hermeneutic. This holds open the possibility of reframing the institutional dimensions of hermeneutics in a manner that remains attuned to Jesus' singularity. The discipleship motif points to this possibility. The two snapshots from respective poles of Bonhoeffer's life reveal a distinctly christological account of the institution. Bonhoeffer gets to the heart of the matter: "The empirical church-community, office, and assembly belong together . . . [because] God wants to walk with God's holy people on a path that leads through the midst of history."[35] Here, in one statement, Bonhoeffer joins the empirical and essential church—and does so within the framework of discipleship. The church exists as a sociohistorical and institutional entity precisely because Christ calls his people to follow after him as they journey through history.

Hermeneutics and Christ's Livelihood. The first step toward unpacking the hermeneutical implications that follow is to ask Bonhoeffer the same question that trips up Jenson: Where does he locate the risen One? Here Bonhoeffer's imagination remains dexterous. Noting Jesus' agile unpredictability in the postresurrection stories, Bonhoeffer refuses to settle for an answer that would restrict Christ's movement. While some theologians proffer the ascension as a means of securing Christ's location, Bonhoeffer recognizes that even though he has ascended, Jesus has not vanished into the heavenly realms. He continues to stride through history, fulfilling his promise to be with his disciples until the end of the age. Because Christ is with his followers in the independence of his being, he remains totally free and irreducibly other. So, where is Jesus? He is leading the church toward the kingdom. Bonhoeffer would answer, in other words, by pointing to the church while simultaneously pointing ahead of it.

This latter move introduces a note of instability into Christian theology. While Christ can certainly be trusted to be with the church, he refuses to be tethered therein. "It is not a church organization that defines Christ," Clifford Green writes summarizing Bonhoeffer, "but Christ who defines the church."[36] As the out-ahead one, he retains the capacity to surprise. As Theo Sundermeier aptly states, "The Son comes to his own, and yet it is a way into the unknown."[37] In terms of scriptural interpretation, this means that the church remains open to the unexpected, trusting that the Spirit will continue to lead the community into truth. Understood in this way, the text's "surplus of meaning" ultimately derives from the mobile freedom of Christ himself. The church returns again and again to Scripture, not only to be reminded of something it may have forgotten but also in search of new insights that will sustain it on the way. The church returns to

---

[35]Bonhoeffer, *Sanctorum Communio*, DBWE 1:236. Even at this early age, the discipleship motif is key to Bonhoeffer's logic.

[36]Clifford Green, "Editor's Introduction," in Bonhoeffer, *Sanctorum Communio*, DBWE 1:15.

[37]Quoted in David W. Congdon, *The Mission of Demythologizing: Rudolf Bultmann's Dialectical Theology* (Minneapolis: Fortress, 2015), 558.

Scripture because Christ continues to work, continues to move, and continues to speak.

The notion of textual surplus can be frightening. One of the most alluring features of an institutionalized account of hermeneutical space is that its stability provides the basis for sorting through the text's surplus in an orderly and predictable manner. T. F. Torrance refers to this allure as the "temptation of orthodoxy." The temptation, he warns, is to achieve epistemic stability at the expense of Christ himself, reducing the truth of Christ to an object that can be easily regulated and preserved.[38] There is certainly something valid animating this temptation, for the truths of the faith were "once for all delivered" (Jude 3, RSV) and need to be handed on with care. The temptation, however, is that the fixity of tradition renders Christ's unique personal agency unnecessary—what he would do as a living agent in the present has been accomplished ahead of time by the institution itself. We must not let the past tense of "once for all delivered" obscure the equally important sense that God's grace is "new every morning" (Lam 3:23). The livelihood of God enacted in Jesus' ongoing history frustrates our longing for epistemic mastery.

While it certainly destabilizes knowledge, subordinating the church's institutional dimensions to its christological dimensions is not an excuse to abandon all notions of ecclesial consistency. Rather, it calls us to reimagine the type of consistency the church possesses. Again we take our cues from Christ. As a living person who acts in freedom, his life is necessarily marked by unpredictability. At the same time, however, he acts in continuity with himself. The one who lives freely ahead of the church, calling it into being, "is the same yesterday and today and forever" (Heb 13:8). Thus, even as it lacks static stability, the church need not fear anarchic chaos. As a creature of Christ's call, it shares in his consistency. Rather than possessing the selfsame permanence of an object that unflinchingly perdures through time, the church in history is marked by continuity of a person.

In his work *Living Tradition*, John Meyendorff helps us understand what this means for the church's institutional memory. Tradition, he claims, is not a static collection of propositions but something that changes while

---

[38]Thomas F. Torrance, "The Deposit of Faith," *SJT* 36, no. 1 (1983): 1-28; and idem, *Karl Barth: An Introduction to His Early Theology, 1910–1931* (London: T&T Clark, 2004), 101-2.

remaining the same. This is possible because tradition's essential content is not a body of abstractions but the living Christ himself.[39] As the living One calls his people into new encounters in new historical circumstances, the church's memory must adapt and grow, even as the essential content of its memory remains the same. Accordingly, when the church recounts its own history, it engages in the distinctly christological task of tracing "the sameness of Jesus across the generations."[40] Given Christ's freedom, this task of tracing his life requires more than mere repetition. James Cone suggests that the church must hold Christ's "wasness" and "isness" in creative tension: "We do not simply ask, 'What would Jesus do?' . . . We ask, 'What is he doing *now*?'"[41] Given Christ's personal continuity, the answer to the latter question emerges from the former even though it is not reducible to it. In this sense, the historical-institutional inheritance helps the church navigate the gap between Christ's past history and contemporary livelihood. The act of tracing the past reveals signposts—touchstones—reminding the church of who Christ has been and thus who he will be.

This further suggests that although the act of remembrance cannot alone secure faithfulness, it can familiarize the church with its Lord. Memory of Christ's past speech attunes the church to the frequency of his dialect. Or, to put this same insight in biblical idiom, the sheep follow the shepherd because they know his voice (Jn 10:4). In this sense, traditioned knowledge functions like personal awareness. The historical-institutional past carries hermeneutical value because Christ speaks from the continuity of his person and because his people, guided by the Spirit, foster a mode of knowing suitable to his personal speech. The church's doctrinal inheritance functions to "prepare the way" for Christ's presence through Scripture.[42] It does not, in and of itself, allow the church to predict Christ's word for the moment. It does not, in and of itself, secure hermeneutical faithfulness. It does not, in and of itself, compel Christ to speak. But it can sketch the

---

[39]John Meyendorff, *Living Tradition: Orthodox Witness in the Contemporary World* (Crestwood, NY: St. Vladimir's Seminary Press, 1978), 8.

[40]John Howard Yoder, "Historiography as a Ministry to Renewal," *Brethren Life and Thought* 42, nos. 3-4 (1997): 216.

[41]James H. Cone, *God of the Oppressed*, rev. ed. (Maryknoll, NY: Orbis, 1997), 110-16, 191.

[42]On the notion of human activity "preparing the way" for God's ultimate word in Christ, see Bonhoeffer's "Ultimate and Penultimate Things," in *Ethics*, DBWE 6:146-70.

domain or context within which this word might arrive.[43] The one who speaks may deliver a new and surprising word, but even in so doing he remains unfailingly himself. As Richard Bauckham suggests, "He may be trusted to be consistent with himself, but he may surprise in the ways he proves consistent with himself."[44] As paradoxical as it may sound, when the church reads Scripture it can expect to have its expectations undone; it can anticipate being surprised.[45]

This refocuses the hermeneutical task. Jenson claims that the church, on the basis of its institutional identity, knows what God will say when God speaks through Scripture. I contend that this is an overblown account of the institution that leads to interpretive overconfidence. I suggest, on the contrary, that even if the church does not know *what* God will say, it knows *who* God is. Such confidence is properly placed. This nuance may seem nitpicky. But when it comes to the posture and practice of reading, it carries significant implications. Whereas an overly institutionalized posture equates the formation of a traditioned rationality with hermeneutical faithfulness, I am arguing that such formation functions penultimately; it cannot secure God's Word, but it can put the church in a position to listen for and discern it anew.

Imagining Christ. I suggest that this gap between *what* and *who* opens space for a unique mode of hermeneutical activity. The recent turn toward imagination as a theological category points in a helpful direction. I argue, in short, that when we locate historical-institutional modes of knowing within christological space, a particular account of hermeneutical imagination rightly comes to characterize the church's reading of Scripture.

When properly deployed, the concept of imagination allows the church to navigate the fine line between the temptation of orthodoxy and the threat of theological anarchy. To be sure, imagination is integral to Christian epistemology more generally, for the risen Christ leads his community into a kingdom we now see only dimly. This eschatological directionality

---

[43]See Gerald McKenny, *The Analogy of Grace: Karl Barth's Moral Theology* (Oxford: Oxford University Press, 2010).

[44]Richard Bauckham, *Jesus and the God of Israel: God Crucified and Other Studies on the New Testament's Christology of Divine Identity* (Grand Rapids, MI: Eerdmans, 2008), 53.

[45]See Shannon Craigo-Snell, *The Empty Church: Theater, Theology, and Bodily Hope* (Oxford: Oxford University Press, 2014), 142.

necessitates a mode of perception not limited to the immediately visible and empirically available. In theological terms, hope is epistemologically consequential. In hermeneutical terms, hope takes shape as imagination.

More specifically, Luke Timothy Johnson implies that my driving question in this project—What does it mean to read within the church?—calls for imagination as a key answer. He notes that the "historical-critical hegemony" that loosed the text from its ecclesial home simultaneously worked to suppress the role of imagination in the process of understanding.[46] Garrett Green expands on Johnson's insight; instead, of the "picture-language of religious *Vorstellung*," modern hermeneutics prized "the translucent purity of the *Begriff*."[47] Scientific reason, not ecclesial imagination, became the ideal mode of engaging Scripture. Yet as the aforementioned hegemony has begun to wane, imagination has reemerged as a hermeneutical category.

Some have referred to this mode of thinking as "traditioned innovation," a way of creatively navigating the new in light of the old.[48] Kavin Rowe suggests that this is a biblical pattern of thinking—not because the Bible commends it but because the Bible exemplifies it.[49] A pattern of traditioned innovation is perhaps most obvious in the Old Testament as editors and redactors in new historical situations responded to inherited texts in innovative ways. But this pattern is evident in the New Testament as well. The four Gospels exhibit modes of thinking that are simultaneously faithful and creative. Consider also Paul's innovative readings of his inherited texts, or Luke's ability in the book of Acts to forge unity between the church and Israel while also representing the distinct newness of a community belonging to the risen Messiah.

If this pattern of thinking is integral to the content of the Bible, I am here considering how it affects the church's reading of it. By suggesting the

---

[46]Luke Timothy Johnson, "Imagining the World Scripture Imagines," in *Theology and Scriptural Imagination*, ed. L. Gregory Jones and James J. Buckley (Malden, MA: Blackwell, 1998), 7.

[47]Garrett Green, *Theology, Hermeneutics, and Imagination: The Crisis of Interpretation at the End of Modernity* (Cambridge: Cambridge University Press, 2000), 182.

[48]See, e.g., Jason Byassee, "Theology and Worship," in *The Routledge Companion to the Practice of Christian Theology*, ed. Mike Higton and Jim Fodor (New York: Routledge, 2015), 204: "Arguably there is no innovation anywhere, inside or outside the Church, without rich tradition; and likewise no tradition kept alive without some form of innovation."

[49]Kavin Rowe, "Navigating the Differences in the Gospels," *Faith and Leadership*, August 17, 2009, https://faithandleadership.com/navigating-differences-gospels.

importance of imagination I am not claiming that God exceeds language and that we must be content to know God metaphorically. Likewise, I am not merely reiterating the common claim that all reading is imaginative in the sense that it expands the horizons of our own vision.[50] I am continuing to pursue the hermeneutical logic of the resurrection. In light of the past, we read Scripture in search of Christ's address to us today. The gap between the past and present tenses of Christ's address constitutes the "hermeneutical breathing room" within which imagination can flourish.[51] It is precisely the ongoing newness of Christ's voice that necessitates the imaginative engagement with the text.

According to Garrett Green, imagination is the "paradigmatic faculty" that enables one to think in terms of a pattern or model.[52] Though Green himself does not make an explicit connection to discipleship, we can expand on his thinking by noting that Jesus is the church's definitive model, the paradigm for faithfulness, and the one whose pattern of existence the church strives to emulate. Christ is the image of the invisible God who grounds ecclesial imagination. The imitation of Christ, in other words, is the church's attempt to reimagine Christ's own image. It is the church's attempt to think paradigmatically—i.e., imaginatively, as Green suggests—as a means of embodying a pattern of action that fits with his. As much as this is the case, the logic of imagination is integral to the logic of discipleship. There can be no imitation without imagination. Rather than a sign that its readings are weak or imperfect, imagination is a necessary aspect of interpretation that aims to catch up to the ongoing life of the living Lord.[53]

---

[50]See Trevor Hart, "Imagination and Responsible Reading," in *Renewing Biblical Interpretation*, ed. Craig Bartholomew, Colin Greene, and Karl Möller (Grand Rapids, MI: Zondervan, 2000), 316.

[51]The phrase comes from Garrett Green, *Imagining God: Theology and the Religious Imagination* (Grand Rapids, MI: Eerdmans, 1998), 135. Here Green draws from Hans Frei: "I would suggest that a good interpretation of a text is one that has 'breathing space,' that is to say, one in which no hermeneutic finally allows you to resolve the text—there is something that is left to bother, something that is wrong, something that is not yet interpreted" (Hans W. Frei, *Theology and Narrative: Selected Essays*, ed. George Hunsinger and William C. Placher [Oxford: Oxford University Press, 1993], 162). Here Frei has in mind the gap between literary meaning and historical referent. Though I am redeploying the notion in a slightly different manner—giving priority to God's voice and not the literary document per se—a similar hermeneutical space emerges, the navigation of which requires a degree of imaginative activity on the part of the interpreter.

[52]Garrett Green, *Imagining God*, 66-82.

[53]Cf., L. Johnson, "Imagining the World Scripture Imagines," 15. N. T. Wright puts forth the metaphor of "improvisation" as a way to maintain hermeneutical balance between innovation and

Richard Hays adds specificity to this account of hermeneutical imagination. The church "will have to formulate imaginative *analogies* between the stories told in the texts and the story lived out by our community in a very different historical setting."[54] Hermeneutical faithfulness requires that one renders the unknown—the new challenge or question the church faces today—in light of the known—the biblical witness to the kingdom. At this point, Jenson's insights remain important. Hays argues, echoing the notion of intratextuality on display in Jenson, that the task of discerning a contemporary word requires the church to place itself within the story.[55] The church must attempt to make sense of its particular hermeneutical moment in light of the larger narrative as a whole. As Trevor Hart notes, this is precisely what imagination equips one to do: "It is . . . the faculty which makes sense of things, locating particular bits and pieces within larger patterns, and in so doing goes beyond what is given."[56]

While much recent work on narrative and imagination proceeds from a literary or philosophical standpoint, James Cone gives these insights a distinctly christological dimension. Though his *God of the Oppressed* preceded Lindbeck's *The Nature of Doctrine*—and obviously differs from it on key material grounds—it does anticipate certain dimensions of Lindbeck's better-known account of intratextuality. Cone states, for example, that the preacher's task is to weave the stories of the congregation into the one biblical story: "Through the reading of Scripture . . . [people] are taken from the present to the past."[57] In short, the church must imaginatively indwell the story. Yet unlike much of the narrative theology emerging in the postliberal tradition, Cone's reasoning remains strictly christological. As with Barth in his famous essay, "The Strange New World Within the Bible,"[58] Cone notes that the scriptural world is a site of encounter, movement, and

---

consistency. See N. T. Wright, "How Can the Bible Be Authoritative?," *Vox Evangelica* 21 (1991): 18-19. For a full exploration of the ethical significance of improvisation, see Samuel Wells, *Improvisation: The Drama of Christian Ethics* (Grand Rapids, MI: Brazos Press, 2004).

[54]Richard B. Hays, *The Moral Vision of the New Testament: Community, Cross, New Creation; A Contemporary Introduction to New Testament Ethics* (San Francisco: HarperCollins, 1996), 298.

[55]Hays, *Moral Vision*, 302.

[56]Hart, "Imagination and Responsible Reading," 319.

[57]Cone, *God of the Oppressed*, 102, emphasis added.

[58]Karl Barth, "The Strange New World Within the Bible," in *The Word of God and the Word of Man*, trans. Douglas Horton (New York: Harper & Row, 1957), 28-50.

surprise. The point of indwelling this strange textual world is ultimately to encounter Christ therein.[59] And since this Christ is not constrained by the story but continues to reign as Lord of all, the encounter with him necessarily presses one into the web of stories that constitute the present world. We indwell the narrative, but we do not stop there—as Cone contends, Christians move into the text and are "then thrust back into their contemporary history."[60] This constant imaginative movement from first century to present context, from text to world, characterizes narrative imagination in a christological key.[61]

Forming hermeneutical imagination. How does one actually form a faithful hermeneutical imagination? Hays points a way forward. He refers to scriptural interpretation as a "complex practice"—here referencing MacIntyre's famous definition of a practice as a socially established activity with its own standards of excellence.[62] If the practice of reading is socially established, then the process of being formed for it requires prolonged and intentional participation in the community that constitutes the practice. It requires the formation of a way of life, a form of embodied wisdom that grows from immersion in the tradition. This account of formation calls to mind Jenson's institutional ecclesiology. Earlier, I gestured toward the notion of catechesis that coincides with it. Indeed, some type of formal initiation into the tradition is necessary for a church that attempts to live

---

[59]In her work, *God Is Not a Story: Realism Revisited* (Oxford: Oxford University Press, 2007), Francesca Aran Murphy wonders if Jenson's narrative theology undermines this possibility. By strongly accenting the narrative dimensions of the text, Jenson risks portraying a closed world, she claims. Jenson's move, following Frei, has the benefit of reminding the reader that the point of reading the text is not to move beyond the text to another realm of textual meaning, but it risks presenting Jesus as what Murphy calls a "screened self." Constrained by the logic of a story, the reader encounters a narrative character who lacks free personality, a storied Jesus who lacks spontaneity, surprise, and extratextual concreteness. As she states, "The presence of Christ to us in narrative theology [like Jenson's] is like that of a screen actor to a movie-viewer. The screened 'self' is both product of a collective imagination and delivered to one. This analogy undermines personality" (Murphy, *God Is Not a Story*, 4).

[60]Cone, *God of the Oppressed*, 102, emphasis added.

[61]Among other things, this account of intratextuality, in contrast to an ecclesiocentric account, leaves open the possibility that one might find resources for faithful reading outside of the church. The movement into the world holds potential to challenge, judge, and expand Christian vision. More on this in chaps. 7 and 8.

[62]Richard B. Hays, "Reading the Bible with Eyes of Faith: The Practice of Theological Exegesis," *JTI* 1, no. 1 (2007): 11. For MacIntyre's definition of practice, see Alasdair MacIntyre, *After Virtue: A Study in Moral Theology*, 2nd ed. (Notre Dame, IN: University of Notre Dame Press, 1984), 187.

faithfully. Yet certain dangers come lurking within this pedagogical vision when the underlying ecclesiology becomes one-sided. Here we would do well to listen to Willie Jennings's warning, particularly as he highlights the pedagogical distortions that follow from an inadequately christological account of the church:

> Christianity is a teaching faith. It carries in its heart the making of disciples through teaching. Yet its pedagogical vision is inside its christological horizon and embodiment, inside its *participatio Christi* and its *imitatio Christi*. . . . [But starting in the colonial period] theology was inverted with pedagogy. Teaching was not envisioned inside discipleship, but discipleship was envisioned inside teaching.[63]

According to Jennings, in other words, troubles arise when we invert teaching and following, when the church's efforts of pedagogical replication trump the ongoing process of imaginative christological imitation. It is precisely the embodied and enacted nature of *imitatio* that thrusts faithfulness beyond the purely cognitive realm, thereby rendering the traditional notion of teaching as transmission pedagogically inadequate.

Jennings's critique of overly pedagogical forms of Christianity maps nicely onto my critique of a one-sidedly institutional church. Indeed, his account of following Jesus runs sharply athwart those who emphasize "discipline at the borders"[64] as a means of securing cultural normativity. He argues that the inversion of pedagogy and discipleship funds a distorted vision of intellectual and cultural judgment—"hyperevaluation," as he calls it—that exerted particularly damaging consequences on the recipients of colonialist instruction and continues to undergird much Christian pedagogical practice today. There is, of course, much more to be said about the effects colonialism has exerted on the theological disciplines. Here I briefly listen to Jennings because he alerts us to the possibility that a strongly institutionalized account of faithfulness, if left unchecked, might work at cross-purposes with the formation of the imagination inherent to discipleship.

---

[63] Willie James Jennings, *Christian Imagination: Theology and Origins of Race* (New Haven, CT: Yale University Press, 2010), 106.

[64] Robert W. Jenson, *The Works of God*, vol. 2 of *Systematic Theology* (Oxford: Oxford University Press, 1999), 205.

Following Jennings, we can affirm that pedagogy exists within discipleship, that *participatio* and *imitatio* are the primary features of formation. Or as Bonhoeffer succinctly puts it: "There is no education without taking discipleship to Christ seriously."[65] By this he means that "Christian education can never be programmatic. . . . It is a matter not of creating a new type of human being, a 'Christian human being,' but of the human being with all his ideals, including Christian ideals, bowing to the dominion of God." Instead of educational ideals and models, which give pedagogical control to the human teacher, there is "only the call to discipleship at a certain point. It is left to God to shape the person according to God's likeness."[66] Bonhoeffer suggests, in other words, that the church's pedagogical practices are not called to manufacture a particular product. Only God can do that. Instead, they strive to hold open the possibility that one may encounter Christ, be called to follow him, and be formed in the process. Any sort of visible changes that may accrue along the way result not from pedagogical techniques but from the grace of Christ, which sustains the journey of discipleship. To believe that education itself can produce faithfulness is to render Christ an ideal and not a living person. Practices of formation must leave space for Christ himself.

Framed within the discipleship motif, the livelihood of Jesus renders problematic any project aimed at hyperevaluation. Faithful hermeneutical imagination in the wake of Christ is more an art than a science, more about wisdom than technique. In the wake of Christ, hermeneutical imagination does not lend itself to tidy procedures and is not easily quantifiable. The act of following, not the act of teaching, is primary. This account of hermeneutical training might look something like apprenticeship, the hermeneutical equivalent of Paul's appeal to "be imitators of me, as I am of Christ" (1 Cor 11:1).[67] As *imitatio*, the formation of hermeneutical faithfulness aims at a lived disposition that is at once located within the tradition and yet alert to the imaginative possibilities that discipleship entails. On this reading, teaching is not simply a matter of conveying content and method;

---

[65]Bonhoeffer, *Theological Education at Finkenwalde*, DBWE 14:539.

[66]Bonhoeffer, *Theological Education at Finkenwalde*, DBWE 14:540.

[67]For a technical account of apprenticeship situated within discussions of modern hermeneutics, see Joseph Dunne, *Back to the Rough Ground: Practical Judgment and the Lure of Technique*, rev. ed. (Notre Dame, IN: University of Notre Dame Press, 1997).

it is also, and most importantly, a matter of exemplifying a way of life that is attuned to Jesus and that faithfully searches the text in hopes of hearing his word.

In many ways, Bonhoeffer imagined his Finkenwalde experiment as an attempt to put flesh on this picture of formation. Here he displays that formation is an embodied, communal, and ongoing process. There is a certain density to Christian pedagogy when the church is considered simultaneously as both the *creatura verbi* and a historical institution. Discipleship is something we do, not just with our minds but with our bodies, not just with reason but with imagination, not just as individuals but as communities. Here we anticipate what is to come in part three. Bonhoeffer's mature pedagogical vision suggests that the traditioning process, the process of being incorporated into this community, shapes both what we know and also how we know, both the content of our minds and also the very pattern and posture of our thinking. Of course, this does not render practices like catechesis meaningless; rather, as Bonhoeffer's Finkenwalde experiment exemplifies, training in hermeneutical faithfulness occurs both in the classroom and in worship, prayer, service, play, friendship, and hospitality. As I express more fully in chapters five and six, Christology has communal implications. The thick account of communal life on display in Bonhoeffer is itself an interpretation of his Christology, for together these practices constitute a christological *habitus*, a way of training and embodying a pattern of existence in the wake of the risen One.

Conclusion: Jenson, Bonhoeffer, and the Church as an Institutional Space

I have argued in part two that we ought to situate the church's institutional dimensions within the christological. The consistency of Christ's call throughout history creates the church's historical-institutional structures. Theologically understood, the institutional form of the church derives from the consistency of Christ to his people. Because Christ is risen, the church is (contra Jenson) not as threatened by the passage of time as any institution. Ecclesial purity always arises as a byproduct of his risenness, is always a gift, and is always received. The church's identity lies beyond itself in the risen One it attempts to follow. A church with an inflated concern for identity maintenance ironically risks forfeiting its identity by becoming a community of an idea about Christ and not the church of the risen One himself.

If an exaggerated account of reading within institutional space forces us to ask the question, What was the church yesterday?, we can also ask Bonhoeffer's driving hermeneutical question: "Who is Jesus Christ for us today?" The church's historical-institutional past is hermeneutically relevant because Christ continues to walk ahead of his people and call them to follow after him. In this way, I have continued to sketch a multidimensional account of the church as a hermeneutical space that issues in a hermeneutic of discipleship.

Though the church fundamentally lives from an eccentric orientation, the process of being incorporated into the tradition remains a key practice. The fundamental asymmetry that characterizes Jesus' relationship with his people suggests that both traditioned rationality and christologically oriented imagination coexist as the church follows after its Lord. For just this reason, the task of hermeneutical faithfulness requires an agile mode of thinking. A one-sidedly christological hermeneutic leaves no room for *traditioned* innovation—imagination would have free reign, and God's word would seemingly be apprehended by means of immediate, ecstatic intuition. Conversely, a one-sidedly institutional hermeneutic would leave no room for traditioned *innovation*—repetition would reign, and the promulgation of technique would overshadow the formation of Christ-directed imagination. As a christological institution the church must remain open to the innovative and imaginative performances that necessarily arise as the Spirit draws Christ's people into his ongoing march toward the kingdom, and it must do so precisely on the basis of Christ's consistent faithfulness.

Because this sort of knowing is simultaneously enabled and limited by the past—and because the object of our knowledge is fundamentally consistent—originality is not necessarily a hermeneutical virtue. Likewise, by suggesting the importance of imagination I am not suggesting that clever readings are necessarily the best, as if those equipped with poetic brilliance are more likely to handle the text faithfully. By situating the imaginative task within space that is at once historical-institutional and christological, I am unsettling any easy adjudicatory criterion. Faithful readings must be consistent with the past, just as Christ himself is consistent, and as such they must ultimately fit within the contours of his ongoing reign.

With this we broach a question that has been lurking in the background throughout: How do we discern whether the voice we hear belongs to Christ or someone else? How do we know when imagination ceases to be traditioned and instead becomes fanciful? On what basis can the church adjudicate its readings? Along the way I have noted key features of an answer—e.g., constant self-criticism, reading canonically, and awareness of the tradition. But this question deserves more attention. Ultimately, the question of adjudication is a question directed to the community that seeks to follow Jesus. No technique or method will solve this problem. Instead, the answer must be worked out in company with others, which requires a host of concrete practices that enable communities to function as such. In this sense, the church is a hermeneutical space not only because it exists in relationship to the risen Lord and not only because it exists in relationship to its historical-institutional past—the church is also a hermeneutical space because within it bodies gather together in concrete relation to each other.

PART THREE

The Church as Congregation: Hermeneutics and Togetherness

5

Reading Together

A CONVERSATION WITH STANLEY HAUERWAS

ONE OF THE GREAT IRONIES of thinking theologically about Scripture is how little Scripture says about itself. Traditionally, certain verses have carried much theological weight: those that speak about Scripture's inspiration (2 Tim 3:16), divine origin (2 Pet 1:20-21), life and activity (Heb 4:12), or ability to instruct (Rom 15:4). In recent conversations about theological interpretation it has become common to note Scripture's own desire to be interpreted christologically (Jn 5:39), spiritually (1 Cor 2:12-16), and in light of the resurrection (Jn 2:20-22).

Yet the surest thing the Bible implies about itself is that its reading is a communal and public event. The biblical narrative rarely portrays the act of reading as a solitary affair. Key hermeneutical moments in the narrative—moments when understanding arises from the text—are also distinctly communal moments. Josiah, upon rediscovering the book of the Law, gathered to himself all the elders and read in their hearing (2 Kings 23:1-2). Ezra, upon returning from exile, assembled the community around the text and assigned teachers to gather with the people to facilitate understanding (Neh 8:1-8). The earliest Christians, upon receiving the Spirit at Pentecost, jointly devoted themselves to the apostles' teaching (Acts 2:42). One of the few things we can surmise about Jesus' reading habits is that he read in public (Lk 4:16-27). The exception that proves the rule is the imprisoned reader who must read alone and who yet longs for community with other

Christians (2 Tim 4:13). One of the few times we encounter a solitary reader—the Ethiopian eunuch alone on the chariot—his reading lacks understanding (Acts 8:26-40). It is only when Philip joins the eunuch, when they enact togetherness by sitting shoulder to shoulder, that the text comes alive as the word of God.

As we have seen, one of the key instances of communal hermeneutics occurs in Luke's resurrection stories. Walking with the two disciples on the way to Emmaus, Jesus performs what we can only assume to be a masterful interpretation, expounding all of Scripture as a text about himself. Yet, to the disciples, this teaching—though firmly christological and existentially penetrating—remains hermeneutically insufficient. In this story, understanding arises not simply when a master teacher expertly exposits the text but when bodies gather around a shared meal (Lk 24:29-31). Understanding arises not in pedagogy but in fellowship. A similar situation unfolds in the very next pericope (Lk 24:36-49). While gathering with the eleven to share a meal of broiled fish, Jesus exposits Scripture and opens their minds to understand it. These stories obviously testify to the gratuitous nature of understanding. Yet they also suggest that hermeneutical grace arrives through the avenue of togetherness.

It is likely, moreover, that most (if not all) scriptural texts were addressed to gathered communities. As Markus Bockmuehl suggests,

> While we cannot climb into the heads of the original authors to discover their intentions, the documents as they stand do . . . assume and address a certain kind of audience. . . . Almost invariably, the implied readers are ecclesially situated. Even where they are directly addressed as individuals (e.g., in Luke-Acts or the Pastorals), it is clear that the readers are never undefined and unrelated singularities. Instead, they are assumed to be related to the (or a) body of Christian believers.[1]

Thus, we can surmise that the canon carries certain assumptions about its "implied reader," that a communal *Tendenz* comes embedded in the text itself. As Bockmuehl goes on to note, this challenges common assumptions about reading: "The implied reader does not approach the text as a

---

[1]Markus Bockmuehl, *Seeing the Word: Refocusing New Testament Study* (Grand Rapids, MI: Eerdmans, 2006), 68-71.

disembodied rational self."[2] This means that the church must attend to the "politics of reading," i.e., to the fact that hermeneutical practices always come enmeshed within the social composition of the reading community.[3] In a significant study, Stephen Fowl and L. Gregory Jones highlight the implications that follow: "As a social activity, interpretation is confirmed, constrained, and determined by the political constitution of those contexts in which interpretation takes place. . . . The political nature of any particular context will both shape [interpretive interest] and constrain the types of resources available to any group of interpreters."[4] The church is a space for reading, then, because of its "political constitution," because within it various bodies navigate difference and create a shared life as they gather around the text.

A key biblical paradigm of communal hermeneutics occurs in Acts 15 when the apostles and elders meet to consider the highly contentious matter regarding the relationship between Jews and Gentiles in the church. The Jerusalem Council enacts its unique politics of reading through a process of shared speaking, listening, and examining Scripture. Only after this political process can they conclude, "It has seemed good to the Holy Spirit and to us" (Acts 15:28). Here in part three I explore the theological anatomy of this key phrase, "and to us," and I consider the ways it might be developed, sustained, and enacted.

Toward this end, I press forward toward a holistic ecclesiology, taking up key strands of thinking that have emerged in previous chapters. The church exists simultaneously in relationship to the risen Christ and its historical-institutional past—and precisely in these two relational dynamics it exists concretely as a local gathering of bodies. By considering the church as bodies gathered I continue to resist the temptation of placing the theological and sociohistorical dimensions of the church in competition. I continue to uphold the fundamental asymmetry and ordered unity that characterizes the church, thereby avoiding easy one-sided patterns of thought that reduce the church to one facet of its complex structure.

---

[2]Bockmuehl, *Seeing the Word*, 71.
[3]See Michael G. Cartwright, *Practices, Politics, and Performance: Toward a Communal Hermeneutic for Christian Ethics* (Eugene, OR: Wipf & Stock, 2006).
[4]Stephen E. Fowl and L. Gregory Jones, *Reading in Communion: Scripture and Ethics in Christian Life* (Grand Rapids, MI: Eerdmans, 1991), 17.

Stanley Hauerwas is especially helpful at this point. His ecclesial ambi-dexterity stands as an example of the multidimensional joining I claim is central to any theologically serious ecclesiology. One may contend that someone who identifies as a high church Mennonite[5] or an evangelical Catholic[6] is theologically confused—but perhaps such an elastic imagi-nation reflects something of the complexity of the church as a social reality corresponding to Christ's ongoing livelihood.[7] Moreover, Hauerwas lu-cidly illustrates the communal nature of Christian existence, indeed of the gospel itself. Following his lead, I attempt in chapter five to sketch an ac-count of hermeneutical practices of togetherness.

Many aspects of Hauerwas's narrative ecclesiology, especially as they emerge in his mature work, accent the historical and institutional dimen-sions of the church. In this sense, his position at times bears a certain resem-blance to Jenson's. The uniqueness of Hauerwas, and one of the reasons he deserves focused attention in this project, resides in his ability to show how a historical-institutional account of the church must also attend to its concretely communal dimensions. He demonstrates, in other words, how there can be no institution stretched through time without the social and material conditions that enable the acts of togetherness through which the institution takes concrete form in history.

Hauerwas's resemblance to Jenson suggests that he is susceptible to some of the same one-sided tendencies. I will show, however, that his theology possesses resources that allow him to deal with them differently. In this sense, I offer a partial defense of Hauerwas in response to some recent critics. While his work, taken as a whole, often appears "ecclesiocentric," not all strands of his thought fit within this qualifier. This becomes especially clear when we consider the different—and perhaps inconsistent—ways he frames the hermeneutical task. At his most ecclesiocentric, Hauerwas overburdens hermeneutical practices of togetherness in a manner analogous to Jenson's overburdening of historical-institutional practices. I suggest that this ten-dency derives from a more basic inconsistency regarding the relationship

---

[5]Stanley Hauerwas, *A Community of Character: Toward a Constructive Christian Social Ethic* (Notre Dame, IN: University of Notre Dame Press, 1981), 6.

[6]Stanley Hauerwas, *Sanctify Them in Truth: Holiness Exemplified* (Nashville: Abingdon, 1998), 77.

[7]See Michael G. Cartwright, "A Reader's Guide," in *The Hauerwas Reader*, ed. John Berkman and Michael Cartwright (Durham, NC: Duke University Press, 2001), 665.

between Jesus and the church. The way forward, I will show, requires a clearer account of Christ's resurrected and ascended existence.

This claim directs me to Bonhoeffer. As I will argue in chapter six, Bonhoeffer unequivocally affirms the social character of Christian existence while also affirming the role of Christ himself in the hermeneutical process. If Hauerwas shows how the church's historical-institutional dimension requires practices of togetherness, Bonhoeffer does the same with the *creatura verbi*. If God speaks, the church must be an addressable community equipped to receive and discern the divine address. This constitution is a gift of grace, the acceptance of which takes concrete form as an array of community-sustaining social practices. Nowhere is this clearer than at Finkenwalde, where Bonhoeffer attempts to put his theory of revelation into practice as he forms a common life that correlates to Jesus' ongoing agency as the risen One.

Listening to both Hauerwas and Bonhoeffer, we see that the two lines of thinking I began pursuing in parts one and two converge in the local community, at the nexus of bodies gathered. The church is a hermeneutical space because it engages in practices of togetherness that sustain a community gathered around the text.

STANLEY HAUERWAS'S COMMUNAL HERMENEUTIC

Though he resists the label of "narrative theologian," no account of Hauerwas's ecclesial hermeneutic can avoid the concept.[8] His assertion that "every community requires a narrative"[9] lies at the heart of his theological ethics, and his unique theological vision takes shape as he unfolds this claim in light of the particular narrative that constitutes the church.

Hauerwas began his career by arguing that morality is dependent upon its narrative context. In this, he proffered a convincing alternative to political liberalism and the modern ethical tradition, both of which rely upon individualistic and universal accounts of rationality. He has subsequently referred to this as a paradigm shift in the field of ethics.[10] Whereas the

---

[8]Stanley Hauerwas, *Performing the Faith: Bonhoeffer and the Practice of Nonviolence* (London: SPCK, 2004), 136: "I hate the idea that I am a 'narrative theologian.' I hate all qualifiers other than 'Christian.'"

[9]Hauerwas, *Community of Character*, 4.

[10]Stanley Hauerwas, "A Retrospective Assessment of an 'Ethics of Character': The Development of Hauerwas's Theological Project," in Berkman and Cartwright, *Hauerwas Reader*, 77.

modern ethical tradition has tended to focus on discrete commands, decisions, and dilemmas, Hauerwas instead focuses on the identity of the ethical agent. Before analyzing what we do, we must consider who we are—and in order to do this we must attend to the stories that give shape and substance to our identity.

As with ethical action more generally, the church's practices gain meaning from their story. According to Hauerwas, these practices in turn sustain the story. In this sense, the logic driving his narrative ecclesiology closely resembles the historical-institutional logic on display in Jenson. As Hauerwas states, the practices specific to the church develop its common rationality and sustain a common history across time.[11] Moreover, his conception of narrative owes much to the MacIntyrean notion of tradition-based rationality that I employed to explicate Jenson's ecclesiology. Both Hauerwas and Jenson view narrative as something more than a formalist or literary concept. Though Hauerwas does not probe the logic of narrative with as much theological rigor as Jenson does, he echoes Jenson's basic argument about the narrative structure of reality: the "appeal to narrative," Hauerwas states, "is the primary expression of a theological metaphysics and is, therefore, an unembarrassed claim about the way things are."[12]

This helps explain his reluctance to move behind the story of Jesus in search of a deeper level of truth or a more solid foundation for meaning.[13] The problem with this extratextual move is not merely that it risks loosing

---

[11]Hauerwas, *Performing the Faith*, 156. On Hauerwas's admiration of and similarity to Jenson, see Stanley Hauerwas, "How to Write a Theological Sentence," *Sewanee Theological Review* 57, no. 1 (2013): 56-72; and idem, "Only Theology Overcomes Ethics; or, Why 'Ethicists' Must Learn from Jenson," in *Trinity, Time, and Church: A Response to the Theology of Robert W. Jenson*, ed. Colin E. Gunton (Grand Rapids, MI: Eerdmans, 2000), 252-68.

[12]Hauerwas, *Performing the Faith*, 146. This claim carries implications for the actual act of reading the text. For example, Hauerwas makes no effort to dig behind the text and instead aims simply "to retell the story [the text] tells"; see Stanley Hauerwas, *Matthew*, Brazos Theological Commentary on the Bible (Grand Rapids, MI: Brazos Press, 2006), 18. He also resists resorting to "consciousness words" as a means of putatively explaining an author's mental state, instead opting to attend to the text itself (Hauerwas, *Matthew*, 20). For more analysis of Hauerwas as a reader of Scripture, see Richard B. Hays, *The Moral Vision of the New Testament: Community, Cross, New Creation; A Contemporary Introduction to New Testament Ethics* (San Francisco: HarperCollins, 1996), 253-65; and Darren Sarisky, *Scriptural Interpretation: A Theological Exploration* (Malden, MA: Wiley-Blackwell, 2013), 145-58.

[13]See Robert W. Jenson, "The Hauerwas Project," *MT* 8, no. 3 (1992): 285-95, in which Jenson wonders, among other things, if Hauerwas adequately deals with the "truthfulness" of Christian claims about reality.

theological reflection from the biblical narrative (as the problem is broadly framed, for example, in Frei's *Eclipse of Biblical Narrative*); the problem, more substantively, is that it risks undermining the content of salvation. Here his reasoning is straightforward: the very person and work of Jesus requires narrative depiction. "Grace is not an eternal moment above history," Hauerwas avers.[14] It is the very story Jesus lives, a historical event that requires narrative representation. Through his life, Jesus makes possible a new mode of existence, thereby inaugurating the kingdom. Going to the cross and being vindicated in the resurrection, Jesus shows that "forgiveness and love are alternatives to the coercion the world thinks necessary for existence."[15] We are saved, Hauerwas therefore claims, by being invited into the kingdom made possible by Jesus' person and work. The church thus comes into existence as the ongoing narrative embodiment of Jesus' story, the form of communal existence that lives into the pattern of life opened up by Jesus.[16] "Salvation," he therefore insists, is "our material embodiment in the habits and practices of a people that makes possible a way of life that is otherwise impossible."[17] The very nature of the gospel implies that it cannot merely be spoken but must also be shown, which is why practices of togetherness are inherent to the narrative logic of salvation. Grace is something one experiences tangibly in community precisely because it provides the rationale for a community that recognizes that self-justification was rendered irrelevant in the story of Christ's death and resurrection.[18] This is why Hauerwas famously refuses to separate ethics from theology. The very logic of salvation (deriving from the logic of Christ himself) entails a communal form of life.

Narrative, togetherness, and scriptural hermeneutics. The central point to keep in mind as we move forward is that Hauerwas's notion of narrative necessarily entails concrete practices of togetherness. The logic of narrative is inseparable from the logic of bodies gathered. Hence, practices of

---

[14]Stanley Hauerwas, *The Peaceable Kingdom: A Primer in Christian Ethics* (Notre Dame, IN: University of Notre Dame Press, 1983), 27.

[15]Hauerwas, *Peaceable Kingdom*, 87.

[16]Hauerwas, *Peaceable Kingdom*, 62. Also see Stanley Hauerwas, *Wilderness Wanderings: Probing Twentieth-Century Theology and Philosophy* (Boulder, CO: Westview Press, 1997), 192-93.

[17]Hauerwas, *Sanctify Them in Truth*, 74.

[18]On this, see Rowan Williams, *Where God Happens: Discovering Christ in One Another* (Boston: New Seeds, 2005), 26-27.

togetherness are in no way ancillary to the substance of the gospel but rather are the necessary corollary of salvation's historical presence.

Consequently, when Hauerwas considers the role of narrative in hermeneutics, he is less concerned with the technicalities of reading the text than with construing the community that does the reading.

> Part of the difficulty with the rediscovery of the significance of narrative for theological reflection has been too concentrated attention on texts qua texts. It is no doubt significant to rediscover the literary and narrative character texts of the Bible. . . . But the emphasis on narrative can only result in scholarly narcissism if narrative texts are *extracted from the concrete people* who acknowledge the authority of the Bible.[19]

With this realization we locate Hauerwas's unique contribution to our account of ecclesial hermeneutics. Though in many ways his larger vision fits within Jenson's historical-institutional project, he is particularly enriching to our conversation because of his ability to press the logic of tradition into the communal realm and thereby to offer a thick and particularist account of tradition. For Hauerwas, narrative requires politics; tradition requires practices of togetherness.

Consider, for example, the very idea of maintaining historical continuity. Such continuity is, at the least, a process involving real people and concrete moments of teaching and learning. Relational structures and conversational skills are therefore necessary to the very existence of tradition, for without them the community would lack the means by which to exist through history. As Hauerwas succinctly argues, Scripture does not convey the story "independently of the existence of a historic people."[20] The historical-institutional dimensions of the church, characteristic of both Jenson's and Hauerwas's narrative theology, require concrete practices of togetherness. Indeed, they are hermeneutically vacuous without them.

This points us toward the importance of discipleship as a motif in his theology. Christianity is not "a system of beliefs that can be or is universally known without the conversion of being incorporated within a specific

---

[19]Hauerwas, "The Church as God's New Language," in Berkman and Cartwright, *Hauerwas Reader*, 152, emphasis added.

[20]Hauerwas, "The Servant Community: Christian Social Ethics," in Berkman and Cartwright, *Hauerwas Reader*, 373.

community of people."[21] As he writes in his commentary on Matthew, "It is important . . . that Peter's knowledge of Jesus as the Messiah not be used to develop a general theory of revelation. Simon does not learn that Jesus is the Messiah by some intuitive or mystical mode of knowing. Rather, Simon learns that Jesus is the Messiah because he obeyed Jesus' command to be his disciple."[22] For Hauerwas, discipleship is an epistemological category; the disciples know the Lord not in theory but in following.

He presses this logic into the hermeneutical realm. Discipleship is not the outcome of faithful interpretation but is ingredient in its very process.[23] His criticism of general hermeneutics parallels his criticism of the modern ethical tradition more broadly. In rejecting the "academic captivity" of Scripture and "the hegemony of the historical-critical method,"[24] he unequivocally insists that hermeneutical excellency is a specifically ecclesial activity. In explicit contrast to both fundamentalism and modern criticism—which he suggests are two sides of the same coin[25]—Hauerwas avers that Scripture is not universally accessible; it requires a very particular sort of reader.

Most obviously, this implies that one must read Scripture in light of tradition.[26] But Hauerwas adds communal tangibility to this logic by emphasizing that "all reading is embedded in a politics."[27] All reading requires an account of the reading community, not just as an entity that conveys ecclesial knowledge but as bodies gathered within a shared story. We should take the Bible out of the hands of individuals, he famously claims, not simply because they do not know the right things but because they do not embody the right story. Here he draws from John Howard Yoder: "To speak of the Bible apart from people reading it and apart from

---

[21]Stanley Hauerwas, *Naming the Silences: God, Medicine, and the Problem of Suffering* (Grand Rapids, MI: Eerdmans, 1990), 53.

[22]Hauerwas, *Matthew*, 150.

[23]Stanley Hauerwas, *Unleashing the Scripture: Freeing the Bible from Captivity to America* (Nashville: Abingdon, 1993), 47-62.

[24]Hauerwas, *Unleashing the Scripture*, 8.

[25]Hauerwas, *Unleashing the Scripture*, 17.

[26]In *Unleashing the Scripture*, Hauerwas favorably quotes Vatican II's "Dogmatic Constitution on Divine Revelation": "Sacred tradition and sacred Scripture form one sacred deposit of the word of God, which is committed to the church" (Hauerwas, *Unleashing the Scripture*, 22); see Hays, *Moral Vision*, 263.

[27]Hauerwas, *Unleashing the Scripture*, 15.

the specific questions that those people reading need to answer is to do violence to the very purpose for which we have been given the Holy Scriptures."[28] Another way of saying this is that the church does not merely have a hermeneutical theory—it is one. To read in light of tradition, Hauerwas maintains, is to read as a community that embodies the politics that the tradition makes possible.

Practices of togetherness. This helps make sense of what is perhaps the most distinctive feature of his scriptural hermeneutic: the church is a space for reading because its narrative, embodied through an array of concrete activities, forms people who possess the skills and dispositions necessary to read the Bible faithfully. Outside of the church, reading Scripture is an eminently difficult task, not because the text is a complex literary artifact but because readers employ it for the wrong ends. The difficulty of reading lies not in the text but in ourselves.[29] In order to read Scripture faithfully the community must have antecedently "learned to live in a way that makes it possible for them to hear that story."[30] He even goes so far as to suggest that it is not good interpretation that produces nonviolence but nonviolence that produces good interpretation.[31] The church's formative practices precede the act of reading, for such practices are the necessary precondition for seeing the text rightly.

According to Hauerwas, this training occurs primarily when bodies gather to worship. Worship, of course, is most fundamentally a work rendered to God. But he notes that it is also a work done *to us*, a work that provides "resistance to the ugliness of [the] surrounding culture."[32] If "it is by doing just acts that the just man is produced," as Aristotle famously suggests,[33] then it is by engaging in worship that the godly person is produced. "It becomes our duty to be a people who submit to the discipline of the liturgy," Hauerwas writes, "as it is there that we are trained with the skills

---

[28] John Howard Yoder, *Royal Priesthood: Essays Ecclesiological and Ecumenical*, ed. Michael G. Cartwright (Grand Rapids, MI: Eerdmans, 1994), 353.

[29] Hauerwas, *Community of Character*, 239n5.

[30] Stanley Hauerwas, *Christian Existence Today: Essays on Church, World, and Living in Between* (Durham, NC: Labyrinth, 1988), 101.

[31] Hauerwas, *Unleashing the Scripture*, 64.

[32] Hauerwas, *Performing the Faith*, 161.

[33] Aristotle, *Nicomachean Ethics*, in *The Basic Works of Aristotle*, ed. Richard McKeon (New York: Modern Library, 2001), 2.4.

rightly to know the story."[34] As he elsewhere states, "the regular, continual pattern of gathering for worship may be viewed as the church's rehearsal. Worship thus becomes a kind of performance before the performance, it is where Christian commitment is 'fleshed out' and given tangible shape."[35]

It becomes evident that worship, for Hauerwas, is no internal or private matter. Liturgy is an embodied and public activity. What might remain formal becomes three dimensional as Christians bump shoulders around the altar. This corporeality is essential to worship's formative capacity. Rather than a mere side effect of gathering, the act of bumping shoulders is itself materially significant, for it allows the community to identify those who ought to be imitated. In other words, the very authority of Scripture, Hauerwas claims, is contingent upon the regular movement of bodies toward each other. The text is mediated not only by worship itself but by the spiritual masters that worship enables the community to identify.[36] He writes,

> The authority of Scripture is mediated through the lives of the saints identified by our community as most nearly representing what we are about. Put more strongly, to know what Scripture means, finally, we must look to those who have most nearly learned to exemplify its demands through their lives. . . . Through the lives of the saints we begin to understand how the images of Scripture are best balanced so that we might tell and live the ongoing story of God's unceasing purpose to bring the world to the peace of the kingdom.[37]

In sum, Hauerwas's narrative theology leads him to emphasize Scripture's location among bodies gathered. The hermeneutical enterprise, then, is always located concretely within a "web of ecclesial practices, skills, and gestures."[38] More specifically, the mutually reinforcing practices of worship and imitation form faithful readers who are fit to handle the text. In my terms, Hauerwas illustrates how the church as a historical institution—a story stretching across time—gains hermeneutical significance by means of concrete acts of gathering that form faithful readers.

---

[34]Hauerwas, *Christian Existence Today*, 108.
[35]Hauerwas, *Performing the Faith*, 98.
[36]Hauerwas, *Unleashing the Scripture*, 16. Also see Cartwright, "Reader's Guide," 634; and Hays, *Moral Vision*, 255-58.
[37]Hauerwas, *Peaceable Kingdom*, 70-71.
[38]Cartwright, "Readers' Guide," 641.

AN OVERREALIZED HERMENEUTIC?

Someone as prolific and provocative as Hauerwas has garnered no dearth of criticism. It is unnecessary here to survey the scope of this criticism. However, we should note one particularly contentious dimension of his narrative ecclesiology, for it carries implications for his ecclesial hermeneutic.

The tendency in question can be articulated in various ways. Most basically, the problem lies in his tendency to equate the kingdom with the church, what some have called an overrealized eschatology.[39] Hauerwas's narrative logic, so the argument goes, implies that Christ's gift of salvation quite simply is the community of followers he creates. Salvation *is* the community. One recent critic has forcefully referred to this as Hauerwas's "onto-ecclesiology"—i.e., his depiction of the church as an objectively given reality, constituted by liturgical practices, that stands empirically as the supreme manifestation of God's salvation.[40]

This line of critique has some traction. Hauerwas indeed claims that the church's practices manifest the peace of God and thus the salvation of the world, which is why he boldly contends that the church in history is what the world can be.[41] He likewise asserts that Jesus "proclaims and embodies a way of life that God has made possible here and now"[42] and thus that his work establishes the new age.[43] The basic problem, critics claim, is that salvation ceases to be an eschatological goal and instead becomes a communal production. If this is the case, then Hauerwas requires practices of togetherness to accomplish a hefty task. Salvation simply is the reality that

---

[39]See, e.g., Michael Horton, *A Better Way: Rediscovering the Drama of God-Centered Worship* (Grand Rapids, MI: Baker Books, 2002), 135.

[40]Ry O. Siggelkow, "Toward an Apocalyptic Peace Church: Christian Pacifism After Hauerwas," *Conrad Grebel Review* 31, no. 3 (2013): 274-297. Here Siggelkow plays with Heidegger's notion of "onto-theology": "By onto-ecclesiology, I mean the attempt to ground the church theologically in terms of its metaphysical correspondence to the reality of Being. . . . Indeed, it is the church's being—objectively given in its liturgical practices and institutional life—that is the 'supreme manifestation' and the 'all-founding' *logos* of the totality of beings as such" (Siggelkow, "Toward an Apocalyptic Peace Church," 275). Milbank's notion of the church as a "counter ontology" lies behind this analysis; on Hauerwas's use of Milbank, see Hauerwas, "Creation, Contingency, and Truthful Nonviolence: A Milbankian Reflection," in *Wilderness Wanderings*, 188-98.

[41]Stanley Hauerwas, *War and the American Difference: Theological Reflections on Violence and National Identity* (Grand Rapids, MI: Baker Academic, 2011), xiii.

[42]Hauerwas, *Peaceable Kingdom*, 83.

[43]Hauerwas, *Matthew*, 150.

these practices make tangible. Salvation simply is the politics they produce. But can ecclesial practices bear such responsibility?

Darren Sarisky has recently criticized the hermeneutical implications of this here-and-now logic, claiming that Hauerwas's "notion of the reader needs to specify more clearly that readers do not reach their end before the *eschaton*."[44] Hauerwas's narrative ecclesiology seems to imply that the various practices of togetherness that constitute the church as a space for reading can be counted on, in and of themselves, to render interpretive faithfulness. Sarisky might ask, Can one participate in the liturgy and emulate the saints and thereby appropriate the traditions and practices of the community and yet offer unfaithful readings? Does formation guarantee hermeneutical faithfulness?

This critique goes further. An overrealized account of hermeneutical space, it would seem, actually deteriorates the logic of reading, rendering superfluous the ongoing hermeneutical process. Within such a space, there is little left for Scripture to accomplish—the work of formation and imitation does the heavy hermeneutical lifting before one even turns to the text. The hermeneutical process itself becomes an afterthought, a byproduct that emanates naturally from a well-formed reader. By the time we have learned to read well, we no longer need to read.

Richard Hays similarly wonders if Hauerwas's strong turn toward the community erodes the leverage by which Scripture can challenge, judge, or change the community.[45] Given Hauerwas's narrative logic, Hays suggests that he has no choice but to offer a muzzled and muted text, one that merely echoes back the church's antecedent speech.[46] To frame this critique within my larger project: If the church is constituted by the practices that instantiate and embody its narrative, in what sense is the church also constituted by Christ? Hauerwas helpfully highlights the ways that the church as a historical entity requires practices of togetherness in order to function as a hermeneutical community, but does he not thereby fall into the same one-sided tendencies that lurk around strongly historical-institutional approaches?

---

[44]Sarisky, *Scriptural Interpretation*, 141.
[45]Hays, *Moral Vision*, 263.
[46]Hays, *Moral Vision*, 265-66.

The deeper issue underlying his account of the church as the narrative instantiation of the kingdom is that it risks undermining the logic of discipleship. Whereas Bonhoeffer's discipleship motif operates under the assumption that faithfulness lies always ahead of the church, an exaggerated account of Christian practice collapses the church's goal into its present form. The worry, then, is that an overrealized hermeneutic fails to direct interpretive activity toward funding the movement necessary to follow Jesus on the way. If for Jenson institutional structures bear the great burden of maintaining ecclesial identity, for Hauerwas practices of togetherness bear the great burden of situating one within these structures and thereby securing faithful interpretive outcomes.

Nicholas Healy has recently argued along similar lines.[47] Though he does not focus his critique on scriptural hermeneutics per se, he does explore the underlying theological rationale that makes Hauerwas's hermeneutic possible. He claims that Hauerwas's theology, taken as a whole, is "ecclesiocentric." Healy uses this label pejoratively to denote the sense in which Hauerwas's enthusiastic turn to the church, its narrative, and its institutions causes him to underplay the ongoing priority of God. On Healy's reading, Hauerwas expects the social and immanent dimensions of the church to do what should more properly be attributed to grace alone. Responsibility that should belong to God instead becomes an attribute of the story itself. Healy writes,

> If, however, we are a Christian, we do not so easily inhabit our tradition, for it is axiomatic for us that we need to make *ongoing efforts to convert* if we are to be a good Christian. It is relatively easy to be a good liberal or a good socialist if you are so inclined; it is never easy to follow Jesus Christ truly. Furthermore, the more one tries, the more explicit (to ourselves, at least) must be our judgments as to what constitutes Christianity and how it should be lived. We have to *think* about being a Christian in a way that does not necessarily pertain to being a liberal; being Christian involves effort, prayer, and fasting, not least because we are to follow One who is our Lord, rather than merely inhabit a tradition.[48]

---

[47]Nicholas M. Healy, *Hauerwas: A (Very) Critical Introduction* (Grand Rapids, MI: Eerdmans, 2014). On Hauerwas's insufficient eschatology, see Healy, *Hauerwas*, 134.
[48]Healy, *Hauerwas*, 106, first emphasis added.

At the core of Hauerwas's mistake, Healy argues, is his tendency to filter his notion of narrative through a nontheological account of tradition (drawing heavily from MacIntyre), thereby reducing Christian discipleship to the process of indwelling a tradition or embodying a story. The danger in this is that discipleship becomes institutionalized and generic. What should be a dynamic, complex, and adventurous affair—the process of continually trying to keep up with Christ—is rendered tame and predictable. What Hauerwas needs, Healy claims, is a more uniquely Christian approach to discipleship that frames ecclesial practices within a theocentric account of the church.

A Hauerwasian Response: Togetherness and Discipleship

These criticisms hold much truth. Yet as a means of nuancing my analysis of Hauerwas I would like to highlight another dimension of his communal hermeneutic. Doing so does not completely absolve him of the aforementioned charges, but it does suggest that there is more going on in his account of ecclesial space than these critics notice. And, as I explore below, it points toward an alternative way of framing his account of hermeneutical practices of togetherness.

We have seen already that practices of togetherness form readers for the text. But Hauerwas also at times suggests that the text itself forms readers to fit within the story of Jesus. Formation, in other words, happens in two directions: from the church to the text and from the text to the church. While Hauerwas sometimes seems to load interpretive agency squarely upon the community and its constitutive practices, thereby falling into an overly realized hermeneutic, he writes in other places that Scripture itself is an agent that "renders" and "shapes a community," making the church into a "story-formed" people.[49] On this reading, the community per se is necessary but not sufficient for faithfulness. More is required than is immanently available. This second account of formation grants Scripture a measure of freedom and leverage vis-à-vis the reading community, thereby relieving communal practices of bearing a burden beyond their capacity. The community exists in relationship to a text that can act on its own.

---

[49]Hauerwas, *Community of Character*, 67, 55.

Scripture does things: it overtakes the reader's world and trains people for Christ's story.[50]

These two accounts of the direction of scriptural formation tend to occur in different places in his corpus. When talking specifically about ethical issues, Hauerwas often notes the priority of the text, whereas when talking specifically about scriptural hermeneutics he tends to focus on the priority of the community. More could be said about this apparent tension and how it might be resolved. Regardless, we can conclude that as much as Hauerwas imagines formation running in two directions, his approach to interpretation might not be as ecclesiocentric as some critics think, and, subsequently, we can reconsider the extent to which he offers an overrealized hermeneutic.

Tradition as an aspect of discipleship. In particular, we can reconsider Healy's contention that "Christianity cannot be anything like a tradition in MacIntyre's sense, because it is engaged with an agent that cannot be explained or controlled or harnessed to human projects of development toward excellence."[51] I certainly agree with the latter half of Healy's claim, as the account of discipleship that has unfolded in this project should make clear. Yet he misapplies the logic of the argument. While a Christ-centered account of discipleship cannot be *entirely* like MacIntyre's notion of tradition, certain dimensions of MacIntyre's thinking actually fund the account of discipleship Healy desires. And I suggest that Hauerwas understands this, not only theoretically but also, most tellingly, at the level of practice.

MacIntyre writes, for example, that "traditions, when vital, embody continuities of conflict."[52] Hauerwas appropriates this logic when he claims that "traditions by their nature require change."[53] He goes on to note that "politics is nothing else but a community's internal conversation with itself concerning the various possibilities of understanding and extending its life . . . [and thereby] *drawing nearer to the truth* about itself and the world."[54] On this reading, practices of togetherness are hermeneutically significant precisely to the degree that they allow the community to

---

[50]Hauerwas, *Peaceable Kingdom*, 74.

[51]Healy, *Hauerwas*, 109.

[52]Alasdair MacIntyre, *After Virtue: A Study in Moral Theology*, 2nd ed. (Notre Dame, IN: University of Notre Dame Press, 1984), 22.

[53]Hauerwas, *Community of Character*, 61.

[54]Hauerwas, *Community of Character*, 61, emphasis added.

navigate conflict and engage in argument. Such practices, in other words, do not determine meaning but enable the process of discovering it.

Though Healy is perhaps right to note Hauerwas's general reluctance to talk about God, we should acknowledge that Hauerwas does at times link the movement of tradition to divine action. The church "must always remain open to revision," he claims, because it constantly faces the temptation of domesticating God.[55] On this reading, to embody the Christian narrative is to engage in a journey, which is why, as Hauerwas suggests, the church must resist foreclosing the story.[56] He also at times claims that the church's material and communal life is not itself the presence of the kingdom but stands only as a foretaste of it.[57] There is more left for the community to discover, for the God of the story cannot be sequestered within the church's telling of it.

Healy and others believe that Hauerwas's narrative theology undermines "ongoing efforts to convert" and precludes the logic of self-criticism or the pursuit of better readings. Yet I suggest that Hauerwas's notion of argumentation, navigating conflict, and "drawing nearer to the truth" can account for this. This is how the "not yet" of the kingdom plays out in practice.

On this second reading, we can imagine Hauerwas's practices of togetherness functioning within an eschatological horizon, even if he does not always frame things this way. Introducing a consistent eschatological dimension would not require Hauerwas to modify his strongly historical account of salvation; we must continue to affirm that grace does not hover above history but takes communal form as the story Jesus makes possible. Hence, narrative and the concomitant account of practices of togetherness remain vital for construing the church as a hermeneutical space. Yet his refusal to engage in suprahistorical reasoning need not imply the converse, that salvation is fully present in history. We can uphold both the essentially material, embodied, and communal nature of the church—the

---

[55]Hauerwas, "God's New Language," in Berkman and Cartwright, *Hauerwas Reader*, 160.

[56]Hauerwas, *Performing the Faith*, 94. On the importance of the journey motif in Hauerwas's narrative theology, see Hauerwas, *Community of Character*, 59-63, 98-99; idem, *Peaceable Kingdom*, 24, 68; idem, "A Retrospective Assessment of an 'Ethics of Character': The Development of Hauerwas's Theological Project," in Berkman and Cartwright, *Hauerwas Reader*, 85-87; and Stanley Hauerwas and William H. Willimon, *Resident Aliens: Life in the Christian Colony* (Nashville: Abingdon, 1989), 49-53.

[57]Hauerwas, *Peaceable Kingdom*, 97.

here-and-now tangibility of the narrative—and the church's being as a community en route.

Hermeneutics en route: practices for the journey. While one can read Hauerwas's theology in a way that funds an overrealized eschatology that undermines the logic of discipleship and overburdens ecclesial practices, I have suggested that it can also elucidate the nature of the Christian life as a journey, another key motif in his writing. On this reading of Hauerwas, Jesus' salvific work both instantiates the kingdom and initiates a community into an adventurous journey toward it.[58] Practices of togetherness, then, do not deliver the meaning of Scripture as much as they enable the ongoing journey of discipleship through which meaning is discovered. This depiction of reading—a hermeneutic en route—calls for a second account of practices of togetherness. If Scripture functions within a community that lives en route toward a kingdom that lies always ahead of it, faithful reading requires the skills and practices that enable the journey.

Implied within this account of practices is the recognition that the kingdom is neither an instantaneous moment that descends timelessly from above (as it can become in some highly revelational models) nor an entity that stands in opposition to time (as it can become in some highly institutional models). In both cases, time itself is rendered an insignificant feature of God's action and is thereby made irrelevant to the hermeneutical process. The notion of Christian life as a journey presents another option. The temporal gap between resurrection and parousia is neither a threat to ecclesial identity nor an unfortunate byproduct of a delayed second coming; rather, it is the proper and necessary context of faithful communal life. Practices of togetherness, on this reading, equip the community to navigate time faithfully.

Most obviously, then, Hauerwas suggests that between resurrection and parousia the church must live patiently.[59] More than a mere tactic for achieving tolerance, patience functions for Hauerwas in a uniquely theological manner. Indeed, it derives from God's very nature. This is evident

---

[58]Hauerwas, *Peaceable Kingdom*, 87.
[59]See "Practicing Patience," in Stanley Hauerwas and Charles Pinches, *Christians Among the Virtues: Theological Conversations with Ancient and Modern Ethics* (Notre Dame, IN: University of Notre Dame Press, 1997), 166-78.

in the act of creation itself for, in creating, God grants creatures time to live with God. It makes sense, then, that patience is fundamental to the embodiment of God's love in the midst of creation. Jesus' nonviolent acceptance of the cross reveals both that patience is a feature of God's love for us and that patience characterizes human faithfulness to God. Patience also underlies the very being of the church, for this unique community exists precisely because God has granted it time between resurrection and parousia.

Christians live together in the midst of this time precisely by reciprocating God's patience in their relationships with each other. In this sense, patience is integral to the very logic of togetherness: "To learn to live with the unavoidability of the other," Hauerwas claims, "is to learn to be patient."[60] Hence he refers to the church as "a people constituted by the virtues necessary to endure the struggle to hear and speak truthfully to one another."[61]

The theological virtues, of course, are easily confused with their semblances.[62] Patience is not a glib optimism that things will turn out in the end but a vigilant commitment to remain alert in the time between the times. Patience is fundamental to a living community that follows a living Lord. The practice of patience leaves the church space to navigate and negotiate, space to recognize a future not reducible to the past. By emulating Christ's patience, the church can freely abandon the goal of securing any particular outcome to history. Patience is thus the communal enactment of the "not yet" of God's kingdom, the community's admission that it only follows and does not lead.

A community of peace constituted by Christ and his story is not a community without conflict or a community where conflict is quickly absolved. It is one where conflict is endured. The specific hermeneutical implications of patience emerge when the virtue is enacted in practices of listening and speaking, in what Hauerwas refers to as the community's "internal conversation" that enables the pursuit of truth.[63] The very togetherness that constitutes the church as a space for reading is sustained by linguistic

---

[60]Hauerwas and Pinches, "Practicing Patience," 176.
[61]Hauerwas, *Performing the Faith*, 15.
[62]Hauerwas and Pinches, "Practicing Patience," 175.
[63]Hauerwas, *Community of Character*, 61.

patience, which is the foundation of a nonviolent hermeneutic. Linguistic violence—the act of foreclosing the other's space for discourse—gridlocks the hermeneutical process. Linguistic nonviolence, on the other hand, leaves space for hermeneutical discourse, for dialogue and discernment, for forms of speech that allow the community to sustain unity in the midst of disagreement, and for discourse that holds open the possibility of modes of life that more closely approximate truth.

When patience is enacted as hermeneutical discourse, the process of seeking understanding can become a genuinely communal reality. One is freed to treat the insight of another as a gift to be received, explored, and cherished. Patience alleviates the fear of hidden agendas and rhetorical games and thereby paves the way for genuine listening. Patience lies at the heart of practices of togetherness because it enables the pursuit of truth and the multidirectional process of teaching, learning, and discerning. Patience willingly sits in ambiguity and uncertainty. The practice of patience therefore admits that one's own way of reading is not the only way, that others have insights into the text that one lacks, that ultimately the text transcends us. Patience allows for—indeed, desires—a community of diverse readers. Patience, and the nonviolent linguistic practices that sustain it, is what results when the priesthood of all believers becomes not merely an idea but a hermeneutical practice.[64]

Within such a hermeneutic, the interpretation of Scripture is neither instantaneous nor individualistic. It instead becomes a social process. Various claims about what interpretive faithfulness entails in a given community and in a given context must be carefully assessed, and the patient enactment of hermeneutical discourse allows a community to continually engage its text as it pursues its Lord.[65]

---

[64]See Kevin J. Vanhoozer, *Biblical Authority After Babel: Retrieving the* Solas *in the Spirit of Mere Protestant Christianity* (Grand Rapids, MI: Brazos Press, 2016), 29-30.

[65]For more on this, see James Wm. McClendon, *Ethics*, vol. 1 of *Systematic Theology*, rev. ed. (Nashville: Abingdon, 2002), 222-29; and John Howard Yoder, "Hermeneutics of Peoplehood: A Protestant Perspective on Practical Moral Reasoning," *Journal of Religious Ethics* 10, no. 1 (1982): 42. McClendon speaks of the "never-ending congregational *conversation*" necessary to discern the will of God in community. For a recent take on the importance of communal virtues for scriptural hermeneutics (and one that employs ethnographic tools to analyze the practices of actual communities), see Andrew P. Rogers, *Congregational Hermeneutics: How Do We Read?* (New York: Routledge, 2016).

This account of patience, I suggest, makes little sense within an ecclesio-centric theology. If the kingdom is present in and as the church, as some-times seems to be the case in Hauerwas's work, there would be no "not yet" standing over the faithful community calling for the enactment of patient hermeneutical discourse. Hauerwas's practical account of togetherness sustained through practices of patience and linguistic nonviolence runs against the grain of his overrealized ecclesiology. Patience is one of the defining marks of a community en route.

SEEKING CHRISTOLOGICAL CLARITY

Hauerwas's narrative ecclesiology, taken as a whole, helps us see that herme-neutical faithfulness is a social skill. The church, for Hauerwas, is the social embodiment of the narrative that Jesus makes possible, and the practices that sustain the community are integral to the logic of salvation. The church is a space for reading, therefore, not simply because it transmits data or forms a certain cognitive makeup but because it sustains discipleship.

In fairness to both Hauerwas and his critics, we must also admit that the notion of discipleship takes two different forms in his work. That is to say, two narrative logics emerge, one that construes the church as itself the nar-rative embodiment of the kingdom and another that construes the church on a journey toward the kingdom. While this might seem overly nuanced, the distinction plays out in practice. Of course, the two sets of practices that Hauerwas's two narrative logics respectively generate do not necessarily stand at odds with each other. Practices of togetherness that form an indi-vidual for the community (e.g., worship, liturgy, imitation) and practices of togetherness that form the community for the journey (e.g., patient dis-course and linguistic nonviolence) are both integral to the church for her-meneutical space. Hauerwas's bidirectional account of scriptural formation, in and of itself, is not the problem. Problems do arise, however, when the logic of the former displaces the logic of the latter. We certainly indwell the story of the church, but this becomes one-sided when the church itself be-comes the end of the story.

I suggest that Hauerwas's tendency at times to drift toward ecclesio-centrism derives from an underlying christological tendency. He tends, at times, to construe the community strictly in terms of Jesus' ongoing story and not in terms of Jesus' ongoing life. For sure, his theology is rightly labeled christological. The problem is that his christological emphasis is often misplaced. He beautifully accounts for Jesus' narrative presence to the community, but lost in his vision is Christ's concrete and personal presence. This tendency becomes especially evident when he places the church "in a narrative relationship to Jesus and the Gospels, within a story that subsumes both."[66] This christological move nicely accents the significance of the church's story; the danger, however, is that the story about Jesus becomes more basic than Jesus himself.

Some critics have picked up on this. Nathan Kerr, for example, suggests that Hauerwas offers a "community-dependent understanding of Jesus' person" that underplays Jesus' ongoing independence.[67] He goes on to argue that for Hauerwas the church thereby inflates to become the subject and agent of the ongoing Jesus-story.[68] According to this logic, Jesus exerts salvific influence as a character from history, as the one who performed the kingdom and thereby opened the way for his followers to perform it as well. Though there is certainly some truth in this narrative depiction of Jesus' significance, it lacks something of his particularity and concreteness, his freedom to act in history apart from the church.[69] Hauerwas accomplishes by reference to story what should be accomplished by reference to the resurrection and ascension. Or, perhaps more precisely, in Hauerwas's work the resurrection becomes a key feature of Jesus' first-century identity but not of his ongoing identity as a singular agent. Thus, Hauerwas struggles to uphold the sense in which the church is the creature of the Word. He can claim that Christ created the church but struggles to say that Christ still does.

Healy helpfully highlights this tendency: "As a result of this sharp turn to the church, Jesus becomes of interest more as an exemplar and guide for us than for who he is as himself."[70] The christological weakness evident at times in Hauerwas is not that Jesus is the church, as in Jenson, but that he

---

[66]Hauerwas, *Wilderness Wanderings*, 192; here quoting John Milbank, *Theology and Social Theory: Beyond Secular Reason* (Malden, MA: Blackwell, 1990), 387.

[67]Nathan R. Kerr, *Christ, History and Apocalyptic: The Politics of Christian Mission* (Eugene, OR: Cascade, 2008), 93.

[68]Kerr, *Christ, History and Apocalyptic*, 106.

[69]On this depiction of Jesus, see Rowan Williams, "Between the Cherubim: The Empty Tomb and the Empty Throne," in *On Christian Theology* (Malden MA: Blackwell, 2000), 183-96.

[70]Healy, *Hauerwas*, 70.

remains merely a historical figure lying behind it. Webster puts his finger on this issue when he names Albrecht Ritschl as Hauerwas's theological progenitor. Webster contends that Ritschl's "conviction that Christian faith is principally a mode of active moral community [is] not far from much that may be found in Hauerwas' corpus."[71] More pointedly, Webster suggests that Hauerwas's theology is plagued by a lingering sense of "moral immanentism." While Webster may overstate the issue (I have considered already how Hauerwas can also speak of a reality that transcends the community), this notion of moral immanentism alerts us to the possible "hermeneutical immanentism" that corresponds to an overrealized ecclesiology.

This further helps us grasp the sense in which a more robust account of the resurrection and ascension would counter the tendency toward an over-realized hermeneutic. Difficulties arise, in other words, when we load the hermeneutical burden on the story-formed community and not on the living subject of the story who forms the community. Hauerwas readily admits that the church is "formed by a savior who *was* . . . always on the move"[72]; a stronger emphasis on the resurrection would allow him to account for a Savior who still *is*. This would subsequently require him to locate hermeneutical practices of togetherness more consistently in relation to the ongoing journey of following after Jesus and thus to articulate hermeneutical practices that focus on the risen One rather than merely on the resources immanent to the community.

Even if Hauerwas lacks the concrete christological vision I am pressing for in this project, his tendency at times to articulate practices of togetherness in terms of the journey metaphor leaves theoretical space for it within his larger body of work. His account of the church's narrative as a journey marked by conflict and growth would carry more force and coherence if framed within a particularist and singular account of the resurrection. This would hold together his multifaceted account of formation and togetherness, and it would prevent him from lapsing into an overrealized hermeneutic. This is precisely where Bonhoeffer can again come to our aid.

---

[71]John Webster, "Ecclesiocentrism," *First Things*, October 2014, 55. Also see Healy, *Hauerwas*, 71n36.
[72]Hauerwas, *Peaceable Kingdom*, 102, emphasis added.

6

Reading as Christ's People

HAUERWAS AND BONHOEFFER are natural conversation
partners. Indeed, Hauerwas acknowledges his intellectual debt to Bonhoeffer. The account of faith's visibility that emerges in *Discipleship* taught
Hauerwas that Christian life requires communal embodiment.[1] For both
theologians, the logic of togetherness lies near the heart of the gospel. Yet
granted these similarities in their accounts of discipleship, Bonhoeffer en-
riches our conversation by framing practices of togetherness in relation to
a concrete and particularist account of Jesus. Jesus is not merely a historical
influence, an exemplar, or the founder of a new community—he is the risen
Lord who remains personally present to his community.

---

[1]Hauerwas claims that reading Bonhoeffer's *Discipleship* prepared him for Yoder's *The Politics of Jesus*; see Stanley Hauerwas, *Performing the Faith: Bonhoeffer and the Practice of Nonviolence* (London: SPCK, 2004), 35. Also see Hauerwas's essay, "Dietrich Bonhoeffer," in *The Blackwell Com-
panion to Political Theology*, ed. Peter Scott and William T. Cavanaugh (Malden, MA: Blackwell,
2004), 136-49. Hauerwas does not explicitly write about Bonhoeffer until the 2000s, but when
he does, he calls it an acknowledgment of a debt long overdue. He claims that he felt prohibited
from writing about Bonhoeffer earlier in his career due to Bonhoeffer's early reception in English
language theology as a death-of-God theologian; see Hauerwas, "Dietrich Bonhoeffer's Political
Theology" and "Bonhoeffer on Truth and Politics," in *Performing the Faith: Bonhoeffer and the
Practice of Nonviolence* (London: SPCK, 2004), 33-54, 55-73. Recent attempts to read Bonhoeffer
as a virtue ethicist suggest that the similarities run even deeper; see Jennifer Moberly, *The Virtue
of Bonhoeffer's Ethics: A Study of Bonhoeffer's* Ethics *in Relation to Virtue Ethics* (Eugene, OR: Pickwick, 2013). Though there are undoubtedly points of resonance between Bonhoeffer and the
virtue tradition, in my estimation the virtue tradition, per se, does not capture the full force of
Bonhoeffer's christological imagination. For a recent theological comparison of Bonhoeffer and
Hauerwas, see Robert J. Dean, *For the Life of the World: Jesus Christ and the Church in the Theologies
of Dietrich Bonhoeffer and Stanley Hauerwas* (Eugene, OR: Pickwick, 2016).

My goal in this chapter, therefore, is to demonstrate how Bonhoeffer's account of Christ's singularity shapes his understanding of communal practices. Bodily acts of togetherness are integral to the process of sustaining the church's narrative embodiment of Christ's story, as Hauerwas shows. Yet such practices also sustain ongoing openness to Christ himself. If Hauerwas shows how the historical institution requires communal embodiment, Bonhoeffer does the same with *creatura verbi*. If the risen One is an agent who speaks to the church, then practices of togetherness are hermeneutically necessary, for they form a community fit to hear his Word. I argue below that this theory takes shape at Finkenwalde. Bonhoeffer's experiment in common life and education stands as a lived attempt at communal faithfulness to the risen Christ—and precisely as such it is a uniquely hermeneutical endeavor.

Creatura Verbi, Sociality, and Hermeneutics

A social account of Christology emerges early in Bonhoeffer's academic career. As a student, his theological imagination was taken with the task of showing how idealism undermines genuine community.[2] In his dissertations he offers what Charles Marsh calls a post-Kantian account of selfhood.[3] Jesus, not the self, is the center of all relationships, the one who mediates between the self and others. Therefore, Bonhoeffer boldly contends that only theology can answer the philosophical problem of selfhood, and only the church can offer genuine sociality.

Bonhoeffer's reasoning remains distinctly christological. Given Christ's unique identity, community is a necessary corollary of his presence. Jesus is indeed an irreducibly singular and utterly unique figure—but Scripture never depicts his identity in isolation from his relationships.[4] His followers

---

[2]Bonhoeffer, *Sanctorum Communio: A Theological Study of the Sociology of the Church*, DBWE 1:45-54.

[3]Charles Marsh, *Reclaiming Dietrich Bonhoeffer: The Promise of His Theology* (Oxford: Oxford University Press, 1994), vii.

[4]Of course, it is not unusual for Christian theology to understand Jesus as "God acting alone" in the sense that Jesus himself, not the community, hangs on the cross and goes to the grave. Yet I would suggest that the Gospel narratives prevent us from imagining Jesus in isolation, quarantined from his relationships. Jesus' identity is always enacted and defined in relationship with others. His solitude on the cross is so stark and shocking precisely because we have come to situate his identity in inextricable relationship with the disciples who have abandoned him.

are integral, not accidental, to his being.[5] Thus, as Bonhoeffer famously puts it, Christ is always "Christ existing as community." This means that in Christ there are no self-contained identities. The encounter with Christ displaces the ego that once blocked the way to others. Through Christ, the *cor curvum in se* is burst open, creating the possibility of genuine togetherness.[6] Christ's revelatory presence creates authentic community where before there was only a conglomeration of individuals. Where there was once separation and discord, salvation creates intimacy and union.

Bonhoeffer's early sociological analysis becomes concrete as he learns to explicate the logic of Christ and community in terms of discipleship. Discipleship, on this account, is nothing less than embodied and enacted Christology. "The bond between Jesus and the disciples who followed him was a bodily bond. . . . A prophet and teacher would not need followers, but only students and listeners. But the incarnate Son of God who took on human flesh does need a community of followers."[7] Consequently, Bonhoeffer claims that whereas one enters into relationship with an idea by means of knowledge, one enters into relationship with an incarnate Lord by means of discipleship. "Because Christ exists, he must be followed."[8]

This helps us more fully understand the *creatura verbi*. Christ's address does not merely convey data; it creates togetherness. It forges connections that would not exist apart from the miracle of his presence. The Christ who constitutes the church by his address and the Christ whose faithfulness throughout history grounds the church's institutional structures is the same Christ who brings bodies into proximity.

This means that within the church, proximity is a christological possibility. Because "the Son of God appeared on earth in the body for our sake and was raised in the body," Bonhoeffer claims, "the believer praises [God]

---

[5]The notion that Jesus' calling and commissioning of his disciples is ingredient in his identity comes from David E. Demson, *Hans Frei & Karl Barth: Different Ways of Reading Scripture* (Grand Rapids, MI: Eerdmans, 1997).

[6]Bonhoeffer, *Act and Being*, DBWE 2:119.

[7]Bonhoeffer, *Discipleship*, DBWE 4:215.

[8]Bonhoeffer, *Discipleship*, DBWE 4:59. For sure, the New Testament word *disciple* (*mathētēs*) carries a didactic dimension in the sense that a disciple is a pupil or a student. Yet as used in the Gospels, the word means more than that. It is telling that the Gospels consistently depict the act of genuine learning within the space of following. In a very real sense the following is the learning. Traditionally didactic elements are obviously an important component of this, but they compose one part of a more holistic learning process.

for the bodily presence of the other Christian." He goes so far as to claim that "the nearness of a fellow Christian [is] a physical sign of the gracious presence of the Triune God."[9] It is hard to imagine greater praise for bodily togetherness. This sentiment not only displays the heart of Bonhoeffer's social Christology, it also provides the foundation for his communal experiment at Finkenwalde. The logic of Christian community is predicated upon the conviction that God's grace takes bodily form as the physical presence of others. Bodies moved by grace into community become a source of grace to each other.

This grace carries epistemological consequences. It changes not only what we know but how we know. Sarah Coakley has something like this in mind when she engages in the bold task of exploring the epistemic conditions necessary for discerning Jesus. She speaks of a "transformation of the believer's actual epistemic apparatus" and a "deepened spiritual perception"[10] that the believer develops over time. In contrast to theories that view revelation as a timeless moment of intuition, Coakley suggests that this transformed epistemic apparatus results from a lifetime of practice, purgation, and prayer. Transformative grace must be enacted through what she calls the church's "epistemological program."[11] Hermeneutical implications follow close behind, for this epistemic apparatus functions as what others have called the "eyes of faith" necessary to read Scripture rightly.[12]

Much more could be said about Coakley's understanding of the church's epistemological program and the hermeneutical implications that follow

---

[9]Bonhoeffer, *Life Together and Prayerbook of the Bible*, DBWE 5:29.

[10]Sarah Coakley, *Powers and Submissions: Spirituality, Philosophy and Gender* (Malden, MA: Blackwell, 2002), 130-31.

[11]Coakley, *Powers and Submissions*, 139.

[12]See Richard B. Hays, "Reading Scripture in Light of the Resurrection," in *The Art of Reading Scripture*, ed. Ellen F. Davis and Richard B. Hays (Grand Rapids, MI: Eerdmans, 2003), 235: "Reading Scripture in light of the resurrection produces an epistemological transformation of the readers. . . . The resurrection produces a 'conversion of the imagination' that causes us to understand everything else differently." While Hays speaks of epistemological transformation, he sometimes equates this with the mere addition of new knowledge (i.e., of the resurrection) that subsequently reframes previously held knowledge. It is not clear that he has in mind a new mode or style of knowing, e.g., the way Coakley does. Webster appears closer to Coakley when he claims that "[Scripture] can only be so read by those in whom a certain change has been wrought." John Webster, "'In the Shadow of Biblical Work': Barth and Bonhoeffer on Reading the Bible," *Toronto Journal of Theology* 17, no. 1 (2001): 81.

from it. I briefly reference her work here because it helpfully frames Bonhoeffer's communal experiment. He would agree that the church has an epistemological program. A mode of knowing suitable to revelation does not just magically appear. It requires something from the knowers. Bonhoeffer would deepen Coakley's analysis by suggesting that the practice of community is itself this program. Or to put the matter a bit differently, the change in one's epistemological apparatus is the change in one's social location. Bonhoeffer's social account of Christ reminds us that our mode of knowing God and our mode of relating to others are inseparably related. By inverting the *cor curvum in se*, Christ's address opens up new possibilities for both. Turned outward toward God and others, we recognize that our proximity to other bodies is a sign of our nearness to Christ himself. In making this claim I continue to assert that revelation is a gift. Christ himself creates the conditions by which his Word is received. But Bonhoeffer's social vision invites us to imagine that the Spirit's act of drawing bodies into community with Christ is itself this condition.

Epistemological change, then, is a gift of grace, and precisely as such it cannot be reduced to a mystical event. Given the unique identity of this grace and the nature of its arrival, its presence necessarily coincides with the emergence of a community. Early in his career Bonhoeffer argued that "the church of Jesus Christ that is actualized by the Holy Spirit is really the church here and now."[13] I suggest that the practices of togetherness that constitute the community at Finkenwalde represent the concrete form of this Spirit-enabled actualization. What was largely a matter of theory in his dissertations becomes a matter of communal practices, an embodied form of life. His Finkenwalde experiment, I therefore contend, should be read as the concrete enactment of "Christ existing as community." As such, it also represents a concrete "answer" to his early epistemological questions. Indeed, revelation "must yield an epistemology of his own," as Bonhoeffer theorizes as a student. By the time he got to Finkenwalde he more clearly recognized that this epistemology is inseparable from the formation of community.[14]

---

[13]Bonhoeffer, *Sanctorum Communio*, DBWE 1:208.
[14]On this, see Derek W. Taylor, "What's This Book Actually About?: *Life Together* and the Possibility of Theological Knowledge," *The Bonhoeffer Legacy*, 6, no 1 (2020).

Finkenwalde: The Formation of an Addressable Community

In the face of the Nazification of the church in Germany, the Dahlem Synod of October 1934 sought to provide institutional distinction and clarity for the newly emerging Confessing Church. Toward this end, it established five independent Confessing seminaries, one of which came to be located in Finkenwalde and fell under Bonhoeffer's leadership.

At that time in Germany, church seminaries often supplemented university education by providing practical instruction and preparation for ordination. As a student, Bonhoeffer's academic elitism led him to look down upon the practical training such seminaries provided.[15] His enthusiasm toward the prospect of leading the Finkenwalde community thus comes as something of a surprise, and it highlights his spiritual and theological development during the early 1930s.

A "different kind of training." Indeed, the years immediately preceding Finkenwalde evidence a marked shift in his Christian faith. Perhaps most shockingly, he came to question the value of academic theological education. "I no longer believe in the university," he wrote to a friend; "in fact I never really have believed in it."[16] Yet he still believes in the task of education. As he expresses in another letter, his loss of confidence in the academy presents one particular challenge: "It's just that I am concerned about the students." Acknowledging the impasse between a defunct form of theological education and the ongoing need to form students for pastoral ministry, he held out hope—"Perhaps other ways will be open to me."[17]

In Bonhoeffer's mind, the confessing seminary at Finkenwalde was precisely this "other way," an opportunity to overcome the education-training dichotomy that characterized theological education in the German academy. Bonhoeffer refers to it as a chance to blaze a new trail by combining scholarly and practical work.[18] In a letter to Barth he refers to it as

---

[15]See H. Gaylon Barker, "Editor's Introduction to the English Edition," in *Theological Education at Finkenwalde: 1935–1937*, DBWE 14:1-2.

[16]Bonhoeffer, *London: 1933–1935*, DBWE 13:217.

[17]Eberhard Bethge, *Dietrich Bonhoeffer: A Biography*, rev. ed., ed. Victoria J. Barnett, trans. Eric Mosbacher et al. (Minneapolis: Fortress, 2000), 410; cf. Bonhoeffer, *London*, DBWE 13:152.

[18]Bonhoeffer, *Theological Education at Finkenwalde*, DBWE 14:253.

a "completely different kind of training."[19] Discipleship was, after all, more than an intellectual exercise, so training in Christian faithfulness must be a holistic endeavor, the formation of a way of life, an education of body, mind, and heart.

Importantly for the hermeneutical argument I am making in this chapter, Bonhoeffer's move away from the academy corresponds with his fresh discovery of the Bible. He recounts in a letter to a friend that the "extremely un-Christian" ambition that characterized his early academic pursuits was disrupted when he came to the Bible "for the first time."[20] This encounter with Scripture entailed more than a simple admiration for the stories and ideas expressed therein; it involved, as he writes, the conviction "that God is speaking to us in the Bible."[21]

Bonhoeffer structured his educational experiment at Finkenwalde as the corollary of this claim. Finkenwalde was for Bonhoeffer a lived attempt at developing the ears to hear appropriate to God's revelatory speech. This was a highly spiritual endeavor. Yet Bonhoeffer recognized that the Spirit is bound to the words of Scripture.[22] He was therefore alert to the deeply hermeneutical nature of this task. In an age when competing spirits were vying for influence in the church, he perceived that Christian faithfulness requires fresh attention to Scripture and the formation of a posture of attentiveness to Christ's word in and through it.[23]

Accordingly, when he attempts to summarize the essential purpose of this new community, Bonhoeffer consistently focuses on the task of hermeneutical faithfulness. "Our main concern," he writes, "is that the Bible be read and prayed again" in churches.[24] This is a pressing task, for students are "empty . . . with regard to familiarity with the Bible."[25] They are approaching the task of ministry with new questions: "How can I learn to pray? How can I learn to read Scripture?"[26] In a letter to Barth he claimed that his guiding purpose at Finkenwalde was to help students

---

[19]Bonhoeffer, *Theological Education at Finkenwalde*, DBWE 14:134.
[20]Bonhoeffer, *Theological Education at Finkenwalde*, DBWE 14:134.
[21]Bonhoeffer, *Theological Education at Finkenwalde*, DBWE 14:167.
[22]Bonhoeffer, *Theological Education at Finkenwalde*, DBWE 14:133.
[23]Bonhoeffer, *Theological Education at Finkenwalde*, DBWE 14:59-60.
[24]Bonhoeffer, *Theological Education at Finkenwalde*, DBWE 14:271.
[25]Bonhoeffer, *Theological Education at Finkenwalde*, DBWE 14:253; also see 14:278.
[26]Bonhoeffer, *Theological Education at Finkenwalde*, DBWE 14:254.

learn to pray and read the Bible—"Either we can help them do this, or we can't help them at all."[27]

It therefore comes as no surprise when Bonhoeffer frankly admits that Scripture "stands at the center of our work"[28] and that "the candidate [in the seminary] will seek constant contact with the Holy Scriptures."[29] "Rather than ritual, it will be the word of the Bible itself and prayer that will guide them through the day."[30]

Given Bonhoeffer's stated convictions, it is not a stretch to claim that his experiment in education and communal living was a sustained attempt at training in hermeneutical faithfulness. And given his commitments regarding the nature of discipleship and the bodiliness of Christian faithfulness, it is no accident that he located hermeneutical training within the context of communal life.

Interpretation as a social practice. The communal nature of interpretive faithfulness is one of the most underappreciated dimensions of Bonhoeffer's scriptural hermeneutic. While scholars have focused on his actual methods for handling the text and his theological construal of God's action in the hermeneutical process, they have directed sparse attention to the essentially social nature of theological interpretation in his thought.[31] The reason for this, perhaps, is that the communal nature of hermeneutics is more evident in his practice than in his theory. Moreover, Bonhoeffer himself admits that hermeneutics was something he did and not something he theorized.[32] I suggest, however, that when we consider what Finkenwalde was all about,

---

[27]Bonhoeffer, *Theological Education at Finkenwalde*, DBWE 14:253-54.

[28]Bonhoeffer, *Theological Education at Finkenwalde*, DBWE 14:111.

[29]Bonhoeffer, *Theological Education at Finkenwalde*, DBWE 14:172.

[30]Bonhoeffer, *Theological Education at Finkenwalde*, DBWE 14:97. For other similar statements, see 14:196, 217.

[31]The significant exception is Stephen E. Fowl and L. Gregory Jones, *Reading in Communion: Scripture and Ethics in Christian Life* (Grand Rapids, MI: Eerdmans, 1991).

[32]It appears that hermeneutical questions were at the forefront of Bonhoeffer's mind during his time at Finkenwalde, even if he was unable to pursue them formally; see Bonhoeffer, *Theological Education at Finkenwalde*, DBWE 14:273: "I am hoping to finish my book during the course of this semester [i.e., *Discipleship*], after which I would really like to try my hand at a book on hermeneutics. There seems to me to be a very great gap here." It seems that Bonhoeffer abandoned this plan in order to take up the issues he pursues in *Ethics*, which presumably appeared more pressing due to political circumstances. One could argue that his initial interest in hermeneutics lies behind his turn toward the "non-religious interpretation of biblical concepts" in prison.

and when we attend to the actual practices Bonhoeffer prescribed to reach this end, it becomes evident that in his mind practices of togetherness are integral to faithful reading.

Here the logic of Christ's singularity continues to structure Bonhoeffer's thought. Hermeneutical practices of togetherness are necessary precisely because Christ is risen and verbally active. Because Christ speaks, communities must learn to listen. While Bonhoeffer expects this word from Christ to be direct, even personal, he never pretends that it would be easily discerned, as if hearing Christ were a mystical moment of lucidity. Rather than a mystical encounter, Christ's speech requires the careful communal work of discovery and discernment. To borrow a phrase from J. Louis Martyn, Bonhoeffer's communal efforts at Finkenwalde aim to facilitate the formation of an "addressable community."[33] According to Martyn, God's grace changes the nature of human agency; though the community obviously consists of individual agents, when called by Christ it becomes an agent itself.[34] Drawn together by the Spirit, this corporate agent becomes fit for God's address, an addressable community. Importantly, this addressability, precisely as communal reality, must be enacted, which is why hermeneutics is a social practice.

A straightforward conviction animates Bonhoeffer's vision at this point: "God puts his word in the mouth of other Christians." He goes on to claim,

> [Christians] watch for this Word wherever they can. . . . It has come and comes daily and anew in the Word of Jesus Christ. . . . But God put this Word into the mouth of human beings so that it may be passed on to others. . . . God has willed that we should seek and find God's living Word in the testimony of other Christians. . . . Therefore, Christians need other Christians who speak God's Word to them.[35]

Importantly, priority continues to rest with the verbal Christ. As Bonhoeffer puts it, the Word of God encountered in Scripture possesses its own inherent movement toward concretion.[36] When one attempts to speak about

---

[33]J. Louis Martyn, *Theological Issues in the Letters of Paul* (Nashville: Abingdon, 1997), 264; and idem, *Galatians*, Anchor Bible 33A (New York: Doubleday, 1997), 535.

[34]See 1 Cor 2:9-16; 12:4-31. Also see J. Louis Martyn, "Epilogue: An Essay in Pauline Meta-Ethics," in *Divine and Human Agency in Paul and His Cultural Environment*, ed. John M. G. Barclay and Simon J. Gathercole (London: T&T Clark, 2008), 173-83.

[35]Bonhoeffer, *Life Together and Prayerbook of the Bible*, DBWE 5:32.

[36]Bonhoeffer, *Theological Education at Finkenwalde*, DBWE 14:511.

the Word of God in Scripture, one is simply attempting to make audible Scripture's own inherent impulse.[37] Put differently, Bonhoeffer believes that God's Word carries an inner compulsion toward sociality—when a word strikes home to the individual, it simultaneously presses to be spoken. Willie Jennings puts it well when he suggests that "the reading and the interpretation of holy word must always bend toward the community, and it must ultimately issue in a joining."[38] This is so because of the identity of the word. Precisely because it is Christ's word, it possesses communal momentum. Thus there exists an integral theological connection between reading the word and letting that word come to speech in the present. Without the latter, Scripture remains abstract and lifeless. Bonhoeffer normally refers to this process by which the word comes to speech as preaching or proclamation. "The word moves on its own initiative; it rises from the Bible and assumes the form of a sermon on its own."[39]

For Bonhoeffer, then, the logic of proclamation is the logic of encountering Christ's word in Scripture through the mediation of others. Proclamation is whatever happens when God's word in Scripture becomes concrete here and now. The word of Christ is "a free word from person to person, not the word bound to a particular pastoral office."[40] This means that not everything that comes from the pulpit on Sunday morning counts as proclamation, and that not all proclamation comes from the pulpit (even if Christians can hope and pray that the pulpit becomes its central avenue). The notion of proclamation is fundamental to Bonhoeffer's theology, not primarily because he believed in the power of liturgy—as if the sermon's liturgical location gives it substance and meaning—but because he believed in Christ's presence. Christ's word to us in Scripture, precisely because of his unique identity, must break out into the social and interpersonal realm. It must become concrete in community, and the primary way this happens is when Christians proclaim the message of Scripture to each other.

For Bonhoeffer, therefore, hearing God's word in Scripture and hearing others within the church are mutually reciprocating events. To have one

---

[37]Bonhoeffer, *Theological Education at Finkenwalde*, DBWE 14:504.
[38]Willie James Jennings, *Acts*, Belief: A Theological Commentary on the Bible (Louisville, KY: Westminster John Knox, 2017), 82.
[39]Bonhoeffer, *Theological Education at Finkenwalde*, DBWE 14:511.
[40]Bonhoeffer, *Life Together and Prayerbook of the Bible*, DBWE 5:103.

without the other is to compromise the logic of the church as a space for receiving Christ's address. This is why the process of gathering and sustaining communicative fellowship with others is integral to the logic of revelation. Indeed, it is precisely the otherness of community members that makes concrete the otherness of God's address. The Christocentrism that de-centers the interpretive subject takes corporate shape through the alterity of those within the community.

While this conviction is most evident at Finkenwalde, it emerged earlier in his career as well. It is no coincidence that Bonhoeffer's famous petition for Christians to read "against ourselves" occurs within the context of an ecumenical conference. Within a gathering like this, the difference inherent to the universal church becomes especially pronounced. Precisely through this difference Scripture stands "against" the church and can be heard as an alien word.[41] The de-centering involved in gathering with others around Christ forges, at least in part, the leverage by which Scripture challenges and changes its readers, and in this it functions as the concrete corollary of Christ's own de-centering presence. Here lies the value of diverse hermeneutical communities. If we control or manipulate the identities of those with whom we engage in the hermeneutical process, it is a safe bet that interpretive outcomes will be amenable to our preconceived sensibilities. In this, the threat of a divine *Doppelgänger* continues to lurk. But if it is really Christ's call that constitutes the church, then individual members will find themselves bumping shoulders with those diverse others who have similarly responded to the call by following after Jesus. As disciples, we do not control the identity of fellow disciples—and thus we do not exert control over the word of address that God mediates through them.

It therefore comes as no surprise that much of Bonhoeffer's own theological development is attributable to God's grace confronting him through the diverse bodies with which he has shared space. Consider, as perhaps the leading example, his participation in the Abyssinian Baptist Church in Harlem. Bonhoeffer's involvement with this community expanded his theological imagination in key ways; it taught him to recognize Jesus' active and personal presence, to affirm a theology of vicarious solidarity with the

---

[41]Bonhoeffer, *Ecumenical, Academic, and Pastoral Work: 1931–1932*, DBWE 11:378.

oppressed, and to develop a concrete account of the *theologia crucis*.[42] Other examples abound. His pacifism arose through friendship with Jean Lasserre, a French theologian he met in the United States. His experiences in Rome as a student first awakened him to the beauty of the universal church that was often muted in German Lutheranism. His communal experiment at Finkenwalde was largely based on Anglican monasteries and free-church schools he experienced while in England. Bonhoeffer was so convinced that God's grace is encountered in others (even outside the church) that he famously contemplated spending time in India learning from Gandhi's example of communal life.[43] Bonhoeffer was convinced, in other words, that just as Jesus mediates others, others mediate Jesus. To borrow a phrase from Rowan Williams, other people are "where God happens."[44] To cast this in specifically hermeneutical terms, Scripture comes alive here and now as the Word becomes concrete through the mouth of another in a moment of proclamation.

PRACTICES OF TOGETHERNESS WITHIN THE *CREATURA VERBI*

The hermeneutical importance of bodies gathered plays out in several concrete ways for Bonhoeffer. If God wants people to speak God's word to each other, they must attend to the conditions by which this speaking can occur. Thus, Bonhoeffer places unusual significance on the literal act of verbalizing Scripture. If the human mouth is the medium of God's word, we must learn to speak the words of Scripture to one another in a manner appropriate to the task. Because the mouth is merely a medium, it should not become the object of focal attention. Consequently, Bonhoeffer argues that the public reading of Scripture should be "plain and simple," more focused on the subject matter than on rhetorical flourish.[45] He further contends that one should avoid "tendentious speaking," "logical and aesthetic tricks," and "flowery speech."[46] To read without simple humility is to divert attention to oneself instead of the word.[47]

---

[42]See, e.g., Reggie L. Williams, *Bonhoeffer's Black Jesus: Harlem Renaissance Theology and an Ethic of Resistance* (Waco, TX: Baylor University Press, 2014).

[43]Bethge, *Dietrich Bonhoeffer*, 408.

[44]Rowan Williams, *Where God Happens*.

[45]Bonhoeffer, *Life Together and Prayerbook of the Bible*, DBWE 5:64.

[46]Bonhoeffer, *Theological Education at Finkenwalde*, DBWE 14:503-4.

[47]Bonhoeffer, *Life Together and Prayerbook of the Bible*, DBWE 5:64.

In an oft-quoted line, he writes, "Proper reading of Scripture is not a technical exercise that can be learned; it is something that grows or diminishes according to my own spiritual condition."[48] Commentators commonly point to this as proof that Bonhoeffer operated with a properly theological hermeneutic. Of course, this is true. Yet it is startling to recognize that he is here referring to the literal act of vocalizing Scripture aloud in a communal gathering, not to the theoretical process of understanding the text. His concern is with the act of reading in the most concrete and basic sense. While he certainly recognizes the spiritual and theological dimensions of understanding, he is equally concerned with the logic of bodies gathered, with the way these bodies might mediate Jesus to each other, and hence with the various practices that facilitate this gathering and speaking.

While this line of thinking might seem conceptually unsophisticated, Bonhoeffer believed that the seemingly mundane practices entailed in shaping togetherness were integral to the process of forming an addressable community. For this reason, communal life at Finkenwalde was explicitly marked by an array of practices intended to facilitate physical proximity and promote camaraderie. For example, he insisted that students make intentional efforts to develop genuine friendships. As one community member recounts, he implemented the rule that "during the session every member of the community was to take at least one long walk with every other member."[49] He likewise insisted that students learn to play together. Although communal life was ultimately a christological endeavor, Bonhoeffer "regarded the inability to enjoy leisure time as a gap in student's education"[50] and "found virtue in spontaneity and play, regarding leisure as a means of soul craft."[51] He insisted that students learn to share meals together. The "gracious omnipresence" of Christ, he claimed "is actualized when Christians break bread in fellowship. . . . In a special way, the daily breaking of bread together binds Christians to their Lord and to one another."[52] Bonhoeffer accents the bodily dimensions of this sharing: "We share our bread. Thus we are firmly bound to one another not only in the

---

[48]Bonhoeffer, *Life Together and Prayerbook of the Bible*, DBWE 5:64.
[49]Quoted in Barker, "Editor's Introduction to the English Edition," DBWE 14:26.
[50]Bethge, *Dietrich Bonhoeffer*, 464.
[51]Charles Marsh, *Strange Glory: A Life of Dietrich Bonhoeffer* (New York: Knopf, 2014), 218.
[52]Bonhoeffer, *Life Together and Prayerbook of the Bible*, DBWE 5:73.

Spirit, but with our whole physical being."[53] He insisted that students learn to sing together, for singing creates unity in the Word.[54] "I can hardly imagine our life together here without daily music making."[55] He insisted that the community engage in acts of hospitality. "We must be ready to allow ourselves to be interrupted by God, who will thwart our plans and frustrate our ways time and again, even daily, by sending people across our path with their demands and requests."[56] Practically, this played out in the community's active willingness to host retreats and accommodate large groups of guests.[57] As one former member recounts, one of the reasons for choosing their location at Finkenwalde was its many rooms and its conduciveness to acts of hospitality.[58]

Other practices at Finkenwalde were more obviously theological, yet equally concrete in their ability to form and sustain communal life. Bonhoeffer insisted, for example, on the practice of the personal confession of sin, for "in confession there takes place a *breakthrough to community*."[59] He insisted that students learn to pray for each other. This act would create genuine togetherness, he claimed, for "I can no longer condemn or hate other Christians for whom I pray."[60] He insisted that students learn to serve each other, for mutual service would hinder the natural drive toward self-assertion and break down walls of separation.[61] In all of this, he was perhaps most concerned to train his students in the art of conversation, at the heart of which lies linguistic patience—the ability to listen to others with genuine attentiveness—recognizing that on the day of judgment one will have to give an account for every wasted word (cf. Mt 12:36). "The *first* service one owes to others in the community," he claimed, "involves listening to them. Just as our love for God begins with listening to God's Word, the beginning of love for other Christians is learning to listen to them."[62]

---

[53]Bonhoeffer, *Life Together and Prayerbook of the Bible*, DBWE 5:73.

[54]Bonhoeffer, *Life Together and Prayerbook of the Bible*, DBWE 5:67.

[55]Bonhoeffer, *Theological Education at Finkenwalde*, DBWE 14:279.

[56]Bonhoeffer, *Life Together and Prayerbook of the Bible*, DBWE 5:99.

[57]Bonhoeffer, *Theological Education at Finkenwalde*, DBWE 14:89, 94.

[58]Bethge, *Dietrich Bonhoeffer*, 433.

[59]Bonhoeffer, *Life Together and Prayerbook of the Bible*, DBWE 5:110.

[60]Bonhoeffer, *Life Together and Prayerbook of the Bible*, DBWE 5:90.

[61]Bonhoeffer, *Life Together and Prayerbook of the Bible*, DBWE 5:94.

[62]Bonhoeffer, *Life Together and Prayerbook of the Bible*, DBWE 5:98.

In order to curtail linguistic waste, one must learn to cultivate the art of silence. Within a community created by Christ's address, silence is more basic than speech. "The Word comes not to the noise-makers but to those who are silent," Bonhoeffer suggests.[63] As Marsh notes, here explicating the logic of Bonhoeffer's communal experiment, "Holy silence reawakens and refreshes, making strange once more the mystery of the Word."[64] This posture of silence and the art of listening it produces are especially relevant to the preached word. For Bonhoeffer, the task of listening to sermons is a skill that one must deliberately cultivate. As Bethge recounts, even the practice sermons students wrote for preaching class "were treated in all seriousness as the expression of the true and living voice of Christ. Nothing, insisted Bonhoeffer, is more concrete than the real voice of Christ speaking in the sermon."[65] The sermon "was to be listened to in all humility, not analyzed."[66] As one student recounts, "Nothing was as chastening as Bonhoeffer's own method of listening to sermons. . . . Homiletics began with the most difficult lesson of all—one's own listening to sermons."[67]

Upon a foundation of silence and listening, true dialogue becomes possible. In the previous chapter, I noted Hauerwas's similar account of patience and nonviolent hermeneutical discourse. Here Bonhoeffer adds a christological dimension to this notion. If Christ mediates relationships, then entrance into his community neither dissolves one's individuality into a monochromatic mass nor establishes atomistic structures of conflict.[68] With Christ, community entails neither bland homogeneity nor the contractual binding of independent egos. This tensional unity-in-distinction funds a

---

[63]Bonhoeffer, *Life Together and Prayerbook of the Bible*, DBWE 5:84.
[64]Marsh, *Strange Glory*, 239.
[65]Bethge, *Dietrich Bonhoeffer*, 441-42.
[66]Bethge, *Dietrich Bonhoeffer*, 442.
[67]Bethge, *Dietrich Bonhoeffer*, 442.
[68]The structure of daily life sustains the dialectic between individual and community. Bonhoeffer encouraged individual members of the community to spend time alone, yet even this practice was bracketed by the community, for the individual always moves from time alone to time with others. Bonhoeffer obviously recognized that Christians can and at times should read the Bible as solitary individuals. But he could never imagine the notion of an essentially private reading. An individual, even when physically alone, always exists in differentiated unity with the community. Even the practice of silent meditation, an important spiritual discipline at Finkenwalde, had a communal dimension, for individuals mediated on a shared text, communally reflected on their experiences, and occasionally meditated in pairs or larger groups (see Bonhoeffer, *Theological Education at Finkenwalde*, DBWE 14:933-35).

distinct set of language practices. The communal struggle for truth is not a game of competition or manipulation nor a veneer hiding a contest of agendas jostling for advantage. Through the togetherness that Christ's on-going life creates, communal dialogue can occur without devolving into competition (the linguistic corollary of individualism) or the glib rein-forcement of groupthink (the linguistic corollary of collectivism).

Such linguistic activity requires practice, which is why, as Bethge recounts, "One evening a week was devoted to discussion of current issues."[69] These open-ended discussions often involved contentious issues and thereby func-tioned as training in a form of dialogue that would concretely instantiate the posture of listening and receptivity inherent to the church as the *creatura verbi*. For Bonhoeffer, to put the matter simply, the process of living in at-tentive orientation to Christ requires intensive dialogue and discernment. The social and conversational skills that sustain life together constitute, at least in part, the "ears to hear" appropriate to Christ's ongoing reign.

These practices can at times seem awkwardly intimate, perhaps even idealistic. But Bonhoeffer was searching for the social conditions nec-essary for "speaking the truth in love" (Eph 4:15). His point was not that such speech should become easy. Naming sin and falsehood never is. But communities that seek to follow Christ should strive to foster the social conditions by which such naming can occur, by which the word of a sister or brother can be heard as the word of Christ himself. Taken to-gether, these practices illustrate Bonhoeffer's larger desire to form a com-munity fit to live in attentive orientation to Christ and bear his address. Practices of togetherness, therefore, are not ancillary to the hermeneu-tical process but are essential to the task of hearing Christ in and through the text.

In this, Bonhoeffer shows how a theory of revelation remains abstract without a practical corollary. If Christ speaks, the community must listen, and this act of listening must be enacted and sustained by practices of togetherness. The receptivity of Christian life in relation to the risen Christ takes concrete form as receptivity to brothers and sisters. There is no turning to Christ without also turning to those in the community. The act

---

[69]Bethge, *Dietrich Bonhoeffer*, 430.

of gathering remains a receptive activity: we receive Christ's call and, sub-sequently, we receive brothers and sisters who likewise receive us.

By this I am not claiming that human works of community building are a prerequisite for receiving God's address, as if this social vision functions as a works-based hermeneutical righteousness in which communal virtues, in and of themselves, produce faithful interpretive outcomes. I continue to affirm that the gathering of bodies is, ultimately, Christ's work through the Spirit. "Eyes of faith" are always only a gift, the reception of which is an ongoing communal event.

ADJUDICATION IN THE CHURCH

This account of practices of togetherness and the communal discourse they enable draws us into a question that has been looming in the background until this point: How does the church deal with interpretive conflict? The obvious reality is that different readers handle the text differently and thus make differing proposals about which interpretive outcomes are most faithful to it. How do we discern the appropriateness of these claims?

Truth that conforms to reality. The hermeneutic of discipleship I have been sketching prevents us from settling such debates by means of a mere theory of textual meaning. To be sure, the Spirit fights only through the text of Scripture, as Bonhoeffer maintains.[70] Any supposedly private revelation must be brought into judgment by the text itself. Even so, final adjudication regarding the content of interpretive faithfulness cannot be settled on the basis of the text alone. The ground of interpretive faithfulness ultimately lies with Christ himself.

The theological rationale for this claim begins to emerge in the famous section in *Discipleship* where Bonhoeffer combats the prevalence of cheap grace. Here he is particularly concerned about those who twist Luther's true statements about grace and render them false by positing them in ab-straction from discipleship. "Grace as presupposition is grace at its cheapest; grace as a conclusion is costly grace. . . . It is the same word of the justifi-cation by grace alone, and yet false use of the same statement can lead to a complete destruction of its essence." He sums up this line of thinking: "That

---

[70]Bonhoeffer, *Theological Education at Finkenwalde*, DBWE 14:132.

means that knowledge cannot be separated from the existence in which it was acquired."[71] To be sure, this gets to the heart of Bonhoeffer's notion of discipleship, yet it also points toward a radical hermeneutical vision. He is suggesting that the same semantic claim can be either true or false, depending on the conditions of the situation in which it is spoken.[72]

In relation to a living Christ, the notion of truth takes on new dimensions. As Bonhoeffer claims in *Ethics*, truth "is the real itself . . . not the abstractly real that is separated from the reality of God, but the real that has its reality only in God."[73] Such reality, of course, is found in Christ, who alone is "the Real one" in whom "all reality is taken on and summed up."[74] Bonhoeffer here suggests that any claim to truth apart from Christ remains at best partial and abstract. In such a case, "the words are true, but they have no weight."[75] He suggests, in other words, that because the ultimate truthfulness of a statement derives from its relation to the real One, it cannot be reduced to a semantic formula. The truthfulness of a statement finally lies not in the words themselves or in their relationship to a certain historical or ideological referent but in the way they fit to Jesus. A true statement, a true doctrine, a true interpretation—all remain false when posited apart from the act of following the Lord. Indeed, any attempt to interpret Scripture apart from discipleship distorts Scripture itself. "Fundamentally eliminating simple obedience introduces a principle of scripture foreign to the Gospel. According to it, in order to understand scripture, one must first have a key to interpreting it. But that key would not be the living Christ himself in judgment and grace."[76] Bonhoeffer states the matter baldly: "The problem of following Christ shows itself here to be a hermeneutical problem."[77]

Bonhoeffer is aware that this line of thinking challenges conventional hermeneutical paradigms. He willingly complexifies the task of

---

[71]Bonhoeffer, *Discipleship*, DBWE 4:51.

[72]For this line of thinking, I owe a debt to J. Patrick Dunn, whose dissertation at Stellenbosch University picks up similar themes. See J. Patrick Dunn, "Prophets, Faust, and First-Years: Bonhoeffer and the Language of Charismatic Experience," *Stellenbosch Theological Journal*, 2, no. 2 (2016): 39-56; and idem, "'To Know the Real One': Christological Promeity in the Theology of Dietrich Bonhoeffer" (MTh thesis, Stellenbosch University, 2016).

[73]Bonhoeffer, *Ethics*, DBWE 6:50.

[74]Bonhoeffer, *Ethics*, DBWE 6:263.

[75]Bonhoeffer, *Ethics*, DBWE 6:371.

[76]Bonhoeffer, *Discipleship*, DBWE 4:82.

[77]Bonhoeffer, *Discipleship*, DBWE 4:82.

understanding Scripture. Speaking specifically of Matthew 5–7, he writes, "We have *heard* the Sermon on the Mount; perhaps we have *understood* it. But who has heard it *correctly*?"[78] Bonhoeffer wants us to see that in relation to the living Christ, the question of hermeneutical truth cannot be reduced to the question, What does this text mean? He would have us ask a more dynamic and concrete question: Which claims about the text have greater purchase on truth? Or, even more concretely: How do various readings open us to the truthful One? Consequently, what Bonhoeffer says about the pursuit of ethical decisions holds equally for the pursuit of hermeneutical decisions: "We can and should speak not about what the good is, can be, or should be for each and every time, but about how Christ may take form among us today and here."[79]

Bonhoeffer is suggesting, in other words, that the overarching question that drives Christian reading is, "Who is Jesus Christ for us today?" In pursuit of Christ, the church should ask of the text, How does it alert us to his ongoing call? Which claims about the text open us to his movement and allow us to witness to his ongoing work? In the wake of Christ, meaning is therefore not a calculable commodity or a fixed quantity. Proposals regarding the truthfulness of competing interpretive outcomes cannot be adjudicated vis-à-vis a static and empirically available yardstick (e.g., authorial intent, the literal sense, or a body of tradition). Even if an interpretation could be deemed semantically true in some empirically verifiable sense, it may nevertheless remain abstract. It may nevertheless fail to conform to reality. The point is not the words but the way they refer to Jesus—not an idea or doctrine about Jesus, but the living One himself. Meaning in this deeper sense is tantamount to active and embodied conformity to Christ. In this, Bonhoeffer presages later hermeneutical developments by implying that language cannot be abstracted from a way of being in the world. The problem he addresses in *Discipleship* is not simply that one's interpretation is correct while the application is wrong. He refuses to tease the two apart. Because our knowledge of God and the language we use to refer to God are bound up in a form of life in pursuit of God, the interpretation-application distinction carries little weight.

---

[78]Bonhoeffer, *Discipleship*, DBWE 4:181, emphasis added.
[79]Bonhoeffer, *Ethics*, DBWE 6:99.

The nature of interpretive decisions. Framing the issue in this way certainly does not solve the hermeneutical dilemma. In a sense, it only makes the matter more perplexing. But it does allow us to make a few claims regarding the nature of interpretive decisions. First, within the framework of discipleship, hermeneutical outcomes are not black and white—not simply right or wrong, good or bad. Just as with one's ongoing imitation of Jesus, readings are faithful to a greater or lesser degree. Indeed, by replacing the qualifier *good* with the qualifier *faithful*, we can more accurately depict what is happening in the hermeneutical process.

It follows, second, that when we locate the hermeneutical process within the framework of discipleship, concrete examples of "good interpretation" are not easily ascertained. Those within contemporary debates about theological interpretation have increasingly demanded examples, actual instantiations of good theological hermeneutics. But even this demand easily remains beholden to the logic of academic space, for the desired example, is almost always another written text. Yet if faithful reading is intimately entwined with Christ's ongoing movement and the community's ongoing participation in him, the object to be adjudicated becomes slippery, as elusive as Christ himself. Examples of interpretive faithfulness are utterly time bound and dated. We are reminded of Bonhoeffer's belief that although faithfulness is always visible, it is not empirically available. Objective methods of study that identify a stable and quantifiable object remain open to a rigorous and methodologically controlled process of policing. But a hermeneutic of discipleship requires us to sit loosely with such procedures.

Third, we thus admit that final adjudicatory certainty lies beyond our reach. Within the framework of discipleship, the hermeneutical process exists within an eschatological horizon. We are operating here with a hermeneutic en route. Between resurrection and parousia, our sight remains dim (cf., 1 Cor 13:12). For this reason, Bonhoeffer writes that "we cannot know with ultimate certainty" the extent to which "a human action serves the divine goal of history."[80] En route, we lack access to an unambiguous standard by which to make such claims. As he was well aware, Christ's address does not lend itself to critical scrutiny. At his most antihermeneutical,

---

[80]Bonhoeffer, *Ethics*, DBWE 6:227.

he even suggests that interpretation is inaction and thus disobedience.[81] By this he clearly does not mean that the process of discernment is unfaithful; he trained his students for just this task. It does mean, however, that even the act of interpretation, if severed from the act of following, is nothing but a sophisticated attempt to evade the force of the text. To map the criteria and methods that would equip one to lay hold of Christ's voice is to succumb again to humanity's original temptation to be *sicut deus*.[82] Following after Christ, we make interpretive judgments in a provisional and ongoing manner, for Christ remains on the move. To conclusively adjudicate an interpretation by means of method would be the hermeneutical equivalent of cheap grace, grace secured as a principle and not from the living One himself.

All of this makes the need for adjudication even more acutely evident. If carelessly handled, a hermeneutic of discipleship risks opening the door to interpretive anarchy. To resist stable and determinate accounts of textual meaning is not tantamount to saying that anything goes. Even with the above qualifications in place, it nevertheless remains the case that some renditions of the text conform to Christ more closely than others and that the church must reject faithless readings. So this again raises the question: To what extent can we make judgments about various renditions of the text, and how might we go about coming to such conclusions? While we should insist on the value of a wide variety of interpretive outcomes, we can make a few claims that frame the task of hermeneutical judgment and prevent it from spilling over into chaos.

Making interpretive judgments. First, and perhaps most obviously, is the foundation of discipleship itself. The most basic thing to say about the task of adjudicating interpretive conflict is that claims to truth should arise from a form of life that takes shape in Jesus' wake. This is not to deny the possibility of truth arising outside of discipleship. It is to say, however, that hearing the text as Christ's address is necessarily bound up with the process of following. This distinctly Bonhoefferian rendering of the Augustinian *credo ut intelligam* implies that in order to adjudicate, one must first follow.

This vision of knowledge resonates with the scriptural depiction of discipleship. Christ only asks "Who do you say that I am?" (Mk 8:29) after

---

[81]Bonhoeffer, *Discipleship*, DBWE 4:182.
[82]See Bonhoeffer, *Creation and Fall: A Theological Exegesis of Genesis 1–3*, DBWE 3:111-14.

first inviting the disciples to put down their nets and follow him (Mk 1:17-18). One's cognitive relationship to truth is contingent upon one's bodily enactment of a relationship with the Lord. In Paul's idiom, we present our bodies as sacrifices in order then to "be transformed by the renewing of [our] minds" (Rom 12:1-2). Knowledge and action are inextricably bound. As Bonhoeffer famously writes, "Only the believers obey; only the obedient believe."[83]

It comes as no surprise, then, when Bonhoeffer asserts that a community is needed for discernment and that isolation is the enemy of sound judgment.[84] If we cannot sketch a precise method or technique that will determine the truthfulness of competing interpretive proposals, we can sketch an account of the posture from which truthfulness might emerge, and this posture is fundamentally social. Scripture's paradigmatic instance of discernment takes just this form: "It has seemed good to the Holy Spirit and to us" (Acts 15:28).[85] In this chapter I have been sketching an account of how this "and to us" might be enacted and sustained.

Within a hermeneutic of discipleship, we can reframe the task of adjudication. We can forgo the pursuit of methodologically driven certainty and, in its place, embrace the communal process. In the place of criteria, we have a form of life. In the place of certainty, we have the ongoing journey. The rules for adjudication, then, are the rules that allow the community to navigate the process of hearing Christ's voice. Bonhoeffer's vision of education and formation is inclined toward this question. He claims that the very purpose of theological education is the discernment of the spirits in the church.[86] As we have seen, he structures his Finkenwalde experiment as a sustained attempt at forming a community capable of doing precisely this.

This is where Hauerwas's account of patience is so helpful. Without the ability to maintain open dialogue, the community is bound to short-circuit the discernment process. Fowl and Jones highlight the specifically hermeneutical implications inherent within Hauerwas's vision: "No particular

---

[83]Bonhoeffer, *Discipleship*, DBWE 4:63.
[84]Bonhoeffer, *Theological Education at Finkenwalde*, DBWE 14:96, 117.
[85]See Stephen E. Fowl, *Engaging Scripture: A Model for Theological Interpretation* (Malden, MA: Blackwell, 1998), 103-13.
[86]Bonhoeffer, *Berlin: 1932–1933*, DBWE 12:432-35. Also see idem, *Theological Education at Finkenwalde*, DBWE 14:95-96, 402.

community of believers can be sure of what a faithful interpretation of Scripture will entail in any specific situation until it actually engages in the hard process of conversation, argument, discussion, prayer, and practice."[87] John Howard Yoder refers to this as a "hermeneutic of peoplehood." He suggests that various practices are necessary to structure a communal process of moral reasoning in which conflict is managed and truth pursued. Within his communal account of ethical deliberation, he notes that the process of deliberation is less a matter of how ideas work than a matter of how communities work.[88] For our purposes, we might modify Yoder's insight: pursuing hermeneutical faithfulness is not merely a matter of how *texts* work. Rather, interpretive faithfulness arises in the process of following after Jesus, and it is bracketed by the practices that structure and sustain a common life en route with him. Before we can make a claim to adjudicate readings of Scripture, we must attend to the communal process that would enable such a claim in the first place.

Yoder's insights are especially fitting in this chapter, for his hermeneutic of peoplehood mediates the type of tensions that might arise between a christological and an institutional hermeneutic (parts one and two of this project). Yoder presents his hermeneutic of peoplehood as a constructive response to the respective extremes of hyperindividualism and hypermagisterialism. In contrast to an individual's own intuition vis-à-vis the revealing God and in contrast to blind repetition of authoritative claims, meaning must always be navigated via a communal process. This fits nicely into the structure of this project. One of the main ways we combat one-sided accounts of individualistic intuition (one of the dangers of locating hermeneutics with the *creatura verbi*) and rigid traditionalism (one of the dangers of locating hermeneutics within the historical institution) is through the gathering of bodies.

Yet all of this seems only to delay the question. Once we have sketched the fundamental communal process and posture by which faithful reading can be pursued and identified, we must still attend to the community's critical responsibility for interpretive possibilities. By "critical responsibility"

[87]Fowl and Jones, *Reading in Communion*, 20. Also see Fowl's *Engaging Scripture*, chaps. 3-4.
[88]John Howard Yoder, "Hermeneutics of Peoplehood: A Protestant Perspective on Practical Moral Reasoning," *Journal of Religious Ethics* 10, no. 1 (1982): 52.

I refer to the community's ability to rule out certain interpretive outcomes. While the positive content of a given outcome is determined by Christ's ongoing freedom as the risen Lord, the community must judiciously and humbly exercise a critical vigilance as one aspect of the larger process of receiving his voice. If we cannot speak for Christ, we can identify competing voices that might lead us astray.

Here we recall the distinction between Scripture's sacramental and regulative capacity. Scripture functions most fundamentally as the medium of Christ's address and the means by which the Spirit draw us into Christ's ongoing movement. At the same time, Scripture regulates the discernment process. As we have seen, the vigilant community must attend to the text itself, for this is where the Spirit speaks. An outcome that loses the text must be treated with suspicion. But how does a community determine whether a reading has lost the text? Here my analysis in part two remains significant. Scripture functions in a regulative mode precisely as a narrative of God's redemption. That is, one of the means by which the church determines whether it has in fact received Christ's word is the degree to which a given interpretive outcome fits within the larger story of God's coming kingdom. Thus, the church's inherited traditions—the memory that has accrued as the church has lived into its story—help sketch its interpretive bounds. The church's critical responsibility requires it to ask if a proposed interpretive outcome fits within the broad contours of the tradition. In other words, Do claims about Jesus' "isness" resonate with the memory of his "wasness"?[89]

Of course, reading within the boundaries of the narrative and the tradition is not tantamount to reading faithfully. Boundaries do not deliver positive content. One can obey all the rules and still fail at the game. What matters is what we do when we are not breaking the rules. But sketching a broad rule at least alerts us to readings that might deserve critical attention. Such criteria can help reveal interpretive failure and mitigate interpretive violence even if they cannot, in and of themselves, positively determine interpretive outcomes. Thus, I continue to affirm that the process of adjudicating readings, like the process of pursuing hermeneutical faithfulness itself, is more an art than a science, which is why the

---

[89]James H. Cone, *God of the Oppressed*, rev. ed. (Maryknoll, NY: Orbis, 1997), 110-16.

cultivation of imagination and innovation remains vital to the church's exercise of hermeneutical responsibility.

CONCLUSION: HAUERWAS, BONHOEFFER,
AND THE CHURCH AS A COMMUNAL SPACE

Life together can be messy. Ideas that fit within one's head possess a neatness that is frustrated by the sheer presence of other bodies. The church is a space for reading because in it we must manage the proximity of others, because being in the church means bumping shoulders with those diverse others Christ has called to himself.

I have argued in part three that this bumping of shoulders is integral to the hermeneutical process, and I have claimed that both the *creatura verbi* and the historical institution require concrete communal enactment and remain hermeneutically vacuous without it. The vertical and horizontal intersect where bodies gather around Jesus and are thereby "joined in holy travel."[90] Since no method can lay hold of divine speech, I have suggested that the church must attend to the posture from which it seeks understanding and from which it enacts critical responsibility; this posture, I have argued, is unreservedly communal, a matter of bodies gathered through practices of togetherness.

This obviously is not meant to downplay the extent to which this process is also textual.[91] Yet as both Bonhoeffer and Hauerwas exemplify, the task of reading the text rightly cannot be sequestered from the task of enacting community with other disciples. In this regard, the two have offered mutually reinforcing visions: the church becomes a hermeneutical space by means of practices of togetherness that allow communities to gather around the text.

This is not to suggest that they have offered identical visions. Indeed, they have achieved different goals. Hauerwas has shown how the narrative logic

---

[90]Jennings, *Acts*, 86.

[91]Bonhoeffer realizes that engaging in practices of togetherness is not an excuse to abandon close readings of Scripture. During his Finkenwalde classes, for example, he required his students to read and memorize the text in the original language and to use an assortment of scholarly aids in the process of listening to the text (see, e.g., Bonhoeffer, *Theological Education at Finkenwalde*, DBWE 14:173). If the Spirit is inseparably bound to Holy Scripture, as Bonhoeffer avers, then careful attention to the text is in fact a spiritual discipline.

of Jesus requires togetherness. Given Jesus' identity, a community that embodies his narrative across time—i.e., the church as a historical institution—requires bodies gathered. Bonhoeffer, on the other hand, has shown how the church as the *creatura verbi* requires bodies gathered in order to function as a hermeneutical space. For him, practices of togetherness function according to the logic of the resurrection. A risen and verbal Lord calls forth an addressable community. The community addressed and gathered is, of course, also sent. With this, we direct our gaze to part four.

The Church as Missional Community: Hermeneutics and the World

7

Reading as a Sent Community

A Conversation with Missional Theology

In PART FOUR I CONTINUE with the task of examining the ecclesiological commitments that inform the practice of theological interpretation. Here I consider the church's relationship to the world, how this relationship shapes ecclesiology itself, and how this ecclesiology in turn affects the practice of reading Scripture. We begin by recognizing that the church's relationship to the world implies a task, a mission. After calling disciples to himself, Jesus sends them into the world in his name, which indicates that some responsibility with regard to the world is inherent to the church's identity. This simple realization carries great significance as the church in the West learns to navigate its changing religious landscape. If, as Wilbert Shenk famously contends, "the Christendom model of church may be characterized as *church without mission*,"[1] a consensus is beginning to emerge that characterizes the post-Christendom church as a church *in* mission.[2] At the very least, the reemergence of mission onto the church's

---

[1]Wilbert R. Shenk, *Write the Vision: The Church Renewed* (Eugene, OR: Wipf & Stock, 2001), 35, emphasis original. Also see Darrell Guder, "Missional Hermeneutics: The Missional Authority of Scripture—Interpreting Scripture as Missional Formation," *Mission Focus: Annual Review* 15 (2007): 111.

[2]For leading works that have paved the way toward this consensus, see David Bosch, *Transforming Mission: Paradigm Shifts in Theology of Mission* (Maryknoll, NY: Orbis, 1991); Darrell L. Guder, *The Continuing Conversion of the Church* (Grand Rapids, MI: Eerdmans, 2000); Darrell L. Guder and George R. Hunsberger, eds., *Missional Church: A Vision for the Sending of the Church in North America* (Grand Rapids, MI: Eerdmans, 1998); Lesslie Newbigin, *Foolishness to the Greeks: The*

theological radar in the twentieth century has reminded us that mission is not merely one ecclesial activity among others but something that characterizes the very essence of the church.[3] Those who are called out of the world are always also sent back into it. To use my terms, the church's relationship with the world is constitutive of its identity; the church that exists in relationship to the risen Christ, to its historical-institutional past, and to concrete communal locations always also exists in relationship to the world.

If hermeneutics presupposes ecclesiology, then this relationship affects how we read. If "mission is the mother of theology," as some have claimed,[4] then one must recognize the hermeneutical consequences that follow. Mission must also be, in some sense, the mother of hermeneutics. As I venture in this direction, I am entering less-traveled terrain. The emerging field of missional hermeneutics has begun to blaze this trail by drawing connections between the church's missional identity and its hermeneutical responsibility. But key questions remain. Here in part four I contribute to these efforts by grappling with the ways the church's missionary nature—its fundamental sentness—impinges upon the task of faithful reading. I am wondering what it might mean for mission to function within our hermeneutical imaginations not merely as a theme but as a practice, not as an idea but as an event. If mission characterizes the nature of the church, then it must shape the context within which Christians read the Bible.

A fundamental issue immediately confronts us. At the heart of the newly emerging post-Christendom paradigm is the recognition, to put it broadly for the moment, that the church is one thing and the world is something else. We have come to assume that at least some distinction exists between the two. Much hangs on how we nuance this distinction. How, theologically speaking, should we depict the church's difference from the world? Care is necessary here, for the church's response at this point shapes its missional self-understanding and strongly determines the nature of the practices that

---

Gospel and Western Culture (Grand Rapids, MI: Eerdmans, 1986); idem, *The Gospel in a Pluralist Society* (Grand Rapids, MI: Eerdmans, 1989); idem, *The Open Secret: An Introduction to the Theology of Mission* (Grand Rapids, MI: Eerdmans, 1995); and Andrew F. Walls, *The Cross-Cultural Process in Christian History* (Maryknoll, NY: Orbis, 2002).

[3] John Flett convincingly argues for the essential "sentness" of the church in Flett, *The Witness of God: The Trinity, Missio Dei, Karl Barth, and the Nature of Christian Community* (Grand Rapids, MI: Eerdmans, 2010).

[4] Bosch attributes this phrase to Martin Kähler (Bosch, *Transforming Mission*, 16).

facilitate its missional movement. In chapter eight I follow Bonhoeffer in critiquing common assumptions about the church's difference from the world. For now, we follow his lead in diagnosing two common errors.

Bonhoeffer recognized that Christian theology faces two opposing temptations—one that stresses the church's distinction from the world and another that stresses the church's solidarity with it. Throughout his writings he names this tension in different ways. He speaks, for instance, about those who abandon the world and those who fixate on improving it, or those who are otherworldly and those who are secularists.[5] This tension is significant. In order for an ecclesiology to be genuinely missional it must avoid sliding to one side of this polarity at the expense of the other. Maintaining this balance, however, is easier said than done.

As a means of creating some terminological clarity, I refer to the first side of the polarity (to put it simply for the moment) as the *culturalist option* because it places special emphasis on the church as a unique culture that stands in contrast to the non-Christian cultures of the world. The temptation here, Bonhoeffer suggests, is to retreat from the world by "build[ing] ourselves a strong fortress within which we can dwell safe and secure with God."[6] The second tendency does precisely the opposite. I refer to it as the *secularist option* because it tends to downplay the distinctiveness of the church for the sake of missional engagement in the realm beyond the church. To be secularist is to dive headlong into the world for the sake of building the kingdom on earth. When this happens, Bonhoeffer worries, "the church [hardens] into an organization of action for religious-moral reconstruction"[7] and risks becoming "a purely functional" community.[8]

Broadly speaking, certain tendencies characterize these respective options. The culturalist option tends to view the church as a distinctly defined space, to prioritize the universal elements of the church, to conceive of mission in terms of cultural protection and replication, to be exclusivist, and to resort to ecclesial triumphalism. The secularist option, by contrast, tends to view the church as a social movement with porous boundaries, to

---

[5]This two-part distinction is especially clear in Bonhoeffer's essay, "Thy Kingdom Come" (*Berlin: 1932–1933*, DBWE 12:285-97).
[6]Bonhoeffer, *Berlin*, DBWE 12:287.
[7]Bonhoeffer, *Berlin*, DBWE 12:287.
[8]Bonhoeffer, *Ecumenical, Academic, and Pastoral Work: 1931–1932*, DBWE 11:377.

prioritize contemporary trends, to conceive of the goal of mission in non-ecclesial terms, to be inclusivist, and to more readily compromise the tenets of orthodoxy.[9] Whereas the culturalist option falls squarely on the church side of the church-world divide, the secular option eagerly embraces the world.

The importance of carefully navigating the culturalist-secularist tension is made even more obvious by the historical results of the modern missionary movement. As Kwame Bediako famously suggests, the "surprise story" of this movement is that the gospel took shape in ways the sending culture did not envision.[10] He highlights the "genuinely and specifically *African* contributions" that resonate "far beyond what the missionary transmission conceived."[11] He therefore claims that "the gospel has no permanent resident culture."[12] W. A. Visser 't Hooft similarly notes that the church's global movement entails "dynamic and costly flexibility." He thus suggests that the church should not be "afraid to leave behind the securities of its conventional structures" but must be "glad to dwell in the tent of perpetual adaptation."[13] This experience of crosscultural movement has often pressured Christians toward the extremes of the culturalist-secularist polarity. On the one hand, one may fear the unpredictability of crosscultural movement and thus double down on cultural normativity. Or, on the other hand, one may come to value the diversity apparent in this movement and downplay the confessional and theological uniqueness of the church. Both options imply that an ecclesial hermeneutic is not a missional hermeneutic.

---

[9]Jennifer McBride also uses the exclusive-inclusive and triumphalism-compromise typologies in her analysis of the church in the United States; see Jennifer M. McBride, *The Church for the World: A Theology of Public Witness* (Oxford: Oxford University Press, 2011), 29-31. McBride draws from the sociological analysis of Robert Wuthnow in his *America and the Challenges of Religious Diversity* (Princeton, NJ: Princeton University Press, 2005), 110-89.

[10]Kwame Bediako, *Christianity in Africa: The Renewal of a Non-Western Religion* (Maryknoll, NY: Orbis, 1996), 205-6.

[11]Kwame Bediako, *Jesus and the Gospel in Africa: History and Experience* (Maryknoll, NY: Orbis, 2004), 56, 15. Also see Andrew Walls, *The Missionary Movement in Christian History: Studies in the Transmission of Faith* (Maryknoll, NY: Orbis, 1996), 146, where he compares the enriching potential of African culture to the role of Greek culture in the early church.

[12]Kwame Bediako, "Scripture as the Interpreter of Culture and Tradition," in *African Bible Commentary: A One-Volume Commentary Written by 70 African Scholars*, ed. Tokunboh Adeyemo (Nairobi: WordAlive, 2006), 4.

[13]W. A. Visser 't Hooft, ed., *The New Delhi Report: Third Assembly of the World Council of Churches* (London: SCM, 1962), 90, quoted in John Flett, *Apostolicity: The Ecumenical Question in World Christian Perspective* (Downers Grove, IL: InterVarsity Press, 2016), 22.

So in part four I'm asking a deeper ecclesiological question: What kind of church can take seriously both the obviously pluriform effects of the gospel's global spread and the distinct universality of the church as the one body of Christ in the world?

Admittedly, this two-part typology is broad, and a great deal of nuance exists within both culturalist and secularist options. But the typology has heuristic value. For one, it helpfully maps the development of Bonhoeffer's missional imagination and therefore allows us to see how he offers a third option that avoids sliding to one extreme or the other. We will also see that hermeneutical implications come embedded within both alternatives. These different ways of construing the church's relationship to the world shape different postures toward Scripture as a feature of the church's missional life. What ultimately emerges as we follow Bonhoeffer in forging a third way beyond culturalist and secularist options is a church that is at once genuinely ecclesial and genuinely worldly. Such a church houses a missional hermeneutic.

THE CULTURALIST OPTION

Bonhoeffer's most direct engagement with the culturalist option occurs in his prison writings as he retrospectively assesses the failed course of the Confessing Church. As I suggest more fully in chapter three, he was particularly disappointed in certain conservative factions within the movement who engaged in a cultural battle aimed at "conservative restoration."[14] Fearing secularity's encroachment, many were tempted to "entrench themselves" behind the "faith of the church."[15] Christian mission, on this account, was tantamount to fighting with the world for cultural space. "Reiterated confession and ceaseless activity"[16] became the church's core missional practice, and survival became their animating goal. The end result of this misguided missionary posture, Bonhoeffer fears, is a ghettoized church, a church at the margins, a church relegated to its own cultural confines. This is why he claims that a church that fights for self-preservation has "become

---

[14]Bonhoeffer, *Letters and Papers from Prison*, DBWE 8:430.
[15]Bonhoeffer, *Letters and Papers from Prison*, DBWE 8:500, 502.
[16]Eberhard Bethge, *Dietrich Bonhoeffer: A Biography*, ed. Victoria J. Barnett, trans. Eric Mosbacher et al., rev. ed. (Minneapolis: Fortress, 2000), 409.

incapable of bringing the word of reconciliation and redemption to humankind and to the world."[17]

While one might be forgiven for thinking that dire political circumstances would warrant extreme ecclesial measures, Bonhoeffer is unrelenting in his criticism. As usual, his reasoning remains christological. Some factions within the Confessing Church had become so concerned with conserving orthodox language and customs, Bonhoeffer suggests, that for them "Jesus disappears from view."[18] Here we see the animating logic of his criticism. A posture of cultural protection is antimissional because it is fundamentally nonchristological. The seemingly noble attempt to fight for God's ongoing relevance actually sequesters the church. Such a church inevitably resorts to a posture of competition with the world. Standing up for a "cause," the church loses sight of its Lord; becoming enamored with its culture, it loses sight of the world.

The "cultural-linguistic" turn in theology. Though the Confessing Church's sociopolitical context was obviously unique, the tendency to over-value ecclesial culture is not. Before Bonhoeffer, Barth similarly criticized those who rendered the church as "an alleged superior world *over against the world*."[19] In the generations after Bonhoeffer, "postliberal" trends pushed many theologians in a culturalist direction. In part two, I note that Alasdair MacIntyre plays a unique role in paving the way for this possibility. Many within the church heard MacIntyre's warning as a call to action and therefore translated his broader warnings about Western society into a particular concern for preserving Western forms of ecclesiology. George Lindbeck adds theological clarity to MacIntyre's vision when he advocates a

---

[17]Bonhoeffer, *Letters and Papers from Prison*, DBWE 8:389. Others have similarly argued that the Confessing Church went awry when it became fixated on social and cultural control; see Shelley Baranowski, *The Confessing Church, Conservative Elites, and the Nazi State*, Texts & Studies in Religion 28 (Lewiston, NY: Mellen, 1986). Manfred Gailus concludes that the Confessing Church's main motivation was "to protect their own religious and ecclesiastic freedom," which explains why they "did not dare to publicly express words of solidarity with persecuted people" (Gailus, "Religion," in *A Companion to Nazi Germany*, ed., Shelley Baranowski, Armin Nolzen, and Claus-Christian W. Szejnmann [Medford, MA: Wiley Blackwell, 2018], 335, 338). Also see Wolfgang Gerlach, *And the Witnesses Were Silent: The Confessing Church and the Persecution of Jews*, trans., Victoria J. Barnett (Lincoln: University of Nebraska Press, 200).

[18]Bonhoeffer, *Letters and Papers from Prison*, DBWE 8:500.

[19]Karl Barth, *The Word of God and the Word of Man*, trans. Douglas Horton (New York: Harper & Row, 1957), 67.

"cultural-linguistic" theology. Religion, Lindbeck suggests, is "a kind of cultural . . . framework or medium that shapes the entirety of life and thought."[20] More recently, Peter Leithart has pursued a similar agenda by depicting the church in an "expansive anthropological sense as the beliefs, values, practices—the whole way of life—of an organized group."[21] The church is a distinct culture, on this account, because its customs, language, and embodied practices structure all of reality. This is not to imply that there is only one style of Christian culture; indeed, the culturalist tendency is broad. In addition to Catholic, Lutheran, and Reformed versions (exemplified by MacIntyre, Jenson, and Leithart, respectively), it has also taken shape in recent years in distinctly evangelical and Orthodox forms.[22] To say that the church is a culture, then, is not to imply one particular form of culture. It is also not simply to say that the church possesses certain unique elements that the world does not. It is to make a much more penetrating claim. The difference is not one of degree but of kind. For the culturalist option, the church is an interrelated whole, a complex autonomous entity that is qualitatively distinct from and incommensurable with competing cultural realities.[23]

J. C. Hoekendijk points toward the missional implications by suggesting that when the church becomes a "well-protected area" with "its own style of life, . . . its own language, [and] its own time," then "direct intercourse between the Church and the world has ceased."[24] Kathryn Tanner is more aggressive in her diagnosis when she suggests that the culturalist option tends "to view influences from other cultures as a source of cultural

---

[20]George A. Lindbeck, *The Nature of Doctrine: Religion and Theology in a Postliberal Age* (Louisville, KY: Westminster John Knox, 1984), 33.

[21]Peter J. Leithart, *Blessed Are the Hungry: Meditations on the Lord's Supper* (Moscow, ID: Canon Press, 2000), 164.

[22]See, e.g., Rodney R. Clapp, *A Peculiar People: The Church as Culture in Post-Christian Society* (Downers Grove, IL: IVP Academic, 1996); and Rod Dreher, *The Benedict Option: A Strategy for Christians in a Post-Christian Nation* (New York: Sentinel, 2017). On the latter, see Derek W. Taylor, "Bonhoeffer and the Benedict Option: The Mission of Monasticism in a Post-Christian World," *Ecclesiology* 14, no. 1 (2018): 11-31.

[23]Kathryn Tanner, "Cultural Theory," in *The Oxford Handbook of Systematic Theology*, ed. John B. Webster, Kathryn Tanner, and Iain R. Torrance (Oxford: Oxford University Press, 2007), 531. Henning Wrogemann refers to this as a "relativistic" concept of culture that views different cultures as separate entities. For a technical treatment of various theories of culture within ethnology, religious studies, and sociology, see Wrogemann, *Intercultural Hermeneutics*, trans. Karl E. Böhmer (Downers Grove, IL: IVP Academic, 2016), chap. 7.

[24]J. C. Hoekendijk, "The Call to Evangelism," *International Review of Mission* 39, no. 154 (1950): 166.

disruption . . . [that] need to be either repulsed or neutralized in ways that allow a culture's overall character to remain unchanged."[25] While this stance toward nonecclesial culture does not necessarily imply that culturalist ecclesiologies have abandoned their missional identity, it does suggest a particular view of what mission entails. Implicit missional commitments emerge, for instance, when Lindbeck suggests that "for the sake of survival" Christians must "develop close-knit groups" that preserve ecclesial culture from contaminating influences."[26] Peter Leithart highlights the missional dimensions of this proposal when he suggests that "central to [the church's] mission" is the task of "maintain[ing] the symbolic boundaries that separate her from worldly culture."[27] The church serves the world, on this view, precisely by being itself. "The church's first mission is to be the church," Leithart claims.[28] Echoing MacIntyre's earlier insights, he suggests that the church fulfills its mission by being "the socioreligious entity" that can withstand the "social chaos" that pervades the wider culture.[29] Given this missional posture, the practice of "discipline at the borders"[30] becomes *the* missional practice, for it repels other cultures (to use Tanner's terminology) and thereby stabilizes intraecclesial life. At best, Christian mission becomes self-referential, "an invitation to become like us."[31] At worst, it becomes a cultural battle against the "increasingly alien and hostile" cultures outside the church.[32] It would seem, then, that in order to be for the world, the church must first be against it. Indeed, some have even embraced a militaristic conception of mission. "We must expect other polities to make war against us," Robert Jenson suggests.[33] In the face of opposition, the church "is responsible to cultivate her culture . . . [or will] lose her identity if she does not."[34] Leithart similarly suggests that the church best serves the world by being a "standing

---

[25]Tanner, "Cultural Theory," 531.

[26]Lindbeck, *Nature of Doctrine*, 78.

[27]Leithart, *Blessed Are the Hungry*, 164.

[28]Peter J. Leithart, *Delivered from the Elements of the World: Atonement, Justification, Mission* (Downers Grove, IL: InterVarsity Press, 2016), 230.

[29]Leithart, *Delivered from the Elements of the World*, 230, 218.

[30]Robert W. Jenson, *The Works of God*, vol. 2 of *Systematic Theology* (Oxford: Oxford University Press, 1999), 205.

[31]McBride, *Church for the World*, 25.

[32]Robert Louis Wilken, "The Church's Way of Speaking," *First Things*, August 2005, 30.

[33]Robert W. Jenson, "Christ as Culture 1: Christ as Polity," *IJST* 5, no. 3 (2003): 329.

[34]Jenson, "Christ as Culture 1," 324.

challenge and rebuke" to existing cultural alternatives, which turns mission into an act of "resistance, a struggle, perhaps to the death."[35]

Given this missional posture, any movement beyond the cultural confines of the church becomes risky business. Perhaps such movement is inevitable due to the contingencies of life, but it is not logically necessary to the existence of the church itself. Framed within a culturally competitive account of the church, therefore, missional movement ceases to carry ecclesiological relevance. The church *is* something before it subsequently (if at all) moves outwards. The defensible boundaries necessary to fund cultural distinction suggest that missional engagement with the world is at best a secondary step that exists as an addendum to the more fundamental task of cultural maintenance. Consequently, missional movement ceases to be one of the distinct practices that constitute the church's unique culture. If the church does turn its attention outward, it usually aims toward something like cultural expansion, toward enlarging its influence by means of a process that Lamin Sanneh critically refers to as assimilation and diffusion.[36] As Leithart claims, exemplifying Sanneh's fears, the church must "seek to form the surrounding culture into something like the culture that exists within the church" and in this way must "seek to remake the world."[37] Within a culturalist understanding of the church, mission becomes a matter of repetition and replication, of expanding the church's normative pattern of life and thereby displacing the alternative cultures the church encounters.[38]

Culturalist hermeneutics. Hermeneutical implications become obvious when we realize that this normative way of life includes a normative way of reading Scripture. For the culturalist option, the church becomes a "quasi-independent universe of meaning"[39] that determines the meaning one might draw from a text. Within a culturalist ecclesiology, in other words, particular cultural artifacts acquire inflated importance, functioning normatively as relics from the past that maintain Christian identity in the

---

[35]Leithart, *Delivered from the Elements of the World*, 234.

[36]Lamin Sanneh, *Translating the Message: The Missionary Impact on Culture*, 2nd ed. (Maryknoll, NY: Orbis, 2009), 33, 72.

[37]Leithart, *Blessed Are the Hungry*, 164.

[38]See John G. Flett, "Communion as Propaganda: Reinhard Hütter and the Missionary Witness of the 'Church as Public,'" *SJT* 62, no. 4 (2009): 472.

[39]Wrogemann, *Intercultural Hermeneutics*, 125.

present.[40] This is particularly true of the church's textual relic. Leithart suggests, for example, that the church must strive to ensure that its predetermined manner of speech becomes "the dominant language of culture." The church must "speak a language distinct from that of the world," he claims, and this unique form of speech must be rooted in and ordered by "the biblical pattern of language."[41] Here we recall Jenson's claim that the church is the culture that speaks "Christianese."[42] As Wilken states the matter, "culture lives by language" that is "formed and carried by the language of the Scriptures."[43] It follows that any modification of traditional biblical language—for example, through translation or vernacularization—should be treated with suspicion. Wilken concludes, "If there is a distinctly Christian language, we must be wary of translation. . . . Jerusalem cannot become Paris or Moscow or New York without losing its rootedness in the biblical narrative."[44] To translate these words into another idiom is to risk creating another religion. This means that encounter with the reality lying beyond the church's distinct space is rendered, at best, hermeneutically superfluous and, at worst, hermeneutically distortive. The location of the church within its wider cultural, historical, and geographical context remains irrelevant to intraecclesial activity. Any linguistic movement remains strictly unidirectional, a translation into the normative language of the church.

This depiction of the culturalist option uniquely relates to the argument I have been unfolding in this book. Put simply, I contend that the contemporary practice of theological interpretation commonly presupposes a culturalist ecclesiology.[45] I contend, in other words, that the same logic that underlies the culturalist option—we are distinctly this community and not another—also animates the basic rationale of theological interpretation— we read within this community and not another. Walter Moberly represents the movement when he highlights the role of the church as the social presupposition—the plausibility structure or preunderstanding—that

---

[40]See Flett, *Apostolicity*, 115. Also see my analysis of Jenson in chaps. 3 and 4.

[41]Leithart, *Blessed Are the Hungry*, 165.

[42]Robert W. Jenson, *The Triune God*, vol. 1 of *Systematic Theology* (Oxford: Oxford University Press, 1997), 18.

[43]Robert Louis Wilken, "The Church as Culture," *First Things*, April 2004, 35.

[44]Wilken, "Church as Culture," 35. Also see Wilken, "Church's Way of Speaking," 29.

[45]For a similar argument, see David W. Congdon, "The Nature of the Church in Theological Interpretation: Culture, Volk, and Mission," *JTI* 11, no. 1 (2017): 101-17.

shapes biblical interpretation. Moberly's account of the church as a space determined by unique forms of socialization, language, and education coheres with the basic contours of the culturalist option.[46] R. R. Reno similarly contends that "the animating culture of the church" ought to shape the hermeneutical process.[47] Indeed, he hints that this hermeneutical return to a normative culture is the church's best response to a situation in which the Western world has been "de-Christianized."[48] To claim that we ought to read "in the church" is therefore to claim (even if only implicitly) that a normative culture provides trustworthy hermeneutical guidance. Amidst the waves of cultural disarray, the church becomes an island of stability. It is no wonder, as Angus Paddison accurately observes, that the practice of theological interpretation has become "robustly situated within the culture of the church."[49]

As I have suggested in earlier chapters, there is something obviously right about this—the church is indeed a thick community that constitutes something like a plausibility structure that provides hermeneutical access to Scripture. But we have reason to pause if this implies that mission must become a secondary feature of ecclesial identity. I worry that the practice of theological interpretation, precisely in being unduly bound to the culturalist option, has become missionally deficient. I suggest, to put the matter differently, that the paucity of missional themes within theological interpretation should make us wary of its ecclesiological presuppositions and, therefore, warrants interrogating the legitimacy of its culturalist underpinnings.

The basic reason animating this missional paucity should be clear: hermeneutical practices that explicitly locate themselves "in and for the church" can easily come to imply that the act of faithful reading and the act of faithful mission take place at a distance from each other. If reading Scripture is essentially something that happens within the culture of the church, then any missionary movement outside of the church becomes a movement away

---

[46]R. W. L. Moberly, "Theological Interpretation, Presuppositions, and the Role of the Church: Bultmann and Augustine Revisited," *JTI* 6, no. 1 (2012): 17. Congdon notes that for Peter Berger, a "plausibility structure" is synonymous with a "cultural world" (Congdon, "Nature of the Church in Theological Interpretation," 106).

[47]R. R. Reno, "Series Preface," in Jaroslav Pelikan, *Acts*, Brazos Theological Commentary on the Bible, ed. R. R. Reno (Grand Rapids, MI: Brazos Press, 2005), 12.

[48]Reno, "Series Preface," 13.

[49]Angus Paddison, "Theological Interpretation and the Bible as Public Text," *JTI* 8, no. 2 (2014): 186.

from the context of hermeneutical faithfulness. Such movement necessarily lacks interpretive significance. It may be the byproduct of faithful interpretation, but not an ingredient within the process of interpretation itself. Even if the recent turn to theological interpretation has not always been motivated by a strong sense of antipathy toward hostile forces outside the church, the logic of cultural separation remains operative, defining the nature and ends of biblical interpretation.

Consider, as evidence, the main interlocutors I have engaged in previous chapters. Each offers a uniquely ecclesial hermeneutic, though none gives sustained attention to how the church's missionary calling might affect its reading practices. Greg McKinzie has recently made a similar argument. He suggests that for Stephen Fowl, one of the forebears of the contemporary reemergence of theological interpretation, the practice of reading tends toward "ecclesiocentric ends."[50] While Fowl helpfully notes that the church's primary aim in practicing theological interpretation "is to interpret Scripture as part of their ongoing struggle to . . . [move] into ever deeper communion with God and others,"[51] he depicts this communion in terms that remain entirely intraecclesial. Thus, while Fowl has rightly drawn attention to the importance of ecclesially normed "interpretive habits and practices,"[52] rarely is anything resembling mission included as one of these practices. As the respective bodies of literature on missional theology and theological interpretation each continue to grow, the overlap between the two is surprisingly sparse.[53]

---

[50]Greg McKinzie, "Missional Hermeneutics as Theological Interpretation," *JTI* 11, no. 2 (2017): 172.

[51]Stephen E. Fowl, *Engaging Scripture: A Model for Theological Interpretation* (Malden, MA: Blackwell, 1998), 3. See McKinzie, "Missional Hermeneutics as Theological Interpretation," 171-72.

[52]See, e.g., Fowl, *Engaging Scripture*, 9.

[53]Michael J. Gorman is one of the few who has explicitly argued that missional hermeneutics is a form of theological interpretation, suggesting that "missional hermeneutics should be seen as a subset, or perhaps an extension, of theological interpretation"; see Gorman, *Becoming the Gospel: Paul, Participation, and Mission* (Grand Rapids, MI: Eerdmans, 2015), 51. However, there is reason to wonder just how significantly the two overlap. Michael Barram suggests, for instance, that "as tempting as that conclusion may be, I suspect that there is indeed something that distinguishes 'theological interpretation' (in all of its diversity) from missional hermeneutics (with its various streams). In the end, it seems to me that what distinguishes these two lines of interpretation is the *conscious and consistent emphasis* on the church as a 'sent' community that undergirds . . . missional hermeneutics." Barram, "Reflections on the Practice of Missional Hermeneutics: 'Streaming' Philippians 1:20-30" (paper, Annual Meeting of the Society of Biblical Literature, New Orleans, LA, November 2009).

Explaining the lack of mission within the theological interpretation of Scripture. Three interrelated tendencies have led to this situation. First, in recent decades the move toward articulating a distinctly ecclesial hermeneutic has emerged in tandem with larger trends that emphasize theological retrieval and *ressourcement* thinking. For many proponents of this movement, theological interpretation has value precisely as a project of ecclesial renewal. The Brazos Theological Commentary Series, one of the hermeneutical landmarks of this movement, explicitly frames its task as one of rehabilitation and recovery. It attempts to move behind the Enlightenment to a time before the "animating culture of the church" had been darkened by the "fetters of worldly habit."[54] Fowl likewise suggests that the interpretive habits and practices that characterize faithful interpretation are premodern in nature.[55] It makes sense, then, that the theme of mission would fall from view. Missiologist David Bosch reminds us that when "reading theological treatises from earlier centuries, one gets the impression that there was only church, no world."[56] While there is certainly value in projects of recovery, they risk presupposing a vision of ecclesial space defined within the social conditions of Christendom. For such a church, the marks of faithfulness are entirely immanent to the community, which means that missional practice and ecclesial faithfulness do not coincide.

A second explanation for theological interpretation's missional paucity is the way the "academy" is construed within the movement. The impulse to relocate Scripture within the church has been catalyzed by a large-scale dissatisfaction with the modern critical enterprise. The danger here is that the antimodern impulse motivating the ecclesial turn in hermeneutics in particular becomes confused with an impulse to flee the modern world in general. By vilifying this particular realm beyond the church, theological interpreters risk making an exaggerated claim, thereby letting a very particular sliver of the world (the modern, secular academy) scare them into a hermeneutical posture whereby they fear the world itself. In truth, however,

---

[54]Reno, "Series Preface," 11-12.

[55]Fowl, *Engaging Scripture*, 9. In the introduction to *The Theological Interpretation of Scripture: Classic and Contemporary Readings,* he claims more generally that "theological interpretation will be non-modern in several respects." Stephen E. Fowl, ed. *The Theological Interpretation of Scripture: Classic and Contemporary Readings* (Malden, MA: Blackwell, 1997), xvi.

[56]Bosch, *Transforming Mission,* 376.

the space characterized by academic secularity does not represent the "world" as a theological category, which means, among other things, that we can rightly criticize certain modern-critical interpretive postures without resorting to hermeneutical insularity.

Third, the lack of missional themes within theological interpretation owes to the movement's postliberal roots. However we narrate the precise history of the reemergence of ecclesial hermeneutics, the role of Lindbeck's cultural-linguistic hermeneutical framework is undeniable. For example, in the lead article of the inaugural volume of the *Journal for Theological Interpretation*, Richard Hays draws from Lindbeck's cultural-linguistic account of Scripture to define the nature and ends of theological interpretation.[57] Kevin Vanhoozer's "Introduction" to the *Dictionary for the Theological Interpretation of the Bible* similarly points to Lindbeck's seminal influence.[58] Daniel Treier explicitly relates Lindbeck's cultural-linguistic project to the emergence of theological interpretation and even highlights the way Lindbeckian hermeneutics functions to repel non-ecclesial cultural influences.[59]

Of course, not all proponents of theological interpretation will agree with this strongly cultural and nonmissional account of the church. Some within the movement recognize the importance of the church's relationship with realities that lie beyond it. For example, one of the nine introductory theses in *The Art of Reading Scripture* claims that the church must read with diverse others outside the church because these are the ones from whom the church needs to learn.[60] This claim carries much truth. It is important to recognize, however, that it implies a particular ecclesiology, one that, at the very least, willingly tolerates some level of cultural discontinuity. If it is indeed true that the church must learn from

---

[57]Richard B. Hays, "Reading the Bible with Eyes of Faith: The Practice of Theological Exegesis," *JTI* 1, no. 1 (2007): 13-14.

[58]Kevin J. Vanhoozer, "Introduction," in *Dictionary for Theological Interpretation of the Bible*, ed. Kevin J. Vanhoozer et al. (Grand Rapids, MI: Baker Academic, 2005), 19-25.

[59]Daniel J. Treier, *Introducing Theological Interpretation of Scripture: Recovering a Christian Practice* (Grand Rapids, MI: Baker Academic, 2008), 81-82; and idem, "Scripture and Hermeneutics," in *Mapping Modern Theology: A Thematic and Historical Introduction*, ed. Kelly M. Kapic and Bruce L. McCormack (Grand Rapids, MI: Baker Academic, 2012), 91.

[60]Ellen F. Davis and Richard B. Hays, "Nine Theses on the Interpretation of Scripture," in *The Art of Reading Scripture*, ed. Ellen F. Davis and Richard B. Hays (Grand Rapids, MI: Eerdmans, 2003), 4-5.

outsiders and that the movement of the gospel is "ever outward—not merely geographically but also culturally,"[61] then we must be willing to tolerate some level of cultural disruption within the church. We must be willing to admit the missional, and thus hermeneutical, limitations of culturalist ecclesiologies.

THE SECULARIST OPTION

Before we think constructively about missional ecclesiology, we must look at the other side of the coin. Though the secularist option has exerted less influence in contemporary discussions of ecclesial hermeneutics than the culturalist option has, it too carries hermeneutical implications. Here Bonhoeffer is again a helpful guide.

Bonhoeffer's critique of the American church. He first encountered this phenomenon during his time as a student at Union Seminary in New York (1930–1931). Reflecting upon his time in New York, he notes that the ecclesiological assumptions evident at Union were "accelerating the process of the secularization of Christianity in America."[62] He depicts this secularized ecclesiology in strongly missional terms. The theology on display at Union was concerned with church growth and social improvement and was heavily weighted toward pragmatism and practice. Marked by a form of missional hyperactivity—endless events, programs, and organizations, as Bonhoeffer suggests—it directed its effort toward the "development of humanity to its greatest potential" and, ultimately, building God's kingdom on earth.[63] He laments that theological reflection at the seminary "is directed as much at political, social, and economic circumstances as toward theological and ecclesiastical" ones.[64] He thus notes the "slow but steady process of decline" through which "pragmatic philosophy" was coming to overtake Christian theology.[65] Emphasis falls on "Jesus's social proclamation," and Christianity is thereby reduced to an ethic.[66] Within the missional imagination he encountered at Union, Bonhoeffer notes that "the dualism of two worlds is

---

[61]Craig L. Blomberg, *A New Testament Theology* (Waco, TX: Baylor University Press, 2018), 424.
[62]Bonhoeffer, *Barcelona, Berlin, New York: 1928–1931*, DBWE 10:309.
[63]Bonhoeffer, *Barcelona, Berlin, New York*, DBWE 10:313; Bonhoeffer, *Berlin*, DBWE 12:237.
[64]Bonhoeffer, *Barcelona, Berlin, New York*, DBWE 10:305.
[65]Bonhoeffer, *Barcelona, Berlin, New York*, DBWE 10:305.
[66]Bonhoeffer, *Berlin*, DBWE 12:238-39.

changed into a monism of an evolutionary theory of history,"[67] meaning that the traditional church-world tension is severed and the church is collapsed into the world. If the culturalist option errs by so strongly accenting the church-world distinction that the world recedes from view, the secularist option errs in the other direction by downplaying—if not outright neglecting—the difference between church and world.

During his time in New York Bonhoeffer encountered the secularist option as a curious onlooker. But the matter would soon become relevant to his own theological vocation. Upon returning to Germany in 1931, he accepted an invitation to participate as a youth delegate in the World Alliance for Promoting International Friendship. The same tendency he encountered at Union Seminary was present in the World Alliance in the form of the Anglo-Saxon tendency to emphasize the "world-improving" potential of the church.[68] As Keith Clements notes, "the World Alliance epitomized . . . idealistic internationalism—some would say utopianism."[69] The desire to promote international peace was, of course, commendable, and in many ways Bonhoeffer was in agreement. The danger, as we will explore below, has to do with the way the World Alliance turns Jesus into a principle for world-improvement and thereby collapses the church into the world. David Bosch gives language to this tendency when he notes that after World War II the early twentieth-century notion of "church as conqueror of the world" (paradigmatically expressed at the 1910 Edinburgh Missionary Conference) became "the church in solidarity with the world."[70] Radical sociopolitical changes—most notably in the form of the civil rights movement in the United States and in the form of postcolonial independence internationally—infused great confidence into movements that sought social change. Bosch suggests that with this confidence came the temptation to secularize the calling of the church, often by highlighting the church's role in the process of "humanization." Bosch worries that with this turn toward humanization, the notion of *mission* devolves into "an umbrella term for health and welfare services . . . projects for economic and social development, the constructive

---

[67]Bonhoeffer, *Berlin*, DBWE 12:240.

[68]Bonhoeffer, *Ecumenical, Academic, and Pastoral Work*, DBWE 11:376.

[69]Keith Clements, "Ecumenical Witness for Peace," in *The Cambridge Companion to Dietrich Bonhoeffer*, ed. John W. de Gruchy (Cambridge: Cambridge University Press, 1999), 155.

[70]Bosch, *Transforming Mission*, 377.

application of violence, etc. . . . . The distinction between church and world has, for all intents and purposes, been dropped completely."[71] Jennifer McBride forcefully suggests that within the secularist mindset there is "little to no sense that Christian life and faith requires the *ecclesia*."[72] When the congregation becomes a practical entity, she suggests, it sees itself in "broad humanistic terms" and thus has little need for the church qua church. When this happens we witness a tendency "to compromise the basic tenets of orthodox faith" and a concomitant "ambiguity about the distinctive nature of Christian faith."[73] Some have even suggested that the church should see itself as a "movement" and no longer as a distinct institution.[74]

Bonhoeffer was certainly impressed by the seriousness with which the secularist option addressed social issues. But he worried that in becoming so preoccupied with producing social outcomes, this particular form of mission willingly abandoned the church's distinct message and task. He diagnoses this tendency when he notes that "in the place of church as the congregation of believers in Christ stands the church as a social corporation."[75] The church may experience some degree of social effectiveness, but "the question of the message of the church is hardly raised at all."[76] The church becomes "the place where one acquires secondary significance as a social entity for this or that purpose," but it is "no longer the place where the congregation hears and preaches God's word."[77] Bonhoeffer worries, in short, that the secularist option's zealous enthusiasm to do good in the world renders the church a mere humanitarian agency or a "purely utilitarian organization"[78]—in either case, no longer the true church of Christ. This is what he means when he claims that the theology he encountered at Union had a "churchless" character.[79] Whatever precisely the church becomes, it has "forgotten what the real point is."[80]

---

[71]Bosch, *Transforming Mission*, 383.
[72]McBride, *Church for the World*, 32.
[73]McBride, *Church for the World*, 29, 31.
[74]Stuart Murray, *Post-Christendom: Church and Mission in a Strange New World* (Milton Keynes, UK: Paternoster, 2005), 19-20.
[75]Bonhoeffer, *Barcelona, Berlin, New York*, DBWE 10:313.
[76]Bonhoeffer, *Barcelona, Berlin, New York*, DBWE 10:309.
[77]Bonhoeffer, *Barcelona, Berlin, New York*, DBWE 10:317.
[78]Bonhoeffer, *Ecumenical, Academic, and Pastoral Work*, DBWE 11:370.
[79]Bonhoeffer, *Barcelona, Berlin, New York*, DBWE 10:312.
[80]Bonhoeffer, *Barcelona, Berlin, New York*, DBWE 10:314.

Reflecting on his time at Union, he notes that for students there, "God . . . is not valid truth, but rather 'effective' truth, that is, he is either active in the process of human life or he 'is' not at all."[81] According to Bonhoeffer, the tendency to conflate God into human processes corresponded to a general reluctance to speak distinctly about the specific person and work of Jesus. He notes that students at Union questioned the necessity of preaching about Christ at all.[82] Or, if Christ was mentioned, emphasis would fall on his "social proclamation" or historical influence—not on the person himself.[83] McBride highlights this tendency when she notes that within the secularist options we see "witness that reflects a general sense of God's love and acceptance, not one that reflects a God who is known in a particular way through the person and work of Christ."[84] Schlabach similarly notes that the tendency to reduce Jesus to "an ahistorical abstract philosophical principle" correlates with the tendency within Protestantism to see the church as "superfluous."[85]

A decade after his initial visit to New York, Bonhoeffer reflects on the theological situation in the United States and adds penetrating clarity to his earlier analysis: in the American church that has traded distinctiveness for effectiveness, thereby becoming collapsed into the world, "The person and work of Jesus Christ recedes into the background."[86]

Secularist hermeneutics. In Bonhoeffer's estimate, the world-improving enthusiasm of the Anglo-Saxon contingent of the World Alliance epitomizes the secularist option. In their enthusiasm to build the kingdom on earth, they became guilty of collapsing the church into the world.[87] The hermeneutical implications of this option became especially apparent to Bonhoeffer when the World Alliance met to discuss the issue of international peace. Their cause, of course, was noble; in the midst of growing international tensions and the question of rearmament, a call for peace carried

---

[81]Bonhoeffer, *Barcelona, Berlin, New York*, DBWE 10:311.

[82]Bonhoeffer, *Barcelona, Berlin, New York*, DBWE 10:309.

[83]Bonhoeffer, *Berlin*, DBWE 12:238.

[84]McBride, *Church for the World*, 31.

[85]Gerald W. Schlabach, *Unlearning Protestantism: Sustaining Christian Community in an Unstable Age* (Grand Rapids, MI: Brazos Press, 2010), 25.

[86]Bonhoeffer, *Theological Education Underground: 1937–1940*, DBWE 15:462.

[87]See Bonhoeffer, *Ecumenical, Academic, and Pastoral Work*, DBWE 11:371. Also see Michael P. DeJonge, *Bonhoeffer's Reception of Luther* (Oxford: Oxford University Press, 2017), 175.

great value. But Bonhoeffer remained uneasy with their theological foundations. Given the apparent need for peace, the World Alliance faced the temptation of reducing Scripture to a bearer of timeless principles that would support their cause. This was a dangerous move, in Bonhoeffer's estimate, because it turned peace into a universal principle, what he calls "an *absolute ideal*."[88] Granted the obvious challenge that one can prooftext biblical principles both for and against war, Bonhoeffer has a deeper concern in mind. He believes that to proceed in this manner would actually undermine their ability to speak authoritatively to the present situation, for it would imply that Christ is not personally present speaking a concrete command. What should be a concrete command for peace today instead hardens into an abstract call for pacifism based on certain principles distilled from Scripture.[89] Bonhoeffer offers a different account of the church's hermeneutical responsibility: "The church . . . can proclaim not principles that are always true but rather only commandments that are true today. For that which is 'always' true is precisely not true 'today': God is for us 'always' God precisely '*today*.'"[90]

This distinction between timeless biblical truths and particular biblical truths gets to the heart of Bonhoeffer's criticism of secularist hermeneutics. As we have seen, he believes that the place vacated by the present Christ is quickly filled with inert cognitive quantities like principles and ideas. Rather than a bearer of the divine address, Scripture functions with the secularist options as something like "a collection of spiritual truths."[91] This is why, in Bonhoeffer's estimate, the secularist tendency to replace Christ himself with ideas about Christ constitutes a "lack of obedience to Scripture."[92] As he powerfully suggests, even the most pious principles drawn directly from Scripture—like "love your neighbor" (Mt 22:39) or the Sermon on the Mount (Mt 5-7)—remain useless in the present moment if they become "once and for all" abstractions.[93] In contrast, Bonhoeffer believes that Scripture functions authoritatively in the moment only when Christ is

---

[88]Bonhoeffer, *Ecumenical, Academic, and Pastoral Work*, DBWE 11:371.
[89]See DeJonge, *Bonhoeffer's Reception of Luther*, 160-72.
[90]Bonhoeffer, *Ecumenical, Academic, and Pastoral Work*, DBWE 11:359-60.
[91]McBride, *Church for the World*, 31.
[92]Bonhoeffer, *Berlin*, DBWE 12:242.
[93]Bonhoeffer, *Ecumenical, Academic, and Pastoral Work*, DBWE 11:362.

present. Michael DeJonge nicely captures Bonhoeffer's position: "It is this Jesus Christ [i.e., the *present* Christ] who provides the necessary illumination for understanding the significance of what is recorded about Jesus in the bible. And it is this Jesus Christ's commandment, rather than simply the biblical Jesus' teaching and actions, that issues the call for peace."[94]

Two key dangers cluster around principle-based scriptural interpretation. The first has to do with *hermeneutical control*. Bonhoeffer recognizes that social principles can be applied to Christianity; the danger with this is not necessarily that doing so distorts the nature of Christianity itself (the principle may in fact be true to the moment). The more serious danger is that when a particular social principle comes to function as a hermeneutical key, the reader of Scripture, armed with knowledge of the principle, now exerts control over the text. This is why, in Bonhoeffer's estimate, "rapturous enthusiasm . . . makes itself lord over the Bible."[95] When Bonhoeffer laments the church's inability to "read against" itself, he is speaking to an ecumenical gathering of the World Alliance. He has the secularist option in his cross hairs.[96] In his experience, it is precisely when the church becomes a "world-reforming" entity that it begins to lose the critical hermeneutical leverage necessary to read against itself. It reads Scripture on the basis of preformed ideas and principles and not from a posture of openness and receptivity.

A second danger is related and has to do with *hermeneutical posture*. In Bonhoeffer's experience, the secularist option believes that the "Spirit of God is in a profound sense not . . . tied to the Word."[97] It follows from this assumption that ongoing attentiveness to Scripture ceases to be a significant hermeneutical practice. If God's Word is unmoored from Scripture, then the task of reading becomes something other than discerning his living voice. This means that when the Bible is opened, the minds of those who read it are already filled with the necessary ideas, such that the act of actually listening for God's word becomes irrelevant.[98] For example, the secularist concern for social and ethical issues often drew students away from

---

[94]DeJonge, *Bonhoeffer's Reception of Luther*, 175.

[95]Bonhoeffer, *Theological Education at Finkenwalde: 1935–1937*, DBWE 14:404.

[96]Bonhoeffer, *Ecumenical, Academic, and Pastoral Work*, DBWE 11:378.

[97]Bonhoeffer, *Barcelona, Berlin, New York*, DBWE 10:316.

[98]See William Stringfellow, *A Keeper of the Word: Selected Writings of William Stringfellow*, ed. Bill Wylie Kellermann (Grand Rapids, MI: Eerdmans, 1994), 136.

Scripture, such that serious exegetical work ceased to function as a meaningful part of their missional imaginations.[99] Coming to the text with ready-made commitments, the community had no need to attend freshly to God's address to the church through it.

Both dangers suggest a certain depiction of the relationship between Scripture and mission. William Stringfellow gives voice to Bonhoeffer's concerns about the secularist tendencies evident at Union when, a generation later, he notes that humanitarian forms of Christian mission at Union had become

> appallingly diffident toward the Bible. . . . Those who were the most self-serious about the analysis of culture and society were most often the dilettantes in Bible study. Apparently, some of the clergy felt that Bible study was unnecessary, since they had already learned all they needed to of the Bible in seminary.[100]

At best, then, reading Scripture and engaging the world are two distinct and sequentially ordered events. Scripture perhaps exerts a missional function for the community as it originally inspires mission. But Scripture no longer functions within mission itself. Scripture may have a role to play at the beginning, but once the principle has been abstracted or the idea secured, the text can be returned to the shelf.

THE COMMON ERROR

The culturalist and secularist options represent two ways of depicting the traditional church-world tension and, subsequently, two ways of depicting the nature of the church's mission. These twin errors of retreating into the church at the expense of the world and moving into the world at the expense of the church both bifurcate church and mission. In both cases, the uniqueness of the church as a distinct entity is constituted apart from missional engagement with the world. Although one option devalues mission and the other devalues the church, the same logic is operative in both. This shapes the nature of faithful hermeneutical activity in the church. To read within such a church is never to read within mission itself.

---

[99]See, e.g., Bonhoeffer, *Barcelona, Berlin, New York*, DBWE 10:266, 317.
[100]Stringfellow, *Keeper of the Word*, 136.

Here we can pause to notice the irony: the secularist option struggles in the same way as the culturalist option. Both imply that when the church embarks on missional movement into the world, it inevitably leaves behind the distinct beliefs, practices, and confessional identity that shaped the sending community. The key difference is whether this movement is cast in negative or positive light. For both culturalists and secularists, therefore, hermeneutical activity lies behind missional activity, never in it. The two moments remain distinct and ordered.

Culturalists and secularists struggle in this similar manner because they make the same core theological mistake: they both objectify the gospel. They do so in different ways, of course. The culturalist option objectifies the gospel within the specific cultural parameters of the church and its particular language, thereby making the gospel distinct from the world outside the church and implying that the world carries little value for the inner constitution of the church. The secularist option objectifies the gospel within the much broader parameters of society at large, thereby implying that the particular language, customs, and practices of the historic church are of little value when it comes to the church's task in wider society. In both cases, the gospel has settled into a particular historical form. In different ways, both claim "to have the Realm of God finally present not only by faith but by sight"[101]—that is, to have a gospel undialectically equated with a given historical situation. When this happens, the church ceases to be an essentially missional community; when the gospel is adequately objectified, the church can, at last, come to rest.[102] At best, the church can step in and out of its missionary task depending on the degree to which it perceives the gospel to be

---

[101]Bonhoeffer, *Sanctorum Communio: A Theological Study of the Sociology of the Church*, DBWE 1:222.

[102]For a compelling account of mission that similarly refuses to objectify the gospel, see David W. Congdon, *The Mission of Demythologizing: Rudolf Bultmann's Dialectical Theology* (Minneapolis: Fortress, 2015). Congdon notes that the dialectical theology of Barth and Bultmann emerged precisely as a rejection of the tendency to conflate the gospel into a particular cultural form. Bultmann uses the term *entweltlichte* ("deworldlized"; see Congdon, *Mission of Demythologizing*, 360-62) to convey this sense. Dialectical theology is, therefore, an essentially missional form of theology. Congdon follows Bultmann in speaking about the kerygma as that which refuses to settle. Following Bonhoeffer, I speak of this reality as the present Christ himself. For Bonhoeffer, to deny the objectification of the gospel is not to claim that it never takes worldly shape for, indeed, Christ is always the incarnate Christ. Rather, because it is the gospel of God, it never becomes undialectically equated with a given worldly form but always stands over and above it—precisely while being intimately present to it—as a word of judgment and hope.

adequately objective in a time and place. But notice that this posture has lost touch with the livelihood of Christ's personal presence. As I explain more fully in the following chapter, if we claim that Jesus remains freely himself, then we must also claim that the gospel never hardens into a particular objectified or ideologized form. The gospel remains eternally consistent, but it is always on the move. Jesus remains himself, and as himself he remains always ahead of the community that follows him. This means that in contrast to the ecclesiological assumptions at play in both culturalist and secularist options, the gospel utterly resists objectification. To use language that I explain in the next chapter, it remains consistently nonideological. When we forget this—when we tie the church's mission to particular cultural or ideological goals—we end up implying that mission is something other than participation in the present work of Jesus. Rather than participation, mission becomes something like cultural construction or world improvement. But when we recognize that the gospel never hardens into any particular cultural pattern, we see that the church lives precisely as it participates in Jesus' own livelihood, precisely as it joins in his own unique proclamation and demonstration of the kingdom of God. Indeed, this is the essence of mission and the essence of the church. What it looks like to join in Jesus' proclamation and demonstration of the kingdom in a particular time and place is never something we can fully predict in advance. But we can say that it involves—with secularists—careful attention to and participation in the life of world. And we can also say—with culturalists—that it requires participation in the distinct community that equips us to discern Christ's presence today.

Missional Hermeneutics

In chapter eight I follow Bonhoeffer's lead in construing a path beyond the culturalist-secularist tension. Before that, however, we should pause to note that recent works in the field of "missional hermeneutics" have begun to point in a similar direction. There are different ways to organize the movement and categorize the concerns that constitute it.[103] In my estimate, when one speaks of the intersection of mission and biblical interpretation, one is usually making one of three claims. First, missional hermeneutics

---

[103]For the most important typology, see George R. Hunsberger, "Proposals for a Missional Hermeneutic: Mapping a Conversation," *Missiology* 39, no. 3 (2011): 309-21.

makes a claim about the content of the canon itself. Rather than being limited to a few explicit sending verses, mission lies at the heart of the biblical narrative.[104] Christopher Wright and Michael Goheen argue, for example, that the Bible tells one unfolding story of God's mission of redemption, that mission is a "central strand" within the canon, and that the interpreter must grasp the overarching missional direction of the canon in order to faithfully exegete a particular text within it.[105] In *Bible and Mission*, Richard Bauckham likewise expounds the "missionary direction" of the Bible, claiming that the overarching movement from particular (i.e., Abraham) to universal (i.e., the eschatological kingdom) is a feature of the canon itself.[106] A similar exegetical vision structures N. T. Wright's work. In *Jesus and the Victory of God*, for example, he suggests that the overarching pattern of God's redemption, specifically in the form of exile and return, serves as the hermeneutical grid through which to filter and interpret the various components of the biblical story.[107] In these and other biblical scholars, a wide-angle missional claim exerts particular hermeneutical force. The church must read missionally because the text itself demands it.

Second, missional hermeneutics suggests that the exegetical claim about the content of the canon points toward a theological claim about the doctrine of God. As Bauckham notes, the missional direction of the biblical story ultimately derives from and corresponds to the missional nature of the biblical God.[108] This theological commitment is paradigmatically on display in David Bosch's important work, *Transforming Mission*. According to Bosch, mission is about what God does before it is about what the church does, an attribute of God before an activity of the community.

---

[104]Hunsberger refers to this as the "missional direction of the story" ("Proposals for a Missional Hermeneutic," 310-11).

[105]Michael W. Goheen and Christopher J. H. Wright, "Mission and Theological Interpretation," in *A Manifesto for Theological Interpretation*, ed. Craig G. Bartholomew and Heath A. Thomas (Grand Rapids, MI: Baker Academic, 2016), 189. The fullest treatment of this theme can be found in Christopher J. H. Wright, *The Mission of God: Unlocking the Bible's Grand Narrative* (Downers Grove, IL: InterVarsity Press, 2006). Also see Michael W. Goheen, *A Light to the Nations: The Missional Church and the Biblical Story* (Grand Rapids, MI: Baker Academic, 2011).

[106]Richard Bauckham, *Bible and Mission: Christian Witness in a Postmodern World* (Grand Rapids, MI: Bakers, 2003), 11.

[107]N. T. Wright, *Jesus and the Victory of God*, vol. 2 of *Christian Origins and the Question of God* (Minneapolis: Fortress Press, 1996). Also see N. T. Wright, "Imagining the Kingdom: Mission and Theology in Early Christianity," *SJT* 65, no. 4 (2012): 379-401.

[108]Bauckham, *Bible and Mission*, 12.

Mission is always God's.[109] Darrell Guder likewise suggests that the main "paradigm shift in twentieth century missiology has been away from the ecclesio-centric understanding of mission shaped by Christendom to the theo-centric and ultimately Trinitarian understanding of mission."[110] The church must read Scripture missionally because the God of Scripture is a missional God.

Third, the theological claim about the missional nature of God paves the way for a unique bibliological claim. Scripture itself is both the product of God's mission and a participant within it. N. T. Wright argues that the scriptural texts "were not simply *about* the coming of God's Kingdom into all the world; they were, and were designed to be, part of the *means whereby that happened*."[111] The Bible is a missional text by virtue of what it does: namely, shape the church to fit within God's ongoing missional activity. Darrell Guder has this in mind when he suggests that "the actual task of these scriptures . . . was to deal with the problems and conflicts, the challenges and doubts as they emerged in particular contexts, so that these communities could be faithful to their calling."[112] Scripture carries the same missional function today: "The basic hermeneutical question that we are constantly asking the biblical text might be formulated in this way: How did this particular text continue the formation of witnessing communities then, and how does it do that today?"[113] The church must read Scripture missionally because in both its divine and human dimensions this is its fundamental purpose.

Whether focusing on the content of the canonical story, the nature of divine being, or the nature of Scripture itself, these recent trends are to be commended for putting mission back on the map of hermeneutical conversations. It is to be noted, however, that none of these trends necessarily

---

[109]Bosch, *Transforming Mission*, 389.

[110]Guder, "Missional Hermeneutics," 117.

[111]N. T. Wright, *The Last Word: Beyond Biblical Wars to a New Understanding of the Authority of Scripture* (San Francisco: HarperSanFrancisco, 2005), 51.

[112]Guder, "Missional Hermeneutics," 108.

[113]Guder, "Missional Hermeneutics," 108. Also see Darrell L. Guder, "Biblical Formation and Discipleship," in *Treasure in Jars of Clay: Patterns in Missional Faithfulness*, ed. Lois Y. Barrett (Grand Rapids, MI: Eerdmans, 2004), in which he suggests that Jesus formed his first disciples for mission so that their testimony (both spoken and written) could become the means of the church's future formation for mission (Guder, "Biblical Formation," 62).

requires us to locate the act of reading in distinctly ecclesial spaces or in the act of mission itself. For sure, ecclesiology has been at the center of broader debates in missional theology. The theocentric turn in twentieth-century missiology has concomitantly called for a renewed and properly ordered emphasis on the church as the primary means by which God carries out the *missio Dei*.[114] The danger is that the ecclesiological claim and the hermeneutical claim remain at a distance from each other, that hermeneutical faithfulness and missional movement remain sequentially ordered events. Without further clarification it remains possible, even given these trends in missional theology, that one could enact hermeneutical faithfulness without actually participating in God's mission. The key practices that fund a missional hermeneutic could remain entirely insular, ideas rather than activities. With this, the temptation to objectify the gospel presents itself again, even if mission is now a key principle within it. In other words, I am not merely suggesting that God's missional heart serves as a hermeneutical key, nor that a hermeneutic is deemed valid only if it motivates the church's mission. I am saying that reading and mission must happen simultaneously. The recent trend to reassert the hermeneutical significance of mission has left underdeveloped the sense in which mission itself—not just an idea about it—is the presupposition of the church's hermeneutical task.

---

[114]Guder, "Missional Hermeneutics," 125. Also see, Jürgen Moltmann, *The Church in the Power of the Spirit: A Contribution to Messianic Ecclesiology*, trans. Margaret Kohl (Minneapolis: Fortress, 1993), 64.

8

Reading in and for the World

I ARGUE IN THIS CHAPTER that while the church reads in a certain way on the basis of what it knows about mission—i.e., that mission is central to God's character, the church's task, and the biblical narrative—mission is also hermeneutically central by virtue of what the church does while it is in mission. The first disciples learn to see and know differently not simply when Jesus tells them to go on mission but when, led by the Spirit, they actually encounter others along the way. The paradigmatic instance of this is the gospel's movement to the Gentiles; it is not the call to mission but the ensuing movement that gives the church eyes to read her story—indeed, to know her gospel and her Lord—in new ways. Mission itself is hermeneutically transformative.

Michael Barram gets at this when he highlights the ecclesial context of missional hermeneutics. If we assume that all interpretation is locational, then we must also assume that for a church that participates in Christ's ongoing work, mission is the social location in which interpretation happens.[1] "Perhaps missional interpretation," he writes, "is best understood in a rather general sense as biblical interpretation conducted from the hermeneutical perspective of the church's social location as a sent community."[2] According to Barram, therefore, missional hermeneutics is similar to theological

---

[1]Michael Barram, "The Bible, Mission, and Social Location: Toward a Missional Hermeneutic," *Interpretation* 61, no. 1 (2007): 42.

[2]Michael Barram, "Reflections on the Practice of Missional Hermeneutics: 'Streaming' Philippians 1:20-30" (paper, annual meeting of the Society of Biblical Literature, New Orleans, LA, November 2009).

interpretation because it shares ecclesial presuppositions, but it differs in that it prioritizes the sentness of the reading community.[3] More recently, Greg McKinzie has developed Barram's line of thinking. He calls for a reorientation of scriptural interpretation around the theme of mission, conceived not as an idea but as a practice. He calls this a "praxeological hermeneutic in which participation in God's mission is an epistemological precondition of faithful interpretation."[4] Participation in the *missio Dei* becomes "nonnegotiable for interpretation." Indeed, this "participation in mission *is* readerly formation."[5] McKinzie powerfully concludes that "mission becomes the *locus theologicus* from which a theological reading emerges."[6]

I want to continue pursuing this possibility. In particular, I want to examine the ecclesiological presuppositions that enable an ecclesial hermeneutic to exist in mission and not merely behind it. In what sort of church is it possible to claim that mission is an epistemological presupposition of faithful interpretation? And what sorts of readerly practices and dispositions can sustain the practice of reading within the movement of mission?

BONHOEFFER'S MISSIONAL THEOLOGY

Bonhoeffer might initially seem like a strange resource for my purposes here in part four. After all, mission never became a formal object of focus in his work, he never engaged missiological literature, and the term *mission* played a very minor role in his theological lexicon.[7] In these ways, he was a child of his times. Indeed, he even appears downright antimissional in some of his early writings. This is especially apparent in a series of lectures he

---

[3]Barram, "Reflections on the Practice of Missional Hermeneutics."
[4]Greg McKinzie, "Missional Hermeneutics as Theological Interpretation," *JTI* 11. no. 2 (2017): 157.
[5]McKinzie, "Missional Hermeneutics as Theological Interpretation," 171.
[6]McKinzie, "Missional Hermeneutics as Theological Interpretation," 157.
[7]See Richard Bliese, "Bonhoeffer and the Great Commission: Does Bonhoeffer Have a Theology of Mission?," in *Reflections on Bonhoeffer: Essays in Honor of F. Burton Nelson*, ed. Geffrey B. Kelly and C. John Weborg (Chicago: Covenant, 1999), 253-66. The International Missionary Council sponsored the Jerusalem Conference (1928) and the Tambaran Conference (1938), but we find no evidence that Bonhoeffer was conversant with these conferences. During his Finkenwalde period, he is cordial to the idea of "missionaries" evangelizing in spiritually dead regions (see Bonhoeffer, *Theological Education at Finkenwalde: 1935–1937*, DBWE 14:214). He does use the word *Volksmission*, but it usually functions narrowly, similarly to the way *evangelism* functions today (see Bonhoeffer, *Theological Education at Finkenwalde*, DBWE 14:519).

delivered in Barcelona in 1928–1929. Reggie Williams has argued that these lectures reveal that underlying nationalistic impulses animate Bonhoeffer's early theology.[8] In a telling passage, Bonhoeffer states:

> Peoples [*Völker*] are like individuals. At first they are immature and need guidance. Then they . . . mature into adults, and they die. This situation is neither good nor bad in and of itself. . . . Growth involves expansion; an increase in strength involves pushing aside other individuals. Every people . . . has within itself a call from God to create its history, to enter into the struggle that is the life of the nations. . . . God calls a people to diversity, to struggle, to victory. Strength also comes from God, and power and victory, for God creates youth in the individual as well as in nations, and God loves youth, for God himself is eternally young and strong and victorious. And fear and weakness will be conquered by courage and strength. Now, should a people experiencing God's call in its own life . . . should not such a people be allowed to follow that call, even if it disregards the lives of other people? God is the Lord of history.[9]

Much can be gleaned from this passage in which Bonhoeffer lays the theoretical groundwork for upholding the superiority of the German people and thereby offers ideological justification for German colonial expansion. If, in God's providence, the German people are to mature, then surely the nation, precisely as a matter of its Christian faithfulness, must disregard and push aside other peoples. The church's mission, then, is tantamount to Germanization.[10] In this blending of nationalism and missional faithfulness, Bonhoeffer was far from unique. Indeed, many German theologians positively correlated the nation's involvement in military struggle with the church's fulfillment of the Great Commission—to pursue one was necessarily to pursue the other.[11] Thus, it is not technically correct to say that Bonhoeffer's early theology lacked missional dimensions; rather, his

---

[8]Reggie L. Williams, *Bonhoeffer's Black Jesus: Harlem Renaissance Theology and an Ethic of Resistance* (Waco, TX: Baylor University Press, 2014), 11.

[9]Bonhoeffer, *Barcelona, Berlin, New York: 1928–1931*, DBWE 10:373. The idea of "pushing aside" others implies the notion of *Lebensraum*, which was key in ideologically justifying Nazi military advances (see Reggie Williams, *Bonhoeffer's Black Jesus*, 145). Clifford Green notes that Germans viewed the peace treaty of Versailles as an attempt to "push aside" the German people. In picking up this theme, Bonhoeffer "adopts categories widespread especially among Germans living in foreign countries" (Bonhoeffer, *Barcelona, Berlin, New York*, DBWE 10:373n34).

[10]Reggie Williams, *Bonhoeffer's Black Jesus*, 12.

[11]See David W. Congdon, "Dialectical Theology as Theology of Mission: Investigating the Origins of Karl Barth's Break with Liberalism," *IJST* 16, no. 4 (2014), 390-413.

missional theology subsumed the church within a more determinative framework, in this case the framework of German nationalism. The particular distinctiveness of the church has been set aside for the sake of a political agenda. Though the ideological presuppositions animating this form of mission differ greatly from the Anglo-Saxon theology he would later encounter, it shares the same secularist tendencies.

The development of mission in Bonhoeffer's thought. The secularist and nationalistic tones in Bonhoeffer's early theology fade as the German Church Struggle intensifies and his trust in the established church-state relationship begins to wane. Precisely as he learns to criticize the perverted two-kingdoms theology of his day, missional themes become more apparent in his writing.[12] The fruit of this development is particularly clear in *Discipleship*. Here he claims that in contrast to mere religious teachers, Jesus does not impart doctrine or ideas; he shares his very self, and thus his very task, with his followers.[13] In following Jesus, the disciples "are reminded of their mission on earth."[14] He goes so far as to suggest that Christ cannot do his work alone and that the first disciples are in fact "doing the work of Christ."[15] Indeed, it is the very movement of Christ that calls forth the church's missional movement. "Jesus goes ahead of [the disciples] to other people, and the disciples follow him. . . . Disciples can encounter other people only as those to whom Jesus himself comes."[16] It is clear, therefore, that Bonhoeffer construes mission in terms of participation in Christ, thus the logic of discipleship necessarily includes the logic of mission. As he plainly states, "The message and the effectiveness of the messengers are exactly the same as Jesus Christ's own message and work. They participate in his power."[17]

Notice, in *Discipleship* this account of mission is explicitly predicated on Christ as a present person and not Christ as an idea. His development beyond his Barcelona lectures is stark. Whereas his earlier lectures advocate

---

[12]On the "perverted" nature of Luther's two-kingdoms thinking in the twentieth century, see William J. Wright, *Martin Luther's Understanding of God's Two Kingdoms: A Response to the Challenge of Skepticism* (Grand Rapids, MI: Baker Academic, 2010), 19-20; see also Michael P. DeJonge, *Bonhoeffer's Reception of Luther* (Oxford: Oxford University Press, 2017), 95-99.

[13]Bonhoeffer, *Discipleship*, DBWE 4:186.

[14]Bonhoeffer, *Discipleship*, DBWE 4:111.

[15]Bonhoeffer, *Discipleship*, DBWE 4:186.

[16]Bonhoeffer, *Discipleship*, DBWE 4:170.

[17]Bonhoeffer, *Discipleship*, DBWE 4:188.

for expansion, overcoming resistance, and pushing aside others, Bonhoeffer now believes that "the Word accepts the resistance it encounters and bears it. . . . Nothing is impossible for the idea," he claims, "but for the gospel there are impossibilities." Whereas "the idea is strong . . . the Word of God is so weak that it suffers to be despised and rejected by people." Indeed, "The Word is weaker than the idea."[18] Whereas the promulgation of an idea requires "propagandists," the presence of a person requires mere witnesses. In contrast to the nationalistic fervor pulsing underneath his earlier theology, he now contends that Jesus' witnesses are moved to encounter others, not because they are fanatically motivated by a "conquering idea," not because of a political agenda, not because of some enthusiasm for a cause, but only because Jesus has called them to follow him into the world.

Navigating the culturalist-secularist dichotomy. It is evident that Bonhoeffer has moved well beyond the secularizing tendencies of his youthful theology. But has he swung the pendulum too far? For instance, he now speaks of a church sealed off from the world: "Just as Noah's ark had to be covered 'inside and out with pitch' . . . so does the journey of the sealed church-community resemble the passage of the ark through the floodwaters."[19] The church, he argues, must draw "a clear dividing line between itself and the world."[20] He even advocates going "into the wilderness"[21] and suggests that the church must pursue a "new kind of monasticism."[22] This imagery suggests a community secluded from the world, not a community that follows Jesus into it. This imagery suggests the culturalist option.

It comes as no surprise, then, that some outsiders viewed Finkenwalde as a pious retreat into a spiritual ghetto. The most famous critical voice belonged to none other than Karl Barth, who worried that Bonhoeffer's monastic tendencies represented an attempt "to flee" the world.[23] If this is the case, it would seem that Bonhoeffer has not in fact overcome the dichotomized worldview he inherited—he has simply flipped it on its head. Rather

---

[18]Bonhoeffer, *Discipleship*, DBWE 4:173.
[19]Bonhoeffer, *Discipleship*, DBWE 4:260.
[20]Bonhoeffer, *Discipleship*, DBWE 4:261.
[21]Bonhoeffer, *London: 1933–1935*, DBWE 13:23.
[22]Bonhoeffer, *London*, DBWE 13:285.
[23]Bonhoeffer, *Theological Education at Finkenwalde*, DBWE 14:266n3. The fact that Bonhoeffer had spent eighteen months in London during the initial phases of the Church Struggle likely contributed to Barth's worry that he was fleeing responsibility.

than prioritizing the secular to the neglect of the sacred, it would seem that he has done just the opposite.

In fairness to Barth and other critics of Finkenwalde, Bonhoeffer is not always as clear as he should be at this point. He can simultaneously speak of the church in strongly sectarian terms (a community against the world) and in distinctly missional terms (a community in and for the world). Yet he displays impulses that suggest he is attempting to chart a third way beyond this lingering church-world tension. He claims, for example, that "the 'unworldliness' of the church is meant to take place in the midst of this world."[24] As he writes in a letter from that period, "The goal is not monastic isolation but rather the most intensive concentration for the sake of ministry to the world."[25]

Bonhoeffer himself later implies that *Discipleship* failed to correlate the poles of communal distinction and missional presence in a coherent manner. From prison he detects an impulse toward withdrawal in his Finkenwalde theology. "I thought I myself could learn to have faith by trying to live something like a saintly life," he recounts, alluding to the rigorous pursuit of holiness that animated his Finkenwalde experiment.[26] He goes on to admit that *Discipleship* emerged from this pursuit. By the time he had reached prison, however, Bonhoeffer had learned to embrace "the profound this-worldliness of Christianity."[27] He thus offers a bold confession: "Today I clearly see the dangers of that book." He admits, in other words, that *Discipleship* could, if read a certain way, lead people away from the world. But granted this danger, he immediately adds an important disclaimer: "I still stand by it." This seemingly offhand remark points toward a significant feature of Bonhoeffer's mature theological imagination. It indicates that he has learned to avoid setting ecclesial holiness at odds with worldliness. Indeed, he immediately suggests that "one only learns to have faith by living in the full this-worldliness of life."[28] The two cannot be neatly teased apart. The danger of his Finkenwalde experiment was not its pursuit of holiness but the possible implication that such a pursuit would require one to step

---

[24]Bonhoeffer, *Discipleship*, DBWE 4:245.
[25]Bonhoeffer, *Theological Education at Finkenwalde*, DBWE 14:96.
[26]Bonhoeffer, *Letters and Papers from Prison*, DBWE 8:486.
[27]Bonhoeffer, *Letters and Papers from Prison*, DBWE 8:485.
[28]Bonhoeffer, *Letters and Papers from Prison*, DBWE 8:486.

back from the world. I suggest, therefore, that during his Finkenwalde period Bonhoeffer is trying to integrate distinction from the world and existence for it into one ecclesiological vision but struggles to do so in a coherent and compelling manner.

CHARTING A THIRD WAY: THE CHRISTOLOGICAL OPTION

An essay from 1942 shows evidence that Bonhoeffer has found a way beyond the church-world tension. "Does the church have a mission in regard to the given worldly orders themselves, in the sense of correction, improvement, that is, of working toward a new worldly order," or is the mission of the church simply "to establish within the church-community its own new order"?[29] Bonhoeffer asks, in other words, whether the church is an agency for secular improvement or a culture-building institution. He answers his rhetorical question with straightforward directness: "These alternatives [are] inauthentic. . . . For both have read past the center of the New Testament, namely, the *person of Jesus Christ as the salvation of the world.*"[30]

Bonhoeffer's christological redescription of reality. As expected, distinctly christological commitments animate his thinking. In this way, his move beyond the culturalist-secularist polarity calls to mind his earlier move beyond the poles of act and being. Whereas his earlier breakthrough relied on the concept of Christ as person, here he more fully appreciates the cosmic dimensions of this person. The Christ who is personally present in and as the church is also the salvation of the world. Bonhoeffer will still say, as he did during his student days, that the church is Christ existing as community. But now he more clearly claims that this Christ who exists as community is the Christ in whom "all things hold together" (Col 1:17). Christ lies at the heart of creation.[31] The Christ whose personal presence constitutes the church is the Christ who has reconciled all things in himself (2 Cor 5:19). Bonhoeffer treats this "all" with utmost seriousness. Christ is an ontologically determinative fact. This means that even manifestly non-ecclesial realities like the state, the economy, science, and nature are most properly located in Christ and find their true being there. Indeed,

---

[29]Bonhoeffer, *Conspiracy and Imprisonment: 1940–1945*, DBWE 16:541.
[30]Bonhoeffer, *Conspiracy and Imprisonment*, DBWE 16:542, emphasis original.
[31]See Rowan Williams, *Christ: The Heart of Creation* (London: Bloomsbury, 2018), 182-217.

Bonhoeffer's vision is utterly universal—"nothing is excluded."[32] Christ is not one item to be categorized alongside others but the basic truth of all reality. In *Ethics*, therefore, Bonhoeffer's Jesus is not merely the God who took on flesh (*Inkarnation*) but the God who became human (*Menschwerdung*). This terminological distinction is symbolic of his unequivocal claim that in the God-become-human we encounter all humanity, and in all humanity we encounter the God-become-human. To be drawn to Christ is to be at the absolute center of reality.

This christological view of reality opens up new possibilities for thinking about the church's relationship to the world. Because all reality shares the same fate—i.e., being reconciled to God in Christ—he no longer needs to construe church and world as two different entities vying for supremacy. By grounding all reality in Christ, Bonhoeffer renders impossible any ontological distinction separating ecclesial and nonecclesial realms. Indeed, any consideration of "the world . . . 'in itself'" is sheer abstraction.[33] To participate in Christ, therefore, is not to participate in a segment of life but in all of it. To participate in Christ is to participate in the very heart of the world. Bonhoeffer powerfully sums it up: "In Christ we are invited to participate in the reality of God and the reality of the world at the same time, the one not without the other."[34]

We can now rethink the traditional ways of theorizing the church's relationship to the world. It becomes obvious, on the one hand, that we must reject the secularist notion that movement into the world is movement away from the church. On the other hand, it becomes clear that the church is not some communal substance standing in distinction from the world. Bonhoeffer invites us to see that the call of Christ that constitutes the church does not create an alternative to the world but rather realizes its true form. When Christ calls the church into existence, he calls those already reconciled pieces of the world into active alignment with his own life and work. The stuff that makes up the church—bread, wine, water, music, cloth, speech, or whatever else is at hand—is simply the stuff of the world that has been

---

[32]Bonhoeffer, *Conspiracy and Imprisonment*, DBWE 16:543.
[33]Bonhoeffer, *Conspiracy and Imprisonment*, DBWE 16:531. Also see Bonhoeffer, *Ethics*, DBWE 6:253.
[34]Bonhoeffer, *Ethics*, DBWE 6:55.

called toward its true and proper end: participation in Christ's ongoing life.[35] Bonhoeffer therefore suggests that the church is what it looks like when Jesus becomes socially present to the world he has redeemed; it "is nothing but that piece of humanity where Christ really has taken form."[36] In this sense, the church becomes at the same time a representation of Christ and a manifestation of the true essence of the world. Indeed, the church is worldliness par excellence.

The distinctiveness of the church in the world. This does not mean, of course, that the church must abandon its distinctiveness by being worldly instead of ecclesial. Bonhoeffer invites us to make the exact opposite claim. The key lies in what precisely distinguishes ecclesial from nonecclesial entities. As we have seen, Bonhoeffer's christological remeasurement of reality prevents us from ontologizing the church. Its distinction must lie elsewhere. Thus Bonhoeffer writes, "The church-community is separated from the world only by this: it believes in the reality of being accepted by God—a reality that belongs to the whole world."[37] There is a sense in which this belief is a matter of knowledge—the church knows that it is reconciled to Christ whereas the world does not. But knowledge per se is not the relevant matter. As I have argued in earlier chapters, in the presence of Jesus, belief takes shape as action and knowledge takes shape as following. The church's uniqueness lies not merely in what it knows but in how this knowledge is embodied in ongoing communal practices that facilitate discipleship. The church's distinction from the world lies not in a noetic quantity (nor in its distinct substance) but in a pattern of existence.

Bonhoeffer would therefore remind us that the church's distinctiveness is not a static quantity. The only relevant difference between ecclesial and nonecclesial realities is the difference between that which reflects the reality of reconciliation in Christ and that which does not—a line that runs through church and world alike, and a line that the church must constantly navigate anew. Put differently, the uniqueness of the church lies not in the stuff of which it is made but the use to which that stuff is put. The activity that is

[35]See William Stringfellow, *An Ethic for Christians and Other Aliens in a Strange Land* (Waco, TX: Word Books, 1973), 126.

[36]Bonhoeffer, *Ethics*, DBWE 6:97.

[37]Bonhoeffer, *Ethics*, DBWE 6:67-68.

unique to the church is the activity that sustains a Christward mode of attention, the goal of which is active conformity to Christ himself. Christ's call that creates the church is an ongoing invitation to embody communal forms of life patterned after his own. The church's uniqueness lies precisely in its ongoing efforts to align itself with Christ.

This alignment with Christ takes shape as participation in his person and work. As Bonhoeffer suggests in his *Ethics* manuscripts, Christian faithfulness means "participating in God's reality revealed in Christ."[38] Indeed, it is precisely as Bonhoeffer lays the christological groundwork for overcoming the culturalist-secularist dichotomy that he simultaneously accents the participatory nature of the church's missional agency. As he writes, "Christian life is participation in Christ's encounter with the world."[39] Here Bonhoeffer's constructive missional ecclesiology—we can call it his "christological option"—stands in marked contrast to the culturalist and secularist options. By failing to account for the christological nature of reality, these alternatives construe mission in nonparticipatory terms. For them, the church functions as the link between God and the world. The underlying assumption is that Christ exists at a distance from reality; the mission of the church is to win space for his presence. Rather than participating in Christ's own mission, the implication is that Christ's value to the world is contingent upon the church's missional agency. Mission, in this sense, bears the greatest possible burden. When it neglects to account for the priority of Christ's action and presence, the church feels the frenzied pressure to pick up the slack, which it does by promulgating the items at its disposal—its practices, culture, language, or ideas. The singular agency of Christ recedes from view and the church's agency expands to fill the space. In both the culturalist and secularist options, therefore, the *missio Dei* becomes the *missio ecclesia*.

Bonhoeffer's christological redescription of reality invites us to see things differently. It is not the church that mediates Christ to the world but Christ who mediates the church to the world. The church is present to the world precisely as it participates in Christ's own prevenient presence. This profoundly shapes the nature and posture of the church's activity. The church's missional practices, in short, function to foster and sustain the church's

---

[38]Bonhoeffer, *Ethics*, DBWE 6:50.
[39]Bonhoeffer, *Ethics*, DBWE 6:159.

participation in Christ's ongoing personal existence. The practices, in and of themselves, are penultimate; they carry no value apart from Christ's particular activity. This distinction invites us to imagine that while various church practices may appear similar on the surface, they operate according to different inner logics. The practice of catechesis, for example, can become a matter of defending borders or a matter of equipping the community for ongoing discernment. The practice of preaching can become propagandistic and reproductive, or it can provide space for Christ to speak. The practice of social justice can become another tool in an ideological battle, or it can be a witness to God's love. Even the practice of the Eucharist can emerge from a posture of cultural defensiveness or from a posture of alertness to Christ. The key issue is not merely the practice itself but the mode of its execution. For Bonhoeffer's christological option, practices that distinguish the church from the world are practices that sustain openness to Christ and allow the church to participate in him. In a very real sense, the church remains one worldly institution among countless others. Its life is sanctified not in that it somehow transcends its worldly constitution but in that its practices allow it to continually reorient itself toward the risen Christ. Its sanctification lies in its ongoing alertness to him.

Its sinfulness, on the other hand, lies in its alertness to itself, in the *cor curvum in se*. Christ overcomes the effects of the fall by breaking down dividing walls of hostility (Eph 2:14) and drawing all things together in himself (Col 1:20); the ongoing power of sin struggles against the christological unity of reality by seeking to re-erect dividing walls, thereby dichotomizing, isolating, and segregating the world. To borrow Miroslav Volf's terminology, the sinful powers erect "impenetrable boundaries" of exclusion.[40] Precisely in so doing, sin forcefully militates against Christ's reconciling work. This helps us better understand the effects of sin on human communities. The powers of sin fund a competitive account of individual and institutional life. In a world of fragmented and self-enclosed entities, persons and institutions turn their focus upon themselves as they jockey for space, as they vie for survival, as they defend their cause at the expense of others. Self-regard is what it looks like for institutions to live under the effects of sin; it is the

---

[40]Miroslav Volf, *Exclusion and Embrace: A Theological Exploration of Identity, Otherness, and Reconciliation* (Nashville: Abingdon, 1996), 67.

modus vivendi of the sinful age. As Bonhoeffer's analysis of the failed Confessing Church makes clear, even the church can fall under the influence of the powers by opting for a morality of survival over a morality of witness. One need not look far to see that the "ethic of maintenance" is as rampant within Christian congregations today as it is within other institutions.[41]

The nonideological nature of the church in mission. We have now reached a vantage point from which to fully appreciate the shortcomings of the culturalist and secularist options. Recall that according to Bonhoeffer the fundamental deficiency underlying both options, granted their obvious differences, is their common failure to account for Jesus. The problem with the culturalist dimensions of the Confessing Church he criticized from prison is that for them "Jesus disappears from view."[42] The problem with the secularist account of mission he encountered in the United States is that "the person and work of Jesus Christ recedes into the background."[43] Certainly, both culturalists and secularists operate according to christological commitments. Christ is present as a doctrine, a model, an inspiration, even an object of worship—but Christ himself and his personal agency have been rendered redundant. As we noted in earlier chapters, Christology is not Christ himself. Without clarity on this point, the significance of Jesus will be found in something other than his living presence. As Bonhoeffer reminds us time and again, when the church loses sight of the present person of Christ, ideas about him expand to fill the void.[44] Ideology replaces Christology. Christianity becomes a religious technology employed toward an ideological end. A human quantity replaces the living Lord. Christ becomes what Bonhoeffer calls a mere "Christ-idea."[45] He becomes a bearer of something other than himself—perhaps a moral blueprint for cultural life (for the culturalists) or a blueprint for social improvement (for the secularists). In either instance, the religious significance of Jesus becomes a human possession, something abstracted from the living person. Indeed, Christian faithfulness becomes possible without recourse to Christ himself. In precisely this way, missional faithfulness becomes tantamount to "the realization of a Christian idea" and

---

[41]William Stringfellow, *A Private and Public Faith* (Grand Rapids, MI: Eerdmans, 1962), 14.

[42]Bonhoeffer, *Letters and Papers from Prison*, DBWE 8:500.

[43]Bonhoeffer, *Theological Education Underground: 1937–1940*, DBWE 15:462.

[44]See Bonhoeffer, *Berlin: 1932–1933*, DBWE 12:302.

[45]Bonhoeffer, *Conspiracy and Imprisonment*, DBWE 16:474.

not "the reality of the living Jesus."[46] By failing to account for *Christus praesens*, both culturalists and secularists expect ideas about Christ to do what only Christ himself can do. They have ideologized the gospel.

Bonhoeffer's untiring focus on *Christus praesens* allows him to construe Jesus in nonideological terms—i.e., to think christologically without resorting to abstraction—thereby opening up a way to imagine the missional nature of the church that is not beholden to ideologizing tendencies. Bonhoeffer recognized that his possibility is grounded exclusively in Christ himself. Indeed, as Bonhoeffer powerfully claims, Jesus was the one and only human "who . . . did not lapse into ideology."[47] Only through participating in him can the church transcend the fragmented and competitive patterns of sinful existence.

This realization frees the church to embrace the movement inherent to its identity as a sent community. Christ himself has overcome any supposed centripetal-centrifugal dichotomy; "go . . . and make disciples of all nations" (Mt 28:19) and "come, follow me" (Mt 19:21) do not take place at a distance from each other. Precisely in coming to Jesus, one walks in, with, and toward the world. This means that the church is not a safe and stable entity at the periphery of the world that subsequently, as a secondary step, moves toward its center. Nor, conversely, must we leave ecclesial identity behind in order to stand at the center of the world. Bonhoeffer's christological remeasurement of reality renders both logics nonsensical. The church lives at the center or it does not live at all. Indeed, the church is most truly the church when it lives at the center, when it lives where Jesus lives. Only a non-ontologized community that refuses to be co-opted into ideological patterns of competition can at once be geographically specific and yet not culturally captive. For such a community, retreat, seclusion, and opposition no longer stand as prerequisites for prophetic leverage vis-à-vis its particular locale, and assimilation and secularization are no longer the only means by which to become present to the cultural moment.

When the gospel is ideologized, mission becomes a matter of implementing the idea, of putting the ideology into action. The mistaken assumption animating the logic of mission in this case is that the church must

---

[46]Bonhoeffer, *Ethics*, DBWE 6:156.
[47]Bonhoeffer, *Ethics*, DBWE 6:263.

control history. The course of history could run any number of directions, it is believed, and thus the church must strive to ensure it moves in the right one. The problem with this view of mission, of course, is that it forgets that history has found an end in Jesus, that he holds all things together, and that he alone brings the kingdom. When the gospel is ideologized, we subsequently imagine that the course of history lies outside of Christ's control. For secularists, this means that the church must provide blueprints and programs to improve the world and thereby create a more kingdomlike future. For culturalists, this means that mission becomes a matter of constructing an alternative to world history.

Notice that in both cases the missional mistake rests upon a fundamental misunderstanding of the nature of reality. Whereas Bonhoeffer sees all reality in Christ, ideologized versions of Christianity relegate Christ to "a partial, provincial affair within the whole of reality."[48] Rather than being the ground and goal of creation, Christ has been collapsed into one particular segment of it. When the gospel is ideologized, the church becomes a bearer of an idea and as such becomes just one program in contest with others. Competition becomes the necessary mode of ecclesial existence.[49] But when the church becomes just one social option among others, Bonhoeffer believes, it forfeits its freedom to participate in God's ongoing mission in the world. Its missional faithfulness is therefore rendered contingent upon its ability to compete with the world. This is what Bonhoeffer means when he claims that collapsing the gospel into a political ideology risks abandoning "the highly political substance of the church."[50] The church indeed has a political substance—for God's kingdom comes on earth. But because this kingdom ultimately belongs to God, the church is freed from the various burdens that plague an ideologized community.

THE FREEDOM OF MISSION IN CHRIST

When the church sees its mission in terms of participation in the person of Christ who has transcended ideological captivity and reconciled all things, it thereby discovers its missional freedom. Because the ultimate fate of the

---

[48]Bonhoeffer, *Ethics*, DBWE 6:57.
[49]See Bonhoeffer, *Discipleship*, DBWE 4:59-61.
[50]Bonhoeffer, *Berlin*, DBWE 12:265.

world belongs to Christ, the church is freed from the pressure to produce a new world. Instead, it is free *to witness*. Because all things are united in him, it need not provincialize itself. Instead, it is free *to cross borders*. Because Christ, the crucified One, is the source of its life, the church need not pursue its own survival. Instead, it is free *to give itself away*.

Freedom to witness. If the church is most fundamentally the reality of Christ's social presence, then the church's mission is to make Christ manifest to a particular time and place. When the church gathers to worship, Christ becomes manifest to those who are gathered. When the church is sent out, it makes Christ manifest to those who are not gathered. There are obviously key differences between gathering and sending, but these are not two distinct realities, for the same underlying logic animates both movements. Ecclesial life is never simply intraecclesial life. The gathered community always encounters those who do not gather. The church exists simultaneously both in its coming and its going. Whether gathered or dispersed, the church's mission is the same: to witness to Jesus, to make his life manifest.

For Bonhoeffer, this witness happens in two general ways. "The church of Jesus Christ is the place . . . in the world where the reign of Jesus Christ over the whole world is to be *demonstrated* and *proclaimed*."[51] To say that witness is an act of proclamation is to say that the church serves the world through raising its voice. "There is no legitimate proclamation by the church that is not proclamation of Christ."[52] Indeed, Bonhoeffer boldly contends that any sort of social engagement apart from proclamation is "unthinkable for the New Testament."[53] Since mission is ultimately a participatory activity grounded in Christ's reconciliation of all things, the goal "is not . . . that the condition of the world be improved by my efforts, but that the reality of God show itself everywhere to be the ultimate reality."[54]

Lest this traditionally verbal account of witness lead to social apathy, Bonhoeffer reminds us that witness to Christ also takes political form. The second form of witness—witness as demonstration—necessarily entails social and material dimensions. One must keep in mind that the church's

---

[51]Bonhoeffer, *Ethics*, DBWE 6:63, emphasis added.
[52]Bonhoeffer, *Ethics*, DBWE 6:399.
[53]Bonhoeffer, *Conspiracy and Imprisonment*, DBWE 16:544.
[54]Bonhoeffer, *Ethics*, DBWE 6:48.

demonstration of Christ's reign is guided by the logic of witness rather than the logic of production. Perhaps we could say that Bonhoeffer's account of witness-as-demonstration calls for social justice in a proclamatory mode, justice as a proclamation of hope for what only Christ can create. Bonhoeffer would remind us that acts of justice gain theological significance not from human effort, intention, or accomplishment but from their ability to demonstrate the reality of Christ's reconciliation. Even if the church is not called to improve the world, "by virtue of its very nature, the church-community stands in a place of responsibility for the world that God in Christ has loved. Wherever the church-community does not perceive this responsibility, it ceases to be a church-community of Christ."[55] The notion that justice is ultimately proclamatory rather than productive is a radically freeing realization. In order to witness faithfully, the church need not espouse any particular social theory, political ideology, or economic program. The church best serves the social, political, and economic dimensions of reality by proclaiming Christ as their ground and telos.[56]

Bonhoeffer would remind the church eager to improve the world that Christ is the Lord of history and that no program for social improvement can ultimately control historical outcomes. "The church leaves the worry for the future to its Lord."[57] He notes elsewhere that the New Testament's eschatological view of history does not allow for social progress or evolution.[58] Precisely because Christ has reconciled all things, the church is freed from the responsibility of turning the world into the kingdom of God.[59] The peace we can create pales in comparison to the peace of God's coming kingdom. Our ideologies cannot compare to Christ himself. Even our best attempts at justice remain mired in the web of sin. Saying this is not an excuse to avoid social responsibility, for Bonhoeffer remains adamant that issues of justice and human well-being are absolutely central to the church's mission in the world—but they remain always penultimate and proclamatory. They are

---

[55]Bonhoeffer, *Conspiracy and Imprisonment*, DBWE 16:543.

[56]Of course, the witnessing community must still make judgments about the political and economic aspects affecting the demonstration of the gospel in a certain time and place. But even in so doing, the church is never constrained by these judgments, and it must never reduce its mission to the logic of any particular political or economic ideology.

[57]Bonhoeffer, *Theological Education Underground*, DBWE 15:434.

[58]Bonhoeffer, *Berlin*, DBWE 12:241.

[59]Bonhoeffer, *Ethics*, DBWE 6:224-25.

motivated not by ideological convictions about how to control history but out of a desire to witness to the one who does.

Freedom to cross borders. The Christ in whom the church participates is the Christ who overcomes social division by breaking down the dividing wall of hostility, reconciling those who were far off to those who were near, and creating one new humanity in his flesh (Eph 2:11-22). The Christ in whom the church participates is the Christ in whom "there is no longer Jew or Greek, there is no longer slave or free, there is no longer male and female" (Gal 3:28). The Christ in whom the church participates is the Christ who sent his followers to all nations (Mt 28:19). The church should expect, therefore, that missional faithfulness will require it to cross the various borders and divisions that sin erects in the world. Indeed, when the danger facing the church is not the world per se but the powers therein that attempt to co-opt the things of the world toward the ends of death (see Eph 6:12), the church is free to transgress borders. It is free to move headlong into the center of reality while remaining free from worldly patterns of segregation and thus free for the world.

We noted in chapter seven that the fear of transgressing cultural boundaries is especially acute in proponents of the culturalist option.[60] This fear takes particularly pernicious shape in a truncated account of the church's apostolicity. Culturally competitive accounts of the church often rely upon a conception of apostolicity that is tantamount to cultural continuity. Robert Jenson suggests, for example, that apostolic succession—along with canon and creed—is one of the touchstones that sustains normative ecclesial standards across time.[61] Apostolicity, on this account, is a matter of cultural production and continuity, a task entrusted to the church to ensure it remains the church.

But if the church's task is to participate in Christ and not to produce a culture, a new notion of apostolicity becomes possible, one in which the church's "sentness" comes to the fore and one that requires the church to

---

[60]However, we should not forget that the secularist option, though more readily embracing the world, similarly feels the temptation to leave the church confined to its own cultural location as it moves away from the church and into the world.

[61]Robert W. Jenson, *Canon and Creed* (Louisville, KY: Westminster John Knox, 2010), 71-76; and idem, *The Works of God*, vol. 2 of *Systematic Theology* (Oxford: Oxford University Press, 1999), 232-34.

cross borders. Apostolicity, on this account, has more to do with the church's relationship with the risen Lord than with a normative pattern of life. As the apostle Paul suggests, his own apostolicity came not "from human authorities" and is "not of human origin" (Gal 1:1, 11) but derives solely from the call of the risen Christ. Paul's institutional authority is derivative of his apostolicity, not its ground. On this reading, apostolicity has unique material significance grounded in Christ himself. As the one who was himself sent, Jesus sends his apostles to participate in his ongoing mission (cf. Jn 20:21). Indeed, it is Jesus' very presence—"I am with you always" (Mt 28:20)—that both establishes and sustains the church's missional existence. For sure, the church is also apostolic in the sense that it is devoted to the apostles' teaching (Acts 2:42), but this should not skew the more fundamental fact that this teaching arises from a commission to move to the ends of the earth as a means of making Jesus manifest to the world (Acts 1:8).

Whereas the notion of apostolicity as cultural continuity is tempted to view the diversity of worldwide Christianity as a regrettable loss or an ongoing process of falling away from a normative culture, apostolicity as sentness views such diversity as the proper consequence of mission. Indeed, such diversity is the ideal outcome of a church that is free to cross borders. As John Flett suggests, "Cross-cultural transmission and local appropriation are necessary to a theological definition of apostolicity."[62] Rather than evidence that the church has given up a normative pattern of ecclesial life, cultural diversity becomes a living expression of the church's apostolicity and, indeed, a fruit of its participation in the ongoing mission of Jesus.

Freedom to give itself away. Underlying the culturalist-secularist dichotomy is the danger that Christ and the world stand in a competitive relationship; as Bonhoeffer puts it, the two are always "bumping against and repelling each other."[63] On this misguided reading, the church that endeavors to follow Christ has no choice but to compete with the world for space. Encounter between the two can only happen in the midst of contest. But if we refuse to ontologize the church, a new possibility emerges. The church predicated upon the person of Christ taken to be an ontological fact

---

[62]John G. Flett, *Apostolicity: The Ecumenical Question in World Christian Perspective* (Downers Grove, IL: InterVarsity Press, 2016), 184.

[63]Bonhoeffer, *Ethics*, DBWE 6:57.

can live noncompetitively. Because all reality exists in Christ, distinction does not necessitate opposition. Distinction emerges precisely in being un-equivocally *for* the world. Bonhoeffer can therefore claim that the church is an instrument and not an end in itself.[64]

Certainly, the church must attend to the quality of its own life. As Bon-hoeffer puts it, "witness to the world can only happen in the right way when it comes out of a sanctified life in God's church-community."[65] Im-portantly, this sanctification is not a matter of buttressing itself from the world. As Bonhoeffer suggests, "the space of the church is the place where witness is given to the foundation of all reality in Jesus Christ. . . . The space of the church is not there in order to fight with the world for a piece of its territory, but precisely to testify to the world . . . that is loved and reconciled by God." He concludes, "The church can only defend its own space by fighting, not for space, but for the salvation of the world. . . . So the first task given to those who belong to the church of God is not to be something for themselves . . . but to be witnesses of Jesus Christ to the world."[66] In this way, Bonhoeffer offers a paradoxical notion of the church's unique identity; he imagines the church as a distinct space precisely in that its distinctiveness allows it to point beyond itself. However, in this en-deavor, the unique activity of the church must remain ordered toward its telos. Its uniqueness is not an end in itself. Indeed, the activity that consti-tutes the uniqueness of the church is activity that would be absurd as an end in itself, activity that only makes sense if Christ himself is the ground and life of the community.

Perhaps the most absurd of such activities is the activity of being for others. "Our relationship to God is a new life in 'being there for others,' through participation in the being of Jesus," Bonhoeffer claims.[67] When he argues that "the church is church only when it is there for others,"[68] he is not reasoning in terms of some sort of works-based righteousness; rather, he is indicating that the church exists precisely as it participates in Christ's history.

---

[64]Bonhoeffer, *Ethics*, DBWE 6:404.
[65]Bonhoeffer, *Ethics*, DBWE 6:63-64.
[66]Bonhoeffer, *Ethics*, DBWE 6:63-64.
[67]Bonhoeffer, *Letters and Papers from Prison*, DBWE 8:501.
[68]Bonhoeffer, *Letters and Papers from Prison*, DBWE 8:503.

Bonhoeffer's path beyond the culturalist-secularist tension becomes especially clear at the very end of his *Ethics* manuscripts. Here he rearticulates the tension between the culturalist and secularist options in terms of the community's "double divine purpose":

> The church as a distinct corporate entity is thus subject to a double divine purpose, to both of which it must do justice, namely, being oriented toward the world, and, in this very act, simultaneously being oriented toward itself as the place where Jesus Christ is present. . . . The danger of Roman Catholicism is that it understands the church essentially as an end in itself, at the expense of the divine mandate of proclaiming the word. Conversely, the danger of the Reformation is that it focuses exclusively on the mandate of proclaiming the word at the expense of attending to the church as a distinct domain and thus overlooks almost completely that the church is an end in itself, which consists precisely in its being-for-the-world.[69]

Here we again see Bonhoeffer's proclivity for charting a third way between opposing alternatives. Again, the paradoxical nature of the christological option becomes apparent; the church can be an end in itself only in its being for others. Though stressing the penultimacy of ecclesial space might seem to undermine the importance of cultivating the space itself, Bonhoeffer makes no such move. For him, a life habituated within the space of the church remains a vital presupposition for missional faithfulness. Whereas some accounts of ecclesial formation place the community in conflict with the world, Bonhoeffer here imagines an account of formation that does the very opposite. The church fosters its unique life precisely because it knows that it is not ultimately an end in itself.

Herein lies the uniquely countercultural force of the church. In contrast to other communities, the church recognizes that cultural defensiveness is not an essential ingredient of cultural identity. In a world marked by self-protectiveness, a community that finds its being in giving itself away will stand out as a radically countercultural force. Following a crucified Lord, the church is free to eschew the morality of survival, and in this freedom it witnesses to a radically different form of life.

---

[69]Bonhoeffer, *Ethics*, DBWE 6:405-7.

Shortly after completing the paragraph quoted above, Bonhoeffer was arrested. There is something fitting about this biographical coincidence. Bonhoeffer was literally giving himself away in service as he theorized the ecclesiological basis for a church that could freely give itself away. His ecclesiological reflections are richest at the point where his faithfulness is most costly.

The Pattern of Bonhoeffer's Missional Hermeneutic: Who Is Jesus Christ for Us Today?

Bonhoeffer would have us see that mission emerges from discipleship, from following the Lord into ever new situations. Because mission is participatory, its particular shape is specific to its context. The precise nature of missional faithfulness, then, cannot be predicted in advance. The key to mission lies in the community's ability to constantly discern anew the form of engagement with the world that corresponds to Christ's presence in a given time and place.

From prison Bonhoeffer gestures toward the hermeneutical dimensions of his missional ecclesiology. If all reality is united in Christ, if all ontological distinction has been eradicated in his person, if God and world are inseparably bound in him, if Christ has overcome ideologizing tendencies—then what does it mean to think, speak, and interpret reality in a distinctly Christian manner? His famous conclusion—that we must interpret biblical concepts in a "non-religious" manner—takes with utter seriousness the presence of the risen Christ while also insisting, with no less seriousness, that the Christ of the church is also Lord of the world. To say that the world has "come of age"—Bonhoeffer's equally (in)famous claim—is thus not to insinuate that all things divine must be collapsed into a secular idiom for the sake of making the faith more palatable to the growing masses of the unchurched. It is actually, on the contrary, to make a strikingly constructive claim about the newly emerging religionless world. Precisely this world has implicitly recognized something about the nature of reality that the church has forgotten—namely, that reality cannot be fragmented. Rather than an unfortunate degeneration into secularity, the world's coming of age actually clears the way for Bonhoeffer to claim that the church can—indeed, must— resist the twin urges to sequester itself in some religious ghetto or to abandon its unique identity. The church must live squarely at the center of reality, and must do so precisely as the church. This happens when the church pursues its Lord, who is himself the center of reality. The church's centrality is therefore a byproduct of its attentiveness to Jesus. The uniqueness of the church is most glaringly evident when it asks the question that gives shape and substance to its thinking: "Who is Jesus Christ for us today?" For Bonhoeffer, this question animates the imagination of the church in a world come of age. This is the question that guides the church's ongoing efforts to discern Jesus' presence. This is, therefore, the hermeneutical question par excellence, the fundamental question that structures the hermeneutic of a church in mission.

The church in mission reads Scripture because and as it asks this question: "Who is Jesus Christ for us today?" Were it to stop asking in this manner, it could stop turning to its text. Christ's mobility is the necessary presupposition for the hermeneutical task, its very raison d'être. If Christ were inert, if he were reduced to a Christ-idea, or if his ongoing life could be conflated into a certain cultural pattern, the hermeneutical problem would vanish. There would be no reason to keep reading. Yet as we have seen, the out-aheadness of the risen One undercuts the notion that any particular representation of him is pure and pristine, abstractly relevant for all times and places. The ongoing livelihood of Christ and the concomitant movement of the gospel compel the church ever anew to embrace the task of understanding. Christ is on the move in the world through the Spirit, and the church continues to struggle with its text because it feels the weight of its missional responsibility to "remain in step with God."[70] For the church, therefore, mission is why hermeneutics exists. And we must flip the equation: for the church the task of hermeneutics is necessarily missional. Mission constitutes the context and aims of the hermeneutical enterprise.

THE HABITS OF A MISSIONAL HERMENEUTIC

We are now in a position to ask the practical question. If mission necessarily shapes the ecclesial context in which Scripture is read, what reading habits and practices follow suit? What sort of readerly activity will sustain a

---

[70]Bonhoeffer, *Letters and Papers from Prison*, DBWE 8:228.

missional hermeneutic? At the least, such a hermeneutic will be ongoing, patient, intercultural, and liturgical.

An ongoing hermeneutic. If one were to reduce Scripture to a bearer of abstract principles or timeless ideals, one theoretically could, with enough time and study, definitively grasp the meaning of the text. After enough interpretive work one could actually extract everything relevant from the text and dispense with Scripture itself. Scripture would become as useless as an excavated mine. Christ's living voice would thereby be rendered superfluous, and the readers themselves would become, as Bonhoeffer fears, "the schoolmasters of the Holy Scripture."[71]

Bonhoeffer points us in another direction. As we have seen, his theological imagination emerges from the straightforward conviction that Christ is personal. Persons are on the move; ideas are not. Thus Bonhoeffer recognizes the obvious: "God speaks differently to his church in different times."[72] This simple recognition deals the deathblow to the "lordship of ideas"[73] and paves the way for a genuinely missional hermeneutic. In contrast to hermeneutical schemes that prioritize thought or abstraction, Bonhoeffer's approach to the Bible allows for no finality. The church never stops asking, "Who is Jesus Christ for us today?" The church never reaches a point where it understands a text so well that it can forgo serious ongoing engagement with it. "God's word is not the sum of a few general sentences that could be in my mind at any time," Bonhoeffer claims; "rather it is God's daily new word addressed to me, expounded in its never-ending wealth of interpretation."[74] Precisely because the gospel "must be sought again and again,"[75] the church never rests content with previous interpretive outcomes. This is why Bonhoeffer repeatedly stresses the ongoing nature of the hermeneutical enterprise. He suggests, for example, that Scripture is given to the church "as the word which becomes God's revelation ever anew,"[76] that it must be "read and pondered anew every day," and that in it we encounter "God's daily new word." He thereby recommends "repeated reading of the

---

[71]Bonhoeffer, *Theological Education Underground*, DBWE 15:501.
[72]Bonhoeffer, *Theological Education Underground*, DBWE 15:439.
[73]Bonhoeffer, *Theological Education Underground*, DBWE 15:519.
[74]Bonhoeffer, *Theological Education Underground*, DBWE 15:517.
[75]Bonhoeffer, *Discipleship*, DBWE 4:45.
[76]Bonhoeffer, *Barcelona, Berlin, New York*, DBWE 10:382.

text until the center comes into view."[77] Instead of resorting to preconceived commitments, a missional community is free to recognize that the "dynamic of pilgrimage and the eschatological tension of exile render *every* answer tentative, partial, and situational in the best sense of the word."[78] A church that walks along the path of discipleship knows that even though the Christ who walks ahead of it is eternally consistent—the same yesterday, today, and forever—he speaks a living Word today.

A patient hermeneutic. As I suggested above, sinful powers strive against Christ's reconciling work by attempting to refragment reality and ideologize the gospel. In so doing, they exert force over the act of reading. The reason for this has to do with the way thinking happens within ideologized space. By erecting dividing walls, the powers trap the church within a self-enclosed echo chamber. Interpretive myopia ensues, for the church's hermeneutical imagination remains confined to itself. In this sense, the powers militate against mission by proffering the seductive words of ideology as a replacement for God's living voice. At first glance, echo-chamber readings possess a certain allure. They tempt the reading community with the prospect of certitude and the assured perpetuation of cultural life. As Bonhoeffer realized, ideologues are never forced into the difficult process of sitting with uncertainty, for they possess at their disposal an unambiguous standard by which to judge every decision.[79] Like the serpent in the garden, ideology promises seemingly easy understanding, knowledge without a cost. Ideology answers the church's hermeneutical questions before they are even asked. Patience is no longer a hermeneutical necessity.

Bonhoeffer offers a very different account of interpretation. He recognizes that the practice of "serious attention, tireless asking, and learning"[80] must characterize the church's interpretive practices. As he says of his own reading, "I need time for God's word and often have to ponder the words for a long time in order to understand the precepts of God correctly."[81] We

---

[77]Bonhoeffer, *Theological Education at Finkenwalde*, DBWE 14:495. He repeats this advice in a later cycle of the same lecture (Bonhoeffer, *Theological Education at Finkenwalde*, DBWE 14:523).

[78]Gerald W. Schlabach, "Deuteronomic or Constantinian: What Is the Most Basic Problem for Christian Social Ethics?" in *The Wisdom of the Cross: Essays in Honor of John Howard Yoder*, ed. Stanley Hauerwas, et al (Grand Rapids, MI: Eerdmans, 1999), 461.

[79]Bonhoeffer, *Ethics*, DBWE 6:227.

[80]Bonhoeffer, *Theological Education Underground*, DBWE 15:508.

[81]Bonhoeffer, *Theological Education Underground*, DBWE 15:517.

noted earlier that the church does not apprehend divine speech in a timeless moment. Here the logic of mission helps us expand on this claim: because the church lives in the world only as it participates in Christ, it can approach its task with a nonchalant seriousness, free from the panicked hyperactivity that would indeed characterize its missional life if mission did not belong to God. Just as the church in mission does not bear responsibility for achieving particular historical outcomes, neither does it bear responsibility for producing particular hermeneutical outcomes. So we must say both that the church's hermeneutical imagination never stagnates—for it is always on the move—and also that it need not rush—for this movement is always derivative of Christ's.

Precisely because the community in mission always exists in a mode of following its Lord, it must continually plead for God's Word anew. The psalmist's words mark the rhythm of a missional hermeneutic: "I live as an alien in the land; / do not hide your commandments from me" (Ps 119:19). Thus Bonhoeffer writes, commenting on Psalm 119, that "the more we receive, the more we have to seek God."[82] "Each realization that I receive," he continues, "only drives me more deeply into the word of God."[83] With no settled place from which to secure answers, the sojourning community necessarily lives in a posture of dependence, which takes shape hermeneutically as a willingness to sit patiently with Scripture as a means of discerning Christ's presence today.

By holding open our attention to Christ, interpretive patience holds open the possibility of surprise. If ideologically produced certainty promotes timeless understanding, then patient reading remains open to the possibility that something unforeseen might spring from the text. At the least, this entails reading Scripture, as much as possible, as if one has not read the text before. This is not a naive suggestion that we somehow ought to become neutral and objective as a means of unearthing the text's one true meaning. As I have been suggesting all along, the most "objective" hermeneutical posture is the one that takes shape in Christ's wake. This means that interpretive objectivity actually entails the capacity to be shocked, disturbed, or interrupted by the text. The church in mission must habitually attune itself to dimensions of the text

---

[82]Bonhoeffer, *Theological Education Underground*, DBWE 15:513.
[83]Bonhoeffer, *Theological Education Underground*, DBWE 15:517.

that unsettle its assumed sensibilities. The church in mission expects to be caught off guard. The church that reads within the ongoing movement of missional discernment must attempt to deliberately acknowledge the preconceptions it brings to the text, and it must attempt to interrogate the extent to which these preconceptions may blind it to Christ's activity in the moment. In short, the church must be open to hearing his voice—and thus must be willing to invest the time and patience that such hearing requires.

An intercultural hermeneutic. Bonhoeffer's christological remeasurement of reality suggests that the church's capacity for discernment is heightened when it moves into the world. If the Word that God speaks through the text is indeed the Word that sustains and unites all things, the church in mission can expect to glimpse God in surprising ways. Mission helps the church learn to see.

Though Bonhoeffer never unpacks the intercultural implications that follow from this christological groundwork, his ecclesiology coheres well with the actual experience of the gospel's worldwide movement. Indeed, we can suggest that Bonhoeffer provides the christological basis for the ecclesiological experience of global Christianity. As Lamin Sanneh suggests, calling to mind Bonhoeffer's discipleship motif, "the God whom the missionary came to serve . . . actually preceded him or her in the field." In order to discover God's true identity, Sanneh continues, the missionary must step beyond his cultural confines and "delve deep into the local culture."[84] Locatedness is key for understanding. We should expect as much from a God who in becoming incarnate gave himself concrete location. As Andrew Walls suggests, "The first divine act of translation [in the incarnation] gives rise to a constant succession of new translations. Christian diversity is the necessary product of the incarnation."[85] Because it follows the incarnate Lord, the church recognizes that there is no good news apart from cross-cultural movement and concomitant acts of translation and interpretation.

---

[84]Lamin Sanneh, "The Horizontal and the Vertical in Mission: An African Perspective," *International Bulletin of Missionary Research* 7, no. 4 (1983): 166. Also see Grant LeMarquand, "African Biblical Interpretation," in *Dictionary for Theological Interpretation*, ed. Kevin J. Vanhoozer, Craig G. Bartholomew, Daniel J. Treier, and N. T. Wright (Grand Rapids, MI: Baker Academic, 2005), 33-34.

[85]Andrew Walls, *The Missionary Movement in Christian History: Studies in the Transmission of Faith* (Maryknoll, NY: Orbis, 1996), 27-28.

We can thus affirm the mutually reinforcing nature of immersion in Scripture and immersion in the world.[86] Meaning moves in more than one direction. There is a sense, therefore, in which "it is the 'missionary' . . . who is the one being evangelized."[87] Bonhoeffer intimates as much when he claims that "mission . . . is both giving and receiving."[88] It comes as no surprise, then, when Bonhoeffer writes, "My recent activity . . . in the worldly sector gives me so much to think about. . . . When I open the Bible again, it is new and delightful to me as never before."[89] Robert Schreiter similarly argues that "information is both lost and gained when crossing a cultural boundary."[90] He goes on to suggest that in "too much reflection on intercultural dynamics of Christian evangelization, there is an overemphasis on whether 'they' (the hearers) are going to get the Christian message right. . . . There is not enough emphasis on the transformation of the speaker."[91] Walls likewise reminds us, "It is a delightful paradox that the more Christ is translated into the various thought forms and life systems which form our various national identities, the richer all of us will be in our common Christian identity."[92] As Willie Jennings suggests, the intercultural logic of the church's mission stands as "an invitation to change, transform, and expand our identities."[93] Perhaps this mindset is on display when Bonhoeffer wonders if the so-called "heathenism" of India contains more Christianity than "the whole of our Reich Church." Because Christianity "has become so westernized and so permeated by civilized thought," Bonhoeffer was convinced that a journey to visit Gandhi would help form authentic faith.[94] He seemed to believe that entering the story of another—what Willie Jennings calls a

---

[86]See Angus Paddison, "Theological Interpretation and the Bible as Public Text," *JTI* 8, no. 2 (2014): 175-92.

[87]David W. Congdon, *The Mission of Demythologizing: Rudolf Bultmann's Dialectical Theology* (Minneapolis: Fortress, 2015), 823.

[88]Bonhoeffer, *Conspiracy and Imprisonment*, DBWE 16:499.

[89]Bonhoeffer, *Conspiracy and Imprisonment*, DBWE 16:329.

[90]Robert J. Schreiter, *The New Catholicity: Theology Between the Global and the Local* (Maryknoll, NY: Orbis, 1997), 38.

[91]Schreiter, *New Catholicity*, 43.

[92]Walls, *Missionary Movement*, 54. Elsewhere Walls claims: "Themes are being recognized in the Scriptures that the West never notices." Andrew F. Walls, *The Cross-Cultural Process in Christian History* (Maryknoll, NY: Orbis, 2002), 46.

[93]Willie James Jennings, *Acts*, Belief: A Theological Commentary on the Bible (Louisville, KY: Westminster John Knox, 2017), 88.

[94]Bonhoeffer, *London: 1933–1935*, DBWE 13:152.

"pedagogy of joining"[95]—would serve as the pathway toward deepening both his understanding of the gospel and his lived expression of it.

This expansion of our identity happens in concrete encounter, which is why Bonhoeffer's life was marked by deliberate attempts to encounter difference by crossing boundaries. It was encountering Gandhi, Bonhoeffer believed, not merely reading his works, that would expand Christian identity; it was sitting with Christians at Abyssinian Baptist Church, not merely reading Black theology, that transformed Bonhoeffer's faith. Bonhoeffer's own practice helps us understand what he means when he claims one must be "bound to a specific place and time" in order to hear God's Word.[96] Though many readily admit that theological reflection must be contextual, this sentiment too frequently construes context in abstract and noetic terms, as if contextual theology were merely a matter of abstracting ideas from a context and somehow incorporating them into one's idea system. Bonhoeffer invites us to see that contextuality is a bodily activity and as such must be a deliberate practice. For sure, in order to discern God's concrete Word for the moment, the interpretive community must know what is going on in that moment. But the interculturality necessary to missional movement invites us to see that mere knowledge of a context is insufficient for hermeneutical faithfulness. What matters is not simply knowing about a location but being there. This is where mission—as an *act* and not merely as an idea—becomes so important for hermeneutics. The church in mission ought to be fully implicated in the life of a place. William Stringfellow captures this insight when he suggests that it does not suffice for Christians to gather "off by themselves in a parish house to study and discuss social issues." Rather, faithfulness "becomes possible only when the Christian is on the actual scene where the conflict is taking place, the decision is being made, the legislation is being enacted."[97] An intercultural dialogue with the world is not simply a cerebral exchange; the church must toss itself in the mix.

It follows, therefore, that in order to read Scripture faithfully—if we indeed read in pursuit of Christ's presence today—the church must read

---

[95] Willie James Jennings, "Reframing the World: Toward an Actual Christian Doctrine of Creation," *IJST* 21, no. 4 (2019): 394.

[96] Bonhoeffer, *Ethics*, DBWE 6:379.

[97] Stringfellow, *Private and Public Faith*, 54.

within a place and in perpetual encounter with it. Active engagement with the world stands as a prerequisite for hermeneutical faithfulness. This further bolsters the claim that missional hermeneutics is necessarily ongoing and patient. And it helps make sense of Bonhoeffer's own manner of dealing with Scripture. As we have seen, his goal in engaging the text is not to understand its original sense or distill timeless ideas from it. Rather, he aims to hear the text as a concrete Word for today. This is why he hesitates to offer once-for-all hermeneutical pronouncements. Take pacifism as an example. Though commentators routinely laud his commitment to nonviolence, we must remember that he was a *particular* pacifist, not a *principled* one. In other words, he did not claim that Scripture categorically requires pacifism; to say as much would be to turn Scripture into a bearer of timeless ideas. His hermeneutical imagination remains unrelentingly located. He reasons in a more particular manner; given this war and this cultural situation, he claims, the church must affirm nonviolence. To understand the Sermon on the Mount now means to hear Christ calling us to peace. How will Christ speak through the text in a future situation? We simply cannot know in advance. In order to hear Christ then, we will have to be there.

This is not to say that the church must refrain from all timeless claims. Indeed, the heart of the Christian faith rests on the notion that Jesus is Lord—not provisionally but universally. Here it is helpful to keep in mind the important difference between Scripture's regulative and sacramental functions. Scripture's informative capacity always works within its performative capacity. For sure, Jesus is Lord. But we more accurately grasp the nature of the Christ's lordship when we know that Jesus is Lord for us today. He is Lord here and now. He is Lord in this place.

It becomes clear, therefore, that interculturality is not merely a matter of second-order application, something practitioners do on the ground after the real work of interpretation is done. Bonhoeffer wants us to see that we are not in search of an abstract word that must be distilled and applied. The word itself is a word for today. To believe that the Bible must first speak abstractly before it then speaks to the present moment is to forget that the text is a living word that witnesses to a Lord active in history. This challenges normal conventions. In most cases, when we speak of "scriptural interpretation," we imagine an abstract conversation between an interpreter and a text. We imagine the act of interpretation culminating in a written product. And if this product is good enough, it can be published—the true sign of interpretive excellence. Admittedly, biblical interpretation that culminates in written form possesses stability across time and place. The problem, of course, is that the living Christ upsets this tidiness.

A missional hermeneutic that pursues him takes form as a conversation between Scripture and a particular slice of the world. The work of the interpreter is to facilitate the discussion. Whatever finished product may ensue will come across as time bound and utterly particular. This is nothing short of an interpretive virtue, the necessary form of a missional community's engagement with a word that is alive and active in the text and in the world. This certainly does not nullify the value of biblical exposition that seeks to shine light upon the text as a historical or literary document. Such works are not meaningless—but they are not interpretation. At best, they are (or, at least, can become) a step along the way. Written productions possess utility within the church precisely in their ability to make readers sensitive to the topography of the text and alert to the linguistic force of its words and phrases—and thereby to lead them ever more deeply into the text itself, where they hope to encounter Christ's word for today.

A liturgical hermeneutic. No doubt at this point some will question whether the hermeneutical posture I have been sketching risks compromising the unique essence of the church. If we assume the traditional tension between ecclesial distinctiveness and worldliness, it will indeed appear difficult—if not impossible—to espouse an ecclesial hermeneutic that is simultaneously a located hermeneutic. If we insist on thinking of the church as an ontologically distinct space, contextuality will never impinge upon the essence of the community. Universality will trump particularity. In this case, intraecclesial practices would bear the responsibility of constituting the church. Rather than missionary movement, it would be liturgy that makes the church. If one were to insist that church and world are two distinct categories, one could argue that it is through liturgy, not mission, that we move ever more deeply into our ecclesial identity. One who argues in this way might then suggest that if we follow Bonhoeffer in refusing to ontologize the church or ideologize the gospel, we would subsequently be forced to devalue liturgical activity and the intraecclesial practices that distinguish the church.

Admittedly, there is a sense in which this is correct. The missional posture I have been espousing in this chapter lessens the importance of the institution. The practices of the church would carry much greater weight if Christ were not present, and liturgy would indeed be of utmost consequence if we asked it to do what only Christ can do. It makes sense, then, that Christ's personal presence demotes church practices to their proper role. This is a problem only if we value the church more than its Lord.

But with this said, Bonhoeffer's missional ecclesiology certainly does not empty the liturgy of significance. In fact, it grants it unique importance. As we have seen in early chapters, Christ wills to be found in the church. The liturgy sustains faithfulness precisely to the extent that it continually reorients the community away from itself and toward the true source of its life. This is precisely why we must recast liturgy in missional terms. Because Jesus is the center of reality, to move ever more deeply into him—a movement that liturgy facilitates—is to move ever more deeply into the world. As Bonhoeffer reminds us, we cannot encounter the world without encountering Christ, and we cannot encounter Christ without encountering the world. Thus liturgy is itself a practice of locatedness, an ongoing practice of moving into the very center of reality, a practice of asking who Jesus is for us today. To relativize the distinction between church and world and to recast the church in nonontological terms is not to deny that the church possesses perduring features or to deny that ecclesial practices are central to faithfulness. It is to suggest, rather, that the significance of the church is found not in these features themselves but in the way of life they facilitate, in the One toward whom they orient the community.

By constantly directing Christians to their Lord, liturgy sustains a mode of perception appropriate to reality. As Christians encounter Christ in the congregation, they become sensitized to his presence in the world beyond the church, the very place into which the liturgy sends them. The church's liturgical practice establishes the rhythm of a missional hermeneutic, a constant movement from text to world and back again. The church's hermeneutical imagination is expanded when it encounters Christ beyond the walls of the church. And its hermeneutical imagination is refined when it encounters Christ in the liturgy. Both movements are necessary if the church is to ask, "Who is Jesus Christ for us today?"

Epilogue

I know the commandment to love my neighbor. But do we really know what that means? What does it mean to "love your neighbor"? What does that mean for the politician who has to make decisions about war and peace? What does that mean in education? In marriage? For the owner of a company? What should he do, and how does he show his love for his neighbor? By expanding this company, giving his people work, and taking it away from a hundred others? . . . And why should it mean exactly this and can't it just as well mean exactly the opposite? Yes, the text "Love your neighbor" does not have a clear meaning, does not say to us unequivocally: You should do this. But just the opposite, by placing ourselves under this commandment, we come to recognize even more deeply that God's commandment is hidden from us.[1]

With insights like this, Bonhoeffer makes the task of scriptural hermeneutics immensely challenging, if not downright impossible. If something as central and seemingly straightforward as "love your neighbor" lacks clear meaning, how are we ever to make sense of Scripture? Bonhoeffer intends for insights like this to be disorienting, but not demoralizing. When he says that God's commandment is hidden, he does not mean that God has withdrawn to some heavenly distance, thereby leaving us bereft of God's voice. On the contrary, it is not distance but presence that makes God so mysterious. God's relentless nearness in Christ prevents the church from achieving hermeneutical finality and therefore preserves divine mystery.

---

[1]Bonhoeffer, *Berlin: 1932–1933*, DBWE 12:437.

Importantly, this is a mystery that promotes the ongoing pursuit of intimacy, not the simple resignation of agnosticism. A God who continually walks with the church must be discerned ever anew. God's presence is a mystery—but it is also a gift and a task. Thus, for Bonhoeffer, the only way forward given the seeming impossibility of proper interpretation is the path of discipleship.

Through this act of following, the message of Scripture becomes clear. But notice, this is a very particular sort of clarity. The act of following is not a methodical procedure through which we acquire proper data from Scripture. No, the clarity we gain is not merely conceptual. In the wake of Christ, the knowledge we gain is deeper, a knowledge stored not in the mind but etched in the body, a knowledge that belongs not to the individual but to the community, a knowledge that exists not in a moment of stasis but in a process of movement, a knowledge gained not in cultural isolation but in perpetual encounter with the world.

For sure, the church can feel confident in its knowledge of Christ. Christ is the same yesterday, today, and forever. But this Christ is lively. Put in hermeneutical terms, this means that Scripture functions in both sacramental and regulative modes, as both a performative and informative text. A regulative text devoid of sacramentality becomes a tool for human control; a sacramental text devoid of regulation risks becoming unmoored from Christ himself. Even as both are necessary, they must be ordered. If discipleship is the structuring motif for Christian life, then Scripture's sacramental function must structure its regulative function. It makes no difference whether Scripture is informative if it is not first performative. It makes no difference whether we articulate Christ rightly if we are not following him today.

Throughout this book I have followed Bonhoeffer in suggesting that Christ's presence constitutes the church as a hermeneutical space. At the heart of his theology lies the conviction that this presence requires certain forms of knowing and that revelation yields an epistemology of its own. It must also yield a scriptural hermeneutic of its own. By examining the church in terms of its identity-defining relationships, I have suggested that this hermeneutic is not a method but a posture and that this posture can be most succinctly summarized as the ongoing act of discipleship. This account of the church implies that no tidy, delimiting definition can be given to theological interpretation. No particular hermeneutical method necessarily corresponds to Christ's presence. No style or form or pattern of biblical interpretation necessarily deserves the designation *theological*. Perhaps the most we can say is that theological interpretation is any form of human readerly activity that seeks to discern Christ in and through Scripture, any readerly activity bent toward the question, Who is Jesus Christ for us today? On this account, the church is the locus and agent of faithful reading because the church lives (or at least attempts to live) in constant awareness of Christ's presence. To say that theological interpretation happens in the church is to say that the church in all its dimensions—its habits and practices, its liturgies, its catechesis, its togetherness, its ongoing missional movement, its pursuit of justice—sustains the posture through which this presence can be discerned. An ecclesial hermeneutic, therefore, is necessarily a hermeneutic of discipleship, a form of reading that takes shape in the wake of Christ's address and hopes for it ever anew.

Bibliography

Adam, A. K. M. "Poaching on Zion: Biblical Theology as Signifying Practice." In Adam et al., *Reading Scripture with the Church,* 17-34.

Adam, A. K. M., Stephen E. Fowl, Kevin J. Vanhoozer, and Francis Watson. *Reading Scripture with the Church: Toward a Hermeneutic for Theological Interpretation.* Grand Rapids, MI: Baker Academic, 2006.

Aristotle. *Nicomachean Ethics.* In *The Basic Works of Aristotle,* edited by Richard McKeon, 2.4. New York: Modern Library, 2001.

Auerbach, Erich. *Mimesis: The Representation of Reality in Western Literature.* Translated by Willard R. Trask. Princeton, NJ: Princeton University Press, 2003.

Augustine. *Against the Epistle of Manichaeus Called Fundamental.* Translated by Richard Stothert. In *Nicene and Post-Nicene Fathers,* 1st series, edited by Philip Schaff, 4:129-50. Peabody, MA: Hendrickson, 1999.

———. *On Christian Doctrine.* Translated by J. F. Shaw. In *Nicene and Post-Nicene Fathers,* 1st series, edited by Philip Schaff, 2:513-97. Peabody, MA: Hendrickson, 1999.

Balthasar, Hans Urs von. *The Theology of Karl Barth.* Translated by Edward T. Oakes. San Francisco: Ignatius Press, 1992.

Baranowski, Shelley. *The Confessing Church, Conservative Elites, and the Nazi State.* Texts & Studies in Religion 28. Lewiston, NY: Mellen, 1986.

Barker, H. Gaylon. *The Cross of Reality: Luther's Theologia Crucis and Bonhoeffer's Christology.* Minneapolis: Fortress, 2015.

———. "Editor's Introduction to the English Edition." In *Theological Education at Finkenwalde: 1935–1937.* English translation edited by H. Gaylon Barker and Mark S. Brocker, translated by Douglas W. Stott, 1-46. DBWE 14. Minneapolis: Fortress, 2013.

Barnett, Victoria J. *For the Soul of the People: Protestant Protest Against Hitler.* Oxford: Oxford University Press, 1992.

Barram, Michael. "The Bible, Mission, and Social Location: Toward a Missional Hermeneutic." *Interpretation* 61, no. 1 (2007): 42-58.

———. "Reflections on the Practice of Missional Hermeneutics: 'Streaming' Philippians 1:20-30." Paper presented at the Annual Meeting of the Society of Biblical Literature, New Orleans, LA, November 2009.

Barth, Karl. *Church Dogmatics.* Vol. I/2, *The Doctrine of the Word of God.* Edited by G. W. Bromiley and T. F. Torrance. Translated by G. T. Thomson and Harold Knight. Edinburgh: T&T Clark, 1980.

———. *Church Dogmatics.* Vol. IV/2, *The Doctrine of Reconciliation.* Edited by G. W. Bromiley and T. F. Torrance. Translated by G. W. Bromiley. Edinburgh: T&T Clark, 1958.

———. *Church Dogmatics.* Vol. IV/3.2, *The Doctrine of Reconciliation.* Edited by G.W. Bromiley and T. F. Torrance. Translated by G. W. Bromiley. Edinburgh: T&T Clark, 1962.

——. *The Epistle to the Romans.* Translated by Edwyn C. Hoskyns from the 6th edition. Oxford: Oxford University Press, 1968.

——. *The Humanity of God.* Translated by John Newton Thomas and Thomas Wieser. Louisville, KY: Westminster John Knox Press, 1960.

——. *The Word of God and the Word of Man.* Translated by Douglas Horton. New York: Harper & Row, 1957.

Barton, John. *The Nature of Biblical Criticism.* Louisville, KY: Westminster John Knox, 2007.

Bauckham, Richard. *Bible and Mission: Christian Witness in a Postmodern World.* Grand Rapids, MI: Baker Academic, 2003.

——. *Jesus and the God of Israel: God Crucified and Other Studies on the New Testament's Christology of Divine Identity.* Grand Rapids, MI: Eerdmans, 2008.

Bediako, Kwame. *Christianity in Africa: The Renewal of a Non-Western Religion.* Maryknoll, NY: Orbis, 1996.

——. *Jesus and the Gospel in Africa: History and Experience.* Maryknoll, NY: Orbis, 2004.

——. "Scripture as the Interpreter of Culture and Tradition." In *African Bible Commentary: A One-Volume Commentary Written by 70 African Scholars,* edited by Tokunboh Adeyemo, 3-5. Nairobi: WordAlive, 2006.

Berkman, John, and Michael G. Cartwright, eds. *The Hauerwas Reader.* Durham, NC: Duke University Press, 2001.

Berkouwer, G. C. *Holy Scripture.* Grand Rapids, MI: Eerdmans, 1975.

Bethge, Eberhard. *Dietrich Bonhoeffer: A Biography.* Edited by Victoria J. Barnett. Translated by Eric Mosbacher et al. Rev. ed. Minneapolis: Fortress, 2000.

Billings, J. Todd. *The Word of God for the People of God: An Entryway to the Theological Interpretation of Scripture.* Grand Rapids, MI: Eerdmans, 2010.

Bliese, Richard. "Bonhoeffer and the Great Commission: Does Bonhoeffer Have a Theology of Mission?" In Kelly and Weborg, *Reflections on Bonhoeffer,* 253-66.

Blomberg, Craig L. *A New Testament Theology.* Waco, TX: Baylor University Press, 2018.

Bockmuehl, Markus. *Seeing the Word: Refocusing New Testament Study.* Grand Rapids, MI: Baker, 2006.

Boff, Leonardo. *Jesus Christ Liberator: A Critical Christology for Our Time.* Translated by Patrick Hughes. Maryknoll, NY: Orbis, 1978.

Bonhoeffer, Dietrich. *Act and Being.* Edited by Hans Richard Reuter and Wayne Whitson Floyd. Translated by Martin H. Rumscheidt. DBWE 2. Minneapolis: Fortress, 1996.

——. *Barcelona, Berlin, New York: 1928–1931.* Edited by Clifford J. Green. Translated by Douglas W. Stott. DBWE 10. Minneapolis: Fortress, 2008.

——. *Berlin: 1932–1933.* Edited by Larry L. Rasmussen. Translated by Douglas W. Stott, Isabel Best, and David Higgins. DBWE 12. Minneapolis: Fortress, 2009.

——. *Christology.* Translated by John Bowden. London: Collins, 1966.

——. *Conspiracy and Imprisonment: 1940–1945.* Edited by Mark S. Brocker. Translated by Lisa E. Dahill. DBWE 16. Minneapolis: Fortress, 2006.

——. *Creation and Fall: A Theological Exegesis of Genesis 1–3.* Edited by John W. de Gruchy. Translated by Douglas Stephen Bax. DBWE 3. Minneapolis: Fortress, 1997.

——. *Discipleship.* Edited by Geffrey B. Kelly and John D. Godsey. Translated by Barbara Green and Reinhard Krauss. DBWE 4. Minneapolis: Fortress, 2003.

——. *Ecumenical, Academic, and Pastoral Work: 1931–1932.* Edited by Victoria J. Barnett et al. Translated by Douglas W. Stott et al. DBWE 11. Minneapolis: Fortress, 2012.

——. *Ethics.* Edited by Clifford J. Green. Translated by Reinhard Krauss, Charles C. West, and Douglas W. Stott. DBWE 6. Minneapolis: Fortress, 2009.

———. *Letters and Papers from Prison*. Edited by John W. de Gruchy. Translated by Isabel Best et al. DBWE 8. Minneapolis: Fortress, 2009.

———. *Life Together and Prayerbook of the Bible*. Edited by Geffrey B. Kelly. Translated by Daniel W. Bloesch and James H. Burtness. DBWE 5. Minneapolis: Fortress, 1996.

———. *London: 1933–1935*. Edited by Keith W. Clements. Translated by Isabel Best. DBWE 13. Minneapolis: Fortress, 2007.

———. *Sanctorum Communio: A Theological Study of the Sociology of the Church*. Edited by Clifford J. Green. Translated by Reinhard Krauss and Nancy Lukens. DBWE 1. Minneapolis: Fortress, 1998.

———. *Theological Education at Finkenwalde: 1935–1937*. Edited by Mark Brocker and H. Gaylon Barker. Translated by Douglas W. Stott. DBWE 14. Minneapolis: Fortress, 2013.

———. *Theological Education Underground: 1937–1940*. Edited by Victoria J. Barnett. Translated by Victoria J. Barnett et al. DBWE 15. Minneapolis: Fortress, 2012.

———. *The Young Bonhoeffer: 1918–1927*. Edited by Paul Duane Matheny, Clifford J. Green, and Marshall D. Johnson. Translated by Mary C. Nebelsick and Douglas W. Stott. DBWE 9. Minneapolis: Fortress, 2003.

Bosch, David J. *Transforming Mission: Paradigm Shifts in Theology of Mission*. Maryknoll, NY: Orbis, 1991.

Bourdieu, Pierre. *Pascalian Meditations*. Translated by Richard Nice. Stanford, CA: Stanford University Press, 2000.

Braaten, Carl E. "The Problem of Authority in the Church." In *The Catholicity of the Reformation*, edited by Carl E. Braaten and Robert W. Jenson, 53-66. Grand Rapids, MI: Eerdmans, 1996.

Briggs, Richard S. *Words in Action: Speech Act Theory and Biblical Interpretation*. Edinburgh: T&T Clark, 2001.

Brock, Brian. "Bonhoeffer and the Bible in Christian Ethics: Psalm 119, the Mandates, and Ethics as a 'Way.'" *Studies in Christian Ethics* 18, no. 3 (2005): 7-29.

Brotherton, Joshua R. "Revisiting the *Sola Scriptura* Debate: Yves Congar and Joseph Ratzinger on Tradition." *Pro Ecclesia* 24, no. 1 (2015): 85-114.

Brown, Judith. "The Pattern of Theological Truth: An Interview with Robert Jenson." *Stimulus: The New Zealand Journal of Christian Thought and Practice* 22, no. 1 (2015): 30-35.

Bultmann, Rudolf. *Existence and Faith: Shorter Writings of Rudolf Bultmann*. Translated by Schubert M. Ogden. New York: World, 1960.

———. *Jesus and the Word*. Translated by Louise Pettibone Smith and Erminie Huntress Lantero. New York: Scriber, 1958.

Burnett, Richard E. *Karl Barth's Theological Exegesis: The Hermeneutical Principles of the* Römerbrief *Period*. Grand Rapids, MI: Eerdmans, 2004.

Byassee, Jason. "Theology and Worship." In *The Routledge Companion to the Practice of Christian Theology*, edited by Mike Higton and Jim Fodor, 203-21. New York: Routledge, 2015.

Calvin, John. *Institutes of the Christian Religion*. Translated by Henry Beveridge. Peabody, MA: Hendrickson, 2008.

Cartwright, Michael G. *Practices, Politics, and Performance: Toward a Communal Hermeneutic for Christian Ethics*. Eugene, OR: Wipf & Stock, 2006.

———. "A Reader's Guide." In Berkman and Cartwright, *Hauerwas Reader*, 623-72.

Chapman, Stephen B. "Studying the Word of God." In *Scripture*, 623-72. Christian Reflection: A Series in Faith and Ethics. Waco, TX: Baylor University Institute for Faith and Learning, 2014.

Clapp, Rodney R. *A Peculiar People: The Church as Culture in Post-Christian Society*. Downers Grove, IL: IVP Academic, 1996.

Clements, Keith. "Ecumenical Witness for Peace." In *The Cambridge Companion to Dietrich Bon-
    hoeffer*, edited by John W. de Gruchy, 154-72. Cambridge: Cambridge University Press, 1999.

Coakley, Sarah. *God, Sexuality, and the Self: An Essay 'On the Trinity.'* Cambridge: Cambridge
    University Press, 2013.

———. *Powers and Submissions: Spirituality, Philosophy and Gender*. Malden, MA: Blackwell,
    2002.

Cone, James H. *God of the Oppressed*. Rev. ed. Maryknoll, NY: Orbis, 1997.

Congar, Yves M.-J. *Lay People in the Church: A Study for a Theology of the Laity*. Translated by
    Donald Attwater. Westminster, MD: Newman, 1962.

———. *Tradition and Traditions: An Historical and Theological Essay*. Translated by Michael
    Naseby and Thomas Rainborough. London: Burns & Oates, 1966.

Congdon, David W. "Dialectical Theology as Theology of Mission: Investigating the Origins
    of Karl Barth's Break with Liberalism." *IJST* 16, no. 4 (2014): 390-413.

———. *The Mission of Demythologizing: Rudolf Bultmann's Dialectical Theology*. Minneapolis:
    Fortress, 2015.

———. "The Nature of the Church in Theological Interpretation: Culture, Volk, and Mission."
    JTI 11, no. 1 (2017): 101-17.

Craigo-Snell, Shannon. *The Empty Church: Theater, Theology, and Bodily Hope*. Oxford:
    Oxford University Press, 2014.

Crisp, Oliver. "Robert Jenson on the Pre-Existence of Christ." *MT* 23, no. 1 (2007): 27-45.

Dahill, Lisa. *Reading from the Underside of Selfhood: Bonhoeffer and Spiritual Formation*.
    Eugene, OR: Wipf & Stock, 2009.

Davis, Ellen F., and Richard B. Hays, eds. *The Art of Reading Scripture*. Grand Rapids, MI:
    Eerdmans, 2003.

De Gruchy, John W. "Editor's Introduction to the English Edition." In Bonhoeffer, *Creation
    and Fall*, DBWE 3:1-18.

Dean, Robert J. *For the Life of the World: Jesus Christ and the Church in the Theologies of Di-
    etrich Bonhoeffer and Stanley Hauerwas*. Eugene, OR: Pickwick, 2016.

DeJonge, Michael P. *Bonhoeffer on Resistance: The Word Against the Wheel*. Oxford: Oxford
    University Press, 2018.

———. *Bonhoeffer's Reception of Luther*. Oxford: Oxford University Press, 2017.

———. *Bonhoeffer's Theological Formation: Berlin, Barth, and Protestant Theology*. Oxford:
    Oxford University Press, 2012.

Demson, David E. *Hans Frei & Karl Barth: Different Ways of Reading Scripture*. Grand Rapids,
    MI: Eerdmans, 1997.

Dreher, Rod. *The Benedict Option: A Strategy for Christians in a Post-Christian Nation*. New
    York: Sentinel, 2017.

Dulles, Avery. *Models of the Church*. New York: Doubleday, 1978.

Dumas, André. *Dietrich Bonhoeffer: Theologian of Reality*. Translated by R. M. Brown. London:
    SCM Press, 1971.

Dunn, J. Patrick. "The Presence of the Ascended: History and Incarnation in Barth and Bon-
    hoeffer." Paper presented at the XII International Bonhoeffer Congress, Basel, Switzerland,
    July 2016.

———. "Prophets, Faust, and First-Years: Bonhoeffer and the Language of Charismatic Expe-
    rience." *Stellenbosch Theological Journal* 2, no. 2 (2016): 39-56.

———. "'To Know the Real One': Christological Promeity in the Theology of Dietrich Bon-
    hoeffer." MTh thesis, Stellenbosch University, 2016.

Dunne, Joseph. *Back to the Rough Ground: Practical Judgment and the Lure of Technique*. Rev. ed. Notre Dame, IN: University of Notre Dame Press, 1997.

Ebeling, Gerhard. *Word and Faith*. Translated by James Waterson Leitch. Philadelphia: Fortress, 1963.

Fish, Stanley. *Is There a Text in This Class?: The Authority of Interpretive Communities*. Cambridge, MA: Harvard University Press, 1980.

Flett, John G. *Apostolicity: The Ecumenical Question in World Christian Perspective*. Downers Grove, IL: InterVarsity Press, 2016.

———. "Communion as Propaganda: Reinhard Hütter and the Missionary Witness of the 'Church as Public.'" *SJT* 62, no. 4 (2009): 457-76.

———. *The Witness of God: The Trinity, Missio Dei, Karl Barth, and the Nature of Christian Community*. Grand Rapids, MI: Eerdmans, 2010.

Fodor, James. "Reading the Scriptures: Rehearsing Identity, Practicing Character." In *The Blackwell Companion to Christian Ethics*, edited by Stanley Hauerwas and Samuel Wells, 2nd ed., 153-69. Malden, MA: Blackwell, 2011.

Fowl, Stephen E. *Engaging Scripture: A Model for Theological Interpretation*. Malden, MA: Blackwell, 1998.

———. "Further Thoughts on Theological Interpretation." In Adam et al., *Reading Scripture with the Church*, 125-30.

———. *Theological Interpretation of Scripture*. Eugene, OR: Wipf & Stock, 2009.

———, ed. *The Theological Interpretation of Scripture: Classic and Contemporary Readings*. Malden, MA: Blackwell, 1997.

Fowl, Stephen E., and L. Gregory Jones. *Reading in Communion: Scripture and Ethics in Christian Life*. Grand Rapids, MI: Eerdmans, 1991.

Frei, Hans W. *The Eclipse of Biblical Narrative: A Study in Eighteenth and Nineteenth Century Hermeneutics*. New Haven, CT: Yale University Press, 1974.

———. "The 'Literal Reading' of Biblical Narrative in the Christian Tradition: Does It Stretch or Will It Break?" In *The Bible and the Narrative Tradition*, edited by Frank McConnell, 36-77. New York: Oxford University Press, 1986.

———. *Theology and Narrative: Selected Essays*, edited by George Hunsinger and William C. Placher. New York: Oxford University Press, 1993.

———. *Types of Christian Theology*, edited by George Hunsinger and William C. Placher. New Haven, CT: Yale University Press, 1992.

Fuchs, Ernst. *Studies of the Historical Jesus*. Translated by Andrew Scobie. Naperville, IL: Allenson, 1964.

Gabler, Johann P. "An Oration on the Proper Distinction Between Biblical and Dogmatic Theology and the Specific Objects of Each." In *Old Testament Theology: Flowering and Future*, edited by Ben C. Ollenburger, 497-506. Winona Lake, IN: Eisenbrauns, 2004.

Gadamer, Hans-Georg. *Truth and Method*. 2nd rev. ed. Translated by Joel Weinsheimer and Donald G. Marshall. New York: Continuum, 1989.

Gailus, Manfred. "Religion." In *A Companion to Nazi Germany*, edited by Shelley Baranowski, Armin Nolzen, and Claus-Christian W. Szejnmann, 333-50. Medford, MA: Wiley Blackwell, 2018.

Gathercole, Simon. "Pre-Existence, and the Freedom of the Son in Creation and Redemption: An Exposition in Dialogue with Robert Jenson." *IJST* 7, no. 1 (2005): 38-51.

Gerlach, Wolfgang. *And the Witnesses Were Silent: The Confessing Church and the Persecution of Jews*. Translated by Victoria J. Barnett. Lincoln: University of Nebraska Press, 2000.

Godsey, John D. *The Theology of Dietrich Bonhoeffer*. Eugene, OR: Wipf & Stock, 2015.

Goheen, Michael W. *A Light to the Nations: The Missional Church and the Biblical Story*. Grand Rapids, MI: Baker Academic, 2011.

Goheen, Michael W., and Christopher J. H. Wright. "Mission and Theological Interpretation." In *A Manifesto for Theological Interpretation*, edited by Craig G. Bartholomew and Heath A. Thomas, 171-96. Grand Rapids, MI: Baker Academic, 2016.

Gollwitzer, Helmut. "The Way of Obedience," in *I Knew Dietrich Bonhoeffer*. Edited by Ronald Gregor Smith and Wolf-Dieter Zimmermann. Translated by Käthe Gregor Smith. London: Fontana Books, 1973.

Gorman, Michael J. *Becoming the Gospel: Paul, Participation, and Mission*. Grand Rapids, MI: Eerdmans, 2015.

Green, Clifford J. *Bonhoeffer: A Theology of Sociality*. Rev. ed. Grand Rapids, MI: Eerdmans, 1999.

———. "Editor's Introduction to the English Edition." In Bonhoeffer, *Sanctorum Communio*, DBWE 1:1-20.

———. "Trinity and Christology in Bonhoeffer and Barth." *Union Seminary Quarterly Review* 60, nos. 1-2 (2006): 1-22.

Green, Garrett. *Imagining God: Theology and the Religious Imagination*. Grand Rapids, MI: Eerdmans, 1998.

———. *Theology, Hermeneutics, and Imagination: The Crisis of Interpretation at the End of Modernity*. Cambridge: Cambridge University Press, 2000.

Guder, Darrell L. "Biblical Formation and Discipleship." In *Treasure in Jars of Clay: Patterns in Missional Faithfulness*, edited by Lois Y. Barrett, 59-73. Grand Rapids, MI: Eerdmans, 2004.

———. *The Continuing Conversion of the Church*. Grand Rapids, MI: Eerdmans, 2000.

———. "Missional Hermeneutics: The Missional Authority of Scripture—Interpreting Scripture as Missional Formation." *Mission Focus: Annual Review* 15 (2007): 106-21.

Guder, Darrell L., ed., with Lois Barrett, Inagrace T. Dietterich, George R. Hunsberger, Alan J. Roxburgh, and Craig Van Gelder. *Missional Church: A Vision for the Sending of the Church in North America*. Grand Rapids, MI: Eerdmans, 1998.

Gunton, Colin E., ed. *Trinity, Time, and Church: A Response to the Theology of Robert W. Jenson*. Grand Rapids, MI: Eerdmans, 2000.

———. "'Until He Comes': Towards an Eschatology of Church Membership." *IJST* 3, no. 2 (2001): 187-200.

Hamilton, Nadine. "Dietrich Bonhoeffer and the Necessity of Kenosis for Scriptural Hermeneutics." *SJT* 71, no. 4 (2018): 441-59.

Harrisville, Roy A., and Walter Sundberg. *The Bible in Modern Culture: Baruch Spinoza to Brevard Childs*. Grand Rapids, MI: Eerdmans, 2002.

Hart, Trevor. "Imagination and Responsible Reading." In *Renewing Biblical Interpretation*, edited by Craig Bartholomew, Colin Greene, and Karl Möller, 307-34. Grand Rapids, MI: Zondervan, 2000.

Hauerwas, Stanley. *Character and the Christian Life: A Study in Theological Ethics*. San Antonio: Trinity University Press, 1975.

———. *Christian Existence Today: Essays on Church, World, and Living in Between*. Durham, NC: Labyrinth, 1988.

———. "The Church as God's New Language (1986)." In Berkman and Cartwright, *Hauerwas Reader*, 142-63.

———. *A Community of Character: Toward a Constructive Christian Social Ethic.* Notre Dame, IN: University of Notre Dame Press, 1981.

———. "Dietrich Bonhoeffer." In *The Blackwell Companion to Political Theology*, edited by Peter Scott and William T. Cavanaugh, 136-49. Malden, MA: Blackwell, 2004.

———. "How to Write a Theological Sentence." *Sewanee Theological Review* 57, no. 1 (2013): 56-72.

———. *Matthew.* Brazos Theological Commentary on the Bible. Grand Rapids, MI: Brazos Press, 2006.

———. *Naming the Silences: God, Medicine, and the Problem of Suffering.* Grand Rapids, MI: Eerdmans, 1990.

———. "Only Theology Overcomes Ethics; or, Why 'Ethicists' Must Learn from Jenson." In Gunton, *Trinity, Time, and Church*, 252-68.

———. *The Peaceable Kingdom: A Primer in Christian Ethics.* Notre Dame, IN: University of Notre Dame Press, 1983.

———. *Performing the Faith: Bonhoeffer and the Practice of Nonviolence.* London: SPCK, 2004.

———. "A Retrospective Assessment of an 'Ethics of Character': The Development of Hauerwas's Theological Project (1985, 2001)." In Berkman and Cartwright, *Hauerwas Reader*, 75-89.

———. *Sanctify Them in Truth: Holiness Exemplified.* Nashville: Abingdon, 1998.

———. "The Servant Community: Christian Social Ethics." In Berkman and Cartwright, *Hauerwas Reader*, 371-91.

———. *Unleashing the Scripture: Freeing the Bible from Captivity to America.* Nashville: Abingdon, 1993.

———. *War and the American Difference: Theological Reflections on Violence and National Identity.* Grand Rapids, MI: Baker Academic, 2011.

———. *Wilderness Wanderings: Probing Twentieth-Century Theology and Philosophy.* Boulder, CO: Westview Press, 1997.

Hauerwas, Stanley, and Charles Pinches. *Christians Among the Virtues: Theological Conversations with Ancient and Modern Ethics.* Notre Dame, IN: University of Notre Dame Press, 1997.

Hauerwas, Stanley, and William H. Willimon. *Resident Aliens: Life in the Christian Colony.* Nashville: Abingdon, 1989.

Hays, Richard B. *The Moral Vision of the New Testament: Community, Cross, New Creation; A Contemporary Introduction to New Testament Ethics.* San Francisco: HarperCollins, 1996.

———. "Reading Scripture in Light of the Resurrection." In Davis and Hays, *Art of Reading Scripture*, 216-38.

———. "Reading the Bible with Eyes of Faith: The Practice of Theological Exegesis," *JTI* 1, no. 1 (2007): 5-21.

Healy, Nicholas M. *Hauerwas: A (Very) Critical Introduction.* Grand Rapids, MI: Eerdmans, 2014.

———. "The Logic of Karl Barth's Ecclesiology: Analysis, Assessment and Proposed Modification." *MT* 10, no. 3 (1994): 253-70.

Hegel, G. F. W. *Encyclopedia of Philosophical Sciences in Outline and Other Critical Writings.* Edited by Ernst Behler. Translated by Steven A. Taubeneck. New York: Continuum, 1991.

Hoekendijk, J. C. "The Call to Evangelism," *International Review of Mission* 39, no. 154 (1950): 162-75.

Holmes, Christopher R. J. "Revelation in the Present Tense: On Rethinking Theological Interpretation in Light of the Prophetic Office of Jesus Christ." *JTI* 6, no.1 (2012): 23-42.

Hooft, W. A. Visser 't, ed. *The New Delhi Report: Third Assembly of the World Council of Churches, 1961*. London: SCM Press, 1962.

Horton, Michael. *A Better Way: Rediscovering the Drama of God-Centered Worship*. Grand Rapids, MI: Baker Books, 2002.

———. *The Christian Faith: A Systematic Theology for Pilgrims on the Way*. Grand Rapids, MI: Zondervan, 2011.

Howard, Thomas. *Protestant Theology and the Making of the Modern German University*. Oxford: Oxford University Press, 2006.

Hunsberger, George R. "Proposals for a Missional Hermeneutic: Mapping a Conversation," *Missiology* 39, no. 3 (2011): 309-21.

Hunsinger, George. Review of *Reclaiming Bonhoeffer*, by Charles Marsh. *MT* 12, no. 1 (1996): 121-23.

Husbands, Mark, and Daniel J. Treier, eds. *The Community of the Word: Toward an Evangelical Ecclesiology*. Downers Grove, IL: InterVarsity Press, 2005.

Jameson, Fredric. *Marxism and Form: Twentieth-Century Dialectical Theories of Literature*. Princeton, NJ: Princeton University Press, 1974.

———. *The Political Unconscious: Narrative as a Socially Symbolic Act*. Ithaca, NY: Cornell University Press, 1981.

Janz, Paul D. *God, the Mind's Desire: Reference, Reason and Christian Thinking*. Cambridge: Cambridge University Press, 2004.

Jennings, Willie James. *Acts*. Belief: A Theological Commentary on the Bible. Louisville, KY: Westminster John Knox, 2017.

———. *Christian Imagination: Theology and Origins of Race*. New Haven, CT: Yale University Press, 2010.

———. "Reframing the World: Toward an Actual Christian Doctrine of Creation." *IJST* 21, no. 4 (2019): 388-407.

Jenson, Robert W. *Canon and Creed*. Louisville, KY: Westminster John Knox, 2010.

———. "Catechesis for Our Time." In *Marks of the Body of Christ*, edited by Carl E. Braaten and Robert W. Jenson, 137-48. Grand Rapids, MI: Eerdmans, 1999.

———. "Christ as Culture 1: Christ as Polity." *IJST* 5, no. 3 (2003): 323-29.

———. *Essays in Theology of Culture*. Grand Rapids, MI: Eerdmans, 1995.

———. *Ezekiel*. Brazos Theological Commentary on the Bible. Grand Rapids, MI: Brazos Press, 2009.

———. "The Hauerwas Project." *MT* 8, no. 3 (1992): 285-95.

———. "It's the Culture." *First Things*, May 2014, 33-36.

———. "A Lesson to Us All." *Pro Ecclesia* 3, no. 2 (1994): 133-35.

———. "On the Authorities of Scripture." In *Engaging Biblical Authority: Perspectives on the Bible as Scripture*, edited by William P. Brown, 53-61. Louisville, KY: Westminster John Knox, 2007.

———. "Once More the *Logos asarkos*." *IJST* 13, no. 2 (2011): 130-33.

———. "The Religious Power of Scripture." *SJT* 52, no. 1 (1999): 89-105.

———. "Response to Watson and Hunsinger." *SJT* 55, no. 2 (2002): 225-32.

———. "Scripture's Authority in the Church." In Davis and Hays, *Art of Reading Scripture*, 27-37.

———. *Song of Songs*. Interpretation: A Bible Commentary for Teaching and Preaching. Louisville, KY: Westminster John Knox, 2005.

———. *The Triune God*. Vol. 1 of *Systematic Theology*. Oxford: Oxford University Press, 1997.

———. *The Triune Story: Collected Essays on Scripture.* Edited by Brad East. New York: Oxford University Press, 2019.

———. *The Works of God.* Vol. 2 of *Systematic Theology.* Oxford: Oxford University Press, 1999.

———. "You Wonder Where the Spirit Went." *Pro Ecclesia* 2, no. 3 (1993): 296-304.

Johnson, Keith L. *Theology as Discipleship.* Downers Grove, IL: InterVarsity Press, 2015.

Johnson, Luke Timothy. "Imagining the World Scripture Imagines." In *Theology and Scriptural Imagination*, edited by L. Gregory Jones and James J. Buckley, 3-18. Malden, MA: Blackwell, 1998.

Jowett, Benjamin. "On the Interpretation of Scripture." In *Essays and Reviews: The 1860 Text and Its Reading*, edited by Victor Shea and William Whitla. Charlottesville: University Press of Virginia, 2000.

Kant, Immanuel. "The Conflict of the Faculties." In *Religion and Rational Theology*, edited and translated by Allen W. Wood and George di Giovanni. Cambridge: Cambridge University Press, 1996.

Kearney, Richard. "What Is Carnal Hermeneutics?" *New Literary History* 46, no. 1 (2015): 99-124.

Kearney, Richard, and Brian Treanor, eds. *Carnal Hermeneutics.* New York: Fordham University Press, 2015.

Kelly, Geffrey, and F. Burton Nelson. "Dietrich Bonhoeffer's Theological Interpretation of Scripture for the Church." *Ex Auditu* 17 (2001): 1-30.

Kelly, Geffrey B., and C. John Weborg, eds. *Reflections on Bonhoeffer: Essays in Honor of F. Burton Nelson.* Chicago: Covenant, 1999.

Kelsey, David H. *Eccentric Existence: A Theological Anthropology.* Louisville, KY: Westminster John Knox, 2009.

Kerr, Nathan R. *Christ, History and Apocalyptic: The Politics of Christian Mission.* Eugene, OR: Cascade, 2008.

Kline, Peter. "Participation in God and the Nature of Christian Community: Robert Jenson and Eberhard Jüngel." *IJST* 13, no. 1 (2011): 38-61.

Kuske, Martin. *The Old Testament as the Book of Christ: An Appraisal of Bonhoeffer's Interpretation.* Translated by S. T. Kimbrough Jr. Philadelphia: Westminster Press, 1976.

Kuske, Martin, and Ilse Tödt. "Editors' Afterword to the German Edition." In Bonhoeffer, *Discipleship*, DBWE, 4:289-314.

LaCocque, André, and Paul Ricoeur. *Thinking Biblically: Exegetical and Hermeneutical Studies.* Translated by David Pellauer. Chicago: University of Chicago Press, 1998.

Lakoff, George, and Mark Johnson. *Philosophy in the Flesh: The Embodied Mind and Its Challenge to Western Thought.* New York: Basic Books, 1999.

Lakoff, George, and Rafael E. Núñez. *Where Mathematics Comes From: How the Embodied Mind Brings Mathematics into Being.* New York: Basic Books, 2000.

Lange, Frits de. *Waiting for the Word: Dietrich Bonhoeffer on Speaking About God.* Translated by Martin M. Walton. Grand Rapids, MI: Eerdmans, 1999.

Lash, Nicholas. *Theology on the Way to Emmaus.* Eugene, OR: Wipf & Stock, 1986.

Legaspi, Michael C. *The Death of Scripture and the Rise of Biblical Studies.* Oxford: Oxford University Press, 2010.

Leithart, Peter J. *Blessed Are the Hungry: Meditations on the Lord's Supper.* Moscow, ID: Canon Press, 2000.

———. *Delivered from the Elements of the World: Atonement, Justification, Mission.* Downers Grove, IL: InterVarsity Press, 2016.

LeMarquand, Grant. "African Biblical Interpretation." In Vanhoozer et al., *Dictionary for Theological Interpretation of the Bible*, 31-34.

Levenson, Jon D. *The Hebrew Bible, the Old Testament, and Historical Criticism: Jews and Christians in Biblical Studies*. Louisville, KY: Westminster John Knox, 1993.

Levering, Matthew. *Participatory Biblical Exegesis: A Theology of Biblical Interpretation*. Notre Dame, IN: University of Notre Dame Press, 2008.

Lindbeck, George A. *The Nature of Doctrine: Religion and Theology in a Postliberal Age*. Louisville, KY: Westminster John Knox, 1984.

———. "Postcritical Canonical Interpretation: Three Modes of Retrieval." In *Theological Exegesis: Essays in Honor of Brevard S. Childs*, edited by Christopher Seitz and Kathryn Greene-McCreight, 26-51. Grand Rapids, MI: Eerdmans, 1990.

Littell, Franklin H. "The Question: Who Is Christ for Us Today?" In *The Place of Bonhoeffer: Essays on the Problems and Possibilities in His Thought*, edited by Martin E. Marty, with Peter Berger et al., 25-50. New York: Association Press, 1962.

Lubac, Henri de. *Catholicism: Christ and the Common Destiny of Man*. Translated by Lancelot C. Sheppard and Sister Elizabeth Englund. San Francisco: Ignatius Press, 1988.

———. *Medieval Exegesis: The Four Senses of Scripture*. 4 vols. Grand Rapids, MI: Eerdmans, 1998.

MacIntyre, Alasdair. *After Virtue: A Study in Moral Theology*. 2nd ed. Notre Dame, IN: University of Notre Dame Press, 1984.

———. *Whose Justice? Which Rationality?* Notre Dame, IN: University of Notre Dame Press, 1988.

Marsh, Charles. *Reclaiming Dietrich Bonhoeffer: The Promise of His Theology*. Oxford: Oxford University Press, 1994.

———. *Strange Glory: A Life of Dietrich Bonhoeffer*. New York: Knopf, 2014.

Martyn, J. Louis. "Epilogue: An Essay in Pauline Meta-Ethics." In *Divine and Human Agency in Paul and His Cultural Environment*, edited by John M. G. Barclay and Simon J. Gathercole, 173-83. London: T&T Clark, 2008.

———. *Galatians*. Anchor Bible 33A. New York: Doubleday, 1997.

———. *Theological Issues in the Letters of Paul*. Nashville: Abingdon, 1997.

Matthews, John D. "Responsible Sharing of the Mystery." In Kelly and Weborg, *Reflections on Bonhoeffer*, 114-26.

Mawson, Michael. *Christ Existing as Community: Bonhoeffer's Ecclesiology*. Oxford: Oxford University Press, 2018.

———. "Scripture" in *The Oxford Handbook of Dietrich Bonhoeffer*. Edited by Michael Mawson and Philip G. Ziegler. Oxford: Oxford University Press, 2019.

———. "The Spirit and the Community: Pneumatology and Ecclesiology in Jenson, Hütter and Bonhoeffer." *IJST* 15, no. 4 (2013): 453-68.

Mawson, Michael, and Philip G. Ziegler, eds. *The Oxford Handbook of Dietrich Bonhoeffer*. Oxford: Oxford University Press, 2019.

McBride, Jennifer M. *The Church for the World: A Theology of Public Witness*. Oxford: Oxford University Press, 2011.

McClendon, James Wm. *Ethics*. Vol. 1 of *Systematic Theology*. Rev. ed. Nashville: Abingdon, 2002.

McCormack, Bruce L. "The Being of Holy Scripture Is in Becoming: Karl Barth in Conversation with American Evangelical Criticism." In *Evangelicals and Scripture: Tradition, Authority and Hermeneutics*, edited by Vincent Bacote, Laure C. Miguélez, and Dennis L. Okholm, 55-75. Downers Grove, IL: InterVarsity Press, 2004.

McKenny, Gerald. *The Analogy of Grace: Karl Barth's Moral Theology.* Oxford: Oxford University Press, 2010.

McKinzie, Greg. "Missional Hermeneutics as Theological Interpretation." *JTI* 11, no. 2 (2017): 157-79.

Merleau-Ponty, Maurice. *Phenomenology of Perception.* Translated by Donald A. Landes. New York: Routledge, 2014.

Meyendorff, John. *Living Tradition: Orthodox Witness in the Contemporary World.* Crestwood, NY: St. Vladimir's Seminary Press, 1978.

Milbank, John. *Theology and Social Theory: Beyond Secular Reason.* Malden, MA: Blackwell, 1990.

Moberly, Jennifer. *The Virtue of Bonhoeffer's Ethics: A Study of Bonhoeffer's Ethics in Relation to Virtue Ethics.* Eugene, OR: Pickwick, 2013.

Moberly, R. W. L. *The Bible, Theology, and Faith: A Study of Abraham and Jesus.* Cambridge: Cambridge University Press, 2000.

———. "Theological Interpretation, Presuppositions, and the Role of the Church: Bultmann and Augustine Revisited." *JTI* 6, no. 1 (2012): 1-22.

Moltmann, Jürgen. *The Church in the Power of the Spirit: A Contribution to Messianic Ecclesiology.* Translated by Margaret Kohl. Minneapolis: Fortress, 1993.

Morse, Christopher. *The Difference Heaven Makes: Rehearing the Gospel as News.* London: T&T Clark, 2010.

Murphy, Francesca Aran. *God Is Not a Story: Realism Revisited.* Oxford: Oxford University Press, 2007.

Murray, Stuart. *Post-Christendom: Church and Mission in a Strange New World.* Milton Keynes, UK: Paternoster, 2004.

Newbigin, Lesslie. *Foolishness to the Greeks: The Gospel and Western Culture.* Grand Rapids, MI: Eerdmans, 1986.

———. *The Gospel in a Pluralist Society.* Grand Rapids, MI: Eerdmans, 1989.

———. *The Open Secret: An Introduction to the Theology of Mission.* Rev. ed. Grand Rapids, MI: Eerdmans, 1995.

Niebuhr, H. Richard. *Christ and Culture.* New York: Harper & Row, 1951.

Paddison, Angus. "Theological Interpretation and the Bible as Public Text." *JTI* 8, no. 2 (2014): 175-92.

Plant, Stephen J. *Taking Stock of Bonhoeffer: Studies in Biblical Interpretation and Ethics.* Burlington, VT: Ashgate, 2014.

Plaskow, Judith. *Sex, Sin and Grace: Women's Experience and the Theologies of Reinhold Niebuhr and Paul Tillich.* Lanham, MD: University Press of America, 1980.

Pribbenow, Brad. *Prayerbook of Christ: Dietrich Bonhoeffer's Christological Interpretation of the Psalms.* Lanham, MD: Lexington Books, 2018.

Porter, Stanley E., and Jason C. Robinson. *Hermeneutics: An Introduction to Interpretive Theory.* Grand Rapids, MI: Eerdmans, 2011.

Rahner, Karl. "Membership of the Church According to the Teaching of Pius XII's Encyclical *Mystici Corporis Christi.*" In *Theological Investigations,* vol. 2, *Man in the Church,* translated by Karl-Heinz Kruger, 1-88. New York: Crossroad, 1975.

Rahner, Karl, and Joseph Ratzinger. *Revelation and Tradition.* Translated by W. J. O'Hara. Freiburg: Herder, 1966.

Reno, R. R. "Biblical Theology and Theological Exegesis." In *Out of Egypt: Biblical Theology and Biblical Interpretation,* edited by Craig G. Bartholomew, Mary Healy, Karl Möller, and Robin Parry, 385-408. Grand Rapids, MI: Zondervan, 2004.

———. "Series Preface." In Jaroslav Pelikan, *Acts*, Brazos Theological Commentary on the Bible, edited by R. R. Reno, 11-16. Grand Rapids, MI: Brazos Press, 2005.

Ricoeur, Paul. *Hermeneutics and the Human Sciences*. Edited and translated by John B. Thompson. Cambridge: Cambridge University Press, 1981.

Robinson, David S. *Christ and Revelatory Community in Bonhoeffer's Reception of Hegel*. Tübingen: Mohr Siebeck, 2018.

Robinson, John A. T. *Honest to God*. Philadelphia: Westminster, 1963.

Rochelle, Jay C. "Bonhoeffer and Biblical Interpretation: Reading Scripture in the Spirit." *Currents in Theology and Mission* 22, no. 2 (1995): 85-95.

Rogers, Andrew P. *Congregational Hermeneutics: How Do We Read?* New York: Routledge, 2016.

Rowe, C. Kavin. "Biblical Pressure and Trinitarian Hermeneutics." *Pro Ecclesia* 11, no. 3 (2002): 295-312.

———. "Navigating the Differences in the Gospels." *Faith and Leadership*, August 17, 2009. https://faithandleadership.com/navigating-differences-gospels.

———. *World Upside Down: Reading Acts in the Graeco-Roman Age*. Oxford: Oxford University Press, 2010.

Rowland, Christopher. "Liberation Theology." In Webster, Tanner, and Torrance, *Oxford Handbook of Systematic Theology*, 634-52.

———. "An Open Letter to Francis Watson on *Text, Church and World*." *SJT* 48, no. 4 (1995): 507-17.

Ruether, Rosemary Radford. *Sexism and God-Talk: Toward a Feminist Theology*. Boston: Beacon, 1983.

Sanneh, Lamin. "The Horizontal and the Vertical in Mission: An African Perspective." *International Bulletin of Missionary Research* 7, no. 4 (1983): 165-71.

———. *Translating the Message: The Missionary Impact on Culture*. 2nd ed. Maryknoll, NY: Orbis, 2009.

Sarisky, Darren. *Scriptural Interpretation: A Theological Exploration*. Malden, MA: Wiley-Blackwell, 2013.

Schlabach, Gerald W. "Deuteronomic or Constantinian: What Is the Most Basic Problem for Christian Social Ethics?" In *The Wisdom of the Cross: Essays in Honor of John Howard Yoder*, edited by Stanley Hauerwas, Chris K. Huebner, Harry J. Huebner, and Mark Thiessen Nation, 449-71. Grand Rapids, MI: Eerdmans, 1999.

———. *Unlearning Protestantism: Sustaining Christian Community in an Unstable Age*. Grand Rapids, MI: Brazos Press, 2010.

Schleiermacher, F. D. E. *The Christian Faith*. Edited by H. R. Mackintosh and J. S. Stewart. London: T&T Clark, 1999.

———. *Hermeneutics and Criticism: And Other Writings*. Edited and translated by Andrew Bowie. Cambridge: Cambridge University Press, 1998.

Schreiter, Robert J. *The New Catholicity: Theology Between the Global and the Local*. Maryknoll, NY: Orbis, 1997.

Schwöbel, Christoph. "The Creature of the Word: Recovering the Ecclesiology of the Reformers." In *On Being the Church: Essays on the Christian Community*, edited by Colin E. Gunton and Daniel W. Hardy, 110-55. Edinburgh: T&T Clark, 1989.

———. "Once Again, Christ and Culture: Remarks on the Christological Bases of a Theology of Culture." In Gunton, *Trinity, Time, and Church*, 103-25.

Sheehan, Jonathan. *The Enlightenment Bible: Translation, Scholarship, Culture*. Princeton, NJ: Princeton University Press, 2007.

Shenk, Wilbert R. *Write the Vision: The Church Renewed*. Eugene, OR: Wipf & Stock, 2001.

Siggelkow, Ry O. "Toward an Apocalyptic Peace Church: Christian Pacifism After Hauerwas." *Conrad Grebel Review* 31, no. 3 (2013): 274-97.

Sinn, Simone. "Hermeneutics and Ecclesiology." In *The Routledge Companion to the Christian Church*, edited by Gerard Mannion and Lewis S. Mudge, 576-93. New York: Routledge, 2008.

Smith, Ronald Gregor and Wolf-Dieter Zimmerman, eds. *I Knew Dietrich Bonhoeffer*. Translated by Käthe Gregor Smith. London: Fontana Books, 1973.

Sonderegger, Katherine. *The Doctrine of God*. Vol. 1 of *Systematic Theology*. Minneapolis: Fortress, 2015.

Spinoza, Baruch. *Theological-Political Treatise*. Translated by Samuel Shirley. 2nd ed. Indianapolis: Hackett, 2001.

Steinmetz, David C. "The Superiority of Pre-Critical Exegesis." In Fowl, *Theological Interpretation of Scripture: Classic and Contemporary Readings*, 26-38.

Stendahl, Krister. "Biblical Theology, Contemporary." In *The Interpreter's Dictionary of the Bible*, edited by George A. Buttrick et al., 1:418-32. Nashville: Abingdon, 1962.

Stout, Jeffrey. *The Flight from Authority: Religion, Morality, and the Quest for Autonomy*. Notre Dame, IN: University of Notre Dame Press, 1981.

Stringfellow, William. *An Ethic for Christians and Other Aliens in a Strange Land*. Waco, TX: Word Books, 1973.

———. *A Keeper of the Word: Selected Writings of William Stringfellow*. Edited by Bill Wylie Kellermann. Grand Rapids, MI: Eerdmans, 1994.

———. *A Private and Public Faith*. Grand Rapids, MI: Eerdmans, 1962.

Swain, Scott. *Trinity, Revelation, and Reading: A Theological Introduction to the Bible and Its Interpretation*. London: T&T Clark, 2011.

Sykes, Stephen. *The Identity of Christianity: Theologians and the Essence of Christianity from Schleiermacher to Barth*. Philadelphia: Fortress, 1984.

Tanner, Kathryn. "Cultural Theory." In Webster, Tanner, and Torrance, *Oxford Handbook of Systematic Theology*, 527-42.

———. *Jesus, Humanity, and the Trinity: A Brief Systematic Theology*. Minneapolis: Fortress, 2001.

———. *Theories of Culture: A New Agenda for Theology*. Minneapolis: Fortress, 1997.

Taylor, Charles. *A Secular Age*. Cambridge, MA: Harvard University Press, 2007.

Taylor, Derek W. "Bonhoeffer and the Benedict Option: The Mission of Monasticism in a Post-Christian World." *Ecclesiology* 14, no. 1 (2018): 11-31.

———. "*Crux Probat Omnia*: Rowan Williams' Scriptural Hermeneutic." *SJT* 69, no. 2 (2016): 140-56.

———. "What's This Book Actually About?: *Life Together* and the Possibility of Theological Knowledge." *The Bonhoeffer Legacy: An International Journal* 6, no. 1 (2020).

Torrance, Thomas F. "The Deposit of Faith." *SJT* 36, no. 1 (1983): 1-28.

———. *Karl Barth: An Introduction to His Early Theology, 1910–1931*. London: T&T Clark, 2004.

Tracy, David. *Plurality and Ambiguity: Hermeneutics, Religion, Hope*. 1987. Reprint, Chicago: University of Chicago Press, 1994.

Treier, Daniel J. *Introducing Theological Interpretation of Scripture: Recovering a Christian Practice*. Grand Rapids, MI: Baker Academic, 2008.

———. "Scripture and Hermeneutics." In *Mapping Modern Theology: A Thematic and Historical Introduction*, edited by Kelly M. Kapic and Bruce L. McCormack, 67-96. Grand Rapids, MI: Baker Academic, 2012.

Treir, Daniel J. and Kevin J. Vanhoozer. *Theology and the Mirror of Scripture: A Mere Evangelical Account*. Downers Grove, IL: InterVarsity Press, 2015.

Vanhoozer, Kevin J. *Biblical Authority After Babel: Retrieving the Solas in the Spirit of Mere Protestant Christianity*. Grand Rapids, MI: Brazos Press, 2016.

———. *The Drama of Doctrine: A Canonical-Linguistic Approach to Christian Theology*. Louisville, KY: Westminster John Knox, 2005.

———. "Introduction." In Vanhoozer et al., *Dictionary for Theological Interpretation of the Bible*, 19-26.

———. *Is There a Meaning in This Text? The Bible, the Reader, and the Morality of Literary Knowledge*. Grand Rapids, MI: Zondervan, 1998.

Vanhoozer, Kevin J., Craig G. Bartholomew, Daniel J. Treier, and N. T. Wright, eds. *Dictionary for Theological Interpretation of the Bible*. Grand Rapids, MI: Baker Academic, 2005.

Volf, Miroslav. *Exclusion and Embrace: A Theological Exploration of Identity, Otherness, and Reconciliation*. Nashville: Abingdon, 1996.

Walls, Andrew F. *The Cross-Cultural Process in Christian History*. Maryknoll, NY: Orbis, 2002.

———. *The Missionary Movement in Christian History: Studies in the Transmission of Faith*. Maryknoll, NY: Orbis, 1996.

Watson, Francis. *Text and Truth: Redefining Biblical Theology*. Grand Rapids, MI: Eerdmans, 1997.

———. *Text, Church, and World: Biblical Interpretation in Theological Perspective*. Grand Rapids, MI: Eerdmans, 1994.

Webster, John. "Barth's Lectures on the Gospel of John." In *Thy Word Is Truth: Barth on Scripture*, edited by George Hunsinger, 125-50. Grand Rapids, MI: Eerdmans, 2012.

———. *Barth's Moral Theology: Human Action in Barth's Thought*. Grand Rapids, MI: Eerdmans, 1998.

———. "The Church and the Perfection of God." In Husbands and Treier, *Community of the Word*, 75-95.

———. "The Church as Witnessing Community." *Scottish Bulletin of Evangelical Theology* 21, no. 1 (2003): 21-33.

———. *Confessing God: Essays in Christian Dogmatics II*. London: T&T Clark, 2005.

———. *Confronted by Grace: Meditations of a Theologian*. Edited by Daniel Bush and Brannon Ellis. Bellingham, WA: Lexham Press, 2014.

———. "The Dogmatic Location of the Canon." *Neue Zeitschrift für systematische Theologie und Religionsphilosophie* 43, no. 1 (2001): 17-43.

———. *The Domain of the Word: Scripture and Theological Reason*. London: T&T Clark, 2012.

———. "Ecclesiocentrism." *First Things*, October 2014, 54-55.

———. *God and the Works of God*. Vol. 1 of *God Without Measure: Working Papers in Christian Theology*. London: T&T Clark, 2016.

———. "Hermeneutics in Modern Theology: Some Doctrinal Reflections." *SJT* 51, no. 3 (1998), 307-41.

———. *Holy Scripture: A Dogmatic Sketch*. Cambridge: Cambridge University Press, 2003.

———. "'In the Shadow of Biblical Work': Barth and Bonhoeffer on Reading the Bible." *Toronto Journal of Theology* 17, no. 1 (2001): 75-92.

———. "Perfection and Participation." In *The Analogy of Being: Invention of the Antichrist or Wisdom of God?*, edited by Thomas Joseph White, 379-94. Grand Rapids, MI: Eerdmans, 2011.

———. *Virtue and Intellect*. Vol. 2 of *God Without Measure: Working Papers in Christian Theology*. London: T&T Clark, 2016.

———. "The Visible Attests the Invisible." In Husbands and Treier, *Community of the Word*, 96-113.

———. *Word and Church: Essays in Christian Dogmatics*. London: T&T Clark, 2002.

Webster, John B., Kathryn Tanner, and Iain R. Torrance, eds. *The Oxford Handbook of Systematic Theology*. Oxford: Oxford University Press, 2007.

Weikart, Richard. "Scripture and Myth in Dietrich Bonhoeffer." *Fides et historia* 25, no. 1 (1993): 12-25.

Wells, Samuel. *Improvisation: The Drama of Christian Ethics*. Grand Rapids, MI: Brazos Press, 2004.

Wilken, Robert Louis. "The Church as Culture." *First Things*, April 2004, 31-36.

———. "The Church's Way of Speaking." *First Things*. August 2005, 27-31.

Williams, Reggie L. *Bonhoeffer's Black Jesus: Harlem Renaissance Theology and an Ethic of Resistance*. Waco, TX: Baylor University Press, 2014.

Williams, Rowan. *Christ: The Heart of Creation*. London: Bloomsbury, 2018.

———. *On Christian Theology*. Malden, MA: Blackwell, 2000.

———. *Where God Happens: Discovering Christ in One Another*. Boston: New Seeds, 2005.

———. *Wrestling with Angels: Conversations in Modern Theology*. Edited by Mike Higton. Grand Rapids, MI: Eerdmans, 2007.

Winter, Sean F. "Bonhoeffer and Biblical Interpretation: The Early Years." *Bonhoeffer Legacy* 1, no. 1 (2013): 1-15.

———. "'Present-ing' the Word: The Use and Abuse of Bonhoeffer on the Bible." *Bonhoeffer Legacy* 2, no. 2 (2014): 19-35.

Wolterstorff, Nicholas. *Divine Discourse: Philosophical Reflections on the Claim That God Speaks*. Cambridge: Cambridge University Press, 1995.

Wrede, William. "The Task and Methods of 'New Testament Theology.'" In *The Nature of New Testament Theology*, edited by Robert Morgan, 68-116. London: SCM Press, 1973.

Wright, Christopher J. H. *The Mission of God: Unlocking the Bible's Grand Narrative*. Downers Grove, IL: InterVarsity Press, 2006.

Wright, N. T. "How Can the Bible Be Authoritative?" *Vox Evangelica* 21 (1991): 7-32

———. "Imagining the Kingdom: Mission and Theology in Early Christianity." *SJT* 65, no. 4 (2012): 379-401.

———. *Jesus and the Victory of God*. Vol. 2 of *Christian Origins and the Question of God*. Minneapolis: Fortress, 1996.

———. *The Last Word: Beyond the Biblical Wars to a New Understanding of the Authority of Scripture*. San Francisco: HarperSanFrancisco, 2005.

Wright, William J. *Martin Luther's Understanding of God's Two Kingdoms: A Response to the Challenge of Skepticism*. Grand Rapids, MI: Baker Academic, 2010.

Wrogemann, Henning. *Intercultural Hermeneutics*. Translated by Karl E. Böhmer. Downers Grove, IL: IVP Academic, 2016.

Wüstenberg, Ralph K., and Jens Zimmermann, eds. *God Speaks to Us: Dietrich Bonhoeffer's Biblical Hermeneutics*. Frankfurt am Main: Lang, 2013.

Wuthnow, Robert. *America and the Challenges of Religious Diversity*. Princeton, NJ: Princeton University Press, 2005.

Yeago, David S. "The Bible." In *Knowing the Triune God: The Work of the Spirit in the Practices of the Church*, edited by James J. Buckley and David S. Yeago, 49-93. Grand Rapids, MI: Eerdmans, 2001.

——. "The New Testament and Nicene Dogma: A Contribution to the Recovery of Theological Exegesis." In Fowl, *Theological Interpretation of Scripture: Classic and Contemporary Readings*, 87-101.

Yoder, John Howard. "Hermeneutics of Peoplehood: A Protestant Perspective on Practical Moral Reasoning," *Journal of Religious Ethics* 10, no. 1 (1982): 40-67.

——. "Historiography as a Ministry to Renewal," *Brethren Life and Thought* 42, nos. 3-4 (1997): 216-28.

——. *The Politics of Jesus*. 2nd ed. Grand Rapids, MI: Eerdmans, 1994.

——. *Royal Priesthood: Essays Ecclesiological and Ecumenical*. Edited by Michael G. Cartwright. Grand Rapids, MI: Eerdmans, 1994.

Ziegler, Philip. "Christ for Us Today—Promeity in the Christologies of Bonhoeffer and Kierkegaard." *IJST* 15, no. 1 (2013): 25-41.

Zimmermann, Jens. "Reading the Book of the Church: Bonhoeffer's Christological Hermeneutics." *MT* 28, no. 4 (2012): 763-80.

Author Index

Subject Index

Scripture Index

New Explorations in Theology

Theology is flourishing in dynamic and unexpected ways in the twenty-first century. Scholars are increasingly recognizing the global character of the church, freely crossing old academic boundaries and challenging previously entrenched interpretations. Despite living in a culture of uncertainty, both young and senior scholars today are engaged in hopeful and creative work in the areas of systematic, historical, practical and philosophical theology. New Explorations in Theology provides a platform for cutting-edge research in these fields.

In an age of media proliferation and academic oversaturation, there is a need to single out the best new monographs. IVP Academic is committed to publishing constructive works that advance key theological conversations. We look for projects that investigate new areas of research, stimulate fruitful dialogue, and attend to the diverse array of contexts and audiences in our increasingly pluralistic world. IVP Academic is excited to make this work available to scholars, students and general readers who are seeking fresh new insights for the future of Christian theology.

Volumes Include:

- *Chrysostom's Devil: Demons, the Will, and Virtue in Patristic Soteriology*, Samantha L. Miller
- *The Making of Stanley Hauerwas: Bridging Barth and Postliberalism*, David B. Hunsicker
- *Karl Barth's Infralapsarian Theology: Origins and Development, 1920–1953*, Shao Kai Tseng
- *A Shared Mercy: Karl Barth on Forgiveness and the Church*, Jon Coutts

Finding the Textbook You Need

The IVP Academic Textbook Selector
is an online tool for instantly finding the IVP books
suitable for over 250 courses across 24 disciplines.

---

ivpacademic.com